Felony Murder

Guyora Binder

Stanford Law Books
An Imprint of Stanford University Press
Stanford, California

Stanford University Press
Stanford, California

©2012 by the Board of Trustees of the Leland Stanford Junior University.
All rights reserved.

Printed in the United States of America on acid-free, archival-quality paper

Library of Congress Cataloging-in-Publication Data

Binder, Guyora.
  Felony murder / Guyora Binder.
    p. cm. -- (Critical perspectives on crime and law)
  "Stanford Law Books."
  Includes bibliographical references and index.
  ISBN 978-0-8047-5535-1 (cloth : alk. paper) -- ISBN 978-0-8047-5536-8 (pbk. : alk. paper)
  1. Felony murder--United States. I. Title.
  KF9306.B56 2012
  345.73'02523--dc23
                              2011046510

Typeset by Bruce Lundquist in 10/14 Minion

For Judith

CONTENTS

PREFACE

Although the felony murder rule is one of the most criticized features of American criminal law, no book has ever been written on the topic before.

Such a book is needed for many reasons. Felony murder liability is part of homicide law in almost every American jurisdiction. It is important that lawyers, lawmakers, and voters understand how it works and how it can be improved. Legal scholars have long viewed it as an irrational vestige of ancient English law that does not cohere with the rest of modern criminal law. This view is unfortunate. Felony murder law is more modern and less harsh than commonly believed. Excluding it from general accounts of criminal law as an archaic exception distorts our understanding of the overarching principles of modern criminal law. This book sets out to correct the historical record, explain modern felony murder law, identify needed reforms, and show how, by taking account of felony murder liability, we can improve our understanding of the basic principles of American criminal law.

I am grateful to many people who encouraged and assisted me in the preparation of this book.

George Fletcher, my teacher at Yale and my supervisor in a research fellowship at U.C.L.A., first awakened my interest in criminal law. In this regard, my experience is not unique. George has enlivened criminal law scholarship the world over and more or less invented the field of criminal law theory in the United States. Thus George not only enabled me to produce this book, but also created an audience for it.

Markus Dubber, my colleague at Buffalo for many years, has made indispensable contributions to this project at every stage. He first attracted my attention to the felony murder problem by inviting me to write a review essay on Samuel Pillsbury's excellent book on homicide, *Judging Evil*. Many opportunities followed to contribute to conferences and symposia too numerous to recount, and many of those papers informed this project. Co-teaching courses with Markus on the history and theory of criminal law led to many conversations on the themes of culpability, common law history, and codification. Markus steadily encouraged me to publish a book on the topic, and eventually suggested that I contribute it to his series, "Critical Perspectives on Crime and Law."

Four other scholars have patiently encouraged the project, and improved it by commenting on its component papers. Robert Weisberg, my coauthor on a criminal law textbook and a theoretical work on law and literature, has taught me a great deal about both statutory and doctrinal interpretation, and instilled a conviction that deep questions lurk in the concrete details of homicide law. The remarkable theoretical work of Mark Kelman and Ken Simons on the concepts of strict liability and negligence has greatly shaped my own thinking. Both have generously shared their reactions and suggestions. Jonathan Simon's path-breaking work on the politics of criminal justice has helped me think about how to bring theoretical scholarship and democratic politics into dialogue on questions of criminal justice. Jonathan has also served as an acute reader.

Others have contributed by commenting at conferences and workshops. This includes audiences at the law schools of Arizona State University, Georgetown University, Pace University, the University at Buffalo, the University of Connecticut, the University of Toronto, and Yale University. I am particularly grateful to Paul Butler, Luis Chiesa, Jack Chin, Russell Christopher, Allison Danner, Antony Duff, Ken Ehrenberg, Angela Fernandez, Heidi Li Feldman, Jim Gardner, Bernard Harcourt, Carissa Hessick, Dan Kahan, Marty Lederman, Cynthia Lee, Allegra McLeod, Tracey Meares, Errol Meidinger, John Mikhail, Tom Morawetz, Jeffrie Murphy, Paul Robinson, Ken Shockley, Jack Schlegel, Mike Seidman, David Sklansky, Simon Stern, William Stuntz, Rick Su, Winni Sullivan, Doug Sylvester, and Leo Zaibert.

Other scholars have helped by commenting on papers or fielding my bibliographical and other questions. I am particularly indebted to Lyndsay Farmer, Barbara Fried, Tom Green, Adil Haque, George Hezel, Leo Katz, Fred Konesfsky, Gerald Leonard, Betty Mensch, Dennis Patterson, John Peradotto, Father Augustine Thompson, and Jim Wooten. Buffalo's indispensable and extraordinarily learned reference librarian Marcia Zubrow deserves special mention.

I have been blessed with very capable and enterprising research assistance from Melanie Beardsley, Alex Bouganim, Robert Carbone, Jenny Chang, Michael Court, Jennifer Johnson, Jared Garlip, Kelly-Anne Kelly-Williams, Jon Lamberti, Scott Ptak, Hisham Ramadan, Helen Root, Alicia Sim, Mark Welchons, and

Huiqun Zhu. A fine student paper by Kate Rebhan was also helpful. The book has also benefited from the exemplary professional assistance of Lois Stutzman and Mary Voglmayr.

Dean Nils Olsen and Dean Makau Mutua of the State University of New York at Buffalo Law School both showed their passionate support of scholarship by encouraging the project in every possible way.

Finally, I am grateful for the patient and cheerful support of my family throughout the preparation of this book. My wife, Judith, to whom this book is dedicated, was a constant source of inspiration and made every day a joy. My children, Ari and Galia, kept me from taking myself or my projects too seriously.

Although many people have helped me research and write this book, all errors and opinions are my own.

This book incorporates substantial portions of three articles. Chapters 1, 9, 10, 11, and 12 include substantial portions of Guyora Binder, "Making the Best of Felony Murder," 91 *Boston University Law Review* 403 (2011), reprinted with the permission of the *Boston University Law Review*. Chapters 5, 6, 7, and 8 include substantial portions of Guyora Binder, "The Origins of American Felony Murder Rules," 57 *Stanford Law Review* 59 (2004), reprinted with permission of the *Stanford Law Review*. Chapters 2, 3, and 4 include substantial portions of Guyora Binder, "The Culpability of Felony Murder," 83 *Notre Dame Law Review* 965 (2008), reprinted with permission of the author.

Felony Murder

Part One

FELONY MURDER PRINCIPLES

1 MAKING THE BEST OF FELONY MURDER

THE FELONY MURDER PROBLEM

A rapist chokes a distraught child victim to silence her. To his surprise, the child dies.[1] A robber aims his gun at a motel clerk's forehead. His finger slips and he "accidentally" shoots his target dead.[2] An arsonist burns down a storefront to collect insurance, coincidentally incinerating the family living on the other side of the wall.[3]

Intent on selfish aims, these killers do not recognize the obvious risks their conduct imposes on their victims. Though unintended, these killings are hardly accidental: such inadvertent but foreseeable killings are negligent. Yet "negligence" does not seem a sufficient epithet to capture the culpability of these killings, nor does "negligent homicide" seem a serious enough charge. These offenders callously impose risks of death in order to achieve other wrongful ends. In each case, the offender's felonious motive for imposing a risk of death aggravates his guilt for unintentionally, but nevertheless culpably, causing the resulting death. Accordingly, in most American jurisdictions, these killings would be punished as murder. The legal concept necessary to this result, the felony murder doctrine, is the subject of this book.

Although the felony murder doctrine is arguably necessary to achieve justice in cases like those described above, it is one of the most widely criticized features of American criminal law. Legal scholars are almost unanimous in condemning it as a morally indefensible form of strict liability.[4] Some have concluded that felony murder rules impose unconstitutionally cruel and unusual punishment by ascribing guilt without fault, or that they violate constitutional due process by presuming malice without proof.[5] Many view contemporary felony murder rules as descended from a sweeping "common law felony murder rule" holding all participants in all felonies responsible for all resulting deaths.[6] Some therefore see felony murder liability as an anachronism, a primitive relic of medieval law. Others may concede that modern "reforms" have ameliorated the doctrine, but they regard these rules as pearl earrings on a pig, merely ornamenting an essentially barbaric principle of liability without fault.

Most criminal law scholars have assumed there is nothing to say on behalf of the felony murder doctrine, no way to rationalize its rules to the lawyers who will apply it, and no reforms worth urging on courts and legislatures short of its utter abolition.[7] Sanford Kadish, author of the leading criminal law textbook, called the felony murder doctrine "rationally indefensible,"[8] and the American Law Institute's Model Penal Code commentaries observed that "[p]rincipled argument in favor of the felony-murder doctrine is hard to find."[9] Such critics argue that felony murder liability is a morally arbitrary lottery, in which punishment depends on the fortuity that an unintended death occurs in the course of a felony, regardless of the felon's culpability for that death.

Now a killing can be very culpable even if it is not intended. Most felony murders are intentional shootings by armed robbers. A felony murder rule makes this type of killing murder without requiring the prosecutor to prove, or the jury to find, that the robber intended to kill. Many readers will not find these typical applications of felony murder liability troubling. Yet felony murder liability is sometimes imposed on felons who do not seem very culpable at all. Consider these ten cases:

1. Seven months after stealing a car, James Colenburg, a Missouri man, was driving down a residential street when an unsupervised two-year-old suddenly darted in front of the stolen car. The toddler was struck and killed. Colenburg was convicted of felony murder predicated on theft.[10]

2. Jonathan Miller, a fifteen-year-old Georgia youth, punched another boy in a schoolyard dispute. The second boy suffered a fatal brain hemorrhage. Miller was convicted of felony murder, predicated on the felonies of assault with a deadly weapon and battery with injury.[11]

3. Wrongly suspecting Allison Jenkins of drug possession, an Illinois police officer chased him at gunpoint. As the officer caught him by the arm, Jenkins tried to shake free. The officer tackled Jenkins and the gun fired as they fell, killing the officer's partner. Jenkins was convicted of felony murder, predicated on battery of a police officer.[12]

4. Jonathan Earl Stamp robbed a California bank at gunpoint. Shortly thereafter one of the bank employees had a fatal heart attack. Stamp was convicted of felony murder.[13]

5. New York burglar William Ingram broke into a home, only to be met at the door by the homeowner, who was brandishing a pistol. The homeowner forced Ingram to lie down, bound him, and called the police. After police took Ingram away, the homeowner suffered a fatal heart attack. Ingram was convicted of felony murder.[14]

6. Also in New York, Eddie Matos fled across rooftops at night after committing a robbery. A pursuing police officer fell down an airshaft to his death. Matos was convicted of felony murder.[15]

7. John Earl Hickman was present when a companion overdosed on cocaine in Virginia. He was convicted of felony murder predicated on drug possession.[16]

8. John William Malaske, a young Oklahoma man, got a bottle of vodka for his underage sister and her two friends. One of the friends died of alcohol poisoning. Malaske was convicted of felony murder predicated on the felony of supplying alcohol to a minor.[17]

9. Ryan Holle, a young Florida man, routinely loaned his car to his housemate. At the end of a party, the housemate talked with guests about stealing a safe from a drug dealer's home. The housemate asked Holle for the car keys. Holle, tired, drunk, and unsure whether the housemate was serious, provided the keys and went to bed. The housemate and his friends stole the safe, clubbing a resisting resident to death. Holle was convicted of felony murder and sentenced to life without parole.[18]

10. North Carolina college student Janet Danahey set fire to a bag of party decorations as a prank in front of an exterior door to her ex-boyfriend's apartment. To Danahey's surprise, the apartment building caught fire and four people died in the blaze. Danahey pled guilty to four counts of felony murder.[19]

These cases are indeed troubling. The *New York Times* featured the *Holle* case in a story portraying the felony murder doctrine as out of step with global standards of criminal justice.[20] Some readers will recognize the *Stamp* case as one that criminal law textbooks use to illustrate the harshness of the felony murder rule.[21] Janet Danahey's supporters present her case as an indictment of the felony murder doctrine.

What should be done about such cases? If the felony murder doctrine is designed to produce results like these, it should indeed be abolished. Yet the three cases described in our first paragraph show that felony murder liability is sometimes necessary to satisfy our intuitions about deserved punishment. Thus it should be possible to identify a principle distinguishing justified from unjustified impositions of felony murder liability and to reform the felony murder doctrine in light of that principle. That is the aim of this book.

I should be clear from the outset about two limits on the scope of my argument. First, this book is concerned only with murder liability for unintended killing in the context of felonies. It is particularly concerned with homicides that would not be graded as murder without the killer's participation in a felony. Thus, it does not address how participation in a felony should affect the grading or punishment of intentional or grossly reckless killings that would otherwise be punished as murder.

This limit gives rise to a second essential limit on the scope of the argument: *this is not a book about the death penalty.* Without venturing an opinion on the legitimacy of capital punishment generally, I proceed from the premise that American law reserves it for the most heinous murders. The Supreme Court has determined that capital punishment is not applicable to those who participate in fatal felonies without intent to kill or gross recklessness (sometimes referred to as "extreme" or "depraved" indifference to human life).[22] It has not explicitly required that felons who kill must also act with intent to kill or gross recklessness, but this is the logical implication of its holdings. Many death penalty jurisdictions treat participation in certain felonies as aggravating circumstances that can trigger capital liability for intentional killings. Such feloniously motivated intentional killings are beyond the scope of this book. This book is concerned only with the imposition of very significant sentences of incarceration for killings that would not be murder without a felonious motive. It argues that murder liability is justified for some feloniously motivated inadvertent killings. *It does not justify capital punishment in such cases.*

CONSTRUCTIVE INTERPRETATION

In proposing principled reform of felony murder rules rather than abolition, this book serves to *make the best* of the felony murder doctrine. By this, I mean two things.

First, like it or not, we are stuck with the felony murder doctrine. To be sure, we could get along without it. We could abolish it and still capture many of the most culpable cases with rules conditioning murder on grossly reckless killing. Yet we are not likely to do so. Legislatures have persisted in supporting felony murder for many decades in the teeth of academic scorn. Although most states revised their criminal codes in response to the American Law Institute's Model Penal Code, only a few accepted the ALI's proposal to abolish felony murder.[23] Today, criminal justice policy is less likely than ever to be influenced by academic criticism, as candidates for office find themselves competing to appear tougher on crime than their opponents.[24] Moreover, as we shall see, in adhering to the felony murder doctrine, legislatures appear to be in tune with popular opinion.[25] Felony murder liability is not going away and we are going to have to learn to live with it.

Second, we should try to make felony murder law better. If felony murder liability is ever justifiable, felony murder rules can be improved by confining them to the limits of their justifying principles. Even readers who disagree with those justifying principles should prefer that felony murder liability be applied in a principled way rather than haphazardly.

Accordingly, this book endeavors to make felony murder "the best it can be," in Ronald Dworkin's phrase. Dworkin's influential account of normative legal argument aims to integrate the concerns of lawyers, judges, legislators, citizens, and legal theorists in a single conversation.[26] Although participating in the legal process in different roles, each of these speakers addresses a common question: how to make the law of some particular political community "the best it can be."[27] For Dworkin, legal reasoning is always at once positive and normative. It draws on the authority of institutions that are accepted as legitimate, while remaining mindful that the legitimacy of those institutions is always open to question and always contingent on the acceptance and commitment of other legal actors. Thus an appeal to settled authority never suffices to warrant a legal claim. Such claims also depend upon some normative legal theory; yet such legal theories are always also interpretations of the history of some particular legal system.

Dworkin uses the concept of "principle" to capture this complex ambiguity of legal argument between claims about how the law is and claims about how it should be. For Dworkin, rules and precedents are never self-interpreting. Decision makers cannot apply sources of law without first constructing some more general account of their purposes and values, and of how they fit within the larger body of law that makes them authoritative. These justifying accounts of the purposes and values of rules within a particular legal system are what Dworkin calls "principles."

Many other legal theorists have also argued that applying rules involves constructing their purposes.[28] But Dworkin adds that these ordering purposes are best understood as moral principles rather than as instrumental policies.

In other words, laws are best understood as setting up cooperative institutions to share the burdens of achieving public goods. Thus interpreted, laws have an additional basis of legitimacy beyond their democratic pedigree and their efficacious consequences: they can be defended as fair, and therefore worthy of the support even of those who opposed them.[29]

A jurisprudence of principle is one kind of "constructive interpretation."[30] Constructive interpretation is a two-part process of judgment as to how to continue a practice. A constructive interpreter must first construct a purpose that explains and justifies the history of that practice and, second, apply that purpose to resolve dilemmas that arise within that practice. The validity of a constructed purpose depends upon two different considerations: how well it fits with or explains the past history of the practice and how normatively appealing it is on its own terms. Thus a legal principle is valid insofar as it explains authoritative legal sources in a way that seems just. The principles that "best" reconcile these two considerations of fit and justice make the law "the best it can be."[31]

Although Dworkin insists that the conventions of legal reasoning require that lawyers and judges treat legal questions as having "right answers,"[32] his account of legal reasoning explains why legal theorists often describe law as indeterminate. After all, the principles that best fit enacted laws may not be the ones that seem most just. Indeed, the descriptive question of the content and validity of enacted laws is not entirely separable from the question of their justice.[33] As Dworkin admits, the constructive interpretation of law is a "creative" process depending on something like aesthetic judgment.[34] Both judges and legislators have discretion, but neither is free to develop laws whimsically; both should maintain the integrity of the legal system even as they improve it.[35] Every legal actor, in every legal decision, should strive to make the legal system as a whole the best it can be.

Because constructive interpretation involves a trade-off between explanation and justification, a constructed purpose need not "fit" past practice perfectly. Like any legitimating rationale it has critical as well as justificatory implications. An interpretive legal theory may demand some reforms as the price of maintaining integrity with the principle justifying the remainder of the law.

THE PRINCIPLE OF DUAL CULPABILITY

Proceeding by the method of constructive interpretation, this book offers a principled defense of the felony murder doctrine, rooted in its history, justifying much current law, and urging reform of the rest. It argues that felony murder liability is deserved for those who negligently cause death by attempting felonies involving (1) violence or apparent danger to life and (2) a sufficiently malign purpose independent of injury to the victim killed. How can merely negligent homicide deserve punishment as murder? Because the felon's additional malevolent purpose aggravates his culpability for causing death carelessly. To impose a foreseeable risk of death for such a purpose deserves severe punishment because it expresses particularly reprehensible values and shows a commitment to put them into action. In defending felony murder liability as deserved in cases like those described in its opening paragraph, this book develops an expressive theory of culpability that assesses blame for harm on the basis of two dimensions of culpability: (1) the actor's expectation of causing harm and (2) the moral worth of the ends for which the actor imposes this risk.[36]

Thus felony murder liability rests on a simple and powerful idea: that the guilt incurred in attacking or endangering others depends on one's reasons for doing so. Killing to prevent a rape is justifiable, while killing to avenge a rape is not. And yet killing to redress a verbal insult is worse, and killing to enable a rape worse still. Even when inflicting harm is wrong, a good motive can mitigate that wrong and a bad motive can aggravate it.

The same considerations can affect our evaluations of risk taking. We justify speeding a critically injured patient to a hospital; we condemn the same behavior in the context of drag racing or flight from arrest. As a society, we tolerate the nontrivial risks of death that ordinarily attend driving, light plane aviation, hunting, boxing, and construction as costs worth paying. For reasons that are far from obvious, our society views the risks of recreational drug use very differently. We are quicker to condemn failure to provide medical care to a child if motivated by cruelty or indifference than if motivated by religious conviction.[37] And most pertinently, we regard the risk of death associated with robbery as less acceptable than the *greater* risk of death associated with resisting robbery.[38] Thus we evaluate action based not only on its expected danger but also on the moral worth of its motives. Indeed, because harm results from the interaction of competing activities, we can hardly assign risk to one activity without evaluating its aims in comparison to those of competing activities.

The intuition that our guilt for causing harm depends on our reasons for acting implies that criminal culpability is properly understood as the product of two factors: the harm reasonably expected from an action and the moral worth of the ends for which it is committed. The expected harm is the *cognitive* dimension of culpability, and the moral worth of the actor's ends is the *normative* dimension of culpability. Let us call the view that the punishment deserved for homicide depends on both dimensions, the *principle of dual culpability*. Today, courts generally explain felony murder as a crime of risk imposition, in which a dangerous activity leads to death.[39] Previously courts explained it as a crime of transferred intent, in which a malicious purpose justifies liability for a different, unintended result.[40] The principle of dual culpability reveals that felony murder must involve both the negligent imposition of risk and a distinct malicious purpose. This book explains felony murder liability as a means of imposing deserved punishment in accordance with this principle of dual culpability.

The dual culpability principle seems to accord with the views of many Americans. Opinion research shows that most respondents think homicides deserve more punishment if they are committed in perpetrating another crime. Paul Robinson and John Darley found that their subjects recommended only ten months' imprisonment for negligent killing, but twenty-two to twenty-seven years for negligent killing by a robber, in the perpetration of a robbery.[41] This is not to say that public opinion would support every felony murder rule currently in force. For example, Robinson and Darley's subjects recommended only a six- to nine-year homicide sentence for a robber whose accomplice killed in the course of the robbery.[42] Nevertheless, this evidence suggests that public opinion supports some degree of penalty enhancement for criminally motivated homicides. So when criminal law theorists dismiss felony murder liability as rationally indefensible, they ignore popular ideas of justice and fail to give legislators guidance on how to realize those ideas in a principled way. This book is intended to provide such guidance.

FELONY MURDER AS A CRIME OF DUAL CULPABILITY

The principle of dual culpability renders some unintended homicides punishable as murder that would otherwise be lesser offenses. Yet it does *not* justify murder liability for otherwise faultless killings in the perpetration of felonies. Imagine that a bank robber drives away from the crime scene with the stolen loot, proceeding at a safe speed. A pedestrian suddenly darts out into traffic and the robber's car hits him fatally. Here the robber's felonious motive has not subjected the pedestrian to any greater risk than he would have faced from any other motorist. The robber's greed has placed other persons at risk, such as those he has threatened, but this death seems outside the scope of that risk. His felonious motive cannot aggravate his responsibility for a death unless it plays some causal role in the death. The felonious motive can aggravate cognitive culpability, but it cannot substitute for it.

While the felonious purpose must motivate a negligent act that creates a risk of death, it must also transcend that risk in order to add culpability. The felony cannot simply be an assault aimed at injuring or endangering the victim. This lacks the additional element of exploitation that compounds the defendant's culpability for imposing risk. Nor can the felony consist simply of an inherently dangerous act, such as firing a weapon or exploding a bomb. These offenses do not require any wrongful purpose. They are punished only because they impose danger. Causing death by means of a dangerous act is merely reckless homicide if one is aware of the danger and negligent homicide if one is not. It can be murder only if there is some further culpability. This culpability is supplied by a wrongful purpose, independent of injury or risk to the victim's physical health. The traditional predicate felonies—robbery, rape, arson, burglary, and kidnapping—all involve a wrongful purpose to do something other than inflict physical injury.

These considerations justify imposing felony murder liability when an actor negligently causes death for a felonious purpose independent of physical injury to the victim killed. But should we also impose murder liability on an accomplice in that felony? When critics claim that the felony murder doctrine holds felons strictly liable for killings in the course of felonies, they often mean they are liable for unforeseeable killings by co-felons. But such a rule would not be justified by the foregoing principles. An accomplice in a felony should be held liable for a resulting death only on the same basis as the principal. Like the killer, the co-felon must be negligent with respect to the resulting death. Moreover, the co-felon must share in the purpose that aggravates this negligence. One who reluctantly provides goods or services that he or she suspects will be used in a crime lacks the exploitative motive for imposing foreseeable risk that warrants condemnation as a murderer. Recall that Robinson and Darley's subjects supported far less punishment for accomplices than for those who killed negligently.[43] In the face of this skepticism, legislatures and courts must take special care to ensure that any accomplices punished as felony murderers are fully as culpable as the perpetrators.

REALIZING THE PRINCIPLE OF DUAL CULPABILITY

A felony murder law can use a variety of different doctrinal devices to achieve these limitations. To understand these doctrinal devices it is useful to analyze felony murder liability into its component parts. Felony murder is a kind of homicide, an offense ordinarily combining an act that causes death with a culpable mental state. Felony murder also requires a felony and some linkage between the act causing death and the felony. Where a fatal felony has multiple participants, felony murder liability may depend on additional criteria of accomplice liability. Thus, a fully specified felony murder rule should provide: (1) any required culpable mental state with respect to death; (2) a list or class of predicate felonies; (3) criteria of causal responsibility for the death; and (4) criteria of accomplice liability.

The most straightforward way to condition felony murder liability on negligence with respect to death is simply to make this culpable mental state part of the mental element of the crime. Yet this is not necessarily the best approach, because negligence is arguably not really a mental state at all but a normative characterization of conduct as unreasonable under the circumstances. Conduct is negligent with respect to a harmful result when an actor engaging in such conduct has reason to foresee the harm (and no sufficiently good reason to risk the harm). This may be true of any instance of conduct generally understood to be dangerous. Examples might be driving much faster than the posted speed limit, driving an unbelted child, or handling a loaded gun without the safety catch on. Indeed, as the speed limit example illustrates, the law can play a role in providing notice to actors that conduct is dangerous. By proscribing and punishing conduct, criminal law can alert actors to its risks, rendering a failure to advert to those dangers unreasonable per se.

Accordingly, felony murder laws can require negligence by requiring apparently dangerous conduct. This can be done by limiting predicate felonies to a list of enumerated dangerous felonies, or to the category of inherently dangerous felonies. Such a limited felony murder offense works as a per se negligence *rule*, defining certain conduct as negligent per se. For reasons we will explore below, dangerousness is sometimes defined in terms of force or violence rather than quantifiable risk. Alternatively, felony murder laws can require an apparently dangerous act committed in furtherance of the felony. This is a per se negligence *standard*, defining conduct as culpably committed if it exhibits a certain quality, foreseeable dangerousness. These per se approaches to requiring negligence have the effect of fully incorporating cognitive culpability for the resulting death into the intent to commit the felony. Thus they accord with the traditional characterization of felony murder, as a crime of transferred intent rather than a crime of strict liability.

If the felony is inherently dangerous to life, the mental element of the felony should itself supply the requisite negligence. But if the felony is dangerous only because of the way it is committed, the felon is negligent only if aware of the particular circumstances making commission of the felony dangerous. Where danger does not inhere in the felony, it is important to prove that accomplices in felony murder shared culpability with respect to a dangerous act or circumstance.

Another approach to requiring negligence is to build a requirement of apparently dangerous conduct into criteria of "killing," or "homicide" or "causation of death." Thus one may require not only that a homicidal act be a necessary condition to the resulting death but also that it impose a foreseeable risk of such a death. This approach resonates with tradition, in that before the twentieth century English and American law usually defined homicide in terms of "killing," which meant causing death by intentionally inflicting physical harm. Rather than defining murder in terms of a mental state, eighteenth-century English law defined murder simply as killing absent certain exculpatory circumstances that would show that the killing was not maliciously motivated.[44] Modern felony murder law may similarly define a measure of culpability into the act element of the offense. Many jurisdictions use a proximate cause test, conditioning causal responsibility on an act necessary to the death that also imposes a foreseeable danger of death. A minority of jurisdictions use an agency approach that excludes liability when an actor who is not party to the felony commits a subsequent act necessary to the resulting death, even if foreseeable. Yet even agency jurisdictions may require that the felon's act create a foreseeable risk of death or involve an intentional battery—and we shall see that most do. An agency rule also can have the effect of requiring that the act deemed to cause death serve the felonious purpose.

Finally, lawmakers may build a requirement of negligence into the linkage between the predicate felony and the resulting death by requiring that death occur in a way that was foreseeable as a result of the predicate felony. This is particularly useful for ensuring that accomplices in the felony are negligent with respect to death.

Like the requirement of negligence, the requirement of an independent felonious purpose can also be achieved in a variety of ways. One approach is simply to restrict enumerated predicate felonies to those involving a purpose independent of injuring or endangering the physical health of the victim. Another approach is an independence requirement sometimes referred to as a "merger" limitation, excluding certain predicate felonies such as manslaughter or assault as lesser included offenses of murder itself. Courts applying such a doctrine may interpret it to require that the felony have a purpose, threaten an interest, or involve conduct independent of physical injury. A third device is a linkage requirement that the act causing death be in furtherance of the felony. A few courts have construed an "in furtherance" standard to require that the act causing death serve a purpose independent of endangering or injuring the victim.

Lawmakers should also ensure that accomplices in felony murder share in the required negligence and independent felonious purpose. One way to do this is simply to require that the predicate felony involved an apparent danger of death and an independent felonious purpose. Then, if criteria of complicity in the felony are sufficiently demanding, an accomplice in the felony will automatically have had the requisite culpability. It does not suffice, however, to require that the felony was committed in a dangerous way without also requiring that the accomplice expected that danger. Most jurisdictions deal with this problem by holding the co-felon complicit in only those fatal acts that were in furtherance of and foreseeable as a result of the felony. This foreseeability test requires that the accomplice's participation in the felony entailed some degree of culpability with respect to the risk of death. If, however, jurisdictions require neither an inherently dangerous felony nor that death was foreseeable to the accomplice as a result of the felony, they leave the accomplice open to strict liability, even when death has been caused in a way foreseeable to the perpetrator. This would violate the principle of dual culpability.

DUAL CULPABILITY IN THE HISTORY OF FELONY MURDER

Constructive interpretation requires that a legal principle, however just, should also cohere with authoritative legal materials. One part of the case against felony murder liability is the claim that modern felony murder rules, even if narrowly predicated on dangerous felonies, are descended from an ancient strict liability rule. Thus American lawyers have long been taught that the English common law imposed strict murder liability on felons for all deaths caused—even accidentally—in the course of all felonies.[45] They have long learned that this cruel and ancient common law rule was automatically received into American law with independence[46] and produced terrible injustice as legislative proscription of new felonies expanded its already sweeping scope.[47] According to this mythology, the English rule remained in force in every jurisdiction until ameliorated by legislatures or courts and indeed remains authoritative to this day in default of such reform.

This widely believed account of the origins of felony murder liability undermines its legitimacy in two ways. First, it implies that modern felony murder rules must be interpreted in light of their supposed origins, with gaps and ambiguities resolved in favor of strict liability. Second, it implies that even limited modern rules are not justified by any principle but represent incoherent compromises between felony murder liability and enlightened principles that condemn it as barbaric.

This book will show that the conventional account of felony murder's origins is misleading in almost every respect. Thus felony murder liability was not an ancient rule of the English common law. Indeed, it was not part of the law of England at any time before the American Revolution and so could not have been received into American law from England. In fact, English constitutional law held that the English common law of crimes had no authority in the American colonies except insofar as received and adapted in each jurisdiction. So we have no reason to think felony murder was part of colonial American law unless we find it enacted in colonial statutes or applied by colonial courts—and we don't. American felony murder rules were enacted primarily by legislatures over the course of the nineteenth century. Thus each jurisdiction's felony murder rule was logically independent of every other jurisdiction's rule; each jurisdiction had only the limited rule that it enacted. England began to apply a felony murder rule in the nineteenth century as well. In both countries felony murder liability developed in the effort to reform the law of murder by codifying its elements. In both countries the rule was limited by concerns about culpability from the very outset. The ameliorative "reform" of the felony murder doctrine was contemporaneous with its enactment into law.

In seventeenth- and eighteenth-century England, murder liability depended primarily on the characteristics of the act. The required act was not the causation of death but "killing," a term historically associated with striking a blow.[48] If death resulted from an intentional and unprovoked blow with a weapon, it was murder whether the intent was to cause death or merely to cause pain and injury.[49] Such an attack was conventionally understood as an expression of "malice," that is, gratuitous hostility undiluted by the respect implied in a challenge to duel and unmitigated by the righteous indignation provoked by a prior attack.[50] A merely dangerous act—driving a coach at an unsafe speed down a narrow street, for example—might cause death but was not therefore a killing and expressed no malice.[51] These rules were unaffected by the context of a felony. A fatal stabbing during a robbery was murder; a

fatal cart collision during a robbery was not. The chief significance of a criminal context for homicide was that resistance to a crime—any crime, not just a
felony—could not constitute provocation. Thus the attempted commission of
a felony did not substitute for intent to kill or any other mental state, because
no such mental state was required for murder.[52] So the English common law
did punish unintended killings in the course of felonies as murder, but only
because it punished *most* unintended killings as murder. But it did not punish
accidental deaths in the course of felonies as murder. It is likely that colonial
Americans understood murder in the same way. Colonial statutes simply punished "willful" or "malicious" murder, with these terms likely signifying intentionally wounding with a weapon, followed by fatal results.

    While a criminal context could not turn an accidental death into murder in
eighteenth-century England, it could implicate the participants in an accomplice's culpable killing. A pair of sixteenth-century cases held that co-felons
who joined in or agreed to violence against resisting victims were liable for any
resulting deaths.[53] By the eighteenth century, some judges had suggested that
mere participation in a crime sufficed to implicate one in a codefendant's murder.[54] It appears that by the late eighteenth century, a few judges were applying this sweeping standard, but most limited accomplice liability for murder to
those who had actually participated in the fatal violence.

    The reform of homicide law in nineteenth-century England and America
took place against this background. Already during the early eighteenth century,
religiously motivated reformers had sought to restrict the number of capital
crimes in some colonies, and such views became common among enlightened
reformers during the revolutionary period.[55] In post-revolutionary Pennsylvania, reformers sought to increase reliance on incarceration and reduce the scope
of capital punishment. Thus in 1794 Pennsylvania enacted an influential statute
restricting capital murder to premeditated intentional murder or murder in the
course of robbery, rape, burglary, or arson.[56] This reform, adopted in many other
states, left the definition of murder unaffected but reduced its punishment in
most cases.[57] Murder still included unprovoked battery with weapons that happened to prove fatal. Murder still did not include accidental death. Many other
states adopted statutes defining murder as killing either intentionally, or in the
course of enumerated felonies, or with an abandoned and malignant heart.

    American reformers did not, by and large, see felony murder liability as strict
liability, but instead saw felonious motive as one of a number of forms of culpability aggravating already culpable homicides to murder, or to murder of a

higher degree. Felony murder liability was limited from the outset to deaths resulting from acts of violence committed in the furtherance of particularly dangerous felonies. We will see that the great majority of the felony murder convictions appearing in reported cases during the nineteenth century involved death from the intentional infliction of a violent blow; and the great majority were predicated on the traditional felonies of robbery, burglary, arson, and rape. Predicate felonies almost always involved a felonious purpose independent of injury to the victim, and a few decisions made this requirement explicit.[58]

Accomplice liability for felony murder was quite limited in nineteenth-century England and America. Early-nineteenth-century English cases established the principle that an accomplice in a felony was not liable for a killing by a co-felon unless he joined in or agreed to the fatal violence.[59] In the United States, few jurisdictions clarified rules governing accomplice liability for felony murder, but where they did articulate standards, courts usually required that the killing be in furtherance of the felony or a foreseeable or probable result of the felony. In almost every case where a felon was held liable for murder without having struck the fatal blow, either he participated in the fatal assault or the felony inherently involved violence or great danger of death. Thus from its inception American felony murder law largely conformed to the requirements of the dual culpability principle.

DUAL CULPABILITY IN CURRENT LAW

This book will also support a constructive interpretation of felony murder as a crime of dual culpability by showing that this principle accounts for many features of contemporary felony murder law. This analysis focuses on three issues: requirements of cognitive culpability, dangerousness, and causal responsibility that condition liability on negligence; standards of complicity and collective liability that determine the culpability required for non-killing participants in felonies; and requirements of an independent predicate felony that condition liability on normative culpability.

A third of felony murder jurisdictions explicitly condition felony murder on the culpable mental states of negligence or malice. Jurisdictions conditioning felony murder on malice have usually interpreted it to require apparently dangerous conduct. Almost all felony murder jurisdictions condition the offense on per se negligent conduct by requiring a dangerous felony. A requirement of an inherently dangerous felony ensures that all participants in the felony are negligent with respect to death. A requirement of foreseeable danger ensures that at least one participant, usually the actual killer, acted negligently. Of twenty felony murder jurisdictions predicating felony murder on unenumerated felonies, all but a few require that these felonies be inherently or foreseeably dangerous. Most felony murder convictions are predicated on enumerated felonies, however. With the important exceptions of burglary and some drug offenses, most such enumerated felonies are dangerous. Finally, most felony murder jurisdictions require negligence indirectly by defining homicide as the foreseeable causation of death. This includes most of the jurisdictions enumerating felonies that are not inherently dangerous.

Most felony murder jurisdictions condition vicarious felony murder liability on negligence, although they use a variety of doctrinal devices to achieve this. A few jurisdictions completely restrict predicate felonies to inherently dangerous crimes. Some jurisdictions define felony murder simply as participation in a felony foreseeably causing death. Most felony murder jurisdictions condition complicity in felony murder on foreseeable or inherent danger, or expected violence. A number of them provide an affirmative defense for accomplices without notice of danger.

Felony murder jurisdictions have usually conditioned causal responsibility and complicity on normative as well as cognitive culpability. Most require an instrumental or causal relationship between the felony and the death. The required linkage between the felony and the fatality implies that culpability is being transferred from the felony to the killing. Thus felonious motive is part of the culpability required for felony murder in most jurisdictions. Negligence toward death and felonious motive combine to justify murder liability as deserved.

The dual culpability required for felony murder—negligence and felonious motive—explains the purpose and the contours of the "merger" doctrine, precluding the predication of felony murder on felonious assault. Felonies aimed at injuring some interest other than the life and health of the victim—such as rape, robbery, arson, or aggravated burglary for purposes of theft—supply normative culpability that aggravates the cognitive culpability implicit in endangering the victim. Requiring an independent felonious purpose ensures that the felony will supply enough normative culpability to aggravate a negligent homicide to murder.

Yet the principle of dual culpability does not require that every predicate felony have an independent felonious purpose. Murder liability may be deserved on the basis of depraved indifference rather than felonious motive when death is caused by a felony entailing depraved indifference to human life. Although the dual culpability principle precludes murder predicated on simple aggravated assaults, it may permit murder predicated on a property offense committed for the purpose of an aggravated assault, an aggravated assault on a vulnerable dependent, or a particularly cruel and demeaning assault, such as mayhem. A legislature may rationally conclude that these predicate felonies express depraved indifference to human life.

Most jurisdictions have limited predicate felonies in conformity with these principles. To be sure, only a few jurisdictions have explicitly adopted the merger doctrine. Yet few other jurisdictions have violated the principles underlying the merger doctrine.

In sum, most felony murder jurisdictions condition the offense on negligence through a combination of culpability requirements, enumerations of predicate felonies, dangerous felony limits, foreseeable causation requirements, and complicity rules. In addition, most jurisdictions condition the offense on felonious motive through a combination of enumerated felonies, causal linkage requirements, and merger limitations. Thus felony murder law conforms to the principle of dual culpability in most respects in most jurisdictions.

A CRITICAL PRINCIPLE

While the American law of felony murder is broadly consistent with the dual culpability principle, it is far from perfect. This much is clear from the ten unjust convictions described earlier in this chapter. Yet the dual culpability principle explains *why* felony murder liability was not justified in those ten cases. In each case, at least one of the two required forms of culpability was missing.

Many of the cases lacked the requisite cognitive culpability. In the first eight cases, the likelihood of death from the defendant's conduct was low, too low even for negligence. To be sure, robbery creates a significant risk of death, but not a significant risk that anyone will drop dead or fall down a hole. In cases three through eight, no participant in the felony caused death directly. There was no fatal act of violence.

Many of the cases lacked the requisite normative culpability. Thus, in case one the defendant's fatal act did not serve the felonious end—it had no felonious purpose. In cases two, three, seven, and eight, the act imposing risk did not advance any independent felonious purpose. Thus felonies like assault and distribution of drugs or alcohol are punished primarily because they endanger life and health, not because they aim at some other wrongful end that justifies aggravating a resulting death to murder. In case nine the defendant assisted in a felony that proved fatal but did not appear to share the felonious end. In case ten, the defendant had no discernible felonious purpose. These two defendants probably should not have been convicted of the predicate felonies, let alone of felony murder.

Thus the injustice exemplified by these ten cases results from misapplication of the felony murder doctrine. We will see that in some of these cases courts misapplied existing law. It should therefore not be necessary to abolish the felony murder doctrine to prevent such cases. It is necessary only to conform it to its justifying purpose. Doing so will require statutory changes in some jurisdictions. But justice can be done in most jurisdictions if courts apply existing statutes with a clearer conception of when and why felony murder liability is deserved. Legal scholars do not encourage principled application of felony murder rules by portraying them as inherently arbitrary and unfair.

Whether or not they approve of the felony murder doctrine, legal scholars should acknowledge the rationality of the popular majorities who support it. By dismissing the felony murder doctrine as rationally indefensible, legal scholars deprive themselves of meaningful roles in reforming felony murder rules. By refusing to acknowledge any common ground with supporters of the felony murder doctrine, scholars offer legislators and voters no reason to listen to them. Moreover, by insisting that felony murder has no justifying purpose, legal scholars perversely encourage lawmakers to make the law of felony murder less rational and less just than it could be. Lectured that felony murder rules necessarily violate desert, legislators may assume they must abandon considerations of justice in designing felony murder rules. Told that felony murder rules reflect cynical political pandering, courts will assume they are properly deferring to legislative intent when they impose undeserved punishment. Instructed by scholars that the felony murder doctrine imposes strict liability, courts will more likely instruct juries to impose strict liability. In demanding abolition rather than reform, legal scholars make their narrow conception of the best the enemy of the good. The result is a self-fulfilling prophecy that encourages the arbitrariness and injustice it professes to condemn.

Because American felony murder rules rest on a widely supported and theoretically plausible moral principle, the most democratic approach to critiquing them is to test them against that principle. The most pragmatic strategy for improving the law of felony murder is to show lawmakers how to bring it into conformity with that principle.

PLAN OF THE BOOK

This book is divided into three parts. The remainder of Part One develops a normative defense of felony murder liability as deserved in some cases based on an expressive theory of culpability combining cognitive and normative dimensions. Chapter 2 first argues that felony murder needs such a retributivist defense, because utilitarian defenses of felony murder liability as enhancing deterrence are not persuasive. Chapter 2 then focuses on the cognitive dimension of culpability and considers several variants of the charge that felony murder rules impose strict liability. It argues that these charges rest on an implausibly formalistic conception of culpability that has little to do with moral fault and that felony murder rules can be conditioned on negligence by various means, including per se negligence rules and causation standards requiring foreseeability.

Chapters 3 and 4 focus on the normative dimension of culpability and critique the view that felonious motive is irrelevant to culpability. Chapter 3 attributes this view to a narrowly cognitive theory of culpability that prevails among criminal law theorists, arguing that this theory cannot give an adequate account of culpability for crimes of result like homicide. It argues that assessments of causal responsibility must involve an evaluation of actors' ends. Chapter 4 develops an expressive conception of culpability. It shows how such a conception makes sense of popular intuitions supporting felony murder liability and argues that an expressive conception better explains many other doctrines of American criminal law than does a purely cognitive conception. Chapter 4 also defends an expressive conception of culpability against the charge that evaluating offenders' motives violates the neutrality required of a liberal state.

Part Two debunks the myth of felony murder's origins in a common law rule of strict liability and shows the deep roots of the dual culpability principle in the history of American law. Chapter 5 demonstrates that England did not develop a felony murder rule until well after American independence. Chapter 6 shows that the English common law of crimes had far less authority in early America than is usually assumed and that nineteenth-century homicide law was largely statutory. Chapter 7 examines the development of felony murder law in jurisdictions with statutes that graded murder as first degree when committed in an enumerated felony. Chapter 8 examines the development of felony murder law in jurisdictions with statutes that imposed murder liability for killing in certain felonies. Both of these chapters show that nineteenth-century felony murder law generally required a dangerous felony and a violent act, while complicity required that the killing be in furtherance and foreseeable as a result of the felony. Thus felony murder law generally conformed to the principle of dual culpability from its inception.

Part Three examines contemporary felony murder law in light of the principle of dual culpability. It demonstrates that contemporary felony murder law conforms to the principle in most respects in most jurisdictions. This has two implications. First, felony murder law sufficiently conforms to the principle to warrant the principle as a constructive interpretation. Second, the principle condemns deviations as anomalies, at odds with the purposes that justify a felony murder rule.

Chapter 9 is concerned with felony murder as a crime of negligent killing. It examines the contemporary use of mental elements, dangerous felony requirements, and causation standards to condition felony murder liability on the killer's negligence. It expresses concern that some enumerated felonies—notably burglary and drug offenses—are not nearly as dangerous as legislatures may assume, but it concludes that other doctrines will usually prevent strict liability for causing death.

Chapter 10 examines criteria of vicarious liability for killings committed by co-felons. It finds that most jurisdictions require that death result foreseeably and in furtherance of the felony in most cases. It expresses concern that some jurisdictions do not adequately require culpability for death on the part of accomplices in felonies that are not inherently dangerous. It also observes that unjust attributions of complicity in felony murder often result from misattributions of complicity in the predicate felony. Finally, it condemns the small minority of statutes permitting felony murder liability without proof of causation or complicity.

Chapter 11 is concerned with felony murder as a crime of felonious motive and focuses primarily on the "merger" problem. It finds that most jurisdictions restrict predicate felonies to those involving either an independent felonious purpose or enough violence to manifest gross recklessness. It urges that legislatures take greater care to ensure that child abuse and other assault offenses enumerated as predicate felonies require extreme indifference. It also urges that all courts adopt merger rules in jurisdictions with unenumerated felonies.

Chapter 12 concludes the volume by reviewing the entire argument. It reiterates that unjust results can be avoided if felony murder law is properly understood and applied in light of its principles, while denunciations of felony murder liability as inherently irrational paradoxically permit its imposition without the constraints of principle.

2 THE CHARGE OF STRICT LIABILITY

In characterizing felony murder liability as rationally indefensible, critics assume that it takes the form of a strict liability rule. Imposing severe punishment without fault self-evidently violates desert. Critics add that felony murder is unlikely to deter killing if it does not condition liability for homicide on the choice to kill. Nor can it deter predicate felonies if it conditions additional punishment on a consequence felons have no reason to expect.

This chapter argues that defenders of felony murder rules need not take on the burden of defending strict liability. The equation of felony murder liability with strict liability depends on an artificially formalist conception of strict liability, which begs the question of desert. In substance, felony murder laws condition liability on negligence rather than strict liability.

Yet a persuasive defense of felony murder rules does need to show it imposes deserved punishment for culpable conduct. Deterrence rationales for felony murder liability are not very persuasive, while undeserved punishment can also impose countervailing social costs. Finally, constitutional due process appears to disfavor strict liability for crimes subject to severe penalties.

DETERRENCE ARGUMENTS

Obliged to impose felony murder liability despite the consensus of scholars that it imposes undeserved strict liability, courts have sought to defend a strict liability rule as a useful deterrent.[1] Do these deterrence rationales justify a strict liability rule? The only empirical study of current felony murder rules finds no discernible deterrent effect on homicide or on predicate felonies.[2] Moreover, we will see that deterrence theory would not predict that felony murder liability would have much deterrent effect.

Courts have sometimes explained felony murder liability as necessary to deter predicate felonies.[3] Yet this reasoning is subject to a traditional objection that remains persuasive. Opponents argue that even felonies we think of as very dangerous, like robbery, rarely lead to unintended death. Thus felony murder liability will increase the penalty otherwise imposed for the felony only in rare cases. This makes felony murder liability a punishment lottery that threatens prospective felons with a small chance of a large penalty. Deterrence theorists have long argued that such lotteries deter less efficiently than lesser but more certain penalties.[4] Empirical investigations indicate that increases in the certainty of punishment are more effective deterrents than increases in the severity of punishment.[5] Many reasons have been proposed for this effect. One is a widespread psychological disposition to discount low-probability dangers.[6] In addition, we may expect a decline in the marginal disutility of imprisonment as sentences lengthen, for three reasons. First, there are some psychic costs of imprisonment that do not depend on length of sentence. For example, incarceration may have a permanently stigmatizing effect irrespective of the length of imprisonment. Second, because of adaptive preference formation, inmates may find the status degradation they experience upon entering prison much harder than the low status they experience in prison.[7] Indeed, criminologist John Darley has even suggested that short-term inmates are relatively more likely to remember and describe their incarceration as harsh.[8] Third, because everyone discounts future welfare to some extent and because offenders may discount the future more than most, offenders should be less deterred by the last years of a sentence than by the first years.[9]

In addition to the declining marginal disutility of incarceration, severe but uncertain punishment may undermine deterrence in other ways. Uncertain punishment may create the impression that extraneous factors, such as corruption or prejudice, determine punishment. Punishment perceived as excessive may erode the moral authority of the law, reducing voluntary obedience to law.[10] This reduction in the law's moral authority may also discourage cooperation with law enforcement and so further undermine certainty of punishment. Thus, felony murder liability could have antideterrent effects if it were presented to the public as an undeservedly excessive penalty for the predicate felony.

Punishment lotteries do have some proponents. Thus, some legal economists have urged the efficiency of inflicting greater punishment on a smaller number of offenders in order to reduce apprehension, litigation, and administrative costs.[11]

In addition, some scholars have speculated—despite contrary empirical evidence—that a small risk of a high penalty could be more salient to potential felons than a slight increase in liability for the underlying felony.[12] Similar intuitions support the widespread assumption that a very small chance of capital punishment must deter murder.[13] However, this assumption has not been confirmed empirically.[14]

Some courts have explained felony murder rules as aimed at deterring reckless and negligent killing by felons.[15] Although such a deterrent effect has not been empirically demonstrated, it is supported by some plausible arguments.

To be sure, we already deter negligent and reckless killing by punishing it. Why should we punish the negligent or reckless killer even more when she kills in the context of a felony? Kevin Cole has offered the clever argument that it is harder to deter felons from culpable killing because they already face a stiff sentence for the underlying felony. An additional sentence for homicide will have a lower marginal disutility, for all the reasons explored above.[16] On the other hand, if an additional sentence for homicide is already too remote in time to deter, it would seem that lengthening that sentence would not add much deterrent effect.

Recently, Michael Mannheimer has further developed Cole's argument, pointing out that the substantial sentence that felons already face not only reduces the marginal disutility of a homicide sentence but also creates an incentive to commit homicide. Thus felons can reduce the certainty of punishment for the felony by eliminating witnesses.[17] This reasoning provides a cogent rationale for using felonious motive as an aggravator for intentional killings, as many jurisdictions do.

Does it also justify aggravating unintended killings on the basis of felonious motive? Or is it vulnerable to the traditional objection that unintended acts are not deterrable? Perhaps reducing the prosecution's burden to prove intent could increase the certainty of punishment for intentionally executing a witness if the defendant gets caught. Thus one who intentionally shot a witness to death might later claim that he shot to wound or intimidate or in struggling over the gun. A negligent felony murder rule convicts on all these scenarios.

Would we increase the certainty of punishment for intentional killings even more by holding felons strictly liable? I don't think so. Recall the ten unjust felony murder convictions reviewed in Chapter 1. Many of these cases involved true strict liability. Yet it is obvious that none of the defendants intended to kill. It seems most unlikely that a strict liability rule would convict intentional killers that a negligence rule would miss. Of course, if the argument of this book is accepted, a negligent felony murder rule also has an important advantage over a strict liability rule: it imposes deserved punishment.

Finally, some courts reason that a strict liability rule better deters negligent killing than a negligence rule, since punishment is more certain if the prosecution need not prove the killer's culpability.[18] However, this argument "proves too much" in two senses. First, we could increase the certainty of punishment for all crimes by lowering or eliminating the prosecution's burden of proof. That we generally forgo the deterrent benefits of conviction without proof in the interests of justice suggests we should do so here as well.

Second, the punishment lottery argument not only disfavors murder liability as a deterrent for felonies but also disfavors homicide liability as a deterrent to the endangerment of life. Thus the most efficient deterrent for negligent endangerment—by felons or anyone else—is attaching a small but certain penalty to each dangerous act, rather than imposing murder liability on the much smaller number of dangerous acts that happen to result in death. Deterrence theory favors punishing risk rather than harm. Because homicide law punishes low-probability harms, it is not a very efficient instrument of deterrence. If our end is to rationalize the law of homicide, deterrence theory seems like the wrong place to begin.[19]

Thus we are probably deluding ourselves in speculating that adjustments to the law of homicide will have any tangible deterrent benefit. As criminal law theorists Dan Kahan and Bernard Harcourt have both argued, in a liberal society committed to the subjectivity of value, we tend to disguise moral arguments about criminal justice as speculative empirical claims about consequences.[20] Yet it seems more intellectually honest and less cynical to punish on the basis of a possibly controversial view of desert than to pretend that we don't care about desert.

Even if the deterrent claims were more convincing, they would not necessarily justify the imposition of felony murder liability on the undeserving. Even if we punish primarily to advance the public welfare by preventing crime, we have strong reasons to restrict punishment to the deserving. Most people obey the criminal law because they approve its demands and see themselves as law-abiding citizens rather than because they fear punishment.[21] Legal scholar Louis Michael Seidman illustrates this by pointing to high levels of compliance with obligations of military service during wartime, despite the fact that such service is often more burdensome than incarceration.[22] Seidman reasons that punishment motivates compliance more by threatening to impose deserved blame than by threatening to inflict suffering.[23] By eroding the law's moral authority and obscuring its commands, undeserved punishment may therefore provoke more crime than it deters.[24]

Moreover, the anxiety aroused by the prospect of undeserved punishment may outweigh the security provided by any reduction in crime.[25] Accordingly, Jeremy Bentham's utilitarianism was centrally concerned with making the process of punishment more regular and transparent, so as to assure citizens that public officials would not use it to oppress them.[26] Thus, even if systematically punishing the undeserving deterred crime, it would not necessarily maximize utility.[27] Other things being equal, punishment discourages crime more effectively, and with less damage to public confidence in government, when it is deserved. Thus even utilitarian defenders of felony murder should meet its critics on the ground of desert and answer the charge that it imposes punishment without culpability.

STRICT LIABILITY

Whether felony murder rules impose strict liability or not depends on what we mean by this phrase. The meaning of "strict liability" is contested, particularly in criminal law.[28] Broadly speaking, strict liability means liability without moral fault. In private and regulatory law, where there are social costs of profitable activities to be distributed, strict liability may be useful and not unfair. In criminal law, however, where liability implies blame and imposes uncompensated suffering, liability without moral fault seems contradictory. In this area of law, "strict liability" implies "undeserved punishment." Accordingly, the power to define the concept of strict liability is the power to define the limits of legitimate criminal lawmaking.

The drafters of the Model Penal Code developed an influential scheme for defining and analyzing offense elements that included a technical definition of strict liability. According to this scheme, the actus reus of any offense can be analyzed into some combination of acts, omissions, circumstances, and results.[29] We can call these objective elements. The mens rea of the offense consists of culpable mental states such as purpose, knowledge, recklessness, or negligence associated with particular acts, omissions, circumstances, or results. We may call these mental states subjective elements.[30] If an offense requires proof of a subjective element such as intent to kill, without a corresponding objective element such as causing death, the subjective element is inchoate. If an offense requires an objective element without a corresponding subjective element, the objective element is a strict liability element. Every offense must involve at least one act or omission and possibly additional circumstance and result elements. Every serious offense requires a culpable mental state of negligence, recklessness, knowledge, or purpose with respect to each objective element. An offense with even one strict liability element is a strict liability offense, and no strict liability offense can be punished by incarceration.[31]

Criminal law theorist Ken Simons has dubbed the Model Penal Code's esoteric conception of strict liability "formal" strict liability.[32] If an offense requires no culpable mental state with respect to any objective element, it involves "pure" formal strict liability. If it requires a culpable mental state with respect to some objective elements, but not all, it involves "impure" formal strict liability. In this terminology the Model Penal Code forbids "impure formal strict liability." Simons calls the more familiar conception (liability without moral fault) "substantive" strict liability.[33]

According to the Model Penal Code's scheme, the offense of "negligently causing death" is not a strict liability crime, because it requires a culpable mental state—negligence—with respect to the offense's only act element. On the other hand, the offense of "causing death by means of maiming with the intent to torture" is strict liability, because it requires no culpable mental state with respect to one actus reus element, causing death. The second crime may involve more culpability than the first and is not substantively a strict liability crime. Nevertheless, formally it is a crime of impure strict liability, barred by the Model Penal Code's scheme.

There is no inherent reason why a felony murder law must employ impure strict liability. A felony murder law is simply a law conditioning murder liability on unintended killing in the commission or attempt of a felony. Such a law might explicitly require proof of recklessness or negligence with respect to a risk of death, and we will see that some felony murder statutes take this form. Yet many felony murder laws do not require proof of such a culpable mental state as a separate element. Thus they would qualify as strict liability offenses under the Model Penal Code's definition. For example, an offense defined as causing death by means of armed robbery or arson might entail negligence with respect to death (reasonable notice of a substantial and unjustifiable danger of death). But because it does not explicitly require proof of any culpable mental state with respect to death, it is formally an impure strict liability offense.

Legal theorist Mark Kelman has shown that there is no necessary correlation between impure strict liability and substantive strict liability. A legislature can discourage the negligent causation of harm by at least four means: (1) punishing those who foreseeably cause harm, (2) punishing those who foreseeably risk harm, (3) "strictly" punishing those who cause harm by knowingly committing designated dangerous acts, or (4) punishing those who knowingly commit designated dangerous acts whether or not these result in harm. The third alternative is an example of impure strict liability, but Kelman argues it should be seen as a per se negligence rule that achieves the same aims that the first alternative achieves by the alternative means of a discretionary negligence standard.[34] The fourth alternative eliminates the third alternative's impure strict liability, yet places less of a burden on the prosecution, punishes everyone punished by the third alternative, and punishes additional people besides.[35] It is not obvious why the third alternative should be seen as less fair than the fourth alternative.

Let us consider a more concrete illustration. Imagine that the legislatures of two states, North Appalachia and South Appalachia, both wish to impose deserved punishment for negligently imposing risk of mesothelioma, a cancer usually caused by breathing asbestos fibers. Imagine further that each adopts a different strategy. North Appalachia applies a flexible negligence standard, incriminating anyone who creates an unreasonable risk of mesothelioma (a risk not outweighed by the benefits of their conduct, of which they should be aware). South Appalachia applies a formal per se negligence rule, punishing those who knowingly or purposely engage in certain conduct that the legislature has determined to impose an unreasonable risk of mesothelioma. Thus South Appalachia adopts a regulatory code for the safe handling of asbestos with criminal sanctions for knowing and purposeful violations. Notice that neither approach involves a strict liability element, but North Appalachia's negligence standard involves an inchoate element. South Appalachia's formal rule may actually seem fairer in that it conditions liability on the higher culpability standards of knowledge or purpose rather than negligence, and it satisfies legality concerns by clearly defining the proscribed conduct.

Now suppose both legislatures decide to be more lenient, and punish only those who actually cause the harm as a result of their negligent action. Each adds a result element to the offense. The North Appalachia statute now punishes those who cause mesothelioma by acting negligently with respect to the risk of that harm. The new offense has neither an inchoate element nor a strict liability element. The South Appalachia statute now punishes those who cause the harm by knowingly engaging in the per se dangerous conduct. The new offense has a strict liability element, the result element. Because it has merely narrowed liability within the class of offenders receiving deserved punishment under the earlier statute, it seems that the new South Appalachia statute does not impose substantive strict liability. Yet it imposes formal impure strict liability. Similarly, a felony murder rule that punishes causing death by means of dangerous felonies may involve formal impure strict liability and yet condition liability on negligence.

So there are three difficulties with equating formal impure strict liability with substantive strict liability. First, some acts may imply culpability with respect to a result element that has no explicit culpability attached. For example, arson may imply reckless disregard of a risk of death. Depending on how we define "killing" and "causing death," these acts may themselves imply culpability with respect to death. Thus, if killing means only causing death by certain dangerous means, killing involves culpability per se. If "causing" a result means foreseeably bringing it about, it entails culpability with respect to that result.

Second, some culpable mental states may imply, but not explicitly require, culpability with respect to a result element. Thus the intent to inflict grievous bodily injury implies recklessness with respect to death. Causing death recklessly and causing death with intent to cause grievous bodily harm may be morally equivalent offenses even though one involves formal strict liability.

Third, an offense definition may require no culpable mental state with respect to one element but may require very severe culpability with respect to some other element, or an inchoate element. Thus causing grievous injury with the intent to rape may be as culpable a form of assault as intentionally causing grievous injury. Similarly, causing death with intent to rape may be as culpable a form of homicide as recklessly causing death. For these three reasons, a felony murder rule may involve formal impure strict liability without substantive strict liability.

If felony murder requires no proof of any culpable mental state with respect to death, it imposes strict liability in the formal sense. Yet it may nevertheless condition liability on moral fault by substituting a per se culpability rule for a culpability standard. A legislature may conclude that certain conduct poses a significant enough risk of death that its commission implies negligence or recklessness with respect to death. By providing notice of this judgment through a statutory rule, the legislature precludes a defendant from pleading ignorance of this risk. A dangerous-felonies limitation provides such a per se rule. Another way of conditioning felony murder liability on conduct inherently dangerous to life is to condition the element of "killing" on violent methods of causing death, as eighteenth-century English law did. In these ways, felony murder rules can substantively require culpability with respect to a risk of death, even when they do not do so formally. Finally, a felony murder rule can require a foreseeable risk of death as part of the proof of causation rather than as a separate mental element. Although formally a crime of strict liability, such a felony murder rule nevertheless requires culpability.

The charge that felony murder liability is a form of strict liability may have a different meaning, however. A critic of felony murder rules might concede that they effectively condition murder liability on negligence with respect to a risk of death, but object that negligence is not a legitimate form of culpability. According to the Model Penal Code's influential definitions of culpable mental states, the imposition of risk is negligent when the actor should be aware that she is imposing a substantial and unjustifiable risk.[36] Thus a requirement of negligence can be satisfied by conduct that a reasonable person would recognize as dangerous, even if the particular actor unreasonably fails to advert to the danger. For example, an armed robber who threatens a victim with a loaded gun might simply expect that he can control the weapon, the victim will obey, the robbery will go according to plan, and no one will get hurt—and so might never advert to the various ways creating such a volatile situation could result in death. The motel clerk killer described in the introduction is such a robber. If we adopt a strictly cognitive view of culpability, however, such unreasonably inadvertent risk imposition is merely stupid, not morally culpable.[37] On this cognitive view, if criminal negligence does not require actual awareness of risk, it cannot be a form of culpability. It follows that if felony murder is conditioned on negligent imposition of a risk of death, it imposes strict liability, even in the substantive sense. The negligent actor might be morally at fault for a wrongful act that inadvertently causes harm, but not for the harm itself.

The defender of negligence liability may respond in one of two ways: either she may insist that negligence is a form of cognitive culpability or she may offer some alternative conception of culpability. If she takes the first approach, she may define negligence as actual awareness of some unjustified risk less substantial than that required for recklessness. Or she might argue that negligence is a second-order cognitive failure. Thus one who fails to inform herself about the risks of an activity or who impairs her own capacity to perceive risks might be seen as cognitively culpable for resulting harms. Some commentators have tried to develop cognitive accounts of unreasonable failure to perceive risks. According to these accounts, actors are cognitively culpable if they are aware of facts from which they would infer risk if they focused their attention on those facts.[38] We might say they have notice rather than knowledge of risk, or that their knowledge of risk is "tacit." This might describe an unreflective armed robber like our motel clerk killer. If asked, he might acknowledge that a gun pointed at a victim might go off if he fumbles it, or if the victim, a witness, or a law enforcement officer startles him, or that one of these parties might pull a gun and fire, perhaps hitting a bystander.

Yet it is not clear that this hypothetical knowledge or notice is really a cognitive state. After all, the robber might never pose questions to himself about how things might go wrong. He might habitually act on the basis of desired or wished-for consequences rather than reasoned expectations. This certainly seems true of many bank robbers, for example, who perform their dramas on camera and in front of dozens of witnesses, and consequently face an 80 percent prospect of apprehension.[39] In other words, the risks that robbers unthinkingly impose on themselves are far greater and more apparent than the risks they impose on others. But when someone systematically tries to enact unrealistic fantasies rather than thinking about likely consequences, does her moral fault really depend upon tacit knowledge of risk? Or does it depend, as some "character theorists" claim, on a faulty process of practical reasoning that dismisses risk as irrelevant?[40] If so, negligence seems to depend on character or motivation, not just on cognition.

This reasoning pushes us to broaden our conception of culpability beyond the cognitive, so as to include the robber's negligence toward victims. On the expressive theory of culpability explored in Chapter 4, the robber's moral fault lies in the social meaning of her actions, the implication that her desires should have priority over the safety of others. On such a view the actor is at fault not for the unexamined and yet tacit cognitive implications of her action, but instead for the unexamined and yet tacit normative implications of her actions.[41] On this view the legitimacy of even the negligence component of felony murder liability will depend on the choice between cognitive and expressive theories of culpability discussed in Chapters 3 and 4. On the other hand, if we accept the account of negligence as tacit knowledge of risk, then the normative component of felony murder's culpability is limited to the felonious end for which the risk is tacitly imposed.

Critics of felony murder tend to elide the difference between formal and substantive strict liability. By calling felony murder a strict liability offense, critics create the impression that felony murder rules impose liability without moral fault. Often, however, their objection really concerns only the form of the offense definition. In other cases, the charge of strict liability disguises an objection to conditioning criminal liability on negligence.

CONSTITUTIONAL CONSTRAINTS ON FELONY MURDER LIABILITY

Some scholars have viewed the strict liability critique as implying the unconstitutionality of felony murder. Accepting the Model Penal Code's definition of strict liability and a purely cognitive view of culpability, Nelson Roth and Scott Sundby argued in an influential 1985 article that a homicide crime must be defined as including some culpable mental state with respect to death. If a felony murder rule requires intent to commit a felony rather than such a culpable mental state, they reasoned, it can be analyzed in only one of two ways. Either it improperly treats the commission of a felony as a conclusive presumption of intent to kill or it unfairly imposes strict liability with respect to death.[42] They argued that the first alternative violates constitutional due process and the right to a jury trial, by circumventing the prosecution's burden to prove an offense element, while the second alternative violates due process and the Eighth Amendment prohibition on cruel and unusual punishment by imposing undeserved punishment. Roth and Sundby were mistaken in assuming that felony murder rules *must* take one of these two forms. As we have seen, jurisdictions can avoid strict liability by conditioning felony murder on dangerous or violent felonies, or foreseeable death. Yet their arguments point to constitutional principles that should influence legislators in drafting, and courts in interpreting, felony murder laws.

The unconstitutional presumption argument treated all murder offenses as having a common mental element, malice. It drew on nineteenth-century British jurist J. F. Stephen's argument that different forms of murder liability all involved the common mental state of a high expectation of causing death.[43] Equating malice with an expectation of death, Roth and Sundby equated judicial pronouncements that a felonious purpose was one form of malice with conclusive presumptions of gross recklessness from the perpetration of a felony. Finally, they invoked the 1979 case of *Sandstrom v. Montana*, requiring the prosecution to prove offense elements and rejecting presumptions of culpability as wrongly lifting this burden from the prosecution.[44] If indeed felony murder rules authorized such presumptions, they would violate due process.

Some courts characterized felony murder rules as presumptions before *Sandstrom*,[45] and a few courts continued to instruct juries that they could "infer" malice from the commission of certain felonies that caused death, even after *Sandstrom*.[46] Some courts have accepted the unconstitutional presumption argument as a reason to abandon felony murder as traditionally defined. Thus courts in Michigan and New Mexico invoked the presumption argument in explaining their decisions to require proof of gross recklessness as an element of felony murder.[47] The South Carolina Supreme Court condemned an instruction defining any killing during any felony as murder, on the ground that it presumed the statutorily defined element of malice. The court recommended permitting juries to infer malice from some particular felonious purpose.[48] South Carolina courts have defined the required malice as "malignant recklessness of the lives and safety of others"[49] or a "heart devoid of social duty and fatally bent on mischief."[50]

Apart from these few jurisdictions, courts have generally rejected the charge that felony murder involves an unconstitutional presumption, reasoning that the intent to commit certain felonies is not evidence of culpability, or a substitute for culpability, but is simply the culpability required for one form of murder.[51] One such court concludes, "[A] felony of violence manifests a person-endangering frame of mind such that malice may be imputed to the act of killing."[52] Thus, an unconstitutional presumption challenge to a felony murder rule can become the occasion for confining predicate felonies to those involving violence or some other danger to life, and for articulating a per se negligence standard.

The strict liability argument can draw on two strands of constitutional doctrine that appear to require that criminal liability be conditioned on culpability at least under certain circumstances. One is based on the Eighth Amendment's cruel and unusual punishment clause, and the other is based on the Fifth and Fourteenth Amendments' due process clauses.[53]

The Eighth Amendment argument notes that the cruel and unusual punishment clause has been held to forbid disproportionate punishment, including lengthy terms of imprisonment.[54] Proportionality is generally identified in one of two ways, comparatively or instrumentally. Comparative proportionality measures punishment against that provided for other offenses, or the same offenses in other jurisdictions. Instrumental proportionality assesses punishment in terms of its service to its justifying purposes.

Comparative proportionality is unlikely to condemn felony murder liability as such because such liability is widespread and because many non-homicide offenses are now punished with lengthy terms of incarceration. Comparative proportionality could possibly condemn an unusually broad felony murder rule that did not require a dangerous felony or a foreseeable death. Thus comparative proportionality could conceivably be invoked against a genuinely strict liability felony murder rule, precisely because most felony murder rules are per se negligence rules.

Instrumental proportionality has been defined far less restrictively for incarceration than for capital punishment. The Supreme Court has justified capital punishment primarily on retributive grounds,[55] and restricted capital punishment to those unimpaired adult offenders capable of full culpability.[56] In considering the proportionality of incarcerative punishments, however, the Court has generally declined to prioritize desert,[57] and has permitted lengthy sentences for nonviolent offenses on the basis of speculative incapacitative considerations.[58] The division between capital punishment and incarceration may be breaking down, as the recent Supreme Court decision in *Graham v. Florida* extended much of the death penalty analysis to life without parole for juvenile offenders.[59] Nevertheless, instrumental proportionality has not yet been held to require that non-capital felony murder liability be conditioned on culpability. Still, a proportionality challenge can provide the occasion for a court to defend felony murder liability as deserved by emphasizing its limits. For example, in 1988 the Iowa Supreme Court rejected a proportionality challenge to a felony murder conviction on the narrow ground that proportionality was satisfied where the defendant killed with reckless indifference to human life.[60]

The due process argument relies on a line of cases requiring a mental element for offenses involving significant penalties and stigma. In *Baender v. Barnett*, the Court held that due process required that an offense of possessing counterfeiting tools be conditioned on culpability, and interpreted the statute to conform to this requirement.[61] Shortly thereafter, in *U.S. v. Balint*,[62] the Court recognized an exception to this requirement for regulatory offenses. In the influential 1952 case of *Morisette v. U.S.*, the Court construed a theft statute as requiring knowledge that the goods taken were property of another. The Court did not explicitly determine that such a mental element was constitutionally required, but ascribed to Congress an intention to confine strict liability to regulatory offenses, criminalizing the imposition of risk rather than harm, triggering low penalties, and implying little moral stigma.[63] Subsequent decisions of circuit courts have taken *Morisette* to imply that due process requires culpability for offenses triggering substantial penalties and moral disapprobation.[64] The Supreme Court has also required a culpable mental state for various offenses regulating otherwise constitutionally protected conduct. Thus, a felon-registration law burdening the right to travel could not be enforced without proof of notice of the duty to register.[65] A regulation of the sale of obscene publications could not be enforced without proof of knowledge of the obscene character of the literature sold.[66]

Does all of this add up to a constitutional requirement that murder be predicated on culpability with respect to death? Certainly, a conviction of felony murder entails severe punishment and implies severe blame. Accordingly, due process may require that it be conditioned on culpability. But this does not necessarily require that it be conditioned on culpability with respect to death—it may be that the culpability entailed in the predicate felony suffices. Professor Alan Michaels has argued that the only constitutional requirement of culpability is that an offender must culpably perform some proscribed conduct that is not constitutionally protected. An offense can constitutionally condition punishment on additional circumstances and results on a strict liability basis. A legislature may treat the underlying conduct as demonstrating insufficient care with respect to these other elements. Michaels proceeds to offer felony murder as an example of constitutional strict liability:

> Although strict liability formally attaches to the element of causing a death, the other elements of the statute—in particular committing a felony—establish imperfect care with regard to the strict liability element. A person guilty of felony murder displayed imperfect care with regard to causing a death because that person was not as careful as possible . . . ; the person could have been more careful by not committing the felony at all.[67]

Michaels suggests that felony murder does involve a kind of culpability with respect to death, "imperfect care" implied by the commission of a felony that caused death. I would add that since most jurisdictions require that the felony must be dangerous or violent, the "imperfect" care is usually negligent per se. Moreover, since most jurisdictions require that death must be foreseeable as a result of an act deemed to cause it, legal causation also seems to require negligence.

Are these negligence requirements optional, or are they constitutionally mandated? There are two reasons for thinking they could be required by due process. First, Michaels' principle requires at least one culpable conduct element. He writes as if that requirement is satisfied by felony murder because the defendant commits or attempts the felony culpably. Yet felony murder is a homicide offense distinct from the predicate felony, leading to a distinct penalty. It is not just a sentencing enhancement adding liability to a felony because death results. Arguably, killing or causing death is the single conduct element that requires corresponding culpability under Michaels' test, while the intent to commit a violent or foreseeably dangerous felony is the mental element that supplies that culpability. On this reasoning, felony murder is not and cannot be a strict liability offense. Second, *Morisette* held that crimes causing actual harm should be read as requiring culpability with respect to that result. Following the example of *Morisette* does not require overturning felony murder statutes for imposing strict liability. Instead, it simply involves reading them as requiring a foreseeable risk of death, as most jurisdictions do, through such doctrines as proximate causation and dangerous felony requirements. This is the same strategy some courts have deployed against unconstitutional presumption challenges.

In sum, the constitution requires that offense elements be proven beyond a reasonable doubt rather than presumed, but leaves legislatures broad discretion in defining them. It may require that crimes involving severe punishment and denunciation for causing harmful results be conditioned on some measure of culpability with respect to those results. When courts interpret ambiguous felony murder laws, they should presume a legislative intent to require as much culpability with respect to death as most jurisdictions in fact do. In so doing they will satisfy comparative proportionality. By conditioning felony murder liability on desert, they will also insulate felony murder laws against instrumental proportionality challenges.

In this chapter we have seen that felony murder liability is best justified as deserved. We have little reason to think that undeserved felony murder liability prevents crime. In addition, we have considered and rejected the oft-repeated claim that felony murder liability is undeserved because it does not require any culpability. Felony murder rules typically require culpability toward the risk of death by conditioning liability on conduct that is culpable per se. Thus felony murder liability generally requires negligence toward a risk of death, as well as a felonious purpose. Whether this culpability suffices to satisfy desert remains to be seen in the chapters to come.

3 CRITIQUING THE COGNITIVE THEORY OF CULPABILITY

Thus far, I have shown that the prevailing view of felony murder wrongly equates formal with substantive strict liability. As a result, it fails to acknowledge that felony murder liability can be—and usually is—conditioned on per se negligence rules. Yet even if a critic were to concede both that a felony murder rule conditioned liability on negligence with respect to a danger of death and that negligence is a legitimate form of culpability, she might insist that negligence is not *enough* culpability to warrant murder liability. My response is that felony murder involves two kinds of culpability: negligently imposing a significant and apparent risk of death, and doing so for a very bad reason.

This response must overcome a fundamental objection. Most criminal law scholars conceive culpability as an actor's expectation of harm at the time he or she acts. According to this purely cognitive conception of culpability, the actor's purposes, motives, meanings, and values are irrelevant. In particular, such goals as completing a rape, demeaning a victim because of her race, or intimidating political opponents are irrelevant to culpability for a killing. Why would one adopt such a narrow conception of culpability? Because judging the values that motivate action might seem improper for a liberal state. A purely cognitive view of culpability comports with a restrictive view of the role of criminal law as opposing harmful conduct but taking no sides in disagreements about values.

This ideal of a value-neutral criminal law has at least two distinct sources in liberal political thought. One is rights theory, concerned with protecting liberty. Rights theorists tend to see state coercion as presumptively illegitimate, justified only by a delegation to the state of an individual right of self-defense against private coercion. On such a view, the state is authorized to use coercion to prevent interference with liberty, but not to perfect the characters of individuals, which would violate their liberty. Individuals must be left free to choose their own ends. A second source of the cognitive culpability theory is utilitarianism, which interprets action as the rational pursuit of gratification. From this morally skeptical perspective, desire is the only source of value and so cannot be judged as better or worse on the basis of its content. The state's role is to maximize gratification, which requires it to discourage actions that impose more pain and frustration than gratification. In short, the state can regulate conduct to minimize social cost but cannot stand in judgment of the desires motivating conduct.[1]

Both traditions support the liberal "harm principle," which permits the state to punish conduct that causes harm to others but not to interfere with each individual's selection of her own ends.[2] The cognitive theory of culpability draws on this eclectic harm principle, reasoning that the liberal state can blame actors for predictably harmful actions, but not for their ends, which are intrinsically valuable expressions of liberty or utility. Actors can be blamed for their choices, but not for the values that guide those choices. The cognitive view of culpability invokes these disparate ideas in barring the criminal law from judging the reasons and values that motivate the choice to cause harm. To the extent that felony murder liability requires us to judge actions based on the moral worth of their motives, it is incompatible with such a cognitive view of culpability. Thus when criminal law scholars insist that no rational defense of felony murder liability is possible, part of what they mean is that it cannot be justified on the basis of a purely cognitive theory of culpability.

The shortcomings of this view of culpability are the focus of this chapter. I argue that the cognitive view does not offer a persuasive value-neutral account of culpability for homicide, and indeed that a value-neutral account of culpability for harmful consequences like death is impossible. I consider two variants of cognitive culpability theory, each drawn from a different source of the liberal harm principle. One conceives harm as disutility, and one conceives harm as rights violation.

Because the disutility of an act is the resulting net future welfare loss to all persons compared to that arising from alternative choices, that disutility is not a discrete injury. A utilitarian approach can therefore condemn types of acts as predictably harmful, but can never determine that a particular act actually caused a particular harm. Thus utilitarian cognitive culpability theory "proves too much." It condemns not just felony murder liability, but murder liability itself.

By contrast, rights theory does identify harm with discrete injuries. Yet attribution of causal responsibility and culpability for such particular results requires evaluation of the actor's ends. Since injuries arise from the interaction of conflicting activities, assignments of responsibility require normative criteria to determine which of the conflicting acts was wrongful. Rights theory responds to this "social cost" problem by privileging certain activities as protected by rights. Since actions and results are amenable to multiple descriptions, attributions of culpability for results require normatively laden interpretive judgments. There is no value free solution to this "multiple description" problem.

In short, a utilitarian account of culpability strives to achieve value neutrality by avoiding blame for actual harm. A rights account places blame, but only by evaluating actor's ends.

COGNITIVE CULPABILITY

A conception of culpability that considers only an actor's expectations of causing harm is purely cognitive. By contrast, a test that examines his reasons in order to identify and assess the values expressed by his act is expressive. Such an expressive test sees culpability as having two dimensions: one cognitive, concerned with expectations; the other normative, concerned with ends.

The cognitive and expressive views of culpability reflect two competing approaches to conceptualizing subjective criteria of liability in the criminal law, one descriptive and one normative. Criminal law theorist George Fletcher explains this distinction in *Rethinking Criminal Law*, as follows:

> One of the persistent tensions in legal terminology runs between the descriptive and normative uses of the same terms. . . . English jurists have sought to reduce the concepts of malice to the specific mental states of intending and knowing. California judges, in contrast, have stressed the normative content of malice in a highly judgmental definition, employing terms like "base, anti-social purpose" and "wanton disregard for human life." For the English, malice is a question of fact: did the actor have a particular state of consciousness (intention or knowledge)? In California, malice is a value judgment about the actor's motives, attitudes and personal capacity.[3]

Fletcher finds the same ambiguity in terms like "intent," "criminal intent," and "culpability"[4] and traces the ambiguity of subjective liability standards to a fundamental theoretical disagreement:

> Descriptive theorists seek to minimize the normative content of the criminal law in order to render it, in their view, precise and free from the passions of subjective moral judgment. . . . [T]he reality of judgment, blame and punishment in the criminal process generates the contrary pressure and insures that the quest for a value-free science of law cannot succeed. . . .[5]

The cognitive view of culpability aims at a value-free description of culpability by reducing it to beliefs about the states of affairs accompanying or resulting from conduct. It is based on a conception of the liberal state as a value-neutral framework for the pursuit of private ends. This conception has roots in two nineteenth-century variants of liberalism, utilitarianism and rights theory. Utilitarians held that while acts could be judged better or worse on the basis of their hedonic consequences for all, all acts were motivated by the same morally neutral desire for pleasure. Since the content of utility was determined by desires, desires themselves could not be evaluated. The utilitarian state could regulate harmful conduct, but not the desires motivating it. Rights theory justified a limited state, with only those coercive powers that rational individuals would concede in a state of nature to secure a sphere of freedom for each individual.[6] Within this tradition, ends were private matters, beyond the competence of the state to regulate.[7] Since individuals had a natural right of self-defense against harm in a state of nature, they could delegate this right to the state as their agent. Thus only harm to others could justify the coercive and punitive power of the liberal state. Both utilitarianism and rights theory seemed to support a conception of the criminal law as a value-neutral scheme for regulating the harmful consequences of action, without regard to its motivating ends. Indeed, the philosopher John Stuart Mill invoked both traditions in articulating this "harm principle."[8] Based on the harm principle, the cognitive view defines culpability in terms of expected consequences rather than ends. Thus it focuses on the risk of harm that is apparent to an actor in choosing one act over another.

The harm principle has broad support among contemporary criminal law theorists,[9] and some limited authority in constitutional law. In *Lawrence v. Texas* the Supreme Court held that moral disapproval was an insufficient reason for punishing private consensual sexual conduct absent some threat of harm.[10] On the other hand, the Court has permitted moral disapproval as a reason to add to the punishment otherwise imposed for harmful conduct. Thus the Court has upheld penalty enhancements for crimes motivated by racial animus,[11] rejecting the arguments that they impermissibly infringe free speech by penalizing unpopular political opinions.

The cognitive conception of culpability is sometimes supported by a second tenet of liberal criminal justice, which we may call the choice principle. This is the principle that criminal liability should be conditioned on willed conduct. On the basis of this principle, several theorists would limit culpable mental states to two kinds: (1) the decision to perform (or forgo) an action and

(2) expectations concerning the consequences of that decision.[12] Choice theorists often exclude from culpable mental states motives, emotions, dispositions, statuses, and most desires, on the ground that none of these are chosen.[13] Notice that the harm principle and the choice principle rest on somewhat contradictory premises. The harm principle presumes that the choice of ends is an important personal freedom that must be protected from government coercion. By contrast, the choice principle presumes that ends are unchosen and so concludes that punishing them is unfair and cruel.

An exemplary cognitive view of culpability is set forth by legal theorist Larry Alexander in his article "Insufficient Concern: A Unified Conception of Criminal Culpability."[14] Alexander argues that all the different forms of culpability can be reduced to one, "insufficient concern," by which he means the conscious imposition of a net risk of harm.[15] He begins with recklessness, defined by the Model Penal Code as the conscious imposition of a substantial and unjustifiable risk.[16] He argues that the substantiality and unjustifiability of the risk should be seen not as two independent criteria but as a single balancing standard.[17] Thus a substantial risk can be justified by a more substantial expected benefit, whereas even a small risk is imposed recklessly if there is no justifying purpose. A purpose of producing a small benefit would be "insufficient" to justify a large risk. Alexander views knowing creation of harm as simply recklessness with awareness of a very high probability of harm.[18] He argues that a purpose of causing harm should be seen as pertinent to culpability only because such a purpose implies (1) some conscious imposition of risk, however slight, and (2) a lack of justification for this risk.[19] Alexander concludes that purpose is just "a special case of recklessness, in which the defendant's reason is presumptively unjustifying."[20] He purports to combine culpable knowledge (i.e., expected harm) and culpable desires (i.e., "unjustifying" purposes) into a single calculus. Yet what matters in Alexander's calculus of "sufficient concern" is only expectation, not desire.[21] For Alexander, a harmful purpose is no worse than a neutral purpose: neither is sufficient to justify risk. Dropping a brick onto a crowded street hoping to kill someone is no worse than doing so hoping to make a loud noise. And even a beneficial purpose is relevant only to the extent the actor expects to achieve it. Ultimately, insufficient concern means nothing more than expected net harm.

Alexander is concerned exclusively with the actor's subjective expectations, not with the objective dangerousness or actual consequences of her conduct. Accordingly, he rejects negligence as a form of culpability insofar as it imposes liability based on the objectively apparent dangerousness of conduct rather than on subjective awareness of risk.[22] Similarly, he would punish completed attempts as severely as completed crimes, since both involve the same subjective expectation of harm.[23] Indeed, since attempting to cause harm is no worse than expecting to cause harm, he would extend this principle to reckless conduct. Thus he would punish reckless endangerment of life as severely as reckless homicide.[24]

Criminal law theorist Kimberly Ferzan embraces a similarly cognitive view of culpability. Criticizing Ken Simons' proposal that culpability be assessed on the basis of desires as well as expectations, Ferzan writes:

> If we are to rest culpability on desires, how should we do this in those cases where the desires conflict? . . . Are we culpable only if the stronger desire is the "bad" one? Arguably, it is the desire that one acts upon that makes one culpable or not. But why? . . . Why does it matter that one desire won the day? Here, the response seems clear—because I chose to act on that desire. But then, it seems that culpability is not dependent upon a . . . desire state but the choice that one makes.[25]

In making this argument, Ferzan relies on criminal law theorist Michael Moore's account of culpability as choice. Moore reasons that only intentions should count as culpable mental states since only they are chosen, whereas desires, emotions, and dispositions or character traits are all beyond our control.[26] Posing the hypothetical case of a defendant who is horrified upon fatally shooting her lover in a game of Russian roulette, Ferzan asks, "Is the Russian roulette player less culpable because she cries when her companion dies? Of course not. [Such] desires are irrelevant because faced with the choice, the actor chose to do wrong."[27] Ferzan argues that assessing culpability on the basis of desire rather than choice may unfairly punish actors for thoughts they are powerless to suppress or character traits they are powerless to change.[28]

Legal philosopher Heidi Hurd offers a similar argument in her critique of hate crime liability. She characterizes a hostile motive toward a group as a kind of emotion that is too imprecise to count as a culpable mental state:

> [H]ate/bias crimes are concerned with defendants' motivations for action in a way that no other crimes have ever been concerned. . . . [These] motivations . . . are emotional states that attend actions (rather than future states of affairs to which actions are instrumental means). . . . [T]he emotional states with which these crimes are concerned constitute standing character traits rather than oc-

current mental states (such as intentions, purposes, choices, etc.). . . . [T]he additional penalties that are imposed on defendants who are found guilty of hate/bias crimes constitute, in the end, punishments for bad character.[29]

According to this argument, enhancing the penalty for doing harm because of an actor's political antipathies punishes her for emotions that express enduring character traits:

> [O]ne may form an intention to do an act . . . without being disposed to do such an act. . . . But one cannot hate or be prejudiced against Asians and women without being a racist and a sexist—that is, without being disposed to . . . believe derogatory things about them and to act in ways that oppress them. . . . [Thus] hate/bias crimes necessarily punish defendants for having bad character.[30]

Hurd sees such punishment as undesirable for two reasons. First, it is unfair because racist and sexist political views, although reprehensible, are beyond the capacity of the perpetrator to control.[31] Second, liberalism precludes punishing any such "conception of the good life" because reasonable people can disagree about such views.[32] Hurd struggles unsuccessfully to reconcile these contradictory views of racism and sexism as (1) wrongful but involuntary emotions and (2) freely and reasonably chosen conceptions of the good.[33]

On cognitivist premises, the worst possible culpable mental state accompanying homicide would be knowledge that the conduct would result in death. A purpose to cause death should not aggravate the actor's culpability,[34] because (1) one who knowingly causes a consequence chooses it as much as one who causes it purposefully and (2) liberal neutrality precludes evaluating the actor's desires and hopes. The liberal state cannot condemn such a desire without judging and prescribing ends for its citizens. Thus the cognitive model also treats the offender as fully culpable for choosing to proceed in a course of conduct certain to cause death, even if he regrets that result. He is just as dangerous to the utility or rights of a victim if he regrets the harm he expects to cause as if he exults in it. Expected harm is the sole dimension of culpability.[35] Thus, if knowingly causing death is murder, causing death with any lesser expectation of doing so must be a lesser crime. Causing death recklessly—i.e., with knowledge of a substantial risk of death—should be manslaughter. Indeed, the logic of the cognitive model requires that a reckless killing should be no more than manslaughter, even if the risk-taker hopes the victim dies and is gratified when she does. If even a purpose of causing death cannot aggravate one's culpability, it follows that a purpose of causing some other harm, like taking property, or violating sexual autonomy, cannot aggravate liability for negligent homicide. Thus, according to the cognitive conception of culpability, a felony murder rule irrationally imposes murder liability for merely negligent homicide.

While utilitarians and rights theorists may share an aspiration to achieve a value-neutral liberal state and converge on a cognitive conception of culpability, they define harm very differently. This in turn gives them very different accounts of how cognitive culpability makes the wrongdoer responsible for harm.

Utilitarianism defines harm as net loss of aggregate utility, and defines culpability as expected net disutility. Because this conception of harm is prospective and speculative, it does not permit the assignment of causal responsibility for particular results. Instead, it justifies punishment only for creating risk. Thus, even if utilitarianism could justify a purely cognitive and so value-neutral conception of culpability, it would not be able to apply that conception to crimes of result like homicide.

Rights theory, by contrast, defines harm as discrete rights violations and so defines culpability in terms of expectations of these particular results. Yet defining particular results as harms and assigning responsibility for these results both necessitate evaluation of actors' ends. Moreover, punishing actual harm rather than risk is hard to justify without adverting to the actors' ends or values. Rights theory can provide a persuasive account of criminal responsibility for particular results only if it evaluates actors' ends, thereby abandoning a purely cognitive conception of culpability.

The cognitive theory of culpability for harmful results that prevails among contemporary criminal law theorists is an incoherent pastiche of these two inconsistent accounts of wrongdoing. It appears that a purely cognitive account of culpability—even if achievable—would preclude liability for results. From the standpoint of such a theory, felony murder liability would indeed be anomalous, but only because all homicide liability would be anomalous. Conversely, a coherent account of homicide liability would evaluate the ends pursued in causing death, as felony murder liability does. Such a theory of culpability would have to be normative rather than descriptive in its aspirations.

UTILITARIANISM AND COGNITIVE CULPABILITY

Utilitarianism justifies inflicting criminal punishment insofar as the suffering avoided by thus preventing criminal offenses outweighs the suffering imposed. Criminal offenses are simply those potentially costly acts deterrable at reasonable cost by proscription and punishment. Because utilitarianism aims at deterrence, it views the choice of whether to offend as a rational calculus of costs and benefits, and assesses it accordingly. The offender is not punished for having selfish aims—that is expected and even necessary if punishment is to deter. The offender is instead punished for failing to consider and internalize the expected costs to others of pursuing those aims. Thus he is punished only insofar as he is aware of these expected costs, or would be with a reasonable investment in information. He is punished only if cognitively culpable.

The idea that the mental element of offenses should not include motive emerged out of the utilitarian tradition. One of legal philosopher Jeremy Bentham's main goals was to develop a lucid, value-free language for policy analysis, legal analysis, and legislative drafting.[36] In developing this language, Bentham distinguished motive from intent.[37] Bentham drew many of his most fundamental ideas indirectly from the Swiss utilitarian Baron Helvetius,[38] who argued that the same basic human passions—the desire for pleasure and satisfaction, and the fear of pain and want—were the motivating force behind both good and bad actions.[39] Differing environmental circumstances might channel the same passions into beneficial or harmful actions. Thus the task of the moral philosopher was to design laws that would shape incentives beneficially, rather than to denounce passions as immoral.[40]

In designing criminal legislation, Bentham agreed that the passions motivating human behavior inhered in human psychology, and so could not be used to distinguish criminal from innocent behavior.[41] Bentham identified motives as the forces that deterrent sanctions were designed to mobilize in controlling behavior; but because these motives were both indestructible and useful, they could not be punished. "[A] motive . . . is to be understood [as] any thing whatsoever, which by influencing the will of a sensitive being, is supposed to serve as a means of determining him to act, or voluntarily to forebear to act, upon any occasion."[42] Bentham objected to predicating liability on motives because he saw the language of motives as saturated with normative judgment.[43] Yet no motive, he argued, is bad in itself, because all motives are reducible to the desire for pleasure and the fear of pain.[44] An action is good or bad only because of its hedonic effects, not because of its motives.

While punishing motives would not serve deterrence, punishing expectations would. Deterrence could work only insofar as actors knew they were or might be engaging in punishable conduct.[45] Deterrence required that punishment be conditioned not on actual harm but on behavior that the actor expected would cause harm.[46] Bentham referred to all expected consequences of voluntary conduct as intended,[47] and predicated criminal liability on intentions rather than motives. In sum, Bentham's distinction between motive and intent combined three ideas: (1) criminal law should reduce discretion by precisely defining offenses; (2) it should define offenses in neutral descriptive language rather than normative language; and (3) it should define culpability by reference to cognitive states like expectations, rather than desiderative states like purposes.

In his *Lectures on Jurisprudence*, legal philosopher John Austin further refined Bentham's distinction between motive and intent. Austin distinguished four concepts: act, volition, intention, and motive.[48] Acts were bodily movements only, as distinguished from any of their consequences.[49] Volitions were desiderative states that could accompany such acts.[50] Intentions were cognitive states, involving awareness of willed acts and their consequences.[51] Finally, motives were desiderative states that caused action[52] but did not include volitions.[53] Thus motives were desiderative attitudes towards the consequences of actions. A motivating desire could only be a desire for a feeling of pleasure or gratification or relief from suffering or fear.[54] In Austin's scheme an intended consequence could also be a desired or motivating consequence.[55] Nevertheless, even when intention and motivation coincided, it was the intention that inculpated, rather than the motivation. Austin considered the desire for pleasure a constant, and not punishable. Only the knowledge that gratifying a desire would create a proscribed harm or risk could subject the actor to punishment.

Austin is responsible for much of the modern conceptual vocabulary of culpability, having pioneered the idea of tying every culpable mental state to some state of affairs in the world. For him, acts were unlawful not in themselves but only by virtue of their consequences.[56] A criminal intent could only be knowledge of some probability of the consequences of action that would render an otherwise innocent action unlawful.[57] Austin therefore distinguished a number of different levels of awareness of probable harm corresponding to the Model Penal Code's concepts of negligence, recklessness, and knowledge.[58] He also permitted purpose or "design" as a criterion of liability insofar as it implied the expectation of harm,[59] while still insisting that motive was irrelevant to liability.[60]

The Model Penal Code represents an effort to apply utilitarian premises in designing a penal code.[61] Reflecting the utilitarian views of its principal author, Herbert Wechsler, the code presents the harm principle as fundamental.[62]

It defines culpability primarily (though not exclusively) in cognitive terms, as purpose, knowledge, recklessness, or negligence.[63] It rejects strict liability[64] and felony murder,[65] deemphasizes negligence,[66] for the most part equates knowledge and purpose,[67] and defines knowledge as awareness of a high probability.[68] The code treats cognitive culpability as almost sufficient by itself for criminal liability. Thus, if an actor undertakes an act that constitutes a substantial step toward a proscribed result in the belief the act will cause the result, she is guilty of an attempt[69]—and is punished as severely as if she had completed the crime by knowingly causing the result.[70] She is held causally responsible for a result if her act was a necessary condition to it, and she expected such an event, or foresaw or should have foreseen the risk of such an event.[71]

Utilitarianism's cognitive model of culpability appears to achieve Bentham's goal of an objective assessment of wrongdoing by translating normative judgments about harm, causal responsibility, and culpability into psychological language so that they seem to be measurements of sensation. It measures harm in hedonic terms as a loss of utility. Utility can be defined in two ways: as happiness and as preference satisfaction.[72] Modern economists and rational choice analysts define utility in terms of preference, so the concept can be used in predicting and explaining choice.[73] Economists also favor a preference conception of welfare because their commitment to the subjectivity of value makes them "reluctant to make substantive claims about what is good or bad for people."[74] Thus the preference satisfaction conception of utility offers the promise of a value-neutral account of benefit and harm. And yet insofar as economic models assume that individual decision makers are rationally self-interested, the preference satisfaction conception implicitly equates what people want with what is ultimately best for them.[75]

Because utility is a comparative concept, used for evaluating alternative acts, it is usually defined in terms of the satisfaction of desires that remain stable over time and in alternative futures.[76] Such "rational" desires supply each individual with hedonic evaluations of every possible state of affairs. An act is harmful if it causes a state of affairs yielding less total utility than would result from some alternative act.[77] Based on utilitarian premises, culpability is the predictable harmfulness of an action given the information available to the actor at the time of action. This predictable harmfulness depends upon the utility of each state of affairs that could result from an action multiplied by its probability. An actor is causally responsible for a harmful result if her action was a necessary condition for the result, and such a result was predictable.[78] But notice that what counts as harm from a utilitarian standpoint is not a particular type of injury, but any set of consequences producing net disutility. Thus, given the utilitarian conception of harm, causal responsibility for a harmful result should depend on the predictability of aggregate disutility rather than of particular types of injury.

This utilitarian model of culpability is an application of what philosopher Susan Hurley called "the subjectivist view that preference determines value."[79] It appears to purify criminal law of value judgments by making blame a function of four kinds of facts about subjective experience: states of affairs, expectations, preferences, and quantities of utility. Yet on closer examination these "facts" are figurative representations of experience, embodying value judgments. The subjectivist account of value is vulnerable to the same sort of pragmatic critique as the logical positivist account of knowledge. Just as pragmatic philosophers have doubted the possibility of a theory-free description of data,[80] they have doubted the possibility of a value-free description of preferences.[81]

A state of affairs is a unit of experience with respect to which different individuals have preferences or hedonic evaluations. Thus it is the common medium that enables utilitarian analysis to assimilate together (1) the desires of different people, (2) the desires of each person at different times, or (3) the expectations preceding and the experiences resulting from acts. Utilitarian psychology presumes that rational actors assign a relative hedonic value or "utility" to every imaginable state of affairs and that this hedonic evaluation is stable over time. This enables rational actors to evaluate and choose actions on the basis of their probability of bringing about states of affairs of higher or lower hedonic value to them. Moral actors and policymakers can estimate and sum the hedonic value to all persons of each state of affairs and evaluate actions according to their expected public utility. Preference-satisfaction utilitarianism presumes that when an action brings about an expected state of affairs, it will in fact have the hedonic value to each person that he or she earlier imagined. Also, it equates the state of affairs imagined and hypothetically evaluated and the state of affairs subsequently experienced.

As used in preference-satisfaction utilitarianism, a state of affairs is not a feature of the world but instead is a necessarily selective verbal description of the world. According to decision theorist Frederic Schick, "the objects of wanting . . . are not facts in the raw, but the facts reported somehow," so that "what a person wants is always that some proposition be true."[82] Yet as Hurley pointed out, the utterance of the same proposition by different people or at different times is a different speech act. The decision to interpret two such actions as equivalent in meaning is therefore a normative decision.[83] My expectation of injuring you and your suffering of that injury can be represented by the same words, but that does not make them the same thing. People adapt to both feared and desired circumstances, so that ex ante and ex post evaluations are often quite different.[84] Moreover, as Schick notes, we can accurately describe the same events in different ways, and attach different utilities to those different descriptions.[85] Sometimes an actor's interpretation and consequent evaluation of an event depend upon a moral choice that he cannot anticipate in advance. Schick argues that when an actor faces conflict between competing obligations, he often experiences his ambivalence as uncertainty between two differently motivated descriptions or "understandings" of his situation.[86]

When we say that someone acted with an expectation or intention regarding a result that came to pass, we are again speaking figuratively. While felony murder rules are criticized for "transferring intent" from the felony to the resulting death, in fact all judgments of culpability for particular results "transfer" it to some degree. Thus a gunman is held responsible for an intentional killing whether he hits his intended victim or someone else entirely.[87] He also "kills intentionally" if he misses his target, a victim's heart, and unintentionally hits the same victim's head on the ricochet. Suppose an arsonist believes that a homeowner may be present in the house he torches but does not foresee that the neighbor's house may catch on fire. If the fire kills the neighbor rather than the homeowner, we typically "transfer" the arsonist's recklessness from the foreseen to the unforeseen victim. We treat mental states like intent to kill or reckless disregard of human life as abstractions referring to a class of morally equivalent expectations. That culpable expectations attach to event types rather than particular events is explicit in the Model Penal Code's provisions defining causal responsibility. An offender is responsible for a result within his "contemplation" or "within the risk of which the actor is aware or . . . should be aware" or which differs from these events "only in the respect that a different person or different property is injured" or which "involves the same kind of injury or harm."[88]

Such "foreseeability" standards of causal responsibility derive from philosopher David Hume's conception of causation as a statistical correlation between classes of antecedent and subsequent events.[89] Formulating such a correlation requires describing a wrongful act by reference to a class of acts and a resulting injury by reference to a class of results, so that we can determine the probability of such an injury as a result of such an act. However, there is no objective way to choose which of the infinity of possible descriptions best applies to a defendant's act and a victim's injuries. If we describe any particular injurious result in sufficient detail, it becomes improbable from an ex ante perspective. If we describe a harm sufficiently generally, it becomes foreseeable.[90] Similarly, once we know that an act resulted in an event we deem harmful, we can describe it in sufficient detail that the harm should have seemed inevitable. Yet the propriety of this description depends on a normative judgment as to whether the actor should have perceived his or her action in this way at the time. Among the circumstances we may include or exclude in such a description is the probable behavior of other actors whose possibly culpable choices might increase the risk. It seems there is no value-neutral way of determining the probability of an injury as a result of an act, or of attributing such an expectation to an actor.

Nor can we eliminate normative discretion by abstracting further, from expected injury types to expected cost. First, calculating expected aggregate cost requires predicting the probability of particular harmful and beneficial events. Second, if we are going to apply the utilitarian conception of culpability to a crime of result like homicide, we will need some way of attributing particular results to a defendant's culpable choice. Third, predicting costs and benefits involves us in all the normative judgments associated with attributing preferences.

The concept of preference depends on normative criteria of rationality to solve two sorts of difficulties: indeterminacy and normative implausibility. The indeterminacy problems arise because of the possibilities of changing and conflicting desires.[91] Presumably, we should not force a couple to abide by their marital vows when they cease to care for each other. Neither should we impose a lobotomy on an unwilling patient merely because his simpler desires will be more easily satisfied after the operation. If we must deem desires consistent before we can recognize them as rational preferences, we are passing them through a normative filter before we admit them to the utilitarian calculus. Moreover, as Hurley points out, the assessment of consistency is itself a normative judgment.

The normative implausibility problem arises because even consistent preferences can be based on false belief; can arise from manipulation, oppression, or neurosis; or can be self-destructive or antisocial.[92] We should not credit the desires of an addict, a sadist, or a happy slave.[93] We may insist that the offender's guilty pleasure in his crime is a cost rather than a benefit. We may refuse to count envy as a cost or schadenfreude as a benefit. We may treat the gratification of anger as inculpatory or exculpatory, depending on whether we regard that anger as justified.

Because of the indeterminacy of preferences and the normative implausibility of valuing all preferences equally, Daniel Hausman and Michael McPherson conclude that "[i]t is more plausible to maintain that well-being is the satisfaction of suitably 'laundered' self-interested preferences than to maintain that it is the satisfaction of actual preferences."[94] At bottom, the decision to equate preference satisfaction with well-being necessarily involves a normative judgment.[95]

Finally, the conception of harm as a relative decline in utility requires aggregating together gains and losses to the welfare of different people. To thus aggregate utility we have to be able to commensurate the different desires of different people at different times on a single scale, by translating them into numerical evaluations of the same "states of affairs." The utility scale makes interpersonal comparisons of welfare possible by ascribing similar feelings and experiences to different people. This supposed similarity enables us to evaluate policy by a test that measures each person's welfare equally and adds these measures together, according each one equal weight. The familiar paradoxes of social choice demonstrate that there is no mechanical or incontrovertible method of adding preferences unless they are put on a common scale of cardinal utility.[96] Yet any such scale for commensurating the different desires of different people is an institutional construct like a poll, or a price, which represents a population by creating data about it that would not otherwise exist. "Utility" is not a fact about aggregate hedonic experience, but an artifact, representing hedonic experience figuratively so as to render it tractable for policy analysis.

A cognitive conception of culpability as expected disutility is supposed to enable a value-neutral assessment of an actor's choices. Yet neither the actor nor the legal system can determine the expected disutility of an act without exercising normative judgment.

UTILITARIANISM AND PUNISHMENT FOR HARMFUL RESULTS

A utilitarian conception of culpability as expected disutility has a more serious drawback for anyone trying to rationalize the law of homicide. Because utilitarian analysis is essentially concerned with risk rather than injury, a utilitarian theory of culpability cannot give a coherent account of result crimes like homicide.

Utilitarianism conceives harm in aggregate and comparative terms, as the net disutility for all persons at all future times of all the consequences of choosing one act over the optimal alternative.[97] But since the actual future is always incomplete and the possible alternative futures are never experienced, the actual harm resulting from any act can never be known.[98] Thus utilitarianism can evaluate actions only prospectively, on the basis of expected rather than actual cost. Accordingly, it can never evaluate any particular injury—such as a death—as an actual harm, since this cost may have been or may yet be offset by a greater benefit.

Moreover, since some social cost is inevitable in a world of rivalrous demands for scarce resources, and since the actor is responsible only for predicting the size of this cost, a utilitarian can never judge that an actor should have foreseen and prevented some particular injury. Utilitarianism can condemn particular actions as predictably harmful but cannot condemn particular results as harms. As Herbert Wechsler argued:

> From the preventive point of view, the harmfulness of conduct rests upon its tendency to cause the injuries to be prevented far more than on its actual results; results, indeed, have meaning only insofar as they may indicate or dramatize the tendencies involved. Reckless driving is no more than reckless driving if there is a casualty and no less if by good fortune nothing should occur. . . . [I]f the criminality of conduct is to turn on the result, it rests upon fortuitous considerations unrelated to the major purpose to be served by declaration that behavior is a crime. . . . A major issue to be faced, therefore, is whether penal law ought to be shaped to deal more comprehensively with risk creation, without reference to actual results.[99]

Wechsler's critique of felony murder expressed this view that punishing dangerous conduct obviates additional punishment for causing harm: "The underlying felony carries its own penalty and the additional punishment for murder is therefore gratuitous."[100] Wechsler's approach to grading offenses in the Model Penal Code also reflected this utilitarian focus on risk rather than result. Thus, in punishing attempted and completed crimes equally, the code essentially eliminates punishment for knowingly or purposely causing actual harm by folding it into attempt liability.[101] The utilitarian legal philosopher H. L. A. Hart agreed that, in typical cases, "there seems no reason on any form of deterrent theory . . . for punishing the unsuccessful attempt less severely than the completed crime."[102]

Criminal law scholar Stephen Schulhofer explains the connection between utilitarianism and a policy of punishing risk rather than harm in his influential article "Harm and Punishment." Schulhofer argues that this policy comports with the deterrence theory principle that increases in the certainty of punishment are more effective deterrents than increases in severity.[103] The early utilitarian reform proposals of Bentham and of Cesare Beccaria were premised on this principle.[104] As explained earlier, the logic behind it is that increases in sentence length have diminishing returns and are subject to a temporal discount, while increases in certainty more clearly link the forbidden conduct to the deterrent threat. Moreover, severe but uncertain punishment seems arbitrary and unfair, can be resisted by discretionary decision makers, and can even glorify offenders as martyrs or high-stakes gamblers.

The principle that mild but certain punishment deters most efficiently implies that all acts that foreseeably impose the same risk of harm should be punished equally, regardless of whether they actually cause harm. Schulhofer argues that conditioning punishment on harm rather than risk creates an inefficient "punishment lottery," punishing fortuitous factors beyond the control of the actor, and hence also beyond the influence of the criminal law's deterrent threats.[105] Utilitarian reformers first introduced the punishment lottery argument in criticizing felony murder liability for punishing felons on the basis of the unintended results of their crimes. Yet the same "punishment lottery" critique is available whenever punishment is conditioned on actual results. By contrast, punishing culpable risk rather than harm achieves the desired increase in the certainty of punishment for conduct with negative expected utility.

Sanford Kadish's article "The Criminal Law and the Luck of the Draw" also expresses these affinities among the ideas of risk, cognitive culpability, and deterrence.[106] Like other utilitarians,[107] Kadish adopts a mixed approach to punishment in this article, requiring that punishment serve utility without exceeding the limits of desert.[108] Although he criticizes punishment for causing harm as both useless and undeserved, he also rejects as "rationally indefensible" the retributivist view that deserved punishment is an intrinsic moral good.[109] He deems punishment, which has the necessary consequence of lowering one person's welfare, as rational only insofar as it deters crime.[110]

In rejecting punishment for harm as both unfair and useless, Kadish reasons that an actor causes harm by creating risk, and that an actor does so wrongly by acting with knowledge (or reason to know) that the risk is excessive (i.e., not justified by expected benefits). The actor's culpability turns on the expectation of harm assignable to her, and her punishment properly turns on her culpability.[111] Kadish argues that if an actor culpably imposes a risk of harm in this sense, the actual occurrence of harm is a fortuity, a species of "moral luck."[112] The actor has done wrong and earned a deterrent sanction as soon as he or she commits an act imposing risk. Whether risk subsequently becomes harm is out of the actor's control, and so should not affect his punishment. Harm cannot add to the actor's desert, and punishment cannot deter it.

This moral luck argument against punishing harm rests on the probabilistic notion of the connection between action and consequence introduced by Hume.[113] From this viewpoint, the riskiness of an act is a prerequisite to its harmfulness because without risk there can be no causation. An action is essentially connected to the foreseeable consequences for an act of its type; it is only contingently connected to its actual consequences. This conception of action as a kind of mental wager is quite prevalent among moral philosophers, even those who do not consider themselves utilitarians. Thus, Michael Zimmerman argues that "[i]nsofar as what happens after one has made a free decision is . . . up to nature, then these events . . . are strictly dispensable in the assessment of moral responsibility,"[114] while Joel Feinberg insists that "moral responsibility is . . . restricted to the inner world of the mind, where . . . luck has no place."[115]

Kadish's critique of felony murder grows out of his moral luck critique of liability for causing harm. If even an intentional killing is a blameless and undeterrable fortuity, surely an unintended death should not be held against a felon. Since the occurrence of a harmful result is irrelevant to the punishment deserved for intentionally risking it, it follows that a harmful result should also be irrelevant to the punishment deserved for any other act of wrongdoing. Thus Kadish rejected the doctrine that "if I do something I should not . . . I become guilty of any harm my action produced."[116] Felony murder is rationally indefensible from the standpoint of deterrence theory, because that is true of murder liability itself.

Critical legal theorist Mark Kelman has exposed still more fundamental tensions between utilitarian premises and liability for causing injury in a critique of causation in tort.[117] Drawing on legal economist Ronald Coase's analysis of harm as "social cost,"[118] Kelman argues that welfare loss is always caused by the interaction of two or more parties who have conflicting desires with respect to scarce resources.[119] Thus acts cannot be condemned as harmful merely because they result in the frustration of someone's desire. Frustration for someone—which is to say "social cost"—is an inevitable consequence of rivalrous desires, regardless of how either rival chooses to act.[120] Even optimal actions will produce such injuries, so injury should not be confused with harm.[121]

Because utilitarianism conceives harm as a net welfare loss rather than as any particular injury, it cannot yield a determinate theory of fault for such an injury. Harm in the utilitarian sense can never be to an individual but is always a conclusion about the net effects of an act on the welfare of all. Moreover, as noted above, whether an action is optimal or harmful can never finally be settled. It depends on future consequences and on the hypothetical consequences of alternative courses of action. A utilitarian evaluation of an action therefore concerns its expected future effects on all rather than its actual past effects on a particular individual.[122] Thus the very idea of discrete injuries depends on recognizing entitlements or legal interests that will trump utility in evaluating acts. Injury, in short, is a rights concept, not a utility concept. This fundamental disjunction between the ideas of disutility and injury makes it impossible to develop a stable conception of causal responsibility for injury on the basis of a culpability standard of expected disutility.

The problem can be illustrated with a thought experiment. How might we develop an account of result offenses like homicide based on a conception of culpable wrongdoing as foreseeably causing disutility? First we would need some conception of a wrongful injury. We might say that wrongful injuries include any welfare loss to an individual for which a wrongful act was a necessary condition, and that an act is wrongful if its expected net effects are harmful. This formula looks plausible, yet it yields four difficulties when we try to assign responsibility for particular injuries to particular acts. We may call these the hypothetical alternatives problem, the accounting problem, the moral demands problem, and the scope of the risk problem.

The necessary condition part of the standard is rendered indeterminate by the hypothetical alternatives problem. Sometimes we cannot determine whether a particular injury would not have occurred "but for" a defendant's dangerous act.[123] This problem is particularly apparent with toxic exposures that correlate statistically with increased rates of already common diseases. We cannot determine which actual cases of illness and death would not otherwise have occurred.[124] The problem is even more acute when multiple wrongdoers have exposed a population to the same toxin.[125] Thus, for some of the worst cases of risk imposition, we can never prove causation. Requiring causation of harm therefore precludes deterrence where it seems most needed.

The accounting problem concerns how much harm the offender is causally responsible for. Let us say that an act, although expected to be harmful in the aggregate, is expected to produce good as well as bad consequences.

And let us also say the act does indeed produce mixed consequences, causing three broken legs, but preventing two broken arms. It seems unfair (and excessively deterrent) to attach a penalty to every injury produced when some injuries have also been prevented. That would make the wrongdoer responsible for more harm than occurred. Yet if we choose to punish only certain injuries contributing to net harm, we have no principled way to choose which injuries to punish and which to justify by reference to hypothetical injuries prevented. This accounting problem gets even worse if we imagine an act expected to be harmful in the aggregate that happens to produce some injuries, but also produces benefits that outweigh these costs. Our definition of wrongful injury now makes the offender responsible for injuries *even though no harm occurred.* Moreover, since we never know the complete welfare effects of any act, we never know that any wrongful act will prove harmful in the end. Therefore, to hold an actor responsible for a particular injury is not really to determine that she caused harm in the utilitarian sense, but simply to use the injury as a metonymic representation of the net harm she expected to cause. We are not really punishing harm but merely using the injury to "dramatize the tendencies involved."[126]

The moral demands problem points to some necessary slippage between the concepts of disutility and wrong. It invokes the standard objection that act-utilitarian ethics make impossible demands on individuals.[127] Of all the possible choices available to us, must we really choose only the one with the greatest expected aggregate utility? Must all other choices be condemned and punished? Such a standard would leave each of us so little freedom to shape our own lives and pursue our own aims that it would blight rather than foster happiness. Utilitarians can respond that public utility is a policy standard, not an ethical standard, and that individuals will of course pursue private utility by maximizing their own happiness.[128] The point of utilitarianism is to shape incentives to serve public utility by enforcing utility-maximizing legal rules, but only insofar as this can be done at a reasonable cost. Surely we cannot maximize public utility by punishing all non-maximizing conduct: in many instances the harm of punishment will outweigh the harm of the crime, not to mention the much smaller deterrent benefits achieved by punishing it. Thus a utilitarian criminal law will have to permit lots of non-maximizing choices. But if so, which ones? Is the standard for unacceptably harmful conduct quantitative? If so, is the wrongdoer responsible for all of the net welfare loss she causes, or for only the net welfare loss that exceeds the acceptable amount? If the latter, which particular injuries? Thus the moral demands problem further complicates the accounting problem. It leaves the utilitarian conception of wrongdoing too indeterminate to generate a standard of wrongful injury.

The scope of the risk problem arises because a disutility standard of harm makes it difficult to narrow causal responsibility on the basis of foreseeable harm. As H. L. A. Hart and Tony Honoré argued in their classic study of legal causation, we cannot treat all necessary conditions as causes, because injuries typically have many necessary antecedent acts, including those of the victim.[129] Hart and Honoré note that a popular test restricts causal responsibility to those necessary conditions foreseeably likely to cause such a result.[130] As noted above, foreseeability standards are threatened by indeterminacy because any result can seem foreseeable if described very generally, and unforeseeable if described very narrowly. A solution to this problem endorsed by Hart and Honoré, and employed by the Model Penal Code, is to restrict foreseeable harms to those within the risk that rendered defendants' conduct culpable.[131] In this way, the Model Penal Code connects causation to culpability by requiring the same expectation of harm for both. An offender is deemed culpable insofar as she acted with an expectation of causing a particular type of harm and is held causally responsible only insofar as such an expected harm occurred. But if harm is simply aggregate disutility, culpability means perceiving excessive risk of all kinds, rather than expecting any particular type of injury to occur by any particular causal process. Any act expected to be suboptimal is culpable and so is a candidate for causal responsibility. Any injury that occurs will be "within the risk" for any culpable act. Thus the aggregate harm concept empties foreseeability of any content, so it no longer limits causal responsibility at all. We have imposed responsibility for results rather than risk only by defining every event subsequent to a risky act as its result.

The difficulties we have in making sense of liability for causing particular results within a utilitarian framework simply confirm what Kadish, Schulhofer, and Kelman argue: that a utilitarian conception of culpability as expected harm justifies punishing only risk, not harm itself. But this means it is not only felony murder liability that seems "rationally indefensible" from the standpoint of utilitarianism's cognitive model of culpability. A utilitarian account of cognitive culpability condemns felony murder liability only because it cannot make sense of murder liability of any kind. A theory of homicide must include an account of responsibility for culpably causing particular harms. A utilitarian variant of cognitive culpability theory cannot supply such an account.

CONTRACTARIANISM AND COGNITIVE CULPABILITY

The utilitarian version of cognitive culpability theory rejects all homicide liability as unnecessary for deterrence, but does not support the prevailing view that felony murder in particular is uniquely unfair. A cognitive culpability theory that condemns felony murder liability as less deserved than other murder liability must rest on some other conception of the liberal state, one compatible with a retributive view of punishment. Insofar as such a theory supports liability for crimes of result like homicide, it must conceive harms as particular injuries to discrete interests. By imposing duties not to injure others in these interests, the liberal state would also recognize rights not to be so injured.[132] Violations of these rights would constitute harms, and the expected violation of a right would be morally culpable and so, presumptively, deserving of punishment. On a theory of harms as injuries to discrete rights, felony murder liability would be subject to criticism for improperly transferring culpability from one kind of right to another. This section explores whether such a rights-oriented cognitive theory of culpability can (1) assign blame for actual harm but (2) without evaluating actors' ends. It concludes that a rights-oriented cognitive theory of culpability must evaluate actors' ends, and that no theory of culpability can achieve both aims.

Rights theory can take libertarian and contractarian forms.[133] A libertarian rights theory of criminal law justifies state punishment as the delegation to the state of individuals' natural right of self-defense against harm, which includes the right to deter harmful acts by threatening and exacting revenge. Mill invoked such a delegated self-defense theory in explaining the harm principle.[134] Because such a theory rests on the natural rights of victims, it need not justify punishment on the basis of the offender's desert, or even his consent to the authority of law.

The difficulty with such a theory, however, is that a natural right of self-defense against harm is potentially so expansive that it sets no limit to the criminal law and so reserves no sphere of liberty from state coercion. As noted above, in a world of scarce resources and opportunities, any action can affect others and interfere with their aims, thereby inflicting "harm."[135] A rights theory needs to set some limit to the proprietary domain of each individual for each to have any freedom of action within that domain. A natural rights theory derives these limits from what is "naturally" due each human being. For Mill, this natural due is what the individual needs in order to flourish and fulfill her creative potential.[136] In addition, Mill limits this natural due insofar as utilitarian regulation can foster human flourishing, leaving the scope of liberty in his theory notoriously indeterminate and vulnerable to ad hoc policy judgments.[137] Thus, in a natural rights theory, which rights the criminal law can legitimately protect from harm depends on which ends best realize human nature. It seems that a natural rights theory of harm cannot be value-neutral: it requires a theory of the good. Thus we can set the libertarian version of rights theory aside as a basis for a value-neutral criminal law.

Contractarianism seeks to rely on a theory of the right rather than the good[138] to limit the rights the law protects. It uses a regime of rights to establish what philosopher John Rawls called the "fair terms of social cooperation,"[139] seeking to secure to each individual the broadest sphere of freedom compatible with like freedom for others. Insofar as some forms of freedom can be enhanced through cooperation in the production of public goods, contractarians could rationally undertake duties of cooperation and authorize the state to coerce the performance of such duties. Indeed, the security of individual rights is itself such a public good, enabled by the mutual forbearance of contracting citizens and their acceptance of the coercive force of law.[140] By virtue of their enjoyment of the rights and other public benefits thereby secured, contracting citizens arguably undertake a duty to cooperate in securing these rights—by obeying law or suffering retributive punishment.[141]

From a contractarian perspective, there are two kinds of harm.[142] Harm to individuals consists of the violation of their rights.[143] Harm, even to individuals, is not a hedonic state: not all frustrations and disappointments constitute harms, but only those that result from violations of rights of a kind secured to all.[144] Such harm is a legal artifact rather than a natural fact.[145] In societies with different assignments of rights, different disappointments would count as harms.

Contractarianism also recognizes violations of public duties as harms to public interests.[146] Such harm is always present whenever the duty to respect individual rights is violated. Like harms to individuals, harms to public interests are also jural rather than hedonic.[147] Violations of public duties are wrongful, not because they affect the welfare of particular individuals but because they violate a contractual obligation to all other members of the public.[148] A violation of a public duty is a harm in itself; it is not merely the imposition of a risk that might eventuate in harm. If an individual has a right against some consequence of the violation of a public duty, this right-violating consequence would be a distinct harm.

Conceived as violations of rights and public duties, harms are discrete: they involve the violation of particular rights of particular persons, or particular duties to all. Criminal culpability with respect to harm is therefore always about particular events. The mugger expects to deprive his victim of her property; he should know he imposes a risk of death by clubbing her with a tire iron. He is guilty of robbery, and of negligent homicide, but not murder. Intention or knowledge cannot transfer from one type of harm to another. Some cognitive theorists go further, insisting that culpability should not transfer among victims. Thus, a gunman misses victim A, whom he expected to kill, but to his surprise kills B, who was standing nearby. He is guilty of attempted murder against A and, perhaps, of negligent homicide against B, but not of the murder of A.[149] Transfer of culpability cannot be avoided altogether: the gunman intends to kill by shooting A in the head, but instead shoots A fatally in the heart.[150] The intended result is morally equivalent to the actual result because both violate the same right. The contractarian might, on similar reasoning, transfer culpability from intended victim A to actual victim B, as long as the right targeted and the right violated are of the same kind.[151]

A contractarian conception of harms as particular jural violations also helps explain the resistance of many cognitive theorists to criminal liability for negligence.[152] Certainly it explains disapproval of per se negligence rules. I may knowingly violate a public duty to comply with a public health regulation. If so, I have culpably brought about harm to the public interest. Unless I understand how the regulation protects against harm to individuals, however, I am not culpable for any resulting injuries to them. But should I not have informed myself about the risks I might impose by violating a law? The contractarian answer is that if I have a public duty to educate myself, I can be punished for violating that public duty. Such duties can be enforced through licensing requirements. On such reasoning, I can be punished for engaging in some activity while culpably failing to inform myself about its risks, but not for culpably causing an injury I had no reason to expect. My actions may be culpable with respect to a public duty and dangerous with respect to an injury to an individual, but that does not make them culpable with respect to the injury. For that, I must actually be aware that violating the duty will impose some risk.[153]

Consider how these principles apply to felony murder. An armed robber may not advert to the risk of death he is creating because he deceives himself into believing he has more control over events than he does. Intoxicated by power, he may expect that a gun will give him command over events, and never imagine that threatened victims might resist or flee, that confederates might get frightened or angry, or that police might intervene. This kind of narcissistic blindness may be morally reprehensible, but it does not amount to awareness of a risk of death and so does not justify liability for homicide on cognitivist premises. Such dangers may be among our reasons for proscribing and punishing robbery, but unless the offender has contemplated those dangers, he is properly punishable only for robbery. If we punish the robber for killing negligently, and then aggravate the robber's liability for negligently causing death because of this same purpose, we are simply transferring culpability from the robbery to what is, from the robber's narcissistically narrow viewpoint, a completely unexpected and therefore accidental death.[154]

Can this contractarian theory assign culpability for causing harm without evaluating an actor's ends? I will argue that it cannot. The problems begin with the indeterminacy of the equal freedom the contractarian rights regime is designed to protect. Very different regimes of rights and public duties can plausibly satisfy contractarianism's fairness test. Moreover, these different fair regimes of rights are incompatible, because securing one kind of freedom for all limits other kinds of freedoms for all. Thus, more freedom to transact means less protection against coercion and fraud. Freedom to use property in some ways interferes with freedom to use it in other ways. In Coase's famous example, the freedom of a spark-spitting railroad to use its narrow right-of-way is inconsistent with the freedom of neighbors to grow flammable crops nearby.[155] Similarly, public duties obviously interfere with some kinds of freedom, even though they may enable others. And since the benefits of cooperation often depend on adopting one among several possible arbitrary conventions (e.g., driving on the right), different inconsistent schemes of public duty are possible. So disputants will be able to defend incompatible rights claims with contractarian arguments.

Since what counts as harm depends upon a choice among equally fair regimes of rights and public duties, the single value of "fairness" is not sufficient to specify the harms justifying criminal punishment. The legal system will have to make value choices favoring some ends over others, treating some disappointments as harmful rights violations and dismissing others as fortuitous or self-inflicted. It will have to choose between incompatible activities, or designate limited times and places for each. The contractarian variant of rights theory cannot achieve its aspiration to prioritize the right (fairness) over the good (the choice of ends), because it needs some conception of the good to give content to the right.[156]

Moreover, the evaluation of ends required to specify a regime of rights cannot be restricted to the legislative function but reemerges when courts interpret legislative directives.[157] When widely valued freedoms conflict, democratically elected legislatures are unlikely to choose one and banish the other. They will often protect both, obliging courts to resolve the value conflict in individual disputes.[158] Determining causal responsibility for harm in individual cases often requires determining the precise scope of conflicting rights, thereby choosing between the conflicting ends of the two parties.

Hart and Honoré defined a legal cause as ordinarily (1) an abnormal,[159] (2) voluntary act[160] (3) necessary to[161] (4) an unusual event,[162] (5) correlating with such a result in normal experience,[163] and (6) not followed by another abnormal (and so unforeseeable) cause.[164] The abnormal act criterion privileges customary activities, making them ineligible as sources of liability. It likewise excludes such customary activities as intervening causes. But is normality just a matter of statistical frequency? Speeding, drunk driving, and jaywalking are abnormal events regardless of how commonly they occur because they violate legal norms. The claim that an activity is too "normal" to count as a cause of harm is essentially a claim that the actor has a right to engage in it because it serves a worthy end. The requirement of a "normal" correlation with the result implicates normative judgment as well. Cocaine use appears to be less dangerous than owning a motorcycle,[165] and yet a fatal overdose will be viewed by many as a probable rather than accidental result.[166] Although resistance is an unusual and extremely dangerous response to robbery, the public sees it as a normal response, and attributes the dangers of resisted robbery to the robber rather than the resister. Inevitably the determinations of which events are abnormal and which activities are dangerous in normal experience are normative judgments requiring the evaluation of ends.[167] Indeed, Hart and Honoré conclude that the principles of legal causation

> have aspects which are vague or indeterminate; they involve the weighing of matters of degree, or the plausibility of hypothetical speculations for which no exact criteria can be laid down. Hence their application, outside the safe area of simple examples, calls for judgment and is something over which judgments often differ.[168]

A similar evaluation of ends is required in determining the "scope" of the risk imposed by an actor, or in deciding whether to "transfer" culpability. The problem is illustrated by the following hypothetical: Officers A and B stop and question suspect C. Believing C to be armed, A fires his pistol at C, intending to kill him and later claim that C drew his own weapon first. He fails to notice that B is close to his line of fire. The bullet grazes B's left armpit, inches from his heart and strikes C in the abdomen, but not fatally. C goes into shock and, in an unconscious state, draws and fires a pistol at B, killing him.[169] Did A cause B's death? If so, did he do so with purpose, with recklessness, or with negligence? Hart and Honoré's test asks whether the death was a normal consequence of A's act. But the answer to this question depends on how we describe the result and the act. Surely a death is a normal consequence of trying to kill someone, but surely the death of B is not a normal consequence of shooting C in the abdomen.

Our contractarian theory precludes us from transferring culpability among violations of different rights, but gives us little guidance in this situation, where we are trying to determine which violations of the right to life A culpably risked when he fired at C. Perhaps the death of B is a normal consequence of shooting in B's direction, or of involving B in a gunfight. We must also decide whether C's shot is an unforeseeable, abnormal event that breaks the chain of causation. Is defensive violence a "normal" and "foreseeable" consequence of an attack? Should we describe C's shot as an instance of such self-defense, or as an exceedingly improbable instance of automatism? The Model Penal Code causation standard restates the scope of the risk problem in explicitly normative terms. It asks whether "the actual result differs from the probable [or designed] result only in the respect that a different person . . . is injured . . . or . . . the actual result involves the same kind of injury . . . as the probable [or designed] result and is not too remote or accidental in its occurrence to have a just bearing on the actor's liability."[170] What is the "same kind of injury"? When is the "only" relevant difference between two injuries the identity of the victim? When is a result not "too remote or accidental" to justly affect liability? These are obviously normative questions and how we answer them will depend on our evaluations of the aims of the actors.

The normativity of ascriptions of causal responsibility also infects assessments of culpability. If the concepts of harm, causation, and risk all depend on normative judgments, then the ability of defendants to anticipate the risks of their actions depends on their sharing these normative judgments. If they merely know the probabilities but lack the proper normative interpretation of those probabilities, they may not be aware of the risk of harm. To nevertheless deem them culpable is to blame them for their values under the guise of holding them responsible for their expectations.[171]

CONTRACTARIANISM AND DESERVED PUNISHMENT
FOR HARMFUL RESULTS

We earlier saw that the utilitarian variant of cognitive culpability is incompatible with punishing harmful results, including homicide. But is the contractarian variant of cognitive culpability any more compatible with punishing actual harm? The most fundamental contractarian value is fairness, and we earlier encountered an argument that punishment for harm unfairly conditions liability on morally irrelevant luck. Philosophers have offered several reasons to hold offenders morally responsible for the harmful results of their crimes. We will consider four responses to the moral luck objection to see whether they can justify punishing harm as fair, but without evaluating the actor's ends. We may call these arguments the determinist reductio, the remorse analogy, the undeserved gratification argument, and the undeserved status argument. I will argue that the last two best explain why culpable injury *fairly* merits retribution. Yet both arguments present retributive punishment as a fair response to the desires and values motivating these injuries. Thus it seems that any retributive justification for punishing homicide must invoke forms of culpability that are not purely cognitive.

The determinist reductio argument, offered by retributivist legal philosopher Michael Moore, relies on an objectivist conception of action. This argument rejects the claim that action inherently involves risk but only contingently involves harm.[172] Instead it begins with a picture of action as embodied willing.[173] To act is to engage with a physical world. Willing must produce some intended consequences to count as action at all.[174] Reducing actual harm to a matter of luck places the theorist on a slippery slope towards a deterministic view of choice and character as matters of luck as well. If an actor cannot be blamed for a consequence that would not have occurred under other circumstances, why should she be blamed for creating a risk that would have been less under other circumstances? Why should she be blamed for a choice she would not have made under less tempting circumstances, or with different physical abilities?[175] To take an example relevant to the felony murder context, suppose an armed robber demands "your money or your life." Why should such a robber be held responsible for killing a resisting victim if he would have left a compliant victim alive, or if better opportunities would have drawn him away from a career as a robber? The point of this reductio is not to say that only results matter. For Moore, desert is determined by the actor's will—but willing is subject to punishment only insofar as it has effects.[176] What Moore's argument leaves unexplained is why wrongful injuries are the particular effects that should trigger punishment. Why not draw the line at bodily movements?

A second argument for punishing harm is the remorse analogy, which appeals to common moral intuitions. Perhaps we feel that harm merits greater punishment,[177] because we normally feel a greater sense of remorse when we cause harm, and a sense of relief when our careless actions cause no harm.[178] Legal philosopher Antony Duff reasons that one whose remorse for a careless action is unaffected by a resulting injury to a victim fails to show the empathy expected of a morally developed person.[179] Moore adds that regretting careless actions but not harmful results expresses a narcissistic focus on one's own moral state and repeats the same indifference to the welfare of others that rendered the imposition of risk wrong in the first place.[180] Just as we hold ourselves more accountable for harmful rather than for harmless wrongdoing, we are more inclined to forgive others when their wrongdoing proves harmless. Duff explains that when we punish harm, we communicate to the offender that an extra measure of regret is morally obligatory, as an expression of the empathy owed the victim.[181] We tie the offender's welfare to that of his victim as an expression that an attitude of indifference to the suffering of others is unacceptable. This argument rejects the view that carelessness is fundamental and that harm is a contingent feature of careless acts. The practice of punishing harm insists that moral reasoning begins with the actual suffering of particular persons, and that the wrongness of imposing risk on populations is derivative from the wrongness of injuring persons.

Notice that insofar as this argument justifies punishing the offender so as to force him to experience morally appropriate regret for the harm he causes, it focuses on his desire states rather than his cognitive states. This desiderative focus is more explicit in a third argument for punishing harm, based on Kantian retributivism: the undeserved gratification argument. Within Immanuel Kant's moral philosophy, a moral act is one determined by a "good will," that is, an act motivated by duties of fair cooperation.[182] An immoral act is determined by a bad will, one that yields to a desire incapable of realization if universalized.[183] Punishment serves to enforce duties of fair cooperation by frustrating such anti-cooperative desires.[184] On these premises, punishment for intentionally causing harm fairly corrects an offender's undeserved gratification for causing it. If we punished attempts and completed crimes equally, successful offenders would be left more satisfied than unsuccessful attempters. Their regret at having been caught and punished would be mitigated by their pleasure in having achieved their criminal aims. From this viewpoint, we are obliged to punish the successful wrongdoer more than the attempter, lest we become complicit in his self-indulgence by permitting his undeserved gratification.[185]

The undeserved gratification argument is, in my view, a very strong argument that punishment for harm is deserved. Indeed, H. L. A. Hart thought it "the nearest to a rational defence" that he knew for "this form of retributive theory."[186] Yet this argument has not been appreciated as such by some who regard themselves as retributivists. For example, Kimberly Kessler writes "whether someone benefits from a crime is not the criminal law's concern."[187] Andrew Ashworth agrees that "the principles of profit deprivation and vindicative satisfaction belong to a separate realm of principles ancillary to punishment—chiefly principles of compensation."[188] Stephen Morse also dismisses this idea, reasoning that "[a]gents who fail may feel less satisfied ex post than those who succeed, but such feelings do not affect the agent's culpability at the time of the criminal conduct."[189]

It is odd, however, to find purported retributivists—who presumably regard the offender's suffering as morally necessary—arguing that the extent of the offender's suffering doesn't matter. While Kant denied that punishment could be evaluated on the basis of its welfare effects for persons other than the offender, he saw the offender's suffering as essential.[190] The essence of wrongdoing was yielding to an immoral desire, and the point of punishment was to correct wrongdoing by resisting that desire and forcing the offender to regret his choice. Kant therefore argued that no penalty should be imposed on a drowning swimmer who wrested a plank from another, because no subsequent penalty could possibly negate his desire to survive.[191] His point was neither that the act was justified nor that punishment would have no deterrent effect on others. It was that such a penalty could not even constitute punishment because it could not frustrate the desire motivating the crime. Absent some such account of why and how much the offender should suffer, a retributive theory cannot justify punishment that imposes suffering as well as blame. Kant's principle of frustrating the offender's attempt at undeserved gratification responds to this challenge. Based on this principle, the successful offender is owed more suffering than the attempter.

The undeserved gratification argument justifies punishing harm on the basis of the actor's ends rather than merely her choices and expectations. It is compatible with contractarianism, but not with a purely cognitive theory of culpability. Yet it may appear to justify punishing only purposeful harm, not knowing or reckless harm. If the actor is indifferent to harm rather than seeking it, there is arguably no extra satisfaction to frustrate through additional suffering. Nevertheless, there are some situations where the reckless imposition of risk expresses hostility rather than indifference, for example when the offender imposes risk sadistically in order to frighten, or contemptuously in order to humiliate and dominate. Such motives are often present in unintended homicides charged as murder on the basis of depraved indifference to human life.[192] Similarly hostile motives feature in many felony murders as well. Criminologist Jack Katz's research on robbery argues that it is often motivated more fundamentally by a wish for power and control over others than by economic motives.[193] A desire to dominate and humiliate is apparent in rape as well.[194] Where endangering a particular victim is a gratifying end in itself, we surely have some retributive justification for punishing harm to that victim. It may seem particularly appropriate to hold offenders responsible for events over which they assumed control by force.

The undeserved status argument justifies punishment for actual harm as necessary to correct the effects of successful crime on the social status of victims and offenders. It draws on moral philosopher Jean Hampton's expressive account of punishment as "defeat."[195] This argument presumes that wrongfully inflicted harm is generally understood to express a kind of insult. The wrongdoer treats the victim as a person of lesser status,[196] whose interests do not count as much as his own. This is an insult felt by the victim or anyone who identifies with the victim. In some cultures, the wronged party is obliged to demand, and if necessary coerce, redress from the wrongdoer. If he fails to do so, he accepts the insult and displays cowardice, thereby lowering his status and perhaps inviting more abuse from others.[197] The wrongdoer may gain in status if his wrong is left unredressed, and he can thus become an increasing threat to others. This dynamic explains the practice of vengeance as an effort to restore the preexisting status equilibrium.[198] In some societies, a patron undertakes to protect the status of dependents by exacting vengeance on their behalf.[199]

In a modern liberal society, private vengeance and private dependence (among competent adults) are suppressed, thus depriving victims of a self-help remedy for status degradation. The liberal state purports to guarantee all adults an equal status and asserts an exclusive right to protect that status by exacting vengeance on behalf of victims. This monopoly on vengeance implies an undertaking to vindicate *particular* victims by avenging *actual* harms, rather than merely deterring the imposition of risk against the public at large.[200] Such deterrence may reduce injury, but does nothing to restore the status of those who have been wrongly injured. In Hampton's view, the liberal state is a cooperative institution, guaranteeing equal status to each citizen in return for his eschewing private vengeance and supporting public retribution. Such a state can justly claim the loyalty and demand the forbearance of victims only if it fulfills its undertaking to vindicate them.

Retributivists have sometimes scorned this sort of argument as a form of revenge utilitarianism, justifying unfair punishment in order to reduce a supposed danger of retaliatory vigilantism.[201] Yet the argument is not ultimately concerned with consequences or welfare effects. It concerns the fairness and integrity of an institution that has undertaken to stand up for the equal status of potential victims while precluding them from doing this for themselves. Like the undeserved gratification argument, it is compatible with contractarianism. But rather than punishing harm on the basis of the offender's desires, it punishes harm on the basis of the expressive meaning of harming a victim, and of permitting such harm to go unredressed. The nature of status as a collectively produced institution helps make sense of Kant's notion that impunity makes all citizens complicit in the offender's crime, because they are all complicit in the victim's unremedied degradation.

We can combine the undeserved gratification argument with the undeserved status argument. If a punishment scheme is indifferent to the wrongdoer's undeserved gratification, it allows a wrongdoer to treat the penalty for wrongdoing as a price. This literally "sells out" the victim by enabling anyone to purchase a license from the state to degrade her. By punishing harmful results, the state prevents this commodification and thereby stabilizes the meaning of punishment as a restoration of the victim's status. This in turn enables the state to offer state punishment to citizens as an institution that underwrites civic status more securely than a system of private vengeance. In recognizing the equal status of its citizens, the state offers them a powerful moral motive to identify and comply with the criminal law. The state thereby persuades citizens to view respecting the rights of others as a public duty inhering in their own status as equal citizens. In pursuing this strategy of social control, the state overtly attempts to influence the moral values of its citizens, less by threatening them with punishment than by offering to punish on their behalf.

The strongest arguments for the fairness of punishing harmful results rely on moral assessments of the values implied by injurious acts and condemn the harm inflicted as an expression of those values. They support a richer conception of culpability than that offered by a purely cognitive theory. While the cognitive theory appears to provide a value-neutral assessment of culpability for harm, that appearance is an illusion. It is based on conflating utilitarianism's cognitive conception of culpability for risk with a contractarian conception of culpability for harm that requires the moral assessment of meaning and motive. It appears that we cannot make sense of *culpability for homicide* on a purely cognitive basis.

Utilitarian accounts of culpability as expected net cost cannot justify punishment of homicide as efficacious. Contractarian accounts of culpability can justify punishment of homicide as fair, but only insofar as they evaluate actor's ends. Punishment of homicide cannot be value-neutral. Thus, felony murder rules cannot be faulted for conditioning homicide liability on the pursuit of bad ends.

4 DEFENDING AN EXPRESSIVE THEORY OF CULPABILITY

A liberal state cannot keep its commitment to secure the equal dignity of all persons subject to its laws without assigning blame and exacting punishment for wrongful injuries like homicide. Yet it cannot assign blame for results without evaluating actor's ends.

In this chapter, I offer an expressive account of culpability, which candidly judges the values expressed by action. This account explains why felony murders like those described in the opening lines of this book deserve severe punishment. Not only does this account of culpability better fit our practice of punishing actual harm than does a purely cognitive account, but it also better accords with other doctrines of criminal law. Finally, although judging offenders' ends, this account authorizes punishment for reasons within the competence of a liberal state.

EXPRESSIVE CULPABILITY AND FELONY MURDER

An expressive account of culpability begins with a conception of action as expressively, rather than instrumentally, motivated. On this view, action expresses value by identifying us with normative social practices. In *The Morality of Freedom*, the legal philosopher Joseph Raz denies that our desires determine our goals, arguing instead that our desires often flow from normative beliefs about what is best for us.[1] Thus, he contends, we act on the basis of normative reasons or values, rather than unreflective wants.[2] Frederic Schick offers a somewhat similar account of motivation in *Understanding Action*.[3] Schick argues that our preferences are formulated in light of larger understandings of our situations given by our commitments and social roles. These commitments and understandings make some options salient to us and others unthinkable. In *Value in Ethics and Economics*, the moral philosopher Elizabeth Anderson offers an institutional account of value as a social practice of recognizing certain kinds of goods, which in turn shape social relations. To value is to participate in such a social practice by assuming a certain role, entailing relations with and responsibilities toward others.[4]

On this account of action as value-motivated, valuing does not mean merely harboring a mental state—an opinion or demand curve—somewhere in one's head. Instead, valuing requires identifying oneself with a social practice through action in relation to others.[5] Thus, to bargain is to value economically by participating in the institution of market exchange; to love is to participate in the very different evaluative practices of romantic courtship or familial attachment. To worship a deity or appreciate art is similarly to participate in the conventions of some cultural community. By contrast to the exclusively instrumental conception of rational action employed in economic analysis, then, Raz, Schick, and Anderson offer an expressive conception. According to this expressive conception, to act rationally is to express values that one reflectively endorses, to identify oneself with corresponding roles with respect to corresponding goods, and to fulfill the responsibilities attendant upon those roles.[6]

On the basis of similarly expressive conceptions of action, the philosopher Jean Hampton has offered an account of criminal culpability as the expression of contempt for or "defiance" of values she sees as particularly important in a liberal political community.[7] Thus, drawing on contractarian ideas, she portrays criminal law as a cooperative institution investing certain rights and public duties with significance as symbols of mutual regard in a society of equally free persons.[8] On this view, to commit a criminal act is to express disrespect for the equal status of others; to punish is to reassert their equal status.[9]

Such an expressive model of culpability can account for the criminal law's attribution of responsibility for causing harm because it does not pretend to achieve value neutrality. Instead, it can acknowledge the social cost and scope of the risk problems that preclude cognitive culpability theory from achieving value neutrality. In other words, it recognizes that all action imposes risk to the welfare of others, so that harm always involves the interaction of competitive activities. Because harm cannot be quantified without evaluating the desires frustrated by competing activities, neither can risk. Attributions of responsibility for causing harm therefore depend on evaluations of the underlying activities of both "offenders" and "victims." An expressive model can acknowledge that these attributions of causal responsibility depend on irreducibly subjective or aesthetic judgments of analogy between unworthy aims and unfortunate results. Where such an aesthetic analogy can be found between a coercive or destructive felony and a resulting unintended death, an expressive account can attribute the requisite culpability and causal responsibility for an aggravated homicide offense. Thus, if robbers and rapists do not advert to risks because they wish to claim for themselves a transcendent power to control events, it may seem just to blame them for the harms they thereby inflict on those whom they coercively recruit into their fantasies of dominion.

By contrast to cognitive theory's aspiration to value neutrality, an expressive conception of culpability overtly defines action as culpable insofar as it expresses a commitment to unworthy values. The evaluative focus of an expressive conception is ultimately on the reasons for action. The various mental states excluded by a cognitive conception of culpability—malign desires, motives, or emotions—are not culpable in themselves, any more than an expectation of harm is culpable in itself. These mental states become culpable when an actor allows them to guide action. In so doing, the actor accepts them as valid reasons for action, reasons that outweigh countervailing considerations. Thus the offender repudiates institutional practices of valuation that acknowledge others as equally free, or identifies himself with institutional practices of valuation, such as gangster roles, that disrespect others. By identifying himself with particular institutional practices of valuation, the actor expresses value judgments. These expressed value judgments are attributable to the actor, but they are implications of a particular act rather than manifestations of the actor's character. Such expressed value judgments may of course be influenced by persistent character traits of the actor, but the actor is blamed for a particular act that expresses bad values, not for persistently adhering to bad values.

On this view, conduct is culpable if done for reasons reflecting a lack of proper regard for others' welfare, autonomy, or equal citizenship.[10] Thus it is culpable to purposely reduce the welfare of others, or to knowingly harm or endanger that welfare for an unworthy purpose. It is similarly blameworthy to deprive someone of a basic right secured to all, whether purposefully or as an expected consequence of action taken for some other unworthy or insufficient purpose. It is reprehensible to act with the aim of establishing personal dominion or authority over an equal citizen. One may exercise legitimate authority as an agent or delegate of a democratic polity, for a limited and publicly determined purpose. However, to assert dominion over another without such authorization and limitation is to impugn the other's autonomy and equality, and to displace all democratic citizens from their proper role in establishing and delimiting such authority. Similarly, to exercise such power for an unauthorized purpose or in defiance of its prescribed limitations is to express disrespect for the autonomy, equality, and citizenship of others. In addition, when a democratic polity has duly imposed public duties on all citizens, knowingly evading those duties for an unworthy purpose disrespects one's fellow citizens as equal participants in collective decision making. Finally, a democratic polity may associate duties of care with certain public offices or private positions of trust. To neglect these role responsibilities in favor of other purposes and pursuits is to improperly value these roles and the persons who rely on their fulfillment.

This expressive conception of culpability does not blame actors only for causing—or risking—a harmful state of affairs. First, it recognizes that a wrongdoer's contribution to wrong need not be causal. Thus we blame accomplices for identifying themselves with a wrong rather than for causing it. An accomplice can become a party to crime by providing redundant assistance to a principal, or by encouraging an already resolute principal. When we hold an actor complicit in a killing because he intentionally encouraged it, we do not thereby absolve the killer of blame on the ground that he was caused to kill. In the famous case of *State v. Tally*,[11] the defendant's brothers-in-law pursued and killed a man who had seduced their sister. The defendant urged a telegraph operator not to deliver a message warning the victim of the killers hot on his trail. It was unlikely that the warning could have been delivered before the killing even without Tally's interference, or that reading the warning would have saved the victim. Indeed, it was unlikely that the unread warning would have told the victim— already in frantic flight from the killers—anything he did not already know. Nevertheless, Tally was held liable as their accomplice for associating himself with their crime by providing this redundant aid. Legal philosopher Christopher Kutz has used the firebombing of Dresden to illustrate how multiple actors can participate in producing harm without any individual bearing causal responsibility.[12] In that situation no single bomb was either necessary or sufficient to produce the catastrophic firestorm that consumed the city and killed tens of thousands of victims. Each act of releasing a bomb linked a bomber crew to these deaths expressively rather than causally. No individual participant authored the result, but each authorized it, identifying himself with values that would justify or permit it.

Second, wrongs are not limited to physical events or changes in "states of affairs." As legal philosopher Meir Dan-Cohen argues in his provocative essays in *Harmful Thoughts*, we can be made worse off by changes in how other people think and feel.[13] I am worse off if my friends cease to like and respect me.[14] Others' thoughts may affect my opportunities, or may sadden me if I know about them, but their harmfulness to me does not seem reducible to these effects on my experience.[15] Dan-Cohen agrees with philosopher Joel Feinberg that if I seek esteem, I can be harmed by a bad reputation even after I am dead.[16] In various ways, then, my well-being depends not just on how the world is but also on how others interpret and evaluate the world. Some of the interpretive constructs that affect my well-being are, like the firebombing of Dresden, products of collective action.[17] Important evaluations are often conferred on persons by institutions. The philosopher John Searle defines institutions as social practices organized by norms applied on the basis of interpretive judgments.[18] The existence of an institution depends on its acceptance by some community of persons. Such socially contingent "institutional facts" include linguistic meaning, market value, legal authority, and social status.[19] Indeed, punishment itself involves an institutional practice of evaluation that confers a social status. Just as the Dresden bombers could participate in wrongful collective action without causing its effects, an individual may participate in an institutional wrong like slavery, gender hierarchy, or mob rule without necessarily causing any particular harmful consequence. By committing an act of violence in order to demean or demoralize a group, one identifies oneself with an unjust institution. In so doing one does not merely express a political opinion. One participates in an unjust practice of evaluation that demeans the dignity and injures the status of its victims.

In the case of a hate crime, a diffuse wrongful aim (to subordinate a group) changes the normative meaning and aggravates the wrong of causing harm intentionally. In the case of felony murder, a more precise wrongful aim (e.g., to expropriate property, to violate sexual autonomy, to destroy a building) changes the normative meaning and aggravates the wrong of causing harm negligently. Why should the criminal law consider the offender's ends in negligently imposing a fatal risk? Because imposing such a risk for an evil purpose expresses wrongful, injurious evaluations of others.

This is especially true when the risk arises from the deliberate use of force. Force has destructive potential, of course, but it also has a political meaning that transcends its destructive effects. Force is the language of rule, of political superiority. It is therefore an anomaly in a liberal society of political equals, where it can be authorized only by democratic assent and justified only by good reasons. The coercive power of the criminal law is authorized on just such a basis. In a state claiming a monopoly on legitimate force, that coercive power is important for its symbolic value as well as for its intimidating effect. Whether or not the criminal law can deter, it sets a standard of conduct for society by identifying certain conduct as wrong enough to warrant a coercive response. Such a response should stand out as an anomaly in a liberal society. Offenses that use force as an instrument of wrongful ends challenge the criminal law's expressive content, using the law's own idiom of coercion. To use force in furtherance of a felony is to demean the autonomy of victims and also to infringe the democratic polity's monopoly on force in opposition to its values. A felony murder rule responds to this challenge to the authority of the democratic sovereign and its central value commitments. It reasserts that only a democratically enacted law can determine the ends for which coercive force may be used.

The moral wrong of felony murder is most apparent when an offender uses fatal violence to coerce a victim's cooperation or overcome her resistance during a crime like rape or robbery. Feminist analysis of the crime of rape has emphasized that it is not merely a selfish act of sexual gratification.[20] It is also a political act, in which an assailant asserts dominion over a fellow human being (of either sex) on the basis of gender hierarchy. The rapist simultaneously controls the victim and degrades her status.[21] Think of the way rape is used in prison to permanently lower the victim's status and mark him as one who must obey;[22] or think of what soldiers express about the political status of an undefended civilian population when they use rape as an instrument of war.[23] The rapist's violence strips the victim of her civic status and makes her his subject and dependent. Within the rapist's domain, the victim is at his mercy: the victim's safety and survival depend on the rapist's choices, not her own. In using force as an instrument of governance, the rapist not only demeans the victim, he also misappropriates political dominion in a way that implicates other citizens.

The criminologist Jack Katz offers a related account of the expressive dimension of armed robbery.[24] Robbers differ from other thieves in that they publicly announce their criminal intentions, waving their weapons and shouting commands.[25] The robber's first aim is to establish control over a situation, over a place and the people in it.[26] The victims of a robbery—and the potential victims of a felony murder—often include everyone on the scene, whether or not they control the loot. According to Katz, robberies are difficult to explain instrumentally. The take is small,[27] and successful robbers typically squander the proceeds immediately.[28] The risks are great: robbers draw attention to themselves, inviting identification.[29] They place their trust in collaborators who are violent, dishonest, and instable.[30] Their menacing behavior can provoke violent resistance.[31] Robbers often compound these risks by persisting in the face of resistance and sometimes use violence against uncooperative victims who pose no real threat to them.[32] According to Katz, the seemingly irrational project of robbery often grows out of an existential choice to cope with the chaos of life in the underclass by assuming the persona of an indomitable "hardman."[33] Having cultivated a character capable of transcending danger with implacable violence, however, the robber invites danger so as to occasion the performance of such a character.[34] Like the rapist, then, the robber uses violence expressively and politically, carving out space for his own identity in a society that has no use for him, by establishing his dominion over others. Like the rape victim, the robbery victim finds himself at the mercy of the offender's fantasies. In both cases, the victim's exposure to danger constitutes the very power by which the felon achieves his wrongful aim. If this danger materializes and the victim dies, it seems fair to attribute the death to the felon who claimed mastery over the situation, and who reduced the victim to an instrument of his will.

Not only is such a felony murderer degrading a victim; he is also violating an important political principle. He arrogates to himself the power to coerce other citizens that, in a democracy, is properly vested only in a democratic state subject to constitutional controls. Moreover, the felony murderer uses this power for purposes that the democratic polity has determined to oppose by force. In this sense, the robber and the rapist challenge the rule of law itself, like gangsters or vigilantes. On a small scale, the robber or the rapist establishes a rival regime that repudiates the ordinary grounds of political legitimacy in consent and cooperation. He disrespects his victims' dignity as members of a liberal political community and tests that community's commitment to equality of status.

Of course the rapist and the robber need not have all this "in mind" in order to degrade their victims. Contempt for victims is often expressed by a failure to recognize their dignity and to accept it as a constraint on self-gratification. This is how philosopher Frederic Schick imagines the "thinking" that typically accompanies the crime of rape:

> The man who rapes and the man who doesn't are the same in their beliefs and desires. They both believe that a show of force might frighten some woman into having sex with them, and they both want sex. They differ in their understandings. The rapist sees rape as raw, rough sex, as tough-guy sex, the way he likes it. The other sees rape as a violation. He wants sex, but not violation, and so the way he understands rape doesn't connect with what he wants, which means that he isn't moved to rape.[35]

On Schick's view, the dignity that protects us from victimization is contingent, a way of seeing, an aesthetic attitude that is easily cast aside. It is sustained only by culture, including expressive practices like punishment. The rapist and the robber are at fault not only for the desires they have pursued, but for the values they have thereby failed to attend to. In sacrificing the dignity of their victims to their desires, they have evaluated them as unworthy of respect. They have thereby expressed very reprehensible values, whether or not they have reflected on them.

On the cognitive conception of culpability, however, the values expressed by the killer's act are irrelevant to his or her culpability for causing death. According to this conception, the criminal law has no business judging the values expressed by acts of treason, terror, persecution, and felony murder. We have seen that cognitivists offer two contradictory arguments against conditioning punishment on the actors' ends. One argument is that the choice of ends is the exercise of a freedom fundamental to liberal society, which should not be chilled by the threat of criminal punishment. That argument is considered in the last section of this chapter. The other argument is that values should not be the object of blame because they are not chosen, but instead are inherent characteristics of the person.

Does liability for crimes of motive like genocide and felony murder punish character rather than choice? Not if by "motives" we mean "reasons for action." We may entertain a desire, an opinion, or an affective attitude without choosing it. Indeed, we may resist such feelings or struggle to rid ourselves of them.[36] But when we choose to express such feelings through action, we endorse those feelings as justifying reasons and identify ourselves with them as values.[37] We are just as responsible for the values we express through our actions as we are for the thoughts we express in speech.

Some cognitivists argue that offenders should not be blamed for illicit desires because they may be helpless to avoid them, and that evil desires by themselves are innocent because an actor may experience such desires but resist acting on them.[38] Yet these arguments militate only against punishing unexecuted desires. They offer no reason to absolve offenders who choose to gratify desires they should resist. The expressive account proposed here blames actors only for the values they express by acting on the basis of bad reasons. It does not blame them for harboring fantasies they don't act on.

Some cognitivists distinguish diffuse motives like bigotry from the "specific intentions" required for many conventional crimes. Thus Heidi Hurd and Michael Moore argue that hatred and bigotry are affective attitudes that cannot be equated with specific goals like extermination of a group.[39] They argue that such affective attitudes are not easily controlled or eliminated because they are emotions rather than thoughts.[40] For Hurd and Moore, bigotry causes action involuntarily rather than providing a reason for voluntary action.[41] Even if accepted, this argument would not cut against felony murder, which aggravates negligent homicide based on the specific intentions required for other conventional crimes.

Nevertheless, this argument should not be accepted, for two reasons. First, hate crimes are not simply assaults accompanied by an inner feeling of hostility. They are assaults aimed at the expressive goals of demeaning a group and demeaning a victim because of membership in this group. Other political motives like terrorism and treason can be defined with similar precision. Second, evaluative attitudes like hostility, anger, resentment, and contempt should not be seen as irrational just because they involve emotion. As moral philosopher Martha Nussbaum and criminal law theorist Dan Kahan have argued, emotion is an inherent aspect of evaluative reasoning.[42] An emotional reaction like outrage upon witnessing cruelty to a child reflects a moral judgment, while moral reasoning can assess the propriety of such evaluative emotions.[43] Evaluative emotions do not merely cause action: they offer reasons for action that can be evaluated as better or worse. Kahan and Nussbaum argue that action motivated by a justified evaluative emotion should be seen as less culpable, as when provoked intentional killings are mitigated to manslaughter.[44] By the same logic, an unjustified evaluative emotion like racial animus should aggravate liability when it motivates crime.

Finally, cognitivists sometimes equate motives with enduring dispositions. Thus Hurd poses the following question:

> At the moment that a defendant is about to throw a rock through his neighbor's window, we are reasonably sure that he can will to do otherwise; but at that moment, can he will away his hatred of his neighbor as a Jew? Can one simply decide not to be selfish, or greedy, or narcissistic? I suspect anyone who can is not very selfish, greedy or narcissistic![45]

Hurd concedes that we may be faulted for not having taken measures to develop a better character, but reasons that when tempted to do wrong, "[w]e cannot abandon our emotions and (dispositional) beliefs the way that we can abandon our goals—i.e., simply by choice."[46]

This argument conflates the values expressed by an act with an actor's inherent or essential identity. The social meaning of action is an institutional phenomenon, not a hidden, psychological phenomenon. The actor constructs and portrays a contingent identity through action, rather than revealing an essential and authentic self.[47] In treating anti-Semitism as a personality trait rather than a collectively produced institution, Hurd reduces persecution to an act of vandalism that happens to involve a bigot and so reduces an event like *Kristallnacht* from a status-altering pogrom to a mere wave of delinquency. Thus, in treating the meaning of action as a psychological trait of the actor, Hurd segregates the act from its social meaning. However, an act is not anti-Semitic because it is committed by an anti-Semite. It is anti-Semitic insofar as it expresses anti-Semitic evaluations by supporting an anti-Semitic movement or practice. An individual can choose to express values without adhering to them consistently over time. For example, in a stratified society, any individual who can be identified with a subordinate group is vulnerable to degradation by anyone (even a fellow subordinate) whether or not that person has any prior history of bigotry. Anyone in competition with such a vulnerable person can exploit this vulnerability to gain an advantage, without necessarily holding bigoted views. The wrong of degrading someone in this way consists in *playing* a bad character, not in *having* a bad character.

Similarly, a felony murder rule should not be seen as some sort of recidivist statute aimed at incapacitating habitual criminals because of their characters. A felony murder rule aggravates negligent homicide because it is committed in pursuit of a felonious purpose, not because it is committed by a felon. We have seen that for the paradigmatic predicate felonies of robbery and rape, the pursuit of a felonious purpose involves claiming dominion over victims. The felon whose coercion causes death is blamed for choosing to act in a destructively domineering way, not for having a domineering personality.

This idea of culpability as role performance resonates with Hampton's conception of culpability as the defiance of legitimate authority. Hampton described an action as culpable when the actor knows what an important value—rationality, morality, or law—demands of her and chooses to act on the basis of some other motivating principle.[48] Hampton viewed such a choice in political terms as overthrowing an authority and choosing to obey the practical dictates of a rival authority that indulgently approves the forbidden act as good.[49] In so choosing, an actor expresses allegiance to a value. Just as Kant asked us to test the moral worth of acts by hypothetically universalizing their motivating principles,[50] Hampton asked us to test acts by imagining social practices of valuing based on their motivating principles.[51] To express a value is to play the role of a participant in such a social practice.

This idea of role playing helps explain negligence as a form of expressive culpability. Legal theorist Jeremy Horder views criminal negligence as a failure to fulfill duties of care inherent in the performance of a role one has knowingly undertaken.[52] Such a duty of care requires not just avoiding dangerous practices, but also maintaining active attention towards certain risks. For example, surgeons and drivers are licensed only after having been taught to pay attention. For one who has undertaken such a duty, a failure to advert to these risks therefore becomes a culpable choice to shirk the obligations of a role. Hampton explained much imprudent behavior as arising from the performance of a different kind of role, an egoistic fantasy of transcending mundane causal laws:

> [A] person can postulate a kind of magical control over the world, so that doing what he wishes will also seem consistent with the commands of practical reason. . . . Or people can decide to believe that they are permitted to try a forbidden activity because they are exempted from the sorts of problems that normally plague those who engage in it. For example, drug users often claim that other people get addicted to heroin, but not them.[53]

Hampton explained "inadvertent negligence" as culpable on the ground that the unreasonable actor is responsible for having "defiantly" developed an imprudent character.[54] Yet, thus conceding the ground of choice to cognitive theorists seems unnecessary: the imprudent actors that Hampton described make culpably irrational choices to be guided by a magical sense of destiny rather than by causal laws.

We can give an expressive account of the felony murderer's negligence with respect to a risk of death by combining Horder's and Hampton's conceptions of negligence. The driver who runs a red light is culpable for a resulting collision even if he confidently believes he "can make it." He knows what the law requires of him and is obliged to inform himself about the risks he creates in violating it. Unlike drivers, armed robbers are not licensed after taking a course in safe theft. But in assaulting and stealing they are violating basic civic duties. They know they are violating the law and probably know they are committing predicates for felony murder. In ordering their equals about at gunpoint they know they are infringing the law's monopoly on coercion. It is fair to expect them to inform themselves about the risks involved in an activity that the law so emphatically condemns. Instead, they blind themselves to such risks by defiantly adopting a role—the ruthless, implacable "hardman"—expressing indifference to the welfare of others and arrogantly claiming an impossible mastery over events.

An expressive theory of culpability measures an actor's culpability for causing harm along two dimensions: her expectation of causing harm and the moral worth of her reasons for imposing that risk. A felony murder rule conditions liability for death on a negligent disregard of the substantial risk imposed by a fatal act and a very malign motive for the act. The dual character of expressive culpability explains a traditional feature of felony murder liability that has long puzzled scholars: the requirement of an "independent felonious purpose."[55] Under this doctrine—which we will examine in greater detail in Chapter 11—felony murder liability cannot be predicated on a felony that simply attacks or endangers the homicide victim's body. Thus, offenses like assault and manslaughter are said to "merge" with the homicide.[56] Some scholars and courts have thought that arson should merge as well, since the felonious act of setting a fire is not independent of the act causing death.[57] Yet the expressive theory of culpability explains why arson has traditionally served as a predicate felony. Rather than viewing felony murder as a combination of two acts, the expressive theory of culpability explains the merger doctrine as a requirement that the fatal felony combines two culpable mental states: indifference to a risk of death and an independent felonious purpose. The combination of these two mental states ensures that the fatal felon is sufficiently culpable to deserve murder liability. In arson, the purpose of destroying a building is the additional bad end that aggravates the negligent killing.

The expressive theory of culpability outlined here both justifies and limits felony murder by requiring a dangerous or violent felony, and an independent felonious purpose. In addition, the expressive theory limits causal responsibility to those deaths that illustrate the felon's culpability. Thus, if the felon's negligence is established by the element of violence or destruction in the predicate felony, death must foreseeably result from the violent or destructive act. Accordingly, felons should not be held liable for deaths resulting unpredictably from a victim's emotional response. We can reasonably hold felons causally responsible for deaths resulting from efforts to flee or resist violence, but not for heart attacks or suicides. These deaths may result from a predicate felony, but they do not illustrate—they do not express—that felony's depravity. On this same principle, felons should not be held responsible for unreasonably violent or dangerous police responses to their crimes. These limitations reconcile felony murder with desert. Yet they are not external constraints at odds with the principles of felony murder liability. Instead, an expressive account of felony murder ensures that the limits of desert inhere in the principles of felony murder themselves.

EXPRESSIVE CULPABILITY IN AMERICAN CRIMINAL LAW

Cognitivists claim that their model of culpability provides an accurate description of American criminal law. Thus Hurd and Moore rest their case against hate crime liability on the charge that it violates the value-neutral approach to defining crime that they claim prevails in American criminal law.[58] They ultimately concede that a bad motive aggravates the moral culpability of an offense:

> Notwithstanding the relative inelasticity of character, we are sympathetic to the view that moral culpability is largely a function of the reasons for which persons act and the emotions that attend their actions. . . . Inasmuch as we can distinguish the mercy killer from the contract killer only by reference to their relative motivations, and inasmuch as the mercy killer appears as nonculpable as the contract killer appears culpable, our theory of moral culpability clearly departs from our doctrines of legal culpability by weighting an actor's motivations for action far more heavily than the intentionality of his actions.[59]

With this concession, Hurd and Moore admit the general principle that badly motivated offenders deserve more punishment. But, they contend, it is invidious and illiberal to single out bigoted motives for more punishment. If bigoted motives aggravate crime, they ask, why should not other bad motives affect liability?

The simple answer is that other bad motives do affect liability: assessment of motive pervades American criminal law. Cognitivists fail to see this for two reasons. First, they artificially separate inculpatory standards like criminal negligence and depraved indifference from exculpatory standards like necessity, duress, provocation, and reasonable mistake of law, which are governed by similar moral principles. Second, they dismiss obviously expressive standards of inculpation like felony murder as anomalous. However, there are too many such anomalies. Indeed, an expressive conception of culpability better accounts for prevailing rules of American criminal law than does a cognitive conception.

The defenses of self-defense and necessity are obvious examples of doctrines conditioning liability on evaluation of purposes and desires rather than on the simple expectation of harm. It may be objected that killing in self-defense and stealing a car to rush a heart attack victim to a hospital are approved on the basis of their consequences rather than their motives. Yet motive determines whether a particular life is worthy of defense and so what counts as a good consequence.[60] Thus, we approve the killing of multiple assailants to repel a rape, and disapprove the rapist killing a resisting victim to save his own life. In the context of necessity, a good motive is often more important than a good consequence. Thus we approve the car theft even if the patient dies on the way to the hospital, but disapprove a car theft committed before the heart attack occurs, even if it turns out to save a life.[61] We limit both defenses to courses of action that express worthy values.

The defense of duress, which excuses coerced crime, is also conditioned on worthy reasons for action. First, the defendant must act out of fear: if she bargains for a share of the loot, she gets no defense. Second, she must have a good reason for fear, based on a credible, imminent threat of violence. A threat to expose an embarrassing secret will not suffice.[62] To do great harm to others because of a minor threat to one's own interests is to indulge an unworthy emotion—to yield to cowardice rather than coercion.[63] As with self-defense, we preclude duress if the defendant brought about the necessity of offending, by joining a gang, for example.[64]

The defense of provocation, which mitigates liability for murder on the basis of the offender's anger, also depends on the grounds for the offender's emotion. A recent unprovoked assault suffices; romantic rejection does not.[65] Since the offender has no right to his victim's affection, the loss of it gives him no justification for losing his temper.[66] Provocation depends not just on strong emotion, but on justified strong emotion.[67]

The defense of reasonable mistake of law, available in some jurisdictions, excuses those offenders who reasonably believed their conduct legal after making good faith efforts to ascertain the law. A belief that the law permits dishonest or destructive behavior is unlikely to be judged honest and reasonable. Conversely, constitutional due process can require notice of a criminal prohibition that interferes with such constitutionally protected aims as speech, worship or travel. The normative worth of the defendants' aims informs the reasonableness of their beliefs that their acts are lawful.[68]

When we move from defenses to offense definitions, we find the same concern with the offender's reasons and purposes. This is clearest with the purely inchoate crimes of attempt, conspiracy, and solicitation.[69] A mere expectation of doing harm will not suffice for these offenses. Only a purpose of doing harm can turn harmless conduct into a punishable attempt.[70]

Purpose and other desiderative attitudes are also important in crimes of result. Traditionally, harm has been seen as most culpable when caused on purpose.[71] The cognitive conception equates knowing and purposeful harm, reasoning that only the expectation of harm, not the desire for it, makes purposeful harm culpable. Yet we punish the intentional wrongdoer for her reprehensible aims, even if the accomplishment of those aims seemed unlikely ex ante. Moreover, we punish the knowing wrongdoer not merely because of her knowledge, but because of the values expressed by her acting in the face of that knowledge. Thus we would not punish a horrified bystander who anticipated a fatal accident but was helpless to prevent it. We punish the knowing wrongdoer because in choosing to cause harm, even reluctantly, she accepts it as the price of some other end she cares about more.[72]

The same is true of those who inflict harm recklessly or negligently: in proceeding with their projects in the face of foreseen or foreseeable risk, they overvalue their own ends and undervalue the welfare of others.[73] Even according to the Model Penal Code, these risks must be unjustifiable and unreasonable in light of the nature and purpose of the actor's conduct.[74] This unreasonableness is not just a matter of the quantity of risk, because when conduct is customary, its dangers—even if great—will be attributed to victims who could have foreseen and avoided them.[75] If customary conduct is seen as part of a valued social role or institution, its risks are seen as "reasonable" and its harms are seen as costs of other conflicting activities. By contrast the risks imposed by robbery will not be ascribed to imprudent victims. Whether costs are assigned to an activity depends on its moral worth.[76]

This kind of evaluation of ends is particularly important in deciding what risks are reckless enough to justify second-degree murder liability.[77] A disappointed suitor sets fire to a Christmas tree inside his date's apartment building;[78] a losing gambler shoots up carnival trucks with a shotgun;[79] a bored youth forces a child to play Russian roulette;[80] a greedy surgeon delegates dangerous procedures to untrained assistants.[81] These cases all exhibit the requisite "depraved indifference to human life" or "abandoned and malignant heart," but what do they have in common? In each case, the murderer imposes a great risk of death for a particularly unworthy reason. Some jurisdictions make this requirement of a depraved motive explicit, requiring an "antisocial purpose" as well as recklessness for depraved-indifference murder.[82] Felony murder involves a similar kind of culpability, but requires a felonious rather than a merely antisocial purpose, combined with merely negligent rather than reckless indifference to human life.

These homicide offenses may seem anomalous because they aggravate responsibility for harm an actor did accomplish based on another harm she wanted to accomplish. But this is true of many partially inchoate crimes that require a result as a means to some other unfulfilled end. The burglar must want to acquire, but need only break in;[83] the robber must want to acquire, but need only threaten or injure;[84] the thief must want to acquire loot permanently, but need only succeed in moving it;[85] the witness tamperer must want to suppress testimony, but need only threaten or assault the witness;[86] the briber must want to influence, but need only offer to pay.[87]

Finally, partially inchoate offenses include controversial crimes of political motive such as genocide,[88] crimes against humanity,[89] civil rights violations,[90] terrorism,[91] and treason,[92] as well as offenses aggravated under hate crime statutes. Such political offenses aggravate conventional crimes of violence based on an interpretive judgment that they express certain political values. An occupying army singles out civilians of particular ethnicity or religion, shooting the men and raping the women.[93] A planter and his overseers horsewhip exslaves lining up for work outside a mill.[94] A dissident group bombs a subway on the eve of an election[95] or holds a theater audience hostage to its political demands.[96] In all these cases, a larger context gives particular acts of violence a political meaning. The specific act of violence is part of a collective program of degrading, excluding, or intimidating a population. This political meaning is part of the offender's culpability, providing a moral ground for a higher sentence,[97] or an extended statute of limitations,[98] or an extraordinary extension of jurisdiction.[99] These political crimes therefore involve two forms of culpability, aiming at specific violence but also at a larger and still ongoing political project.

Felony murder liability is not anomalous in conditioning liability on a bad motive as well as expected harm. The moral evaluation of desires, purposes, and projects is found throughout criminal law. Bad motives do aggravate the moral culpability of offenses, as even cognitivists concede. The only remaining question is whether it is politically illegitimate to incorporate such moral judgments into our criminal law.

PUNISHING MOTIVES IN THE LIBERAL STATE

Does liberalism require a value-neutral criminal law? Does it preclude the evaluation of motives for acts of violence? Not according to Hampton:

> It is currently fashionable for many liberals (for example Rawls) to portray the liberal state as "morally neutral"—one that does not take moral sides as it governs a pluralist society. However, were a state to try to be morally neutral, it would be unable to inflict retributive punishment. The demands of retribution

require a legal institution not only to take moral sides, but also to strive to implement a moral world in which people are treated with the respect their value requires. As I see it, no liberal state would be worth supporting if it did not assume this role. A state that would truly be neutral about morality could not be animated by any conception of its citizens' worth as it punished offenders, and whatever its punishment goals, could not be properly responsive to that which matters most deeply to all of us: our value.[100]

Hampton offers here a vision of a liberal state as one that actively fosters a liberal political community in which each person is recognized as having equal status. She presents state punishment as a crucial expressive medium for reducing the status of those who have asserted mastery over others and restoring the status of their victims. She acknowledges no unfairness in the state's taking sides between those who claim a superior authority to govern others and those who assert merely an equal right to govern themselves.

Why then should the liberal state be neutral? Neutrality might serve to legitimize the liberal state in two ways: as a foundational principle limiting the legitimate competence of the state, or as a practice instrumental to certain values that contribute to legitimacy. If neutrality is a foundational principle, it applies to all state functions, including punishment. But if neutrality is simply a pragmatic device, it need not characterize every institution of the liberal state, and the desirability of a value-neutral criminal law becomes a practical question.

Why might we view the state as fundamentally incompetent to regulate values? Perhaps we are value skeptics, holding that values are simply arbitrary matters of taste that cannot be validated or criticized. But if value judgments cannot be rationally defended, it is hard to see how we can defend the value of the liberal state.[101] Thus the principle of value skepticism would seem to preclude any defense of the legitimacy of the liberal state and the obligation to obey its law.

Legitimating the liberal state in the face of cynicism is not merely a theoretical problem. Since the end of the Cold War, liberals have had to learn that liberalism is a feature of societies, not just of states. The fate of putatively liberal governments in transitional societies like post-Soviet Russia and post-invasion Iraq has shown that the power and authority of the liberal state is precariously dependent on widespread public attitudes of mutual tolerance and respect for law. Without a sufficiently "civic" culture,[102] governing institutions will dissolve or become instruments of corruption, coercion, or chauvinist demagoguery.

Thus liberalism would be pointlessly self-defeating if it demanded an attitude of tolerance and impartiality only of the state, and not of its citizens. As I have argued, the criminal law influences behavior far more effectively by inculcating values than by threatening punishment. Indeed, a polity that relied primarily on coercion rather than social norms to maintain social control would be a police state, not a liberal state. Thus a liberal state that undertakes to secure a life of freedom for its citizens cannot afford an attitude of indifference to their values. It cannot treat those values as given, but must make them an object of public policy.

Several liberal political philosophers have drawn on such arguments in denying that liberalism requires value neutrality. William Galston, for example, has argued that purportedly value-neutral accounts of the liberal state treat certain goods as fundamental, such as the fulfillment of human purposes.[103] He holds that the case for liberal government ultimately rests not on any principle but on its ability to secure a number of different goods.[104] These include social peace; the security and predictability provided by a rule of law; tolerance and inclusion of members of diverse communities; protection from extreme poverty, epidemic disease, and private violence; scope for personal development; freedom of inquiry and discussion; and access to information.[105] On this conception, liberalism involves both a vision of a good—or at least an adequately decent— society, and views about some of the constituents of a good life. A good enough society is one in which members can flourish in certain ways, particularly by making informed, uncoerced choices about their own development. This conception of liberalism as the means to a good society suggests several reasons why a liberal state can legitimately take an interest in the values of its citizens.

First, liberal views on the good society and on human flourishing have implications for what individuals should value. If liberalism is right that a good society enables individuals to develop autonomously, it follows that individuals should aspire to do so. Insofar as autonomous development depends on living in a culturally diverse society, individuals should appreciate diversity. If liberal society should protect liberty rights and provide a rule of law, it follows that individuals should value these as well. If liberal society should be decently humane, individuals should respond compassionately to extreme suffering. If a liberal society properly treats its members as political equals, those members should also treat each other as equals and should not endeavor to rule one another. In short, if liberalism is justified by the fact that liberal society is a good, it follows that everyone has reason to realize the good of liberal society, not just the state.

Stephen Macedo develops such an argument in *Liberal Virtues*.[106] Macedo associates the liberal values of autonomy and equality with a practice of rational discourse among disparate normative viewpoints.[107] Differences of opinion are inevitable, because the citizens of a liberal society are never free of the mutual interference and frustration implied by the problem of social cost.[108] But when they resolve their conflicts through an appeal to reason, they confirm their status as political equals, ruled by a collectively produced law rather than by a political superior.[109] Thus the loser of a dispute may suffer injury, but not the additional insult of subordination. To claim status as an equal subject of law, however, commits the liberal citizen to respect the rights and the rationality of her equals.[110] Although legal institutions help to constitute the good of mutual respect among political equals, individuals express that respect anytime they make an appeal to reason in interacting with others.[111] Macedo adds that the good of liberal autonomy is not simply a matter of not being ruled.[112] The autonomous subject determines her own values and commitments through an internal process of deliberation modeled on the debate among diverse views that she witnesses throughout liberal society.[113] Thus, for Macedo, the good of liberalism is maximized insofar as liberal principles are reflected not only in the design of institutions but also in the culture of society generally, and in the principles and practices of its members.[114] So the belief that liberal values are good provides a prima facie reason for the liberal state to encourage liberal virtues among its citizens.

A second reason for the liberal state to take sides on value questions is that it arguably cannot realize the good of liberal society without ensuring the prevalence of certain values and virtues among its population. Legal philosophers Joseph Raz and Stephen Gardbaum both argue that far from being indifferent to the moral views of individuals, liberalism requires a pluralistic society containing a range of moral views, all bounded by the liberal values of mutual tolerance and respect.[115] In *The Morality of Freedom*, Raz presents liberalism as centrally concerned with realizing the values of autonomy and dignity by fostering social conditions enabling individuals to shape their own ends through meaningful choices.[116] This requires the liberal state to support education, to foster a plurality of social institutions offering fulfilling roles, and to protect individuals from private coercion, which attacks both autonomy and dignity.[117] The liberal state discourages private coercion primarily through the criminal law, which deploys both disapprobation and coercion.[118] While Raz concedes that coercion by a democratic state infringes autonomy, he argues that it does not infringe dignity by subordinating one person to another.[119] Moreover, because he views autonomy as a positive good, dependent on actual social conditions, rather than as a negative right against state interference, his view of state coercion is pragmatic.[120] Thus the state is free to inculcate liberal moral views, even by coercive means, if it thereby enhances autonomy overall.[121] Raz has a similarly pragmatic view of neutrality as a policy instrument rather than a principle.[122] Thus the state may advance autonomy by creating locally neutral arenas for choice among certain alternatives, while making value choices in defining, organizing, and protecting those arenas.[123]

Of course it might be objected that the state is the wrong institution to teach liberal values, and that liberal values are best inculcated exclusively through exposure to a pluralistic private sector. Political philosopher Patrick Neal responds that a value-neutral state is not possible because the liberal state cannot help influencing values.[124] Neal argues that individual ends depend upon socialization in an institutional context that is largely shaped by law.[125] He reasons that even if government may be neutral among the preferences that prevail in a modern market society, it cannot be neutral toward other preferences that would prevail in a very differently organized society.[126] Neal invites us to imagine that

> Ralph, who wishes to lead a virtuous life . . . [has a preference] for a small, socially homogeneous polis in a preindustrial setting, for only in such a setting does he think it possible to develop . . . moral virtues . . . . Ralph can express his preference [in contemporary American society] but he can in no way live it. Nor should we say liberalism allows him to pursue his conception of the good privately, because his conception of the good entails an alternative understanding of the nature of "private" and "public" to that of the liberal. Ralph's conception of the good cannot be translated into a liberal language of private preferences without losing its essential character. . . . In order to respond to Ralph the liberal needs a defense of this translating activity and . . . of the form of life which results thereby, not an invocation of neutrality.[127]

Rather than offering its members a choice among all possible conceptions of the good life, liberal society offers only a life of gratifying private preferences by choosing among different purchases, investments, occupations, avocations, and social attachments. These choices are available within arenas constructed by legal rules defining competence, consent, coercion, and fraud. Thus whether or not liberal lawmakers intend to inculcate moral values, they inevitably do so simply by establishing institutions that enable the pursuit of some values while precluding the pursuit of others.

Taken together, these arguments tend to refute the view that the liberal state must, on principle, maintain strict value neutrality in all its actions. If we accept the premises that (1) the liberal state exists to realize the good of liberal society, (2) the good of liberal society depends upon widespread support for liberal values, and (3) the liberal state cannot avoid inculcating some values and suppressing others, it follows that the liberal state may—and probably should—inculcate liberal values. Where, when, and how it should do so, however, is a pragmatic question. Thus, even if value neutrality is not a defining principle of liberalism, it could be good policy in the area of criminal justice.

Should the liberal state use the coercive means of the criminal law to inculcate liberal values? One argument against doing so is that freedom of speech is a centrally important good in liberal society. Thus a pragmatic liberal state might best achieve the good of a liberal society by defining political debate as an arena for unrestricted choice, even at the cost of permitting illiberal hate speech that undermines the dignity and equality of some citizens. But the pragmatic decision to protect and value speech without regard to its content does not imply equal respect for every value expressed in speech. Nor does it require the liberal state to maintain the same neutrality toward values expressed through violent conduct.

Consider the implications for criminal law of Bruce Ackerman's procedural theory of justice in a liberal state. Ackerman views justice as the outcome of a rational and neutral discursive process, defining rationality and neutrality as follows:

> Rationality. Whenever anybody questions the legitimacy of another's power, the power holder must respond not by suppressing the questioner but by giving a reason that explains why he is more entitled to the resource than the questioner is.[128]
> Neutrality. No reason is a good reason if it requires the power holder to assert:
> (a) that his conception of the good is better than that asserted by any of his fellow citizens, or
> (b) that, regardless of his conception of the good, he is intrinsically superior to one or more of his fellow citizens.[129]

Notice that Ackerman's neutrality principle implies that neither expressions of bigotry nor expressions of conceptions of the good make any positive contribution to a legitimate political process. Because his rationality principle militates against punishing such expressions, Ackerman's liberalism forbids punishing hate speech. But, surprisingly, it has the opposite implication for hate crimes— that is, crimes of violence that express bigotry. Ackerman's rationality principle draws a fundamental distinction between two different modes of advancing political views: persuasion and coercion. Since hate crimes express political views by means of coercive force rather than rational persuasion, they are not protected by Ackerman's neutral dialogue.

The liberal state has a right not only to suppress violence but also to discriminate among the ends promoted by violence. In assuming the power to punish, the liberal state acknowledges that violence may be used legitimately for certain ends, and also claims a monopoly on the legitimate use of violence. When anyone uses violence, she assumes the liberal state's enforcement power and exercises a kind of governance, a power properly subject to democratic supervision in a liberal state. In such a state, violence is legitimate only insofar as it is justified by democratically chosen reasons that are consistent with achieving some version of the good of liberal society. By usurping the liberal state's monopoly on violence, private actors properly subject their ends to the same kind of political evaluation applied to public policy. The democratic public has a responsibility to consider whether the actor's ends justified, mitigated, or aggravated every act of violence. Liberal criminal law therefore should assess the values expressed by violence in imposing punishment. This principle supports aggravating liability for crimes of violence that express group hatred, or other antiliberal values. It also justifies aggravating homicide liability when violence is used to enable some other wrong forbidden by democratic decision, like a serious felony. A felony murder rule therefore fits within a democratic state's exclusive competence to determine the ends for which violence should and should not be used.

A near consensus of the criminal law academy holds that felony murder liability is undeserved. Because this consensus is rarely challenged, and because felony murder is usually dismissed as "rationally indefensible," the case against felony murder is rarely spelled out in any detail, or examined critically. Our argument so far has accomplished two things.

First, it has explicated the case against felony murder and exposed a contradiction at its heart. The view of felony murder liability as undeserved presumes a purely cognitive model of culpability as expected danger. Such a model, however, proves too much: it rejects liability for causing harmful results in favor of liability for imposing risk. Thus it rejects not just felony murder liability specifically, but also homicide liability of any kind. A theory of culpability for homicide must assess the offender's aims as well as her expectations. It must then determine if the fatal result sufficiently expresses the values on which she acted to warrant attributing that result to her. This inherently evaluative question is unavoidable in any criminal justice system that punishes for actual harm.

Second, our argument has presented a rational defense of felony murder liability as deserved, based on an expressive account of culpability that assesses ends as well as expectations. This theory understands rational action as motivated by the desire to express identification with values that one endorses upon reflection, by carrying out the responsibilities of a role within a normative social practice. A liberal state expects its citizens to collaborate in conferring a measure of equal dignity on one another by respecting certain fundamental legal rights. The culpability that justifies punishment as deserved includes the disrespect for victims expressed by certain offenses. To compel another by force to acquiesce in the violation of an important right is to express contempt for a victim's autonomy and status by asserting mastery over him or her. The death of a victim under the offender's dominion and as a result of the offender's coercion typifies the wrongfulness of assuming power over another's fate in order to wrong her. Felony murder rules appropriately impose liability for negligently causing death for a very depraved motive, as long as the predicate felony involves coercion or destruction, and a very malign purpose independent of the fatal injury. In evaluating the offender's reasons for action, felony murder rules are compatible with other rules of American criminal law, and with the limits of criminal law in a liberal state that promotes autonomy and that fairly distributes the burdens and the authority of democratic citizenship.

FELONY MURDER ORIGINS

Part Two

5 THE MYTH OF THE COMMON LAW FELONY MURDER RULE

Criticism of felony murder liability rests on oft repeated but seldom examined claims about its origins. Many commentators and courts suppose that a rule imposing strict liability for any death in any felony long prevailed in the English common law, was received into American law upon independence, and remains the law except where modified by enlightened legislation or judicial decision. William Clark and William Marshall summed up this prevailing view on the origin of American felony murder rules in their early-twentieth-century treatise on crimes:

> At common law, malice was implied as a matter of law in every case of homicide while engaged in the commission of some other felony, and such a killing was murder whether death was intended or not. . . . On this principle, it was murder at common law to unintentionally kill another in committing, or attempting to commit, burglary, arson, rape, robbery, or larceny. The doctrine has repeatedly been recognized and applied in this country, and is to be regarded as still in force, except where it has been expressly abrogated by statute. The decisions at common law do not require that the act done shall have been of such a nature as to endanger life, or threaten great bodily harm. . . . If it had been otherwise, the doctrine would have been altogether unnecessary, because the killing would be murder because of the tendency of the act, without regard to its being done in the commission of a felony.[1]

Contemporary commentators continue to instruct lawyers and law students that England bequeathed America a sweeping default principle of strict liability for all deaths caused in all felonies. According to Wayne LaFave's treatise, "[a]t one time the English common law felony-murder rule was that one who, in the commission or attempted commission of a felony, caused another's death, was guilty of murder, without regard to the dangerous nature of the felony involved or to the likelihood that death might result from the defendant's manner of committing or attempting the felony."[2] Similarly, the American Law Institute's Model Penal Code commentary describes "the common-law felony-murder doctrine"[3] as declaring "that one is guilty of murder if death results from conduct during the commission or attempted commission of any felony. . . . As thus conceived, the rule operated to impose liability for murder based on . . . strict liability."[4] According to Joshua Dressler's textbook, "At common law, a person is guilty of murder if she kills another person during the commission or attempted commission of any felony. This . . . felony-murder rule applies whether a felon kills the victim intentionally, recklessly, negligently, or accidentally and unforeseeably."[5] Arnold Loewy's *Criminal Law in a Nutshell* informs students that "[a]t early common law, felony murder was a simple proposition: any death resulting from a felony is murder. Thus a totally unforeseeable death resulting from an apparently non-dangerous felony would be murder."[6]

All of these texts imply that this harsh common law rule was incorporated into American law at independence, where it persists to this day, except where mitigated by judicial or legislative reforms. Similar accounts of the development of American felony murder rules appear in other treatises and texts,[7] in court opinions,[8] in scholarly articles,[9] and in law review comments.[10] On the basis of such accounts, critics attack modern rules as "anachronistic" legacies of a morally regressive age.[11]

Yet none of these accounts identifies when this supposed common law rule of strict liability for all deaths resulting from felonies became the law in England. None identifies a single case in which it was applied in England before American independence. These accounts are equally hazy about early American law. None of them documents application of such a rule in colonial America, or in the early American republic. In short, there is something suspicious about our received account of the origins of American felony murder rules.[12] Our review of the history of homicide law will vindicate such suspicion and expose the harsh "common law" felony murder rule as a myth. We will retrace the origins of American felony murder rules in order to reveal their modern, American, and legislative sources, the modesty of their original scope, and the fairness of their original application, and discover that the draconian doctrine of strict liability for all deaths resulting from all felonies was never enacted into English law or received into American law.

Americans did not receive a felony murder rule from England for the simple reason that there was no such rule in English law before the American Revolution. English law traditionally imposed murder liability for most deaths caused by the intentional infliction of injury. Such killings were murders whether or not they occurred in the context of a felony, while a felony could not transform an accidental death into a murder. While a broad felony murder rule was proposed in some eighteenth-century English treatises, and discussed favorably in some eighteenth-century English cases, it was not applied. Prior to the American Revolution, English courts had gone no further than to impose murder liability on persons who killed one person in an attempt to kill or wound another; killed while defending themselves against resistance to a crime; or agreed with another to use deadly force for a criminal purpose and then killed for that purpose. The distinction between felonies and other offenses was of no particular significance in these cases. In the last decades of the eighteenth century, a few English courts extended accomplice liability for murders committed in the course of crime to those who had agreed only to the crime and not to the fatal wounding. But others disagreed, and this did not become the general rule.

Felony murder did not become law in England until the second half of the nineteenth century. The rule adopted then was much narrower than the one proposed a century and a half before. It did not apply to all felons, and it did not hold felons strictly liable for purely accidental deaths. Instead, English law conditioned felony murder liability on causing death through an act of violence or an act manifestly dangerous to human life, in the perpetration or attempt of a felony. To the traditional conception of murder as death from unexcused intentional violence, this felony murder rule added only unintended deaths resulting from acts of indiscriminate destruction like setting fires or exploding bombs. Accomplices in a felony were not liable for a death resulting from that felony unless they intended the dangerous or violent act that produced death. Thus the felony murder rule eventually adopted in England was at least as mild as the "reformed" law of felony murder prevailing in contemporary America. The "common law" was late in developing a felony murder rule, and never held felons strictly liable for causing death accidentally.

HOMICIDE IN THE COURSE OF CRIME IN EARLY ENGLISH LAW

The moral principle that an actor is responsible for the unintended harms resulting from an unlawful act is ancient, with roots in Christian ethics and canon law.[13] Augustine wrote, "Accidents which, without our will, happen to others through good and lawful actions of ours . . . must not be imputed to us."[14] This implied that accidental harms arising from *wrongful* acts *may* be imputed to us. In the mid-thirteenth century, Aquinas seized on this implication in trying to reconcile Augustine's statement with canon law sources that seemed to treat accidental killings as homicides.[15] He wrote:

> [A]ccidental happenings are neither intended nor voluntary. And because every sin is, as Augustine says, voluntary, it follows that accidents as such cannot constitute sins. What is not willed or intended as such may nevertheless be incidentally willed or intended. We may incidentally cause something by removing the obstacle against that thing happening. It follows that somebody who does not remove such occasions of homicide as he could and should remove will in some way be guilty of voluntary homicide. This can come about in two ways—when a person engages in nefarious activities which he should not have engaged in, or when he does not take due care. This is why the [canon] law lays down that if a man engages in legitimate activities and uses due care, he is not guilty of any homicide that may ensue; if, on the other hand, he engages in illicit activities, or even fails to take due care in some legitimate enterprise, he is guilty of any homicide that may occur.[16]

Notice this principle does not distinguish murders from lesser homicides and is not concerned with criminal punishment. The canon law system was concerned primarily with penance for sin and fitness for clerical office.[17] Nor did Aquinas clarify whether he was proposing liability for the unexpected consequences of all wrongs or only for the foreseeable consequences of dangerous wrongs.

Canon law influenced the practice and theory of English criminal law in the later Middle Ages. Manuals written to guide English clergy in administering penance for sin instructed them that accidental killings were blameless. Consistent with such ideas, some thirteenth-century juries tried to induce the Crown to pardon homicides by describing them as resulting from misdirected attacks on animals.[18] The thirteenth-century English jurist and cleric Henry de Bracton applied canon law ideas to the crime of homicide.[19] Bracton held that accidental killing was no homicide "because a crime is not committed unless the intention to injure exists" and "[i]n crimes the intention is regarded, not the result."[20] Bracton included within intention what we would call motive. Thus even a legally mandated execution could become a criminal homicide "if done out of malice or from pleasure in the shedding of human blood."[21] In discussing homicide "[b]y chance, as by misadventure, when one throws a stone at a bird . . . and another passing by unexpectedly is struck and dies," Bracton wrote:

> But here we must distinguish whether he has been engaged in a proper or an improper act. Improper, as where one has thrown a stone toward a place where

men are accustomed to pass, or while one is chasing a horse or ox someone is trampled by the horse or ox and the like, here liability is imputed to him. But if he was engaged in a lawful act, . . . and if he employed all the care he could . . . liability is not imputed to him.[22]

Bracton apparently based this discussion on Raymond de Penafort's penitential manual, *Summa de Poenitentia,* which discussed chasing a horse or ox in an attempt to steal it.[23]

Understanding Bracton's position requires grasping the moral ambiguity of a verdict of death by "misadventure." While royal criminal jurisdiction had formerly been confined to stealthy killings, by the middle of the twelfth century, royal courts treated all homicides as breaches of the king's peace, punishable by death unless justified as acts of law enforcement or pardoned by the king.[24] In the thirteenth century, accidental and defensive killings were not considered entirely innocent, but merely eligible for a royal pardon, for which the defendant would generally have to pay.[25] By the Statutes of Gloucester of 1278, a verdict of death by misadventure or of self-defense qualified the defendant for a royal pardon, but such verdicts were not acquittals,[26] and did not imply moral innocence: "accidental" deaths included those we would today call reckless or negligent.[27] Bracton should be understood as urging that a criminal motive should preclude the purchase of a pardon for a careless killing.[28]

In fourteenth-century England, as highway robbery became prevalent, complaints were heard that royal pardons were being too frequently bestowed.[29] A 1390 statute provided that pardons would not be granted lightly to those committing "murders," killings by ambush or assault, and killings with "malice prepensed."[30] While scholars believe "murder" connoted stealthy killings, they disagree as to the meaning of malice prepense at this time.[31] Nevertheless, all three forms of homicide were capital felonies,[32] unless subject to ecclesiastical jurisdiction. This exception eventually assumed importance, however, as laymen claimed "benefit of clergy" with increasing ease.[33]

DISTINGUISHING MURDER AND MANSLAUGHTER IN THE SIXTEENTH CENTURY

By the end of the fifteenth century, the earlier association of "murder" with stealth had been forgotten, and the term was probably interchangeable with felonious homicide.[34] Beginning in 1496, however, statutes began to restrict benefit of clergy, and by the middle of the sixteenth century, all murders "of malice prepensed" were no longer clergyable.[35] During the same period, judges and juristic writers proposed a distinction between nonclergyable murder, characterized by "malice prepense," and a residual category of clergyable homicides, referred to as "manslaughter," involving killing by "chance-medley."[36]

Two important sixteenth-century cases explored the boundaries of malice for homicides committed in the course of crime. In the 1535 case known as *Lord Dacre's Case*,[37] a group resolved to enter a park and poach game, and to kill anyone who resisted them. When one member of this group killed a gamekeeper, all the rest were held liable, whether or not they were physically present at the scene of the killing. The decision's innovation lay in its expansion of accessorial liability rather than its expansion of malice. Since all the participants had agreed to kill if necessary, their malice prepense consisted in their willingness to kill rather than in their intent to commit an unlawful act. While *Lord Dacre* did not expand the notion of malice prepense beyond intent to kill, it was important to the reasoning of another sixteenth-century case that did.

Mansell & Herbert's Case was decided in 1558, and resulted from an attack upon the house of Sir Richard Mansfield by a gang of ruffians under the command of one George Herbert.[38] A servant of Herbert's threw a stone at a member of Mansfield's party, but instead struck and killed a bystander. A majority held that Herbert and his men were guilty of murder, on the basis of three premises. First, *Lord Dacre* had established that all who agree to overcome resistance by killing are guilty of any such killing. Second, the majority reasoned, it was settled law that one who caused the death of a person in an attempt merely to hurt or injure him was guilty of murder.[39] Third, the judges asserted, an unsuccessful attempt to kill one person that resulted in the unintended death of another should be viewed as murder. This transferred-intent principle would later be confirmed by the 1573 murder conviction of one Saunders, whose daughter ate a poisoned apple he had prepared for his wife.[40]

From these three premises, it seemed to follow that anyone who agreed to an act of violence was liable for the murder of any person killed as a result. The "malice" shown toward the intended victims of a violent assault would transfer to the death of the unintended victim. This principle predicates murder on participation in an act of violence rather than a felony per se. A substantial minority, including Judges Brooke and Staundford, held that Herbert and his men were guilty only of manslaughter because the actual victim was not one of the intended victims of the violent acts agreed to. They viewed the killing of such an unintended victim in the course of an unlawful act as an example of chance-medley.[41]

Another view of the distinction between malicious murder and manslaughter was propounded in the 1553 case of *R. v. Salisbury*.[42] Richard Salisbury and two conspirators ambushed Richard Ellis and killed one of his servants. Salisbury's servant, though not a conspirator, came to Salisbury's aid during the fight and wounded the man who died. The jury was instructed that Salisbury's servant should be convicted of murder only if he had acted with malice prepense. Because Salisbury's servant had premeditated neither Salisbury's ambush on Ellis nor his own attack on the dead man, the jury convicted him only of manslaughter.[43] This identification of malice prepense with premeditation was confirmed in the 1576 case of *R. v. Robinson*, where the defendant was convicted only of manslaughter rather than murder, when he pursued and killed his fleeing victim "in un continuing fury" after they had gotten into a sudden fight.[44] William Lambarde wrote in his late-sixteenth-century treatise that a killing occurring suddenly upon an unexpected meeting would be manslaughter, because in such a case "men are medled . . . by meere chaunce, and upon some unlooked for occasion, without any former malice or evil mind . . . to offer hurt to the person of the other."[45]

Lambarde also offered a discussion of implied malice, which could be imputed to those who drew a weapon and attacked without provocation, who killed an officer of the law, or who caused death in the course of certain unlawful acts. Thus:

> [I]t is taken for a rule . . . that wheresoever a man goeth about an unlawfull acte, as to beate a man, or to disseize him of his lands, &c., and doe (in that attempt) kill him, it is Murder: because the lawe presupposeth that he carieth that malicious mind with him, that he will achieve his purpose though it be with the death of him against whom it is directed. And therefore, if a thiefe doe kill a man whom he never saw before, and whom he intended to rob onely, it is Murder in the judgement of law, which supplieth a former malicious disposition in him rather to kill the man, then not to have his money from him.[46]

Lambarde's reasoning leaves us uncertain whether he is proposing a formal rule of liability or an evidentiary maxim. Robbery, he implies, is a rational motive for murder. A use of deadly force to overcome resistance suggests a willingness to kill if necessary. Perhaps the unlawful aim does not substitute for malice prepense, but supplies evidence of it. In any case, it is important to realize that Lambarde's discussion of implied malice is concerned not with accidental killing but with intentional killing. The dispute provoked by a robbery was not to be treated as a chance or sudden quarrel, justifying a partial defense of provocation. Justified resistance to a planned attack could not be considered provocation, and so it was fair to treat violence used to overcome justified resistance as premeditated.

From a modern perspective, the results in *Herbert* and *Saunders*, which punish unintended killings as murder, may seem at odds with the results in *Salisbury* and *Robinson*, which punish intentional but unpremeditated killings as manslaughter. Yet the murder convictions in cases like *Herbert* and *Saunders* are reconcilable with the new requirement of premeditation if we bear in mind the roots of the law of murder in the fourteenth century's efforts to suppress organized criminal violence. While Herbert and Saunders killed unintended victims, both deaths resulted foreseeably from the defendants' premeditated acts of criminal violence. All four cases associate malice with a planned use of violence, rather than a sudden loss of temper in the course of an unexpected quarrel.[47]

REJECTING UNLAWFUL ACT MURDER IN THE SEVENTEENTH CENTURY

Francis Bacon's *Elements of the Common Law* used *Saunders* to support a maxim that intent could be transferred among crimes of like gravity. Bacon reasoned:

All crimes have their conception in a corrupt intent, and have their consummation and issuing in some particular fact; which though it be not the fact at the which the intention of the malefactor levelled, yet the law giveth him no advantage of the error, if another particular ensue of as high a nature. Therefore if an impoisoned apple be laid in a place to impoison I.S. and I.D. cometh by chance and eateth it, this is murder in the principal that is actor, and yet the malice in individuo was not against I.D.[48]

Bacon's use of *Saunders* suggests that he was merely transferring intent among alternative cases of the same crime. But he also asserted that intent could transfer from murder to suicide, while questioning whether intent could transfer from a murder to a petty treason.[49] While Bacon's discussion is an early precursor of the ideas of general intent and the notion of the transferability of intent among all felonies, it does not appear to have influenced subsequent common law commentators.

In 1619, Michael Dalton stated the general proposition that accidental killing in the course of an unlawful act was felonious: "But if a man be doing of an unlawfull act, though without any evill intent, and he happeneth, by chance, to kill a man, this is felony, viz. manslaughter at the least, if not murder, in regard the thing hee was doing, was unlawful."[50] Dalton added that if a man unlawfully threw a stone at an animal and thereby killed a man, it would be manslaughter only.[51] On the other hand, killing resulting from an unlawful beating would be murder.[52] Similarly, "if a Theefe that offereth to robbe a true man, killeth the true man in resisting him, it is Murder, of malice prepended."[53] Thus one who caused death in the course of an unlawful act might be guilty of manslaughter or murder, depending on the nature of the unlawful act. In Dalton's scheme, only unlawful acts of violence implied malice.

Edward Coke adopted what appeared to be a much harsher approach to unlawful act killing in his 1628 *Institutes of the Law of England*.[54] Yet Coke never mentioned the new statutory distinction between clergyable and nonclergyable offenses and so ignored the whole question of which homicides were clergyable. He used the term "manslaughter" interchangeably with "homicide," encompassing felonies with and without malice, as well as nonfelonious misadventure.[55]

Coke's discussion of murder is equally confusing. In his chapter on murder, he defined that crime as unlawful killing with malice forethought, express or implied.[56] He defined express malice as the intent to "kill, wound, or beat"[57] and repeated Lambarde's example of killing in the course of robbery as one illustration of implied malice.[58] As George Fletcher comments, "the point of Coke's holding that this case was one of implied malice was to make it clear that provocation could not be a defense on behalf of someone whose robbery induced the victim's provocative act."[59] In his chapter on homicide, Coke initially reiterated the connection of murder with malice, but then offered a puzzling discussion of unlawful act killing as murder seemingly without malice:

There is an homicide, that is neither forethought, nor voluntary. As if a man kill another per infortunium, seu casu, that is homicide by misadventure. . . . Homicide by misadventure, is when a man doth an act, that is not unlawfull, which without any evill intent tendeth to a man's death.

Unlawfull.] If the act be unlawful it is murder. As if A. meaning to steal a deere in the park of B., shooteth at the deer, and by the glance of the arrow killeth a boy that is hidden in a bush: this is murder, for that the act was unlawfull, although A. had no intent to hurt the boy, nor knew not of him. But if B. the owner of the park had shot at his own deer, and without any ill intent had killed the boy by the glance of his arrow, this had been homicide by misadventure, and no felony.

So if one shoot at any wild fowle upon a tree, and the arrow killeth any reasonable creature afar off, without any evill intent in him, this is per infortunium: for it was not unlawful to shoot at the wilde fowle; but if he had shot at a cock or hen, or any tame fowle of another mans, and the arrow by mischance had killed a man, this had been murder, for the act was unlawfull.

Without any evil intent.] If a man knowing that many people come in the street from a sermon, throw a stone over a wall, intending only to feare them, or to give them a light hurt, and thereupon one is killed, this is murder; for he had an ill intent, though that intent extended not to death. . . .[60]

Coke did not treat these scenarios as instances of implied malice. But neither did he classify any killings involving unlawful acts or culpable mental states as manslaughter or chance-medley. At least one commentator has suggested that the clumsiness of Coke's terminology may have caused him to say more than he meant. According to David Lanham,

[t]he message that Coke was evidently trying to convey was that if there was an unintentional killing in the course of an unlawful act the killing would be felonious. The appropriate word would have been "manslaughter" but unfortunately Coke had precluded himself from using that word by holding that some manslaughters were not felonious.[61]

In other words, Coke may have characterized unlawful act killing as "murder" for want of a better general term for felonious homicide. Thus it is possible that Coke did not mean to characterize accidental killings in the course of unlawful acts as murder in the technical sense of a nonclergyable felony. After all, "murder" referred simply to atrocious killings in ordinary speech, and it was only murders with malice prepense that were excluded from benefit of clergy by statute.

Fletcher argues that Coke's discussion of unlawful act killing was anachronistic, reflecting the law of homicide before development of the doctrine that murders with malice prepense were nonclergyable. On this interpretation, Coke was simply expressing a traditional view that the unlawfulness of an act causing death would deprive the defendant of the excuse of accident, or per infortunium. The unlawfulness of the act causing death meant the prosecution's prima facie proof of felonious homicide remained undisturbed.[62] According to Fletcher, this doctrine preceded and had nothing to do with the later doctrine that felonious homicides committed with malice prepense were nonclergyable. Fletcher argues that Coke clearly did not regard the unlawful act as a source of malice prepense.[63]

Fletcher's argument that Coke wrote in an anachronistic idiom is supported by Coke's citations, which were all to sources preceding the sixteenth century.

Coke obviously offered his examples of shooting a deer or a bird in order to echo Bracton's discussion of throwing a stone at a bird, which Coke cited.[64] Yet Bracton merely ascribed liability to one who kills accidentally in an unlawful act, not murder liability or capital punishability.[65] Coke also cited three cases. Two of these simply confirm that in the late Middle Ages, accidental killers were considered liable for homicide until they received their inevitable pardons.[66] The third, dating from 1496, says that it is a felony to kill another in consensual combat (a duel or joust), unless the combat was at the king's command, and that it is a felony to kill with the intention of beating.[67] Both of these hypothetical killings meet Coke's test for express malice (the intent to kill, injure, or beat). Hence the jousting case does not show that an unlawful act can substitute for malice. As of 1496 there was not yet any distinct offense of murder, since all felonious homicides were still clergyable. Coke's reliance on this case supports Lanham's suggestion that Coke was using "murder" to mean only felonious homicide.

James Fitzjames Stephen scoffed that Coke's discussion of unlawful act killings is "entirely unwarranted by the authorities which he quotes."[68] This condemnation was fair if we take Coke to have staked out the extreme position that killing accidentally in the course of any unlawful act was nonclergyable murder with malice prepense. But Coke's authorities accord much better with the limited position that Lanham and Fletcher attribute to him: that while killing accidentally in the course of a lawful act is excusable as death by misadventure, killing in the course of an unlawful act is not excusable and is therefore (clergyable) felonious homicide. In sum, it seems unlikely that Coke intended to say that deaths resulting from unlawful acts were malicious and therefore nonclergyable murders.

In any case, no unlawful act murder rule ever achieved legal authority in England. Two seventeenth-century cases squarely rejected such a rule. In a 1647 case, Sir John Chichester was fencing with his servant with covered swords, apparently illegally. Unbeknownst to the fencers, the cover of Chichester's sword fell off and he struck his servant a fatal blow. The unlawful act murder rule later attributed to Coke would have made this accident a murder. The court held it to be manslaughter because the servant's death, while resulting from an unlawful act, came with no intent to harm.[69] In a 1664 case, the defendant, Hull, shouted a warning and then threw a piece of lumber off a roof, killing a fellow workman below. While Hull was indicted for murder, all the judges agreed that if he had acted with unlawful carelessness, he would be liable for manslaughter only. A majority found him innocent of any wrongdoing, however.[70]

The 1663 case of Sir Charles Stanley does offer support for some form of unlawful act homicide rule. Stanley resisted arrest by firing a pistol at the arresting bailiff. Servants of both antagonists joined the fray, and some of Stanley's servants ultimately killed a servant of the bailiff's. Stanley was deemed guilty of this murder because of his initial act of violence, a result consistent with Herbert. Yet some of the language suggests a rule broader than the result: "[W]hen several men joyn in an unlawful act they are all guilty of whatever happens upon it; as in The Lord Dacre's case . . ."[71] Later the justices agreed that one who, coming upon the scene of an arrest, draws his sword against the arresting officers is guilty of murder if an officer is killed, even if he did not understand he was interfering with an arrest:

> For a man must take heed how he joineth in any unlawful act as fighting is, for if he doth, he is guilty of all that follows. And it being murder to kill those who come to execute the law; every one who joins in that act is guilty of murder, and his ignorance will not excuse him, where the fact is made murder by the law without any malice precedent, as in the case of killing a bailiff.[72]

In this scenario, as in *Lord Dacre's Case*, the unlawful act triggering murder liability is an act of violence. The background circumstance of a lawful arrest precludes any mitigating claim of provocation or sudden quarrel. One can certainly argue that this principle should be confined to those who are aware that they are resisting a lawful arrest. Nevertheless, this is hardly strict liability for accidental death.

Subsequent writers rejected any substitution of an unlawful act for malicious intent as an element of murder. Thomas Hobbes complained that Coke had no authority for treating accidental killing in the course of an unlawful act as if it were committed with "prepensed malice."[73] Matthew Hale insisted that a killing in the course of an unlawful act was manslaughter only, unless accompanied by malice, which he defined as an "ill intent"[74] or an "intention to do harm."[75] Hale added that "[t]hough the malice did not rise so high as death, but intended only to beat the party, yet if malitious, it is Murder if death ensue."[76] Hale followed Lambarde and Coke in offering the killing of a resisting robbery victim as an illustration of implied malice.[77] He supported the rule in *Saunders* that the accidental killing of one person in the attempt to kill another was malicious.[78] Finally, following *Lord Dacre*, he concluded that "[i]f a person . . . comes with a general resolution against all Opposers, if the act be unlawful, and death ensue, it is Murder . . ."[79]

Hale commented on one further instance of unlawful act homicide. He considered death resulting from the administration of a potion to induce abortion to be murder, "for it was not given to cure her of a disease, but unlawfully to destroy her child within her, and therefore he, that gives a potion to this end, must take the hazard, and if it kills the mother, it is murder, and so ruled before me at the assizes at Bury in the year 1670."[80] This position looks harsh to the modern reader, but fits with Hale's conception of malice as the intent to injure, since he regarded abortion as manslaughter.[81]

While Hale confined the mental element of murder to an intent to harm, he also restricted the act element of murder to killing. Homicide required not just causing death, but causing death by means of a battery, "for the ... death without the stroke or other violence makes not the homicide ..."[82] He added that

> [i]f a man either by working upon the fancy of another or possibly by harsh or unkind usage put another into such passion of grief or fear, that the party either die suddenly, or contract some disease, whereof he dies ... it cannot come under the judgment of felony, because no external act of violence was offered, whereof the common law can take notice, and secret things belong to God ...[83]

Thus Hale's conception of killing would have precluded homicide liability in cases where the frightened victim of a robbery dies of a heart attack, or the despondent victim of a rape commits suicide. Hale's conception of violent acts of course included blows, strangling, and poisoning. However, it also included forcible exposure to danger such as abandoning an infant, or confining a prisoner in dangerous conditions.

Summing up Hale's position, Fletcher concludes that an illegal act could inculpate a killer in one of two ways. If death resulted from intentional violence, an illegal aim could preclude provocation and so prevent mitigation of murder to manslaughter. If death did not result from intentional violence, an illegal act could preclude the defense of accident and so convict the killer of manslaughter.[84] For Hale, there was no murder without malice.

PROPOSING A FELONY MURDER RULE IN EIGHTEENTH-CENTURY ENGLAND

A felony murder rule made its first appearance in English case law as a dictum regarding accomplice liability for collateral crimes in the 1701 case of *R. v. Plummer*. Plummer was one of a group attempting to export wool illegally. A second member of this group killed a third. While the court concluded that Plummer was not guilty of murder on these facts, Chief Justice Holt discoursed at length on the circumstances under which participation in a fatal unlawful act would merit murder liability. For the most part, his conclusions tracked those of Hale. He wrote that "[t]his notion that hath been received, that if divers persons be engaged in an unlawful act, and one of them kills another, it shall be murder in all the rest, is very true; but it must be admitted with several qualifications." These qualifications were (1) "the abettor must know of the malicious design of the party killing," (2) "[t]he killing must be in pursuance of that unlawful act, and not collateral to it," (3) "the unlawful act ought to be deliberate," and (4) "it ought to be such an act as may tend to the hurt of another either, immediately, or by necessary consequence."[85]

Yet Holt then identified what he thought was a conflict between the views of Hale and Coke and offered the following reconciliation:

> Shooting at a deer in another's park is an unlawful act: if the arrow glanceth and kills a man, this is but manslaughter, which is contrary to 3 Inst. 56 [Coke], that holds it to be murder: but Lord Hale 31,(2) saith it is but manslaughter . . .
>
> The design of doing any act makes it deliberate; and if the fact be deliberate, though no hurt to any person can be foreseen, yet if the intent be felonious, and the fact designed, if committed, would be felony, and in pursuit thereof a person is killed by accident, it will be murder in him and all his accomplices . . .
>
> So if two men have a design to steal a hen and one shoots at the hen for that purpose, and a man be killed, it is murder in both, because the design was felonious. So is Lord Coke 56,(3) surely to be understood, with that difference, but without this difference none of the books quoted in the margin . . . do warrant that opinion; nor indeed can I say that I find any to warrant my opinion, but only the reason is submitted to the judgment of those Judges that may at any time hereafter have that point judicially brought before them.[86]

Holt's dictum was, by his own confession, an innovation, no better supported by precedent than the more sweeping rule he mistakenly attributed to Coke. He justified it as a moderation of Coke's supposed doctrine.

Holt's compromise was taken up by the early eighteenth-century treatise writer William Hawkins, who attempted to reconcile the divergent positions of Hale and Holt in the following terms:

> [I]f a man happen to kill another . . . in the willful commission of any unlawful act, which necessarily tends to raise tumults and quarrels, and consequently cannot but be attended with the danger of personal hurt, to someone or other;

as by committing a riot, robbing a park, &c. he shall be adjudged guilty of murder.

And a fortiori, he shall come under the same construction, who in the pursuance of a deliberate intention to commit a felony, chances to kill a man, as by shooting at tame fowl, with an intent to steal them, &c. for such persons are by no means favored, and they must at their peril take care of the consequence of their actions; and it is a general rule, that wherever a man intending to commit one felony, happens to commit another, he is as much guilty as if he had intended the felony which he actually commits.[87]

Here Hawkins equates malice with the knowing imposition of a risk of death or injury; reasons that such risk is inherent in any crime likely to provoke resistance; and treats felonies as a subset of such inherently dangerous crimes. Hawkins was willing to assume that all felonies were dangerous in order to reconcile Holt's dictum with Hale's "intent to harm" standard.[88]

Hawkins did not require a very close causal connection between the danger inherent in the predicate felony and the resulting death. Thus "not only in such cases where the very act of a person having such a felonious intent, is the immediate cause of a third person's death, but also where it in any way occasionally causes such a misfortune, it makes him guilty of murder."[89] Indeed, Hawkins' proposed felony murder rule applied only to felonies that did not aim directly at physical injury to the victim: "Such killing shall be adjudged murder which happens in the execution of an unlawful action principally intended for some other purpose, and not to do a personal injury to him in particular who happens to be slain."[90] Thus Hawkins reasoned that murder liability should only be predicated on a felony with a purpose independent of the death or injury of the victim.

Hawkins' "general rule" equating the dangers of all felonies raises the question of whether all felonies were indeed dangerous at the time that Holt and Hawkins wrote. The term "felony" had by this time come to be associated with capitally punishable crimes,[91] including those for which benefit of clergy was available. Yet felonies included petty larcenies and mayhem, which were not punishable by death, and did not include some crimes, like treason, which were. Coke mentions only eight common law felonies: murder, manslaughter, rape, burglary, arson, robbery, theft, and mayhem.[92]

Of the traditional common law felonies, all but burglary and theft involve a direct threat to the person. Burglary, which then required breaking into a dwelling at night to commit another felony, is still generally thought to justify resistance with deadly force. Only theft would strike the modern reader as not necessarily dangerous to life. But theft was a narrower crime in seventeenth-century England, requiring a "trespassory" taking from possession, that could alarm an observer and provoke resistance.[93] And indeed, deadly force was considered justifiable in resisting any felony in one's home[94] or when necessary to apprehend a felon.[95] The situation was quite different by the end of the eighteenth century. Statutory felonies had greatly proliferated, including such pacific variants of theft as forgery.[96] Thus the rule proposed by Hawkins and Holt was plausible when proposed but could have become quite harsh by the end of the eighteenth century, *if* it had been adopted.

It has sometimes been suggested that a felony murder rule could have had no practical significance in the common law because all felonies were capitally punishable anyway.[97] This is not entirely true, for three reasons. First, a few felonies remained clergyable at the beginning of the eighteenth century: mayhem, petty thefts, and thefts that were not from the person.[98] Second, pardons were widely available and were the norm for less serious felonies.[99] Third, both Holt and Hawkins wished to extend felony murder liability to deaths caused in the course of attempting felonies. There was no general doctrine of attempt liability before the late eighteenth century.[100] Where punished, attempts were not viewed as felonies or punished capitally.[101] Blackstone concluded that "a bare assault, with intent to kill, is only a great misdemeanor."[102] Thus a felony murder rule could raise a fatal attempted felony from a misdemeanor to a capitally punishable felony. Indeed, we can think of the proposed felony murder rule as an early conception of attempt liability, developed at a time when crime was still seen as requiring an actual injury.

Holt's dictum was approved, though not applied, in the 1722 case of *R. v. Woodburne*.[103] The defendants were charged with a form of mayhem, maiming with intent to disfigure. They claimed they had lacked the requisite intent to disfigure but instead had intended to kill (which would have made their attack the mere misdemeanor of attempted murder!). The judge, Sir Peter King, encouraged the jury to find that the defendants had intended to kill by means of disfiguring, and so had fulfilled the statutory requirement of intent to disfigure. King approved Hawkins' idea of transferring intent, and illustrated the transfer of intent with the claim that an accidental killing in the course of shooting at a fowl would be murder "if he had had an intention of stealing this tame fowl . . . ."[104] Yet King held that intent could not transfer to certain crimes—including maiming with intent to disfigure—requiring what would later be called a "specific intent." Thus, while King approved Holt's felony murder dictum, the case afforded him no opportunity to apply it. Despite the judge's endorsement of a felony murder rule, the actual result in *Woodburne*, like that in *Plummer*, conferred little authority upon it.

Notwithstanding the dicta in *Plummer* and *Woodburne*, the prevailing practice of English courts in murder cases was closer to the views of Hale than those of Hawkins during the century preceding the American Revolution. Journalistic accounts of murder trials at London's Old Bailey Courthouse reveal that murder liability turned on proof of death caused by an intentional stabbing, shooting, or bludgeoning. Prosecutors generally made no effort to prove, and defense attorneys made no effort to disprove, intent to kill or felonious motive.[105] For example, in a 1718 case, John Price was interrupted in the act of raping and robbing Elizabeth White, who died of wounds to her head, throat, and abdomen.[106] The testimony and questions at Price's murder trial were directed only to proving the fatal assault rather than the theft or the rape. Because any serious assault established malice, there was no need to allege an attempted felony where the defendant intentionally attacked the body of the victim. On the other hand, the Old Bailey reports do not reveal any murder convictions without such intentional acts of violence during the century before the American Revolution.

Although the proposed felony murder doctrine had not yet been put into practice on the eve of the American Revolution, it received further scholarly support in Michael Foster's 1762 treatise, *Crown Law*. Like Hawkins, Foster attempted to reconcile Holt's felony murder rule with Hale's requirement of evil intent. This evil intent was established by the intent to do any unlawful act that was *malum in se*. If this unlawful act *malum in se* were a felony, a resulting death would be murder; if a trespass, the resulting death would be manslaughter.[107] Foster's embrace of felony murder liability flowed from his conception of malice, which differed from Hale's. For Foster, malice meant a wicked disposition or character, which could be manifested by deliberately committing any wicked act. "For the law by the term Malice . . . meaneth, that the fact hath been attended with such circumstances as are the ordinary symptoms of a wicked, depraved, malignant spirit."[108] "Implied malice" referred to "circumstances as carry in them the plain indications of an heart regardless of social duty and fatally bent on mischief."[109] It followed that a felonious motive implied malice.

A few years after the appearance of Foster's *Crown Law*, Blackstone published his *Commentaries on the Laws of England*, which became the standard reference work on the common law for American lawyers.[110] Blackstone offered a version of Hawkins' general principle that the intent to commit one felony could transfer to an unintended felonious result. Blackstone reasoned that while every crime required both a "vitious act" and a "vitious will,"[111] the vicious act implied a vicious will unless the defendant was incapable of controlling his action, by virtue of some excusing circumstance. Blackstone then analyzed accident and mistake as such excusing conditions. Citing Hale, he wrote: "[I]f a man be doing anything unlawful, and a consequence ensues which he did not foresee or intend, as the death of a man or the like, his want of foresight shall be no excuse; for, being guilty of one offence, in doing antecedently what is in itself unlawful, he is criminally guilty of whatever consequence may follow the first misbehaviour."[112] Murder, according to Blackstone, required malice aforethought, express or implied,[113] and Blackstone adopted Foster's conception of malice as any evil motive, reflecting a malignant heart.[114]

Blackstone offered two divergent discussions of how to grade unintended homicide in the course of crime. In a discussion of involuntary manslaughter, Blackstone followed Foster:

> [I]n general, when an involuntary killing happens in consequence of an unlawful act, it will be either murder or manslaughter according to the nature of the act which occasioned it. If it be in prosecution of a felonious intent, it will be murder; but if no more was intended than a mere trespass, it will amount only to manslaughter.[115]

But in discussing murder with express malice, Blackstone followed Hale in emphasizing the dangerousness of the predicate crime rather than its felonious quality. Thus,

> if two or more come together to do an unlawful act against the king's peace, of which the probable consequence might be bloodshed; as to beat a man, to commit a riot, or to rob a park; and one of them kills a man; it is murder in them all, because of the unlawful act, the malitia praecogitata, or evil intended beforehand.[116]

Of implied malice, Blackstone wrote:

> [I]f one intends to do another felony, and undesignedly kills a man, this is also murder. Thus if one shoots at A and misses him, but kills B, this is murder; because of the previous felonious intent, which the law transfers from one to the

other. The same is the case, where one lays poison for A; and B, against whom the prisoner had no malicious intent, takes it, and it kills him; this is likewise murder.[117]

Blackstone's use of examples of transferred intent to kill suggested a restriction of the rule to predicate felonies involving intended bodily harm. Notably, Blackstone omitted any discussion of the poaching examples offered by Bracton, Coke, Holt, Hawkins, King, and Foster.[118]

There is little evidence that Foster's views reflected the actual state of English law at the time of the American Revolution. Murder still seemed to require the intentional infliction of an injury or wound.[119] For example, the 1773 decision of *R. v. Lad* overturned a murder conviction in a case where a girl of "about nine years old" died after languishing from "grievous" lacerations to "the private parts and inside of the body" sustained in a rape.[120] The court held the indictment defective because it failed to allege that the defendant wounded the victim mortally. This decision has sometimes been read as clearly rejecting a felony murder rule,[121] but that puts it too strongly, since the missing element was the killing rather than the intent to kill. Perhaps the more important point is that intent to kill was not required for any murder at this time, whether or not in the context of a felony.

Although eighteenth-century courts appeared reluctant to convict felons of murder unless death resulted from an act of violence, they were sometimes willing to treat participation in a crime as a basis for complicity in such a fatal battery.[122] Journalistic accounts of Old Bailey trials reveal that during the last two decades of the eighteenth century, judges sometimes instructed juries that participants in crime were accountable for killings or murders in furtherance of the criminal plan. In one 1786 case, for instance, a youthful member of a ring of pickpockets was held liable for murder when one of his adult confederates fatally stabbed a pursuer while the youth merely looked on.[123] However, this case seems to have been exceptional. Other cases confined collective liability to participants in crimes of violence like robbery,[124] or found no linkage between the killing and the crime agreed to.[125]

By the time of the American Revolution, the rule that an accidental death in the course of any felony was murder had become a standard theme in scholarly writing. Yet no English court had ever actually applied such a rule. An unlawful act murder rule was explicitly rejected in seventeenth-century cases. Early-eighteenth-century cases offered felony murder rules as dicta, but these were not put into practice. In the late eighteenth century some judges treated co-felons as automatically implicated in any murder committed in attempt of a felony, but most did not. By and large, eighteenth-century English law conditioned murder on intentional violence leading to death, and used a criminal motive only to preclude self-defense and provocation.

THE BELATED EMERGENCE OF FELONY MURDER LIABILITY IN ENGLAND

After the American Revolution, the leading English commentators came to accept Foster's relatively broad formulation of a felony murder rule as an accurate statement of English law. Yet it took the English courts much longer to accept felony murder liability. The rule they finally did accept was much narrower than Foster's rule, and instead reflected Hale's more nuanced approach to homicide in the course of crime. Courts applying the felony murder rule required either an act of violence or an offense otherwise dangerous to human life, such as arson.

Edward East's 1806 treatise held that "if the act on which death ensue [is] . . . done in prosecution of a felonious intent, however the death ensued against or beside the intent of the party, it will be murder."[126] East did not, however, report any cases applying this rule, instead citing *Plummer* and *Woodburne*, as well as Foster.[127] William Russell's treatise, first published in 1819, agreed that "[w]henever an unlawful act, an act malum in se, is done in prosecution of a felonious intention, and death ensues, it will be murder . . ."[128] Russell cited the treatise literature through Foster, but no cases other than *Plummer*. Yet learned opinion did not support a felony murder rule unanimously. In 1834, the Bentham-influenced First Criminal Law Reform Commission found such a rule "totally incongruous with the general principles of our jurisprudence."[129] Subsequent commission reports argued on deterrence grounds that murder liability should always be predicated on the actor's subjective awareness of a danger of death.[130] Scholarly opinion had already turned against the rule before it was established as law.

Felony murder liability was still not established in the case law by the middle of the nineteenth century. An 1855 edition of Russell cited only one new case, *R. v. Smithies*.[131] This 1832 case involved a defendant found guilty of "the wilful murder of Ellen Twamley by setting fire to his own house."[132] There is nothing in the report of the case to indicate that the jury was instructed that murder liability depended on the fire being set feloniously or to indicate that the death was accidental. Even if the death was unintended, murder liability could be justified on the basis that burning a dwelling exhibits gross recklessness, rather than on the basis that arson is a felony.

So *Smithies* provided no support for a felony murder rule. On the other hand, two other cases from the 1830s firmly rejected Hawkins' "general rule" that culpability could be transferred from one felony to another felony, at least as far as accomplices were concerned. In an 1831 case, *R. v. Collison*,[133] a pair of watchmen caught two men in the act of stealing apples. One of the thieves assaulted one of the watchmen, but the other thief was held not to be complicit in the assault because he had not agreed to it, even though the assault was in furtherance of the theft to which he had agreed. In an 1830 mayhem case, *Duffey's & Hunt's Case*, the court approved a similar doctrine, instructing the jury that

> if three persons go out to commit a felony, and one of them, unknown to the other, puts a pistol in his pocket and commits a felony of another kind, such as murder, the two who did not concur in this second felony will not be guilty thereof, notwithstanding it happened while they were engaged with him in the felonious act for which they went out.[134]

An 1841 decision, *R. v. Holland*,[135] suggests that murder liability for unintended death still turned on an act of violence or an intention to injure, rather than a felony. Holland was convicted of murder for beating his victim and cutting him with "an iron instrument," inflicting "divers mortal blows and wounds," including a wound on his finger that became fatally infected with tetanus.[136] The issue in the case was only one of causation, it being taken as given that the intentional and unjustifiable[137]—not necessarily felonious—infliction of a wound would be murder if the wound caused death.

By the middle of the nineteenth century, then, the "common law rule" of felony murder, although supported by leading treatises, remained controversial and still had not been applied in a single English case. Some of the earliest reported jury instructions on the felony murder rule allude to its unpopularity, and seem to invite the jury to ignore it. The 1857 case of *R. v. Greenwood*[138] presented a scenario similar to that in *Lad*. The defendant was found to have raped a child under the age of ten, infecting her fatally with venereal disease. The court offered the jury the odd instruction that these findings "would justify them in finding him guilty of murder," but that "it was open to them to find the prisoner guilty of manslaughter" and that "they might ignore the doctrine of constructive malice if they thought fit."[139] The jury convicted the defendant of manslaughter rather than murder.

In the 1861 case of *R. v. Franz*,[140] the victim was found in her recently burglarized home, suffocated by a gag. Justice Blackburn instructed the jury that "[a]s a matter of law," if the accused had caused her death by "violence . . . to enable [him] to commit a burglary (or any other felony), although . . . [he] might not have intended to kill her," he was guilty of murder.[141] He added, "[Y]ou need not take on yourselves the responsibility of that. I take that on myself."[142] Yet he also offered that "[i]t would be more agreeable to you and to me, and to everybody, that the evidence should not lead us to consider the prisoner guilty."[143] Perhaps taking the hint, the jury acquitted altogether.

Some cases from this period accepted the felony murder rule, but conditioned its application on some form of culpability. One case required that the felony be foreseeably dangerous. In the 1862 case of *R. v. Horsey*, the accused set fire to a barn, unaware of a tramp sleeping inside, who was trapped and burned to death. Justice Bramwell charged the jury that though it "may appear unreasonable," the law held that "where a prisoner, in the course of committing a felony, caused the death of a human being, that was murder even though he did not intend it."[144] Yet, he proceeded, the defendant caused the death only if it was "the natural and probable result" of his arson.[145] Bramwell finally offered the jury the preposterous suggestion that the victim had entered the barn after the fire was set. The jury acquitted the convicted arsonist of murder, apparently on the view that the death of the tramp was not a "natural and probable" result from the standpoint of the defendant. Thus, they used Bramwell's formulation of a proximate cause standard as a culpability standard, requiring recklessness or negligence.

The 1864 decision in *R. v. Lee* applied the approach taken in *Collison* and in *Duffey & Hunt* to a killing in the course of a felony.[146] Lee and Costen, charged with murder, had followed an elderly man out of a pub. Lee pushed the old man into a ditch and summoned Costen to help him rob the victim. Costen did so, and the victim, bruised and severely chilled, crawled home and died. Judge Pollock urged the jury at least to acquit Costen. He instructed them that "if a man in the committal of a felony uses violence to the person, which causes death, even although he did not intend it, he is guilty of murder, and that if two or more persons go out to commit a felony, with intent that personal violence shall be used in its committal, and such violence is used and causes death, then they are all equally guilty."[147] Pollock added that an accomplice who did not share in this violent intent would not be guilty. The instruction in *Lee*, like that in *Franz*, presents felony murder liability as predicated not only on a felony but also on an act of "violence" to the person of a victim.

In the 1868 case of *R. v. Desmond*, the defendants were convicted of murder after they set off an explosion in a crowded street in order to free a prisoner, killing many bystanders. Justice Cockburn instructed the jury that they could find murder on either of two theories: causing death by an illegal and extremely dangerous act or causing death in the attempt to commit a felony. The jury convicted, but whether they found felony murder or gross recklessness murder is unclear.[148]

Thus, when English courts first applied the felony murder rule in the second half of the nineteenth century, they identified it as controversial and linked it to actual participation in a violent or obviously dangerous act. Justices Blackburn, Bramwell, and Stephen also expressed their views that the felony murder rule should be so limited in reporting to a parliamentary committee on homicide law revision in 1874.[149] Stephen commented that a rule imposing murder liability for accidental killing in the course of a felony such as theft would be "perfectly barbarous and monstrous." He claimed that he was aware of many cases of accidental deaths caused by felonies but that "[t]he judge never really wishes to press the matter or to stand strictly on the law, and the jury have a sort of common sense notion in their own heads that it ought not to be held murder, that the man ought not to be hanged, and they find manslaughter." Bramwell agreed that the supposed rule imposing murder liability for accidental death in the course of any felony was "preposterous," and acknowledged that he had persuaded the jury to subvert it in *Horsey*. Blackburn assured the committee that such a broad rule had never been applied and was not then the law. The true rule, Blackburn averred, was that an act of personal violence committed in carrying out a crime could give rise to murder liability. He approvingly mentioned a case in which a rapist had been found guilty of murder for unintentionally smothering his victim. The justices took Russell's treatise to task for its vigorous support of a sweeping felony murder rule.[150] The next edition of Russell's treatise responded with sheepish equivocation: "The law appears to be that anyone who deliberately attempts to commit a felony and thereby occasions death, is guilty of murder. But in this respect, the law seems unreasonable."[151] In 1879 the second English Criminal Code Commission proposed a detailed statute providing that "culpable homicide" would be murder if it resulted from (1) an act likely to cause death, committed for an unlawful object, or (2) any effort to seriously injure, sedate, or suffocate perpetrated in the attempt of or flight from the offenses of piracy, prison break, resisting arrest, murder, rape, kidnapping, robbery, burglary, or arson.[152]

By the end of the nineteenth century, English law clearly conditioned felony murder liability on a foreseeably dangerous act. The famous 1887 case of *R. v. Serné* made this requirement of foreseeable dangerousness explicit. Like *Horsey*, the case involved murder liability predicated on the felony of arson. Serné was charged with causing the death of his two sons by burning down his home and shop to collect an insurance policy. Here the defendant clearly knew the victims were in the building. Justice Stephen charged the jury as follows: "I think that, instead of saying that any act done with intent to commit a felony and which causes death amounts to murder, it would be reasonable to say that any act known to be dangerous to life, and likely in itself to cause death done for the purpose of committing a felony which caused death, should be murder."[153] Here, too, the jury acquitted. In the 1898 case of *R. v. Whitmarsh*, the defendant was convicted of murder after administering mercury to a woman in an attempt to cause an abortion, then a felony in England. The court instructed the jury, somewhat equivocally, that if the defendant "may not have contemplated the possibility of death," or if he "as a reasonable man, could see no possibility of death," the verdict should be manslaughter rather than murder.[154] A 1914 update of Blackstone's Commentaries concluded that "[a]fter much difference of opinion . . . it may now be taken that homicides resulting from the commission of a felony, not involving danger to life, amount only to manslaughter."[155]

Finally, in the 1920 case of *Director of Public Prosecutions v. Beard* the House of Lords returned to the "violence" formula of *Franz* and *Lee*. Beard appealed his murder conviction for suffocating a thirteen-year-old girl in the course of raping her. The House of Lords rejected Beard's argument that the jury should have considered whether his intoxication negated the intent to kill. The court held that his intoxication was relevant only to the intent to commit rape, because rape was a sufficiently "violent" predicate felony to trigger the felony murder rule, thereby rendering intent to kill unnecessary for murder liability.[156] A 1933 treatise reported, however, that juries were then being instructed according to the dangerousness formula of *Serné* rather than the slightly different "violence" formula of *Franz, Lee,* and *Beard.*[157] From their first applications of the felony murder rule, the English courts consistently resisted the notion that the mere intent to commit any felony supplied the malice required for murder. Some intent to injure or at least endanger a person was required.

In 1957 England abolished the felony murder rule by statute.[158] Its provenance as a valid doctrine of English law was surprisingly brief, perhaps only a century. During that time, it never became a rule that felons were strictly liable for accidental deaths in the course of any felony. Instead, the felony had to be violent or manifestly dangerous. The death had to be at least foreseeable, and so had to be caused with a degree of culpability amounting at least to negligence. The much-criticized and supposedly ancient rule of strict liability never existed in English law. It was not part of the common law at the time of the American Revolution, and therefore it could not have been inherited. Such a rule could have become part of the law of any American jurisdiction only if that particular jurisdiction enacted it.

6 THE ABSENT AMERICAN COMMON LAW OF FELONY MURDER

Contrary to what lawyers are generally taught, English courts did not impose felony murder liability before the American Revolution. Yet influential treatises did present felony murder liability as part of the common law. This raises an important question: did early American courts receive and apply a mythical common law felony murder rule, by mistake?

There is little evidence that American courts did so. Colonial American criminal law was distinct from English law. Some of the newly independent states received doctrines of English law selectively, while others continued preexisting law in force. Moreover, Americans seemed to prefer legislative to judicial definition of crimes. By and large, American felony murder laws were enacted by American legislatures, not received or discovered by courts applying any form of common law.

HOMICIDE IN THE COURSE OF CRIME IN COLONIAL AMERICA

Had the English common law developed a felony murder rule in the eighteenth century, such a rule would not have been automatically applicable in the colonies. Some colonies were settled in the early seventeenth century by religious dissenters eager to legislate for themselves. As Gerhard Mueller argued, "[I]t is rather difficult to accept the frequently held notion that the English common law of crimes was transplanted to, and continued an uninterrupted existence in, America."[1] Indeed, the authority of the English common law in colonial America depended on discretionary local reception. Coke's 1608 decision in *Calvin's Case*[2] held that English law, whether customary or statutory, did not automatically extend to conquered territories. While territories conquered from other Christian sovereigns retained their foreign law, territories conquered from infidels were to be governed by natural equity until the Crown legislated for them. Late in the seventeenth century, Chief Justice Holt held that English settlers took English law with them to uninhabited territory, but not to conquered territory.[3] Yet Holt clearly understood that the colonists had settled inhabited land, holding in a case involving slavery that "the laws of England do not extend to Virginia, being a conquered country their law is what the King pleases."[4] On the eve of the American Revolution, Blackstone agreed.[5] The colonial charters conferred by the Crown did not declare the applicability of the common law as such.[6] Instead, they generally authorized local authorities to promulgate laws as compatible with English laws as was "convenient."[7] Andrew Hamilton drew on this principle in persuading the jury at John Peter Zenger's 1735 trial that truth should serve as a defense to seditious libel in colonial America, despite contrary English law.[8] Similar assertions of the primacy of local law were made in defense of other dissidents in the run-up to the American Revolution.[9] Thus the applicability of common law rules depended on local decision making.[10]

Nevertheless, a few colonial jurisdictions passed statutes declaring the common law and certain British statutes to be in force.[11] Moreover, some scholars claim that belief in the authority of the common law was widespread in eighteenth-century colonial America.[12] Yet even where the common law was formally accepted, its authority remained an abstraction. Few colonial Americans were trained in the law or had access to law books.[13] Courts were often administered by lay judges until well into the eighteenth century.[14] Because juries were often considered to be judges of the law as well as of the facts, they would not necessarily have been instructed on the elements of offenses.[15] It seems probable that the common law exerted little influence over the administration of justice before the eighteenth century, but a good deal by the middle of the eighteenth century.[16] Nevertheless, the common law put into practice in any particular colony may have differed a great deal from the common law in England.[17]

About half of the colonies enacted murder statutes of their own, usually imposing the death penalty for "willful" or "malicious" murder, often without further specification.[18] William Penn's 1682 law for Pennsylvania imposed the death penalty for anyone who "shall with Malice or premeditation Kill or be accessary to the death" of another.[19] The following year willfulness was substituted for malice in this formula,[20] and a 1705 Pennsylvania statute provided "[t]hat if any person within this Province shall willfully and premeditately Kill another Person, or willfully and premeditately be the Cause of, or accessary to the Death of any person, such person ... shall suffer Death ..."[21]

Some scholars have seen reformist significance in the substitution of willfulness for malice. Edwin Keedy argues that willfulness was a higher degree of culpability than malice, and that the substitution reflected an effort to avoid

Coke's expansive conception of implied malice.[22] I am dubious, however. Coke was not the first to use the terms "malice" and "implied malice." The term "wilfull" was taken from the 1675 Duke's Laws, rather than being an innovation of Penn's. Willfulness and malice were used together, in colonial murder statutes in Massachusetts Bay, Plymouth Colony, New Hampshire, and North Carolina.[23]

The one colonial murder definition coming closest to a felony murder rule is found in a 1647 code of laws for the Providence Colony decreeing that

> murder is, when a man, upon malice pretended, precedent and with his will, doth kill another feloniously, that is, with a premeditated and malicious mind; and for a man to kill an officer or any of his aid, in the execution of his office, shall also be adjudged murder: So for a thief to kill a true man, shall be judged murder: All that are present aiding and abetting are principals, though they never give a stroke.[24]

This is the one colonial statute apparently drafted in contemplation of the concept of implied malice developed by English jurists. The phrase "true man" refers to one resisting a theft or robbery, and is a clear reference to Dalton's discussion of implied malice.[25] The Providence statute does not mention other felonies, nor does it indicate whether it covers accidental or only intentional killing. But in relying on Dalton, it incorporated Lambarde's implied-malice concept, which precluded mitigation to manslaughter of intentional killings provoked by violent resistance to crime.

No other colonial statute or case established a rule predicating murder liability on the attempt to commit a collateral crime. Cases involving homicide in the course of crime may have been rare. Of thirty homicide cases brought to trial in the colonies before 1660, in only one, *Plymouth v. Arthur Peach*, does the homicide appear to have been committed in the course of a felony.[26]

Nevertheless, the scholarly support for a felony murder rule that developed in eighteenth-century England had some influence on American scholarly writing. George Webb's 1736 treatise on Virginia law defined murder as killing with malice aforethought, express or implied.[27] Express malice included cases where "a Man is resolved to do an unlawful Act, as to rob, or steal, and Death ensues," and "if a Man intends to kill, stab, shoot, or poison another, and the Death of a Third Person ensues."[28] Webb did not explicitly limit predicate crimes to felonies. His term "*resolved* to do an unlawful Act" seemed to refer to *Lord Dacre's Case* and so implied a resolve to overcome resistance. Webb added that "[i]f several Persons come with Intent to rob, kill, or steal, or to commit any other unlawful Act, and One of them commits Murder, tho' not in View or Presence of the Rest, all are principal Murderers."[29] Finally, he added, "Malice may be collected out of Circumstances, shewing the Temper and Intent of the Person killing; as if one assaults another with Intention to rob, but being resisted, kills the Person he assaulted, it's Murder."[30] Richard Starke's 1774 treatise *The Virginia Justice* endorsed the felony murder rule proposed by Hawkins and Foster. Starke cited Coke's account of unlawful act murder,[31] but then favored Foster's view that the accidental killing of a man in the attempt to shoot another man's domesticated fowl would be murder because of the felonious intent.[32] He also invoked Hawkins' "general rule" transferring intent among different felonies.[33] It is unlikely that Webb's or Starke's treatise affected verdicts, as colonial Virginia judges lacked the authority to instruct jurors on the law.[34]

COMMON LAW AND STATUTE IN THE NEW REPUBLIC

During and after the Revolution, a number of states enacted statutes or constitutional provisions accepting the common law in default of legislation, either with respect to crimes in particular or more generally. A 1777 Georgia statute continued in force the criminal law imposed by the statute and common law of England,[35] as did a 1778 North Carolina law.[36] A 1776 Virginia statute recognized the authority of "the common law of England . . . [and] all statutes . . . made in aid of the common law prior to the fourth year of the reign of king James the first . . ."[37] This was understood to apply only to presettlement common law.[38] This statute was also binding in Kentucky.[39] Similar ordinances were adopted for the Northwest Territories and later became law in Indiana and Illinois.[40] However, most of the original states adopted constitutional or statutory provisions continuing in force either (1) preexisting law,[41] or (2) the common law and British statutes as previously applied in that particular jurisdiction.[42] Vermont initially adopted "common law, as it is generally practised and understood in the New-England States,"[43] later modifying this to "so much of the common law of England, as is applicable to the local situation, and circumstances, and is not repugnant to the constitution . . ."[44] Connecticut enacted no provision applying the common law,[45] and waited forty years to adopt a provision continuing in force preexisting law.[46] Ohio initially passed, but then quickly repealed, a statute authorizing application of the common law.[47]

Insofar as state constitutions and statutes applied common law to resolve unprovided-for cases, what common law did they apply? Arguably, their own, since English law made common law rules authoritative in the colonies only insofar as local lawmakers enacted them. Most of the original states authorized application of the common law only as locally practiced. Thus, in the event of a conflict between local and English precedent, local precedent would be authoritative. Hugh Brackenridge's 1814 treatise on Pennsylvania law held that only so much of the common law "could have been carried by the emigrants to this state, as was applicable to their situation and therefore so much of it only in force. What of it was applicable must be determined by the courts . . ."[48] An early Virginia decision held that the statute authorizing application of the common law conferred no authority on contemporary British decisions.[49] Indeed, the Pennsylvania, New Jersey, and Kentucky legislatures, and the New Hampshire Supreme Court, forbade the citation of postindependence British cases.[50] George Tucker, Blackstone's American editor, agreed that independence deprived subsequent British decisions of any authority.[51] He also argued that the common law was different in each state because it was a creature in each state of local decisions during the colonial period.[52] Madison agreed.[53] Zephaniah Swift, author of a 1795 treatise on Connecticut law, held that common law rules were authoritative in Connecticut only insofar as Connecticut courts had approved them on grounds of their reason and expedience.[54] In general, then, the common law applicable in American jurisdictions after independence derived its authority from local enactment and was a different law in each jurisdiction.[55] The common laws of the states were independent of the common law of England, and independent of one another.

Many post-Revolution Americans were particularly skeptical of English criminal law. Tucker commented that he could not "find any more reason for admitting the penal code of England to be in force in the United States, (except so far as the states, respectively, may have adopted it, within their several jurisdictions) than for admitting that of the Roman empire, or of Russia, Spain, or any other nation, whatever."[56] Reformers saw the English criminal law, with its great abundance of capital crimes, as archaic and bloody.[57] Jefferson particularly objected to the felony murder rule described by Foster and Blackstone. His 1779 proposed Virginia criminal code precluded homicide liability

> where persons meaning to commit a trespass only, or larceny, or other unlawful deed, and doing an act from which involuntary homicide hath ensued, have heretofore been adjudged guilty of manslaughter or of murder, by transferring such their unlawful intention to an act, much more penal than they could have in probable contemplation; no such case shall hereafter be deemed manslaughter unless manslaughter was intended, nor murder, unless murder was intended.[58]

Jeffersonians objected not just to the content of the English common law of crimes, but to its undemocratic source. Particularly after the political struggles of the 1790s, Republicans associated the judicial power to punish common law crimes with politically repressive prosecutions for sedition and conspiracy.[59] Strong opposition therefore developed to the exercise of extrastatutory criminal jurisdiction by federal courts.[60]

Ironically, the notoriously partisan Federalist, Justice Samuel Chase, formulated the most influential argument against a federal common law of crimes.[61] Chase argued in the 1798 case of *United States v. Worrall* that the diversity of common law rules in the different states, and their independent sources in local enactments, meant that there was no judicially administrable standard of general criminal law to apply in federal cases.[62] While Chase may have initially stood in the minority among his colleagues on the Supreme Court,[63] and may even have changed his mind,[64] his arguments ultimately triumphed. The Court eventually yielded to public opinion[65] in its 1812 decision in *United States v. Hudson & Goodwin*,[66] holding that there was no federal common law of crimes. Only Justice Story continued to argue that such a power was needed to ensure cooperation with federal maritime policies during the War of 1812.[67] Justice Johnson invoked *Calvin's Case* in arguing against this exception,[68] and the Supreme Court eventually adopted his view.[69]

Concern about judicial definition of crimes extended beyond the federal context as well. Vermont Chief Justice Nathaniel Chipman declared that "no Court, in this State, ought ever to pronounce sentence of death upon the authority of a common law precedent, without the express authority of a statute."[70] Zephaniah Swift criticized courts' common law power to define misdemeanors as "not only incompatible with justice, and dangerous to civil liberty, but unnecessary for the preservation of government."[71] He added that "[t]he supreme excellency of a code of criminal laws consists in defining every act that is punishable with such certainty and accuracy, that no man shall be exposed to the danger of incurring a penalty without knowing it, and which shall not give to courts . . . an unbounded discretion in punishment."[72] Swift argued that punishment could fulfill its principal purpose of deterrence only if based on statutes clearly defining proscribed conduct in advance.[73] The Ohio attorney John Goodenow argued in 1819 that criminal laws were positive rather than natural law, and were properly enacted only by a representative legislature in a democracy.[74] Edward Livingston based his proposed Louisiana criminal code on such sentiments,[75] while Robert Rantoul demanded in his 1836 "Oration at Scituate" that "a uniform written code" replace the common law, which "had its origin in folly, barbarism, and feudality," and "from its nature, must always be ex post facto."[76]

In sum, early-nineteenth-century Americans generally believed that the common law's authority depended on local enactment and was subject to local modification. American reformers were critical of English criminal law's excessive reliance on the threat of capital punishment. Jeffersonian Republicans were particularly fearful of the potentially repressive uses of judicial definition of the criminal law, and sought to ground criminal liability in legislation. In this context, a supposed English felony murder rule would not have been legally authoritative unless and until it was adopted in some particular jurisdiction.

LEGISLATIVE REFORM OF HOMICIDE LAW

Following independence, the first homicide statutes resembled their colonial predecessors. A 1790 federal statute punished "wilful murder" or "murder" in places subject to federal jurisdiction.[77] Similar statutes were enacted in New York, Massachusetts, Connecticut, and Vermont.[78] Many states retained this simple approach to defining murder, or left murder undefined by statute, until well into the nineteenth century. Nevertheless, most American states reformed their homicide laws during the nineteenth century, adopting more-detailed statutes that included provisions addressing homicide in the course of crime.

The most popular legislative reform involved dividing murder into degrees. This new and distinctively American approach to homicide jurisprudence originated with Pennsylvania's 1794 reform statute, which restricted capital punishment to first-degree murder. The Pennsylvania statute was an outgrowth of a protracted movement to reduce and differentiate penalties inspired by such Enlightenment figures as Montesquieu and Beccaria and promoted by James Wilson, Benjamin Rush, and Pennsylvania Supreme Court Justice William Bradford.[79] A report prepared in 1792 by Justice Bradford for Pennsylvania's governor concluded that the death penalty should be reserved for "deliberate assassination."[80] This report prompted a resolution of one legislative house that "all murder . . . perpetrated by means of poison, or by lying in wait, or by any other kind of wilful, deliberate and premeditated killing shall be deemed murder in the first degree," and that all other kinds of murder shall be murder in the second degree.[81] The following year, a bill along these lines was presented to both houses. During legislative debates, murder in the course of enumerated felonies was added to the category of first-degree murder.[82]

While the Pennsylvania statute did not formulate a felony murder rule, or define the elements of murder at all, it identified participation in certain felonies as a grading element that aggravated murder liability. Thus, it prescribed that

> all murder, which shall be perpetrated by means of poison, or by lying in wait, or by any other kind of wilful, deliberate and premeditated killing, or which shall be committed in the perpetration or attempt to perpetrate any arson, rape, robbery, or burglary, shall be deemed murder in the first degree; and all other kinds of murder shall be deemed murder in the second degree . . .[83]

By implication, murder in the course of the enumerated felonies did not require willful, deliberate, and premeditated killing. Yet this language was compatible with a requirement that all murder required intent to kill or wound. There was nothing in the statute's language to suggest that the mere causing of death in the course of a felony was always murder. Any felony murder rule found in a statute of this form would have to be put there by construction. We will call statutes like Pennsylvania's aggravated murder liability based on participation in certain felonies "felony aggravator statutes."

The Pennsylvania statute was enormously influential, shaping homicide re-form statutes in two-thirds of the states by the end of the nineteenth century. Twelve states adopted Pennsylvania's grading scheme with little or no modifi-cation,[84] and another nineteen adopted somewhat modified grading schemes.[85] These modifications took three major forms. A few states aggravated murder to first-degree murder if committed in the attempt of any felony, not just enu-merated felonies. Many states combined Pennsylvania's grading scheme with a simple definition of murder in terms of malice. Finally, a large number of states combined the Pennsylvania grading scheme with statutory provisions impos-ing felony murder liability.

Felony murder liability was the other major legislative innovation in nine-teenth-century American homicide law. Georgia passed a felony murder law in 1811, but it never went into effect.[86] In 1817, however, Georgia enacted a code de-fining murder as unlawful killing with malice aforethought either express or im-plied by the absence of provocation or circumstances showing an "abandoned and malignant heart."[87] In defining involuntary killing in the course of an un-lawful act as manslaughter, the code added that an "involuntary killing . . . in the commission of an unlawful act which in its consequences, naturally tends to de-stroy the life of a human being, or is committed in the prosecution of a feloni-ous or riotous intent, shall be deemed and adjudged to be murder."[88] An almost identical statute went into effect in Illinois in 1827, missing only the reference to riot.[89] Two years later New Jersey enacted a statute that included within murder killing "in committing, or attempting to commit sodomy, rape, arson, robbery, or burglary, or any unlawful act against the peace of this state, of which the probable consequence may be bloodshed . . ."[90] That same year, New York passed a statute defining murder as including killing "without any design to effect death, by a person engaged in the commission of any felony."[91] By the end of the nineteenth century, nineteen states had adopted such felony murder statutes.[92]

The Georgia, New Jersey, and New York homicide reform statutes illustrate three different strategies for defining felony murder: (1) predicating murder liability on implied malice as well as a felony, as in Georgia; (2) predicating murder liability on dangerous felonies, as in New Jersey; or (3) predicating murder liability on any felony, as in New York. The implied-malice strategy was the most popular, employed by a total of ten states. Six of these states also employed Pennsylvania's grading scheme, elevating murder in the course of enumerated dangerous felonies to the first degree. New York's broad rule imposing murder liability for killing "without design to effect death" in the course of any felony was also influential in several states. Three other states adopted similarly broad rules for parts of the nineteenth century and three additional states defined killings committed without design to effect death during felonies as murders in the third degree, meriting as little as seven years in prison. Finally, two states joined New Jersey in explicitly limiting felony murder to killings committed in attempting enumerated or dangerous felonies.

By the end of the nineteenth century, all but eight American jurisdictions (the United States, Kentucky, Louisiana, North Dakota, Rhode Island, South Carolina, South Dakota, and Vermont) had legislation on the subject of homicide in the course of crime, in the form of a felony murder statute or a felony aggravator statute. Indeed, by the start of the Civil War, about three-quarters of American jurisdictions had adopted legislation on the question of homicide in the course of crime. Moreover, beginning in the 1830s, almost every new state adopted such legislation within a few years after its admission, usually as part of a comprehensive criminal code. By codifying their criminal law, new states avoided the intractable problem of identifying what kind of common law—presettlement British, pre-Revolution British, general American, or local—would govern. Common law development of penal law was largely confined to the original states and to the antebellum period. Americans deliberately left little scope for common law definition of homicide.

AMERICAN VIEWS ON FELONY MURDER AS COMMON LAW

Insofar as American courts wished to decide the proper treatment of homicide in the course of crime under local common law, what sources did they have to draw upon? American scholarly writing on criminal law during the nineteenth century was sparse.[93] Until the middle of the century, most American lawyers relied on American editions of such English treatises as Blackstone, East, and Russell.

In a few of the states without reformed homicide statutes, lawyers could turn to treatises on their own state's common law. In antebellum Connecticut, lawyers could consult Swift's treatise. Swift followed the approach of Hawkins and Hale in treating the commission of a dangerous or violent offense as evidence of malice prepense. In particular, "[w]here two, or more assemble for the purpose of doing any unlawful act against the peace, and of which the probable consequence may be bloodshed, as to beat a man, or commit a riot, and one of them kills a man, it is murder in all, because of the illegality of the act, and the premeditated wickedness of the design."[94] Rather than endorsing a felony murder rule as such, he held that in Connecticut unintentional killing was murder only if committed in the course of another capital crime:

> The general rule is, that when an unintentional homicide happens in consequence of an unlawful act, it will be murder or manslaughter, according to the nature of the act which occasioned it. If it be in the commission, or in the attempt of committing a capital crime, it will be murder: as if a man should kill a woman in attempting to commit a rape, it would be murder: if the crime be not capital . . . it will be manslaughter.—There can be no doubt of the justice and propriety of making the unintentional killing of a person, murder, where the real intent was to commit a crime of as high nature.[95]

Consistent with his jurisdictionally specific account of the authority of the common law, Swift adapted what he believed to be the English common law felony murder rule to the local circumstance of Connecticut's more humane schedule of punishment. The logic of transferring intent among crimes of like gravity had a narrower application in a democratic society than in a hierarchical one. An enlightened democratic society graded crime on the basis of harm to societal interests rather than on the basis of disobedience to social authority. Only if all violations of law were equal in expressing defiance of superior authority could intent transfer among them all. Swift's treatise implies a political rationale for what became the prevailing American approach to felony murder: its restriction to a very narrow group of very heinous predicate felonies.

Another early treatise on local criminal law took a different approach to the problem of homicide in the course of crime. The Kentucky legislature authorized an official summary and interpretation of the penal laws, published in 1804–06 by Harry Toulmin and James Blair. While Kentucky adopted Pennsylvania's grading statute in 1798, it replaced it in 1801 with a cryptic statute identifying murder in the course of enumerated felonies as one of several forms of felonious capital homicide. Toulmin and Blair defined murder as "killing . . . without lawful authority, not by accident, nor in self-defence, nor on sudden quarrel, but with malice aforethought, either express or implied, or in the perpetration or attempt to perpetrate any arson, rape, robbery, burglary, or any other unlawful act."[96] They explained that "[t]he law presumes malice in cases where a murder happens in the execution of an unlawful action, principally intended for someother purpose, and not to do a personal injury to him in particular who happens to be slain."[97] They added that "whenever a man happens to kill another in the execution of a deliberate purpose to commit any felony; he is guilty of murder . . ."[98] Toulmin and Blair concluded that the 1801 statute did not change what they regarded as the common law rule.[99]

Yet Toulmin and Blair qualified this sweeping rule by restricting "killing" to causing death directly by means of a "wound or blow" or indirectly by "deliberately doing a thing which visibly and clearly endangers another's life. . . ."[100] They listed five examples of "killing" in the execution of an unlawful action: (1) killing by striking blows against one who resists a theft;[101] (2) poisoning an unintended victim while attempting to kill another by poison;[102] (3) killing a pregnant woman by administering an abortifacient;[103] (4) unintentionally killing one who attempts to break up an assault;[104] and (5) killing by any of several conspirators who "resolve generally to resist all opposers in the commission of any breach of the peace, the execution of which is attended with such circumstances as naturally tend to produce tumult & disorder."[105] Thus a "killing" was not necessarily intentional, but it was never faultless.

The first general treatises on American substantive criminal law appeared at midcentury. The most influential antebellum American commentators were Francis Wharton and Joel Prentiss Bishop. Bishop's 1856–58 treatise offered a particularly broad felony murder rule. Bishop wrote that "whenever one does an act with the design of committing any felony, though not a felony dangerous to human life, yet if the life of another is accidentally taken, his offence is murder. In the application of this rule, statutory felonies are the same as felonies at common law."[106] For the most part, Bishop cited English sources; his only American source was the 1851 case of *State v. Smith*, which applied Maine's grading statute to impose second-degree felony murder liability for the non-enumerated felony of abortion.[107]

Bishop offered a general analysis of culpability based on Hawkins' rule of transferring intent among felonies. According to Bishop, crimes ordinarily required a "general" intention to do some "wrong," combined with a harmful result. Yet the resulting harm did not have to be the intended harm. As long as the intended result was roughly as bad as the result produced, the unlawful intent would transfer to the actual, but unintended, result. There were exceptions to this rule, crimes requiring a "specific intent" to achieve only a particular harm. But aside from these "specific intent" crimes, liability required only a general intent to cause harm.[108] For Bishop, a broad felony murder rule was integral to the logic of Anglo-American criminal law.

Wharton's 1855 treatise on homicide also supported a broad felony murder rule, on the basis of similar evidence. Wharton cited English treatises, the English cases of *Plummer* and *Woodburne*, and Maine's *Smith* decision.[109] He wrote:

> . . . if the act on which death ensue be *malum in se*, it will be murder or manslaughter, according to the circumstances; if done in prosecution of a felonious intent, but death ensued against or beside the intent of the party, it will be murder; . . . As where A. shoots at the poultry of B., and, by accident, kills B. himself: if his intent were to steal the poultry, which must be collected from circumstances, it will be murder, by reason of that felonious intent . . .[110]

Wharton discussed the application of this felony murder rule to situations of riot:

> Each individual is not only responsible for such acts of his associates as spring from the general design, but for such collateral acts as may be committed by his associates, with this distinction, that if the original unlawful act was a trespass, the murder, to affect all, must be done in prosecution of the design. If the unlawful act be a felony, it will be murder in all, although the death happen collaterally, or beside the original design.[111]

Wharton cited a jury charge issued by Justice Story in support of this rule, but then proceeded to undermine it. He attempted to distinguish "collateral acts growing out of the general design" (for which co-felons would be liable) from "independent acts growing out of the particular malice of individuals" (for which they would not).[112] He also discussed the *Plummer* case, which explicitly rejected accomplice liability for killings collateral to the intended crime.[113]

Wharton's second edition repudiated his original endorsement of felony murder. Published immediately after Stephen, Bramwell, and Blackburn testified against a broad conception of the rule, Wharton's treatise quoted their arguments at length. In his preface, Wharton identified himself with a reform movement that, he said, had revolutionized the law of homicide in the twenty years since his first edition. Wharton claimed that modern law treated malice as an actual mental state rather than a "presumption[] of law," required "that between the defendant's malice and the deceased's death there should be established a causal connection, consisting of the sequence of ordinary and well recognized physical laws," and rejected "the old doctrine that a collateral felonious intent can be tacked to unintended homicide, so that a man who in stealing a fowl accidentally kills the fowl's owner, can be held guilty of murder."[114] Wharton commented:

> [T]here is reported no modern conviction of common law murder, in a case in which there was no evidence of malicious intent towards the deceased, and in which the felonious intent proved was simply an intent to commit a collateral felony. And that an intent to commit larceny cannot be now used to prove an intent to kill is emphatically declared by a learned English judge (Blackburn, J.) in his testimony in 1874, before the Homicide Amendment Committee . . . [115]

Wharton added that if the common law did not impose felony murder, American grading statutes modeled on the Pennsylvania statute did not alter the situation.[116] Thus, Wharton argued, neither the common law nor the most prevalent American statutes established the felony murder rule.

Wharton next argued that "when there is no statutory enactment, the doctrine that the intent to commit a felony, when collateral to an accidental homicide, constitutes murder, must be rejected . . . ." He reasoned that "a malicious intent to take life or to do grievous bodily harm is essential" to murder, and that presuming such malice would violate the "presumption of innocence." He added that the intent to steal is "not a general felonious intent, but simply an intent to do a particular thing which is utterly distinct from the killing of a human being." If a thief accidentally killed a man in shooting at his chicken, the right response "would be to indict the offender for the larceny of the chicken, and for manslaughter of the chicken's owner."[117] Wharton approvingly quoted the arguments Lord Macaulay had made against the felony murder rule in his report on the penal code he drafted for India. Macaulay had begun by arguing that it would be "barbarous" to hold someone liable for an "innocent" act that produces unforeseeable harm. He had added that placing such an unforeseeably dangerous act in the context of a crime should not change a defendant's desert with respect to the resulting death. He gave the example of a non-negligent but fatal boat accident occurring in the course of an act of obstruction of justice, kidnapping, smuggling, or espionage. Finally, Macaulay turned to the deterrent value of punishment and argued that holding felons liable for causing deaths non-negligently can do nothing to deter killing but can only deter felonies, and that such a punishment lottery is an ineffective way of doing so: "Surely the worst mode of increasing the punishment of an offence is to provide that, besides the ordinary punishment, every offender shall run an exceedingly small risk of being hanged. The more nearly the amount of punishment can be reduced to a certainty the better . . ."[118]

Wharton illustrated his own view of the common law of murder by discussing homicide in the course of arson:

> No doubt if a person sets fire to a dwelling-house under such circumstances that its inmates, as an ordinary sequence of the fire, are burned and die, then . . . malice is to be inferred . . . The case would be that of a reckless and malicious firing into a crowd, which is murder at common law, if death ensue. But suppose that when perpetrating the arson the defendant, in accidentally discharging a gun, killed some one either in the house or in its neighborhood. Now . . . the malice aforethought necessary to constitute murder cannot be inferred, in face of the fact that the killing was in no way within the scope of the defendant's plan . . . .[119]

Wharton, the foremost American authority on the law of homicide, joined the English reformers who had rejected the concept of felony murder in favor of gross recklessness murder.

Oliver Wendell Holmes also questioned the rationality of a broad felony murder rule in his 1881 commentary on the common law. Of the familiar example of the trigger-happy chicken thief, Holmes offered the argument that

> [t]he only blameworthy act is firing at the chickens, knowing them to belong to another. It is neither more nor less so because an accident happens afterwards; and hitting a man, whose presence could not have been suspected, is an accident. The fact that the shooting is felonious does not make it any more likely to kill people. If the object of the rule is to prevent such accidents, it should make accidental killing with firearms murder, not accidental killing in the effort to steal; while, if its object is to prevent stealing, it would do better to hang one thief in every thousand by lot.[120]

Holmes argued that such a rule could be rational if particular predicate felonies were known by the legislature to be "peculiarly dangerous,"[121] yet he concluded by expressing skepticism that a broad felony murder rule was justifiable on such grounds or likely to be applied "in this country."[122]

So although American lawyers were taught to believe that the English common law imposed felony murder liability in the eighteenth century, they did not necessarily see this supposed English rule as applicable in America even in default of legislation. The American common law was local, and rejection of the English proliferation of capital crimes arguably gave Hawkins' intent-transferring theory a much narrower scope in America. By thus narrowing the scope of intent-transferring, American lawyers developed the idea of predicating felony murder liability only on a small number of enumerated serious crimes. This logic may explain the Pennsylvania grading statute; certainly it would shape the application of such statutes in nineteenth-century America. By the end of the nineteenth century, American scholars had come to recognize that felony murder liability had little foundation in English customary law and little support among modern English scholars. Under the influence of these scholars, American writers reinterpreted enumerated felony murder rules as dangerous-felony murder rules, recharacterizing felony murder as a form of recklessness rather than a form of transferred malice.

Nineteenth-century American courts trying to apply common law treatises to determine whether a criminal motive aggravated a particular killing to murder would have faced a ticklish problem. The treatise literature suggested that a felonious motive could aggravate a homicide, but only if sufficiently malicious or dangerous. Some felonies would warrant murder liability and others would not. Such a standard could not be applied without the exercise of considerable discretion, in a political context that disfavored judicial definition of crimes. It should not be surprising that courts generally left the definition of felony murder liability to legislative determination.

THE ABSENCE OF COMMON LAW FELONY MURDER CASES

While most states eventually adopted either enumerated felony grading statutes or felony murder statutes, many jurisdictions left murder undefined by statute for parts of the eighteenth and nineteenth centuries. These included the United States,[123] South Carolina,[124] Rhode Island,[125] and Vermont[126] up through the end of the nineteenth century, and twenty-seven other jurisdictions for shorter intervals.[127] If a common law felony murder rule were operative in the

United States in the eighteenth and nineteenth centuries, we would expect to find it being applied in these jurisdictions. Yet, as we shall see, almost none of the courts that could have developed a common law felony murder rule did so.

The opportunities for courts to define the law of homicide were largely gone by the Civil War, by which time three-quarters of the states had adopted felony murder or felony aggravator statutes. While common law definition of crime was an early-nineteenth-century phenomenon in America, felony murder liability was a late-nineteenth-century phenomenon. Felony murder liability was almost always imposed under a felony murder statute or a statute grading murder liability on the basis of participation in a felony. I have identified eighty-five reported nineteenth-century American cases that concluded with a valid felony murder conviction.[128] Table 6.1 organizes these cases chronologically, identifying whether these convictions were under felony murder statutes, felony aggravator statutes, or common law felony murder rules. Of the eighty-five cases, only three occurred in the first half of the nineteenth century, when judicial definition of homicide crimes was common. On the other hand, eighty-five percent of the convictions were in the last three decades of the century, when over eighty percent of American jurisdictions had legislation on homicide in the course of crime. Only three felony murder convictions were obtained in jurisdictions that left the definition of murder to common law development.[129] All three were near the end of the nineteenth century.

Only a handful of American courts considered the question of felony murder liability without legislative prompting. One early North Carolina opinion implied the existence of some form of unlawful act murder.[130] In discussing the adequacy of provocation required to reduce a killing from murder to man-

Table 6.1. Convictions Under Various Murder Liability Regimes, 1791–1900

	Total number of convictions	Convictions under a felony murder statute	Convictions under a felony aggravator statute	Convictions under common law felony murder rules
1791–1840	0	0	0	0
1841–1850	3	1	2	0
1851–1860	6	3	3	0
1861–1870	4	2	2	0
1871–1880	13	7	6	0
1881–1890	19	15	3	1
1891–1900	40	25	13	2
Total	85	53	29	3

slaughter, the judge defined malice as "a circumstance attending the fact, that cuts off the slayer from all manner of excuse."[131] He then listed among these excuses killing "undesignedly" while "doing a lawful act in a proper manner."[132] In this way, he implied that an unlawful act might render an unintended death malicious, but he did not expand upon the point.

An early judicial effort to establish felony murder liability can be credited to Justice Story, in the 1813 case of *United States v. Ross*.[133] This case may be seen as part of Story's failed attempt to launch a federal common law of crimes as an instrument of naval warfare. Ross led an armed band in seizing a vessel. One member killed a resisting passenger, and all were charged under the 1790 federal statute punishing murder on the high seas. Ross argued that as the unlawful seizure of a vessel was not defined and punished as a felony, his participation in this crime did not implicate him in the ensuing murder. Story reasoned that even if the crime planned was not a felony, the conspirators would still be liable for a death caused in furtherance of the conspiracy, especially if the planned crime was very dangerous. This was consistent with Hale's position and with *Mansell & Herbert's Case*. Story added that all should be held liable for murder if the conspirators had resolved to kill any who might oppose them, the rule of *Lord Dacre*. Yet he also went beyond English law by instructing the jurors that if death ensued from a conspiracy "to commit a felony, it is murder in all, although the death take place collaterally, or beside the principal design."[134] This was directly contrary to Holt's dictum in *Plummer*, which required that murder predicated on a felony be in furtherance of, rather than collateral to, the felony.[135] Since the killing was in furtherance of the conspiracy, the seizure was not a felony, and the jury acquitted of murder, the case did not test the furthest extent of Story's instructions.

Story's effort to read a felony murder rule into federal criminal law won at least one adherent. District Judge Davis discoursed on felony murder in his jury charge in the 1814 case of *United States v. Travers*,[136] even though there was no allegation that Travers had killed in the course of a felony. Davis opined that "when an involuntary killing happens in consequence of an unlawful act . . . in the prosecution of a felonious intent . . . it will be murder . . . ."[137] Yet there were no reported federal felony murder convictions during the nineteenth century. So far as we know, no federal court ever applied Story's rule.

The next reported federal case to address homicide in the course of crime, the 1890 case of *United States v. Boyd*,[138] followed the recklessness approach favored by Stephen and Wharton and rejected Story's broad felony murder rule. Boyd shot his victim in the course of a robbery. The trial court instructed the jury that killing in the course of an unlawful act that is violent or otherwise dangerous to life is murder. The court included the traditional felonies of robbery, burglary, arson, and rape among such violent or dangerous crimes, but did not emphasize their status as felonies.[139] The court explicitly rejected Coke's claim that an accidental shooting in the course of stealing chickens would be murder, calling this rule deficient in justice and humanity.[140] On the other hand, the court approvingly cited an Illinois case requiring awareness that the predicate crime is dangerous to life.[141] Finally, the court reinterpreted Story's murder instruction in *Ross*, emphasizing the dangerousness and violence of seizing a ship by force and the determination of the conspirators to accomplish their end by violent means if necessary. The dangerous and violent character of an offense, not its grade, supplied the requisite malice. In short, the *Boyd* court rejected the felony murder rules proposed by Holt, Hawkins, Foster, and Story in favor of the dangerous-unlawful-act doctrine favored by Hale, Stephen, and Wharton. However, the court held that the four traditionally enumerated felonies were sufficiently dangerous to life to imply malice, thereby endorsing results consistent with felony murder rules as actually put into practice in most states.

We might expect to find felony murder rules in antebellum Connecticut and Kentucky, where early treatises on local law endorsed such rules. In Connecticut, however, no felony murder rule developed until long after the 1846 adoption of a felony aggravator statute. In Kentucky, a common law felony murder rule did emerge eventually, but not until late in the nineteenth century.

While Kentucky abandoned grading in 1801, it retained the Pennsylvania statute's enigmatic discussion of killing in the course of crime. According to the new statute, "[a]ny person . . . who shall be guilty of murder, and . . . who shall commit the same in the perpetration, or attempt to perpetrate any arson, rape, robbery, or burglary, shall be deemed a felon; and every other . . . killing . . . committed with malice aforethought, either express or implied, will be deemed felony, and shall be punished with death."[142] A year later the legislature decreed that the law "shall not be so construed as any way to alter or change the idea of murder as it stands at common law."[143] Although Toulmin and Blair read a broad felony murder rule into these provisions, the Kentucky courts never applied their interpretation. Moreover, Toulmin and Blair's comments arguably became a dead letter in 1825 when the legislature repealed the 1801 provision on murder and manslaughter without passing any replacement.[144] In 1827 the legislature passed another statute declaring that "nothing in the before recited act, or any other act, shall be construed to alter or change the definition and punishment of wilful murder, by the common law . . ."[145] An 1873 statute restated this agnostic position more directly: "If any person be guilty of willful murder, he shall be punished with death, or confinement in the penitentiary . . ."[146]

The first Kentucky cases to address the felony murder question were decided the same year. Each endorsed a form of felony murder. In the 1873 case of *Chrystal v. Commonwealth*, the court approved Wharton's original view that "a party whose negligence causes the death of another is in like manner responsible, whether the business in which he was engaged was legal or illegal. If the business was of such a character as to be felonious, the offense, it is clear, is murder. . . ."[147] Of course, Wharton's revised treatise would soon repudiate this formulation. In *Mickey v. Commonwealth*, also decided in 1873, the court held that the defendant could not be "convicted of murder upon the hypothesis that he aided and abetted the parties committing the homicide unless it is made to appear . . . that he had confederated with them to make the attack or to commit a felony or trespass . . ."[148] The 1888 decision in *Peoples v. Commonwealth* formulated, but found inapplicable, a rule that "whenever an unlawful act, one malum in se, is done in the prosecution of a felonious intention, or the perpetration of a collateral felony, and death ensues, it is murder."[149] Finally, in 1895, Kentucky actually imposed felony murder liability on this basis. In *Reddick v. Commonwealth*,[150] the Kentucky Supreme Court affirmed a felony murder conviction based on the dictum in *Peoples*. The court approved an instruction that if the defendant "willfully, maliciously, and feloniously set fire to and burned" a hotel being used as a residence and thereby caused death he was guilty of murder. The court commented:

> The offense of feloniously, willfully, and maliciously burning the hotel . . . was a felony. It clearly belonged to the cases "malum in se," and not merely "malum prohibitum." The felonious intent and purpose of accused in doing which, if guilty, the law certainly transfers to a consequence and result of same so natural as that the inmates of the house might by such fire lose their lives.[151]

Thus at the end of the nineteenth century, Kentucky courts regarded as murder any death foreseeably caused by an act that was (1) negligent and (2) motivated by a felony that was (3) *malum in se*.

Like Kentucky, Louisiana repealed its grading statute (though not until 1855) and left the definition of murder to the common law. It had no decisions addressing the felony murder question until *State v. Deschamps* in 1890.[152] The victim died of a drug overdose. The trial court instructed the jury that if the victim died as a result of a drug administered for the purpose of rape, it would be murder. The defendant's murder conviction was upheld and the instruction approved.[153]

South Carolina had three cases during the nineteenth century addressing homicide in the course of crime. In the 1867 case of *State v. Jenkins*, two defendants were convicted of murder when they participated in a fatal mob attack by throwing bricks at the victim. The appellate court upheld the conviction on ordinary principles of culpability and complicity, rejecting the applicability of unlawful act murder.[154] In the 1889 case of *State v. Alexander*, a South Carolina court upheld a murder conviction on an instruction that an assault and battery supplied the requisite malice for murder and that intent to kill was not required.[155] The trial court added that malice embraced both the intent to kill and the intent to violate the law.[156] The appellate court narrowed the latter proposition, requiring an unlawful act "in prosecution of a felonious intent, or in its consequences naturally tended to bloodshed."[157] The case involved an inherently dangerous assault (with an axe) but no independent felonious aim, so the court may not have seen it as a felony murder case.

Two years later, the South Carolina Supreme Court applied a sweeping felony murder rule in the troubling case of *State v. Levelle*.[158] Levelle alleged that he had killed his wife accidentally in attempting suicide. The trial court instructed the jury that suicide was unlawful and that unintended killing in the course of any unlawful act was murder. The appellate court approved this instruction but on the contrary theory that the act causing unintended death must be in pursuit of a felony, *malum in se*.[159] While admitting that suicide was not criminally punished in South Carolina, the court argued that suicide should still be considered a felony because the South Carolina statute providing forms for coroner's inquests referred to suicide as "felonious."[160] This broad conception of felony murder was unique in Anglo-American criminal law.

So was there a common law felony murder rule in nineteenth-century America? Certainly there was no general common law rule. Of thirty jurisdictions that were without legislation on the subject of homicide in the course of crime during some part of the nineteenth century, only three applied a felony murder rule—and they did so in only a handful of cases, almost all at the end of the nineteenth century, after felony murder had become a common feature of American criminal codes.

7 EARLY FELONY AGGRAVATOR STATUTES

Most American states adopted new homicide statutes during the nineteenth century. The most popular reform involved dividing murder into degrees. Such statutes usually aggravated murder to the first degree if it was committed in the attempt of one of several enumerated felonies. These enumerated felony aggravator statutes did not necessarily reduce the culpability required for murder in the course of these felonies. Nor did they necessarily impose second-degree felony murder liability for causing death unintentionally in the course of other, non-enumerated felonies. A felony aggravator statute leaves the criteria of murder liability to judicial discretion.

Felony aggravator statutes were enacted in twenty-two states.[1] In six of these states—Indiana, Iowa, Maine, Nebraska, Ohio, and Washington—the statute also defined murder as requiring the culpable mental state of malice.

We will now examine the application of these felony aggravator statutes to impose felony murder liability. Our primary aim is to see whether courts based felony murder liability on the grading provisions or on the term "murder" itself, and whether courts restricted felony murder liability to enumerated predicate felonies. Some felony aggravator statutes conditioned murder liability on the mental element of malice, and we will also see how such provisions affected felony murder liability.

FELONY MURDER IN PENNSYLVANIA

The Pennsylvania legislature gave its grading statute an authoritative construction in 1810 in an instruction manual for grand jurors. The manual conditioned murder on malice express or implied, defining the latter as "doing an act that apparently must do harm, with an intent to harm" or acting with "deliberation and cruelty," "a mind grievously depraved," and "motives highly criminal."[2]

The grand juror manual assimilated homicide in the course of unlawful acts into homicide by risk taking.

[I]f a person do a wanton, idle action, which cannot but be attended with manifest danger; or an action unlawful in itself, deliberately, and with an intention of mischief, either to particulars, or indiscriminately, fall where it may, and death ensue, though against the original intention of the party, it will be murder. . . . If one throw a stone over a wall, among a multitude, intending only to frighten them, or hurt them lightly, and a man is killed, it is murder upon the same principle. The act was unlawful. But if such mischievous intention does not appear, but the act was done heedlessly and incautiously, it is manslaughter . . . .[3]

This offered no separate theory of unlawful act murder, let alone felony murder. The unlawful act here was simply the malicious or spiteful endangerment required for grossly reckless murder.

A more extensive discussion of homicide in the course of crime was primarily concerned with accessorial liability for killings committed pursuant to a criminal plan.

When a man does an unlawful act, and death ensues, it is murder; as if a man rob an orchard, and being rebuked by the owner, kills him. So, if a man commits a riot, and in doing it, another is killed. Divers come to commit a riotous, unlawful act, in pursuit of which, one of them commits murder or manslaughter, all are guilty. Divers come to steal deer in a park, the park-keeper shot at them; they fled, he pursued, they returned and killed the park-keeper, held to be murder in all. The law presumes they came with intent to oppose all that should hinder their design. So, if A. begins a riot, which continues for an hour, and then B. is killed by another, it will be murder in A. So, if A. assaults B. to rob him, though without any precedent intention of killing him; yet if in the attempt, whether B. resists or not, A. kills him, it is murder. . . . But to render it murder, the killing must be in pursuit of that unlawful act they were all engaged in. Thus, smugglers assemble to run wool; officers oppose; a smuggler fires a gun and kills another smuggler. If it does not appear that it was leveled at the officers, the other smugglers present are not guilty. For it does not appear it was in prosecution of the purpose for which they assembled. So, divers committing an unlawful act, one of them meets with D. with whom he had a former quarrel, and kills him, the rest are not guilty, for it was not within the compass of their original intention. Three soldiers go to rob an orchard, two get up the tree, the third stands at the gate with a drawn sword; the owner's son comes and seizes him; he stabs him. Those in the tree are not guilty, otherwise, if they had come with a general resolution against all opposers, which may be collected from their number, arms, or behaviour, at, or before.[4]

This paragraph concerned unlawfully motivated fatal violence. The first clause, taken in isolation, seemed to imply that causing death in the course of any unlawful act is murder. Yet we know from the previous discussion that unlawfulness did not suffice for murder without gross recklessness. All of the deaths described resulted from an intentional battery; many seemed to be intentional killings. Thus the paragraph made two claims, one about liability for principals and one about liability for accomplices. First, one who strikes a fatal blow in overcoming resistance to a crime receives murder liability rather than the manslaughter liability ordinarily meted out to the survivor of a fatal fight. Second, any participant in the crime who agreed to the use of force to overcome resistance is an accomplice in murder if such force causes death. Nothing in the paragraph conditioned murder liability on the crime being a felony.

The grand juror manual's final discussion of murder in the course of crime concerned second-degree murder:

All murder which follows felonious acts, which were not formerly capital crimes . . . , or in consequence of offensive language, which has been deemed to be no provocation, and the murder not premeditated, or on revenge predetermined; or in consequence of acts prohibited by law, called mala prohibita; in consequence of riots and unlawful assemblies; in consequence of trespasses committed upon the property or possession of another; in all similar cases where it is evident there has been no precedent intention to kill; and more particularly in cases closely bordering on manslaughter, will be but murder in the second degree . . . .[5]

While this paragraph discussed murder in the course of non-enumerated felonies, it did not quantify all deaths caused in the course of felonies as murders. Instead, it treated murder in the course of non-enumerated felonies in exactly the same way that it treated murder in the course of such other unlawful acts as *mala prohibita*, riots, and trespasses. It characterized these murders as involving "no precedent intention to kill," but neither said nor implied that second-degree murder could be committed without gross recklessness or intent to injure.

The first formulation of a felony murder rule in Pennsylvania law came in the 1826 case of *Commonwealth v. Green*,[6] in which the defendant was convicted of second-degree murder after fatally shooting one who had earlier assaulted him. The trial court ascribed a felony murder rule to the common law, criticized it as inhumane, and then implied that it had been retained for enumerated felonies. Noncapital or second-degree murder liability remained available for unintended killing by means of a violent assault:

> Some of [the common law's] . . . features, are . . . hardly accordant with either [reason or humanity]. Among these are the whole doctrine of what may be termed constructive murder, in which a party taking human life is involved in the guilt of murder, when all the circumstances of the homicide, clearly negative any intention to kill. Thus, if in shooting a tame fowl, with intent to steal it, the death of a man accidentally ensues . . . [it is murder] at common law, and punishable with death, and . . . [was] so in Pennsylvania, previous to our act of Assembly.
>
> . . . By the admirable act of 1794, [however,] the whole doctrine of constructive murder, as it may be called, ceased in Pennsylvania, so far as to involve the life of the accused; such murders being nothing more than murders in the second degree. To constitute murder in the first degree, the unlawful killing must be accompanied by a clear intent to take life. . . . In England, if death ensues from any unlawful act of violence, the slayer, although there existed no intention to kill, but only to do bodily harm, is guilty of murder. In Pennsylvania, except in the cases enumerated in the act of Assembly, the malice in any homicide must be directed against the life of an human being, in order to render the slayer guilty of murder in the first degree.[7]

This passage was open to two interpretations, depending on whether read as preserving the harsh rule it misattributed to English and colonial law and then disapproved. Possibly second-degree murder now included accidental killing in the course of nonviolent felonies like theft. More likely second-degree murder was limited to death resulting from an "unlawful act of violence," involving the "intention . . . to do bodily harm." If so, murder in the course of enumerated felonies although not requiring "intention to kill" probably also required an act of violence and an intent to do bodily harm.

A doctrine of second-degree murder liability for unintended killings in the course of non-enumerated felonies was asserted as dictum in the 1855 case of *Johnson v. Commonwealth*.[8] Yet the case reports do not record a single second-degree felony murder conviction in Pennsylvania during the nineteenth century. Certainly the Pennsylvania courts did not impose second-degree murder liability for accidental death in the course of nonviolent felonies. Instead, the Pennsylvania courts imposed second-degree murder liability for deaths caused in violently overcoming resistance to a criminal act, whether it was a felony or a misdemeanor. Thus, in the 1844 case of *Commonwealth v. Hare*, the court instructed the jury that rioters who fired shots at one another were all guilty of manslaughter if one among them was killed, but second-degree murder if an innocent bystander was fatally hit. The court reasoned that the killing of an opponent in a fight was provoked, whereas an innocent bystander could offer no provocation. The intent to do bodily harm would transfer, while the defendant's "hot blood" would prevent the deliberation required for first-degree murder.[9] In the companion case of *Commonwealth v. Daley*, the court instructed the jury that second-degree murder required malice, but that malice included any intended violence and was not restricted to the intent to kill.[10] As riot was a misdemeanor,[11] no felony murder rule played a role in either case. An 1869 case confirmed that where no enumerated felony was involved, a criminal motive played an indirect role in aggravating the defendant's liability: precluding justification and provocation.[12] Felony murder based on non-enumerated felonies remained a myth, a supposed vestige of ancient English law invoked only to emphasize the modernity and humanity of Pennsylvania's reforms.

By contrast, Pennsylvania courts embraced and applied the doctrine of murder liability for unintended killings in the course of enumerated felonies. In the 1844 case of *Commonwealth v. Flanagan*,[13] an appellate court affirmed a first-degree murder conviction, based on a felony murder instruction, for a killing in the course of a burglary. This is the earliest reported felony murder conviction I have come across. This instruction held that

> in cases of homicide committed in the perpetration of certain offences, viz., arson, rape, robbery, burglary, all idea of intention was excluded. The act in which the malefactor was engaged was of such a nature, so deep a crime, involving such turpitude of mind, and protection against which was so necessary to the peace and welfare of all good citizens, that our Legislature considered the intention as of no consequence . . . .[14]

This instruction placed the enumerated felonies in a special category of dangerous offenses, justifying murder liability without intention based on an alternative form of culpability: great "turpitude of mind." The *Flanagan* court's reasoning was restricted to the enumerated felonies.

Felony murder convictions were appealed in eight Pennsylvania cases between the *Flanagan* decision and the turn of the century. All involved first-degree murder convictions predicated on enumerated felonies. Two convictions were overturned on the ground that there was not a tight enough temporal and instrumental connection between the killing and the predicate felony.[15] The other six were upheld. Thus, in the 1860 case of *Commonwealth v. Miller*, two men were convicted of murdering a third by drowning him. The trial court instructed the jury that "if death ensues in the perpetration or attempt to perpetrate any ... robbery ... , the offence is murder of the first degree. ... ." While the evidence suggested that the victim had been robbed, one of the defendants was convicted of second-degree murder and one of first-degree murder.[16] In *Commonwealth v. Hanlon*, the defendant was convicted of first-degree murder, on the basis that he killed in perpetration of rape, without regard to his intent. Hanlon strangled his six-year-old victim in the course of a rape producing extensive injuries, but claimed he was only trying to quiet her.[17] In *Brown v. Commonwealth*, the defendant was convicted on a felony murder instruction for bludgeoning his victim during a robbery. The instruction did not restrict the felony murder rule to enumerated felonies: if killing "was done in the perpetration of some felony . . . the law implies malice and the killing is murder."[18] In *Commonwealth v. Manfredi*, the defendant broke into his victim's home and shot his victim fatally in the chest in the course of a struggle. The Pennsylvania Supreme Court affirmed a conviction on an instruction that a killing in the course of burglary or robbery is murder in the first degree.[19] In *Commonwealth v. Eagan*,[20] the defendants fatally beat, bound, and gagged an intended robbery and burglary victim, but were frightened from the scene before taking any money or entering his house. The Pennsylvania Supreme Court upheld a first-degree murder conviction on the grounds that the acts causing death were committed in the attempt to perpetrate robbery and burglary, and that the killing was also premeditated. Finally, in *Commonwealth v. Epps*, the defendant strangled a robbery victim in her home, with an accomplice. The Pennsylvania Supreme Court affirmed the defendant's first-degree murder conviction, reasoning that "whether it was his intent to kill the victim he had robbed was wholly immaterial; the killing occurred in the perpetration of a robbery by him . . ."[21]

While courts in these cases repeatedly emphasized that intent to kill was not required for first-degree murder liability in the course of enumerated felonies, none of the cases involved what we might call accidental death. All of the deaths resulted from batteries aimed at killing, injuring, or overcoming a victim by force. These killings would certainly have been manslaughter at least, without the enumerated felony. If unprovoked, such killings might have been considered second-degree murders without the context of a felony. And if committed in overcoming resistance to a crime of any degree, such killings could not have been considered adequately provoked. In sum, it seems that the Pennsylvania legislature accepted, and the Pennsylvania courts enforced, traditional English rules that an unprovoked intent to do bodily harm sufficed as the mental element of murder, that such an intent could transfer to an unintended victim, and that a criminal motive barred mitigation on the ground of provocation. The Pennsylvania legislature reduced such murder liability for unintended killing to noncapital murder, except when committed in the course of enumerated felonies. The Pennsylvania courts interpreted the statute to eliminate any requirement of intent for first-degree felony murder, although in practice they confined the element of killing to causing death by a battery, a blow committed with the intent to do bodily harm. A felonious motive, as such, had no significance in Pennsylvania homicide law. What mattered was the motive to commit an enumerated felony, characterized by great danger and moral turpitude.

THE PENNSYLVANIA MODEL IN OTHER STATES

In 1796 Virginia adopted a comprehensive criminal code based on Thomas Jefferson's draft, first proposed in 1779. Jefferson's draft, which explicitly disapproved felony murder liability,[22] was rejected by the Virginia legislature by one vote in 1786. The 1796 draft that passed the legislature replaced Jefferson's murder provisions with the Pennsylvania formula.[23] The Pennsylvania statute was also adopted by Kentucky from 1798 to 1801; Maryland in 1810; Louisiana, which entered the Union with it in 1812 and retained it until 1855; Michigan in 1838; Arkansas in 1838; New Hampshire in 1842; and Connecticut in 1846.[24] West Virginia entered the Union with Virginia's statute in 1863.[25] Substantially similar statutes were adopted in Tennessee in 1829, Delaware in 1852, and Massachusetts in 1858, differing only in their list of enumerated predicate felonies for first-degree murder.[26] Kansas, upon admission in 1861, and North Carolina in 1893, adopted statutes grading murder in the first degree when committed on the basis of any felony.[27] We will next review the application of these Pennsylvania-influenced felony aggravator statutes.

Felony murder liability was imposed very rarely during the nineteenth century in the states adopting enumerated felony aggravator statutes. Courts approved the doctrine in Virginia, Tennessee, New Hampshire, Arkansas, Michigan, and Massachusetts before the Civil War, but only Tennessee actually applied it during this period.[28] The doctrine was not actually applied until after the Civil War in New Hampshire, Delaware, and Massachusetts, and not until the last decade of the nineteenth century in Virginia, Michigan, North Carolina, and Connecticut.[29] Maryland and Kansas courts never endorsed or applied a felony murder rule during the nineteenth century. Arkansas never applied it, and Louisiana neither applied nor approved such a rule until after repealing its grading statute. West Virginia never applied it during the nineteenth century but perhaps inherited Virginia's approval of it. Kentucky kept the Pennsylvania grading structure for only three years and had no felony murder cases in that brief time. On the other hand, not a single state with a Pennsylvania-style felony aggravator statute explicitly rejected felony murder liability. I have identified eleven reported felony murder convictions in these states during the nineteenth century.[30] Seven were first-degree murder convictions based on the enumerated felonies of robbery[31] and rape.[32] One was a first-degree murder conviction predicated on theft in a jurisdiction that aggravated murders in the course of all felonies to first degree. The facts in this case would also have supported robbery or burglary under modern law: the defendant shot and killed a shopkeeper while breaking into his store to steal.[33]

Courts in six of the states (Delaware, Massachusetts, Michigan, New Hampshire, Tennessee, and Virginia) appeared to endorse predicating second-degree murder on non-enumerated felonies,[34] but only Tennessee and Delaware did so. In the Tennessee case, the predicate felony was attempted murder of a different victim.[35] In one of the two Delaware cases, the predicate felony was robbery,[36] an enumerated felony in most other states. In the other Delaware case, the predicate felony was abortion.[37]

Several courts rooted the authority of felony murder rules of varying scope in the English common law. Opinions in the 1828 Virginia case of *Whiteford v. Commonwealth*[38] and the 1892 Delaware case of *State v. Lodge*[39] both invoked Coke's claim that killing accidentally in shooting at poultry in order to steal it was murder at common law. In the 1849 case of *State v. McNab*,[40] the New Hampshire Supreme Court invoked the authority of Russell and East in support of a felony murder rule. In the 1875 Massachusetts case of *Commonwealth v. Pemberton*, the court cited Hawkins for the proposition that "at common law, where the homicide happens 'in the execution of a deliberate purpose to commit any felony,' it is murder, as, 'where one sets upon a man to rob him, and kills him in making resistance.'"[41] In the 1858 case of *People v. Potter*, the Michigan

Supreme Court wrote that Michigan retained the "common law" definition of murder, according to which "if death ensued from an act accompanying an unlawful collateral act . . . the killing would be murder . . ."[42]

On the other hand, some courts rooted felony murder rules in the felony aggravator provisions themselves. Thus opinions in the 1829 Virginia case of *Commonwealth v. Jones*,[43] the 1849 Tennessee case of *Bratton v. State*,[44] and the 1850 Arkansas case of *Bivens v. State*[45] read felony aggravator provisions to obviate proof of intent to kill. The 1882 Connecticut decision in *Smith v. State* viewed the felony aggravator clause as a source of "implied malice" attending killings in the course of enumerated felonies.[46] Other opinions read felony aggravator provisions to authorize application of a common law rule to enumerated felonies.[47]

A few courts justified the imposition of felony murder liability on the basis of the felon's malicious motive. In an 1859 decision the Michigan Supreme Court explained that "where, in the attempt to commit some other offense which is malum in se . . . , human life is taken without an express design to take it, . . . the crime is held to be murder, because resulting from the same species of depravity or maliciousness which characterizes that offense when committed designedly."[48] A later Michigan decision treated a felonious motive as inherently malicious, while reasoning that a misdemeanor could be malicious if very dangerous.[49]

Two Massachusetts decisions offered a fuller account of the kind of depraved or malicious motive that could substitute for intent to kill. The 1875 decision in *Commonwealth v. Pemberton* treated killing the resisting victim of a robbery as a paradigm case of malice implied by a felony:

> In such a case the presumption of malice is not rebutted even if the circumstances show a desire on the part of the assailant not to kill. . . . If the purpose of the defendant was to commit robbery, and if in the execution of that purpose, and in order to overcome the resistance and silence the outcries of the victim, he made use of violence that caused her death, no further proof of premeditation or of wilful intent to kill is necessary. Robbery committed by force and violence, and in spite of all resistance, is of course malicious, and if in the perpetration of that crime the person robbed is killed, it is a killing with malice aforethought; in other words, it is murder, and by the express terms of the statute, it is murder in the first degree.[50]

Here the deliberate use of violence to overcome the will of the victim made the felony murder "malicious" in the absence of intent to kill. A similar account of implied malice appeared in the jury instructions in the 1895 case of *Common-wealth v. Gilbert*,[51] where the defendant had raped and killed a nine-year-old girl. The court emphasized the felon's pursuit of his unlawful end in reckless disregard of the will and welfare of his victim:

> The wilful purpose of carrying out one's own determinations without any re-gard for the rights of others is enough of itself in the meaning of the law to constitute malice. This word comprehends every unlawful motive, every wicked intent or mischievous purpose. Any taking of human life with such an unlawful purpose or from such an unlawful motive is, accordingly, malicious. . . . [Did] this defendant . . . take the life of this girl . . . while engaged . . . in the prosecu-tion of his own unlawful ends, without regard, with a wanton disregard, of her rights? . . . If . . . [he] did, why then he has murdered her.[52]

THE PENNSYLVANIA MODEL MODIFIED:
FELONY AGGRAVATOR STATUTES WITH CULPABILITY

Several states adopted Pennsylvania's grading scheme, but added an explicit definition of the mental element of murder. These statutes forced courts to explain how any homicide punished as murder exhibited the required mental states. This did not preclude felony murder liability, since courts could char-acterize a felonious motive as supplying the requisite culpability. But the need to link killing in the context of crime to a specific mental state put pressure on courts to develop moral and psychological rationales for felony murder li-ability, and to conform the scope of felony murder liability to these rationales. Courts differed as to whether the attempt of some or all felonies supplied the requisite culpability for murder. Views ranged from rejecting felony murder altogether to conditioning felony murder on non-enumerated as well as enu-merated felonies.

Ohio adopted its modified version of Pennsylvania's grading statute in 1815,[53] and its courts ultimately construed this formula as precluding a felony murder rule. The Ohio statute provided "[t]hat if any person shall purposely, of deliberate and premeditated malice, or in the perpetration or attempt to perpetrate any rape, arson, robbery or burglary, kill another, every such per-son . . . shall be deemed guilty of murder in the first degree, and upon convic-tion thereof shall suffer death."[54] Second-degree murder was defined as killing "purposely and maliciously, but without deliberate and premeditated malice."[55] In the 1857 case of *Robbins v. State*,[56] the Ohio Supreme Court held that, as de-

fined by this statute, both first- and second-degree murder required intent to
kill. This was explicit in the second-degree murder provision. The court argued
that this fact, combined with the placement of the comma immediately after
"purposely" in the first-degree murder provision, required reading that provision as requiring purpose both for premeditated murder and for murder in the
course of the enumerated felonies.[57] Four other states adopted Ohio's statutory
formulation of murder—Indiana, Nebraska, Washington, and Wyoming—but
only Ohio explicitly repudiated the felony murder rule in all cases.

Indiana adopted first- and second-degree murder provisions in 1852 that
were very similar to Ohio's.[58] Thus Indiana, like Ohio, clearly required intent
to kill for second-degree murder.[59] Yet Indiana's first-degree provision had no
comma after the word "purposefully," which suggested that the attempt of an
enumerated felony or the use of poison might substitute for purpose as well
as premeditation in supplying the mental element of first-degree murder. The
1855 decision in *Stocking v. State* upheld a murder conviction on an instruction
that "to kill a man purposely, and with premeditated malice, or to kill a man in
the commission or in the attempt to commit a crime—a robbery or an arson—
is murder in the first degree."[60] The defendant and his accomplices had, after a
robbery and assault, returned to strike more blows against their prostrate victim, and then set the building where the robbery occurred on fire and left the
victim to burn. Although the killing was clearly purposeful, the decision established that purpose was unnecessary for first-degree murder when the killing
was pursuant to an enumerated felony.

The authority of this first-degree felony murder rule was confirmed in the
1876 case of *Bissot v. State*,[61] in which burglars returned fire from a watchman,
killing him. The Indiana Supreme Court specified that felony murders need not
be intentional, and could be provoked or defensive killings. It did not clarify
whether such killings could be accidental:

> The intention of the legislature, in enacting the section, was, doubtless, to class
> certain homicides in the highest degree of murder without containing the in-
> gredient of premeditation, malice, or intention, which otherwise could not
> possibly be of a higher degree than manslaughter, and, in many cases, might
> not amount to criminal homicide at all. In this case, take away the elements of
> burglary which surround it, and the prisoner might plausibly contend that he
> had committed nothing more than excusable homicide; for it appears that the
> deceased shot at him first, and thus put his life in immediate jeopardy.[62]

The court revisited this question four years later in *Moynihan v. State*,[63] affirming the first-degree murder conviction of a robber who fatally beat his victim. The court upheld an instruction that no intent to kill is required for felony murder, and that an arsonist unaware of a victim inside a building he burned would be guilty of first-degree murder.[64] The court based this conclusion not on the language of the statute, but on the "depravity" of those felonies:

> [T]hese offences, [involve] great moral depravity and an utter disregard of the rights of person and property. . . . The party who perpetrates, or attempts to perpetrate, [one of] those offences, intends a great wrong in the commission of the offence, and if death ensue he must take the consequences which result.[65]

In 1873 Nebraska adopted the entire Ohio criminal code, including its definitions of first- and second-degree murder.[66] The Nebraska courts did not consider the implications of this statute for felony murder until 1897. In *Henry v. State*, while overturning a first-degree murder conviction on other grounds, a court approved an instruction permitting first-degree murder if the defendant "unlawfully, purposely, and of deliberate and premeditated malice," or, in the perpetration or attempt of robbery or burglary, "unlawfully" killed the victim.[67] Later that year, a court explicitly overruled *Robbins* as authority in Nebraska, in affirming a first-degree murder conviction for killing an eleven-year-old girl in the course of rape.[68] The court noted that many other states had read felony murder rules into felony aggravator statutes.[69] The court quoted at length from Stephen's opinion in *Serné*, endorsing his proposition that "death resulting from a known dangerous act, done in the commission of a felony" is murder.[70] The court invoked Stephen's example of a rapist strangling a victim while attempting only to overpower or silence her, and approved his comment that "[i]f a man once begins attacking the human body in such way he must take the consequences if he goes further than intended when he began."[71] As in Ohio and Indiana, the Nebraska statute clearly precluded second-degree felony murder.

Washington also adopted Ohio's murder and manslaughter provisions, including its explicit rejection of second-degree felony murder.[72] First-degree felony murder liability was imposed in the 1895 case of *State v. Myers*,[73] where the victim died in a hotel fire set by the defendant. Surprisingly, the defense failed to cite *Robbins* or argue that first-degree murder required purpose to kill.

Wyoming's first murder statute replicated Indiana's variation on the Ohio statute.[74] Thus it explicitly rejected second-degree felony murder, and could be read to endorse or reject first-degree felony murder. But as there were no reported felony murder cases in Wyoming before the end of the nineteenth century, it cannot be said that Wyoming had a felony murder rule at that time.

Maine, in 1840, adopted a statute defining murder as killing with malice aforethought, express or implied, and providing that "[w]hoever shall commit murder with express malice aforethought, or in perpetrating or attempting to perpetrate any crime, punishable with death, or imprisonment . . . for life, or for an unlimited term of years, shall be deemed guilty of murder of the first degree. . . ."[75] All other murder was deemed second degree. In the 1851 case of *State v. Smith*,[76] a Maine court instructed the jury that this statute imposed murder liability for unintended "killings" in the course of any felony. The court offered, as an example of such an unintended killing, death resulting from a blow struck with a deadly weapon in overcoming resistance to a robbery. The court added that "[a]s the wilful causing of an abortion is 'punishable in the state prison,' it is a felony; and if, in the perpetration of that offence, a killing occurs, the malice, making it murder in the second degree, may be implied."[77]

Iowa adopted the Pennsylvania language with respect to the grading of murder in 1851.[78] Yet the Iowa murder provision, like the Maine statute, also defined murder as killing "with malice aforethought either express or implied . . . ."[79] The most extensive discussion of the law of first-degree felony murder was in dictum in an 1883 case of murder by poisoning:[80]

> It has been held under similar statutes that, where murder is committed in the perpetration of rape or robbery, it is not essential that there should be established that there was a specific intent to kill. It is sufficient if death ensues from violence inflicted when the defendant is engaged in the commission of the offenses named.[81]

So felony murder required violence inflicted for an appropriate felony. Iowa used such a standard in convicting two robbers of first-degree felony murder during the 1880s.[82]

Two Iowa cases considered the problem of accomplice liability for felony murder. The 1859 case of *State v. Shelledy* approved an instruction, based on Story's dictum in *Ross*, that would have imposed liability on co-felons for all "collateral" deaths.[83] *Shelledy* was not in fact a felony murder case, however. In the 1895 case of *State v. Weems*, the court disapproved an instruction that "[i]f two or more persons conspire or confederate together to commit an unlawful act, and, in pursuit of such conspiracy and commission of such unlawful act, such persons, or either of them, aided and abetted by the other, takes the life of or kills a human being, such taking of life is murder."[84] Nevertheless, the court upheld a first-degree murder conviction because it was clear that the unlawful act in question was the felony of robbery.[85]

Iowa courts considered the scope of predicate felonies for second-degree felony murder liability in a series of cases on the problem of illegal abortion resulting in the death of the pregnant woman. In the first of these, the 1868 case of State v. Moore,[86] the court upheld a second-degree murder conviction, even though abortion was only a misdemeanor, because the act causing death was both unlawful and dangerous to life. Two later cases upheld second-degree murder convictions after abortion had been graded a felony.[87]

The combination of an enumerated felony grading provision with a requirement of purpose or malice creates an indeterminate text. States adopting such statutes embraced disparate interpretations. Ohio and Wyoming recognized no felony murder rule and imposed neither first- nor second-degree felony murder liability. Indiana, Nebraska, and Washington confined felony murder to felonies enumerated by statute. Maine and Iowa equated felonious motive with "implied malice" and approved both first- and second-degree murder liability.

PATTERNS IN THE CASES

In all, twenty-two states had felony aggravator statutes in force during some part of the nineteenth century, without statutory felony murder rules.[88] In fourteen of these jurisdictions, courts created felony murder rules through statutory interpretation[89] imposing felony murder liability in a total of twenty-nine reported cases. Only four jurisdictions imposed second-degree felony murder liability for killing in the course of non-enumerated felonies,[90] in a total of six reported cases. Many courts rested the authority of first-degree felony murder liability on statutory felony aggravator provisions.[91] A number of courts explained the imposition of felony murder liability for killings in the course of enumerated felonies by asserting the special "depravity" or dangerousness of these crimes.[92] Some particularly emphasized the exploitative character of robbery and rape, which endanger their victims while appropriating them as instruments of the perpetrator's will.[93]

In addition to these limits on the predicate felonies, some courts appeared to restrict felony murder to causing death by "violent" acts, or attempts to commit bodily harm.[94] Application of felony murder rules in felony aggravator states generally conformed to this restriction. Exceptions were four second-degree murder convictions predicated on abortion, and one first-degree murder conviction predicated on the obviously reckless felony of arson.

Courts in felony aggravator jurisdictions had little to say on the question of accomplice liability for felony murder. The Pennsylvania grand juror manual appeared to condition accomplice liability for murder in the course of crime on agreement to use deadly force against resisters. One Iowa court suggested that any killing in the course of a felony would implicate all co-felons in murder,[95] while another implied that the accomplice must aid or abet a killing in furtherance of the felony to be liable for it.[96]

8 EARLY FELONY MURDER STATUTES

The majority of reported decisions imposing felony murder liability during the nineteenth century were made pursuant to felony murder statutes. Nineteen states enacted such statutes during the nineteenth century, imposing felony murder liability in fifty-three reported cases.

IMPLIED MALICE FELONY MURDER STATUTES

Ten states enacted statutes combining felony murder provisions with a requirement of "malice, express or implied." These statutes took three forms. Several were ungraded and defined implied malice by reference to Foster's phrase "abandoned and malignant heart." Another group added Pennsylvania's grading provision to this formula. Finally, Texas eschewed the "abandoned and malignant heart" phrase, added Pennsylvania's grading provision, and also added a provision transferring intent among felonies.

1. Ungraded Abandoned and Malignant Heart Statutes

Georgia's 1817 code defined murder as unlawful killing with malice aforethought either express or implied by circumstances indicating "an abandoned and malignant heart."[1] In defining unlawful act manslaughter, the code provided that an "involuntary killing . . . in the commission of an unlawful act which in its consequences, naturally tends to destroy the life of a human being, or is committed in the prosecution of a felonious or riotous intent, shall be deemed and adjudged to be murder."[2] Illinois's 1827 felony murder statute resembled Georgia's, but without riot as a predicate crime.[3] Other states adopting this basic formula were Nebraska, for a brief period,[4] and Colorado.[5] Neither appears to have applied it in a reported case during the nineteenth century.[6]

The Georgia statute appears to have been applied only once in a reported case during the nineteenth century. In the 1860 case of *McGinnis v. State*, the trial court defined riot as a "violent" act committed by two or more persons, and instructed the jury that rioters would be liable only for killings done in prosecution of the riotous intent.[7] The appellate court upheld this instruction, and offered, as an example of an unintended murder in pursuit of riotous intent, a crowd of men forcibly tying a victim to a hot air balloon that later crashed.[8]

The Illinois felony murder rule was not clarified in a reported case until the late nineteenth century.[9] In the 1879 case of *Lamb v. People*, a policeman was shot by one of a group of burglars unloading their stolen goods at a pawnshop after the burglary. The defense successfully established that accessorial liability for felony murder required agreeing to a criminal plan likely to involve the taking of life or requiring the use of force or violence.[10] The court cited the English cases of *Horsey*, which conditioned felony murder liability on the foreseeability of the death, and *Lee*, which conditioned felony murder liability on intent to commit violence.[11]

In the 1884 case of *Adams v. People*, the defendants robbed victims at gunpoint and forced them to jump from a moving train, resulting in one victim striking his head and dying.[12] The defendants appealed the trial court's refusal to instruct jurors that murder liability required that the defendants intended to kill "or that the killing was the probable and reasonable result of such jump."[13] The court responded that death need not have been probable so long as it resulted from an unlawful act committed with an intent to injure. "Malice may be inferred where an act unlawful in itself is done deliberately, and with intention of mischief or great bodily harm to those on whom it may chance to light, and death is occasioned by it."[14]

2. Graded Abandoned and Malignant Heart Statutes

Several western states combined the Georgia "abandoned and malignant heart" formula with the Pennsylvania grading rules that aggravated murder on the basis of enumerated dangerous felonies. California adopted statutory language almost identical to Illinois's in its 1850 penal code,[15] and then added Pennsylvania's grading scheme in 1856.[16] In 1874, California added mayhem to the list of enumerated felonies.[17] California courts discussed the felony murder rule in a number of nineteenth-century cases.

Dicta in several early cases suggested that there were limits to the concept of killing involuntarily in the pursuit of a felonious intent. An opinion in the 1861 case of *People v. Bealoba* implied that felony murder might require intent to harm or injure, "as if the criminal shot at the deceased for the purpose of disabling him, or the like."[18] In the 1864 case of *People v. Foren*, the California Supreme Court explained that the felony murder rule "imputed" the intent to kill required for murder on the basis of acts "malum in se" which "natural[ly]" result in death.[19] The trial court in the 1867 case of *People v. Nichol* instructed the jury that the "infliction" of "a mortal wound" under circumstances of a felony is murder.[20] California's first reported felony murder conviction was the 1865 case of *People v. Pool*,[21] in which stagecoach robbers were convicted of murder when one intentionally killed an arresting officer. The court approved an instruction that if several conspire to rob and kill all opposers if necessary, and death ensues in "the prosecution of the design, it is murder in all who are present aiding and abetting in the common design."[22]

Later California cases suggested a broader rule. In the 1874 case of *People v. Doyell*, the California Supreme Court invoked Bishop's theory of transferred or "general" intent in advocating a rule imposing murder liability for accidental death in the pursuit of any felony:

> Whenever one, in doing an act with the design of committing a felony, takes the life of another, even accidentally, this is murder. . . . The thing done having proceeded from a corrupt mind, is to be viewed the same, whether the corruption is of one particular form or another.[23]

In the 1875 case of *People v. Vasquez*, the California Supreme Court upheld a first-degree murder conviction on the instruction that

> [i]t is no defense to a party associated with others in, and engaged in a robbery, that he did not propose or intend to take life in its perpetration, or that he forbade his associates to kill, or that he disapproved or regretted that any person was thus slain by his associates. If the homicide in question was committed by one of his associates engaged in the robbery, in furtherance of their common purpose to rob, he is as accountable as though his own hand had intentionally given the fatal blow . . .[24]

The court thereby erased *Pool*'s implication that accomplice liability for felony murder depended on a contingent agreement to use deadly force if necessary.

In upholding a felony murder conviction in the 1889 case of *People v. Olsen*,[25] the California Supreme Court expanded the scope of California's felony murder rule in three ways. First, the defendant's second-degree murder conviction was predicated on larceny, confirming that non-enumerated felonies could support felony murder liability.[26] Second, the court rejected the defendant's argument that an accomplice should be liable for his co-felon's intentional killing only if it was "the ordinary and probable effect of the wrongful act especially agreed on."[27] Third, the court approved *Doyell*'s transferred-intent formula.[28]

California's legislative approach to unintended homicide was followed by several western territories. Nevada, which entered the Union in 1864, adopted the California provisions in its territorial code of 1861.[29] One early case hinted that unintentional killing in the course of any felony might be murder.[30] Nevada's first reported felony murder conviction occurred in the 1885 case of *State v. Gray*.[31] In the course of a burglary and robbery, the defendant confronted a victim with a gun. The defendant claimed he shot the victim by accident when he stumbled in trying to escape the victim's grasp. The court concluded that intent to kill was not required for a murder in the course of enumerated felonies, and that abandonment of an attempt did not eliminate a defendant's causal responsibility for its results.

The territories of Idaho and Montana also adopted the California homicide provisions and applied these statutes to provide first-degree murder liability for killings during enumerated felonies even when there was no proof of intent or premeditation.[32] Shortly before statehood, however, Idaho adopted a version of the California statute that excepted from unlawful act involuntary manslaughter any killing in the course of a felony, but did not explicitly provide that involuntary killing in the course of a felony was murder.[33] Utah adopted a similar statute,[34] which was applied in the 1900 case of *State v. Morgan*,[35] where the defendant shot and killed a pursuing officer in a gunfight after the defendant and his accomplice fled from a robbery. Citing the California case of *Bealoba*, the court reasoned that Morgan would have been guilty of first-degree murder even if his accomplice had fired the shot and had intended only to disable rather than kill. A shared commitment to forcibly resist arrest for the felony would make a co-felon guilty of first-degree murder.[36] Implicitly, mere participation in the felony would not.

3. The Texas "Transferred-Intent" Statute

Texas was the site of about one-fourth of the reported American felony murder convictions during the nineteenth century. The Texas penal code, as amended in 1858, provided that "[e]very person with a sound memory and discretion, who shall unlawfully kill any reasonable creature in being within this State, with malice aforethought, either express or implied, shall be deemed guilty of murder."[37] It included a grading scheme based on the Pennsylvania statute, which aggravated murder committed with "express malice" or in the perpetration or

attempt of enumerated felonies.[38] The code defined two other homicide offenses: voluntary manslaughter and negligent homicide. Voluntary manslaughter was confined to intentional killing.[39] Negligent homicide in the second degree comprised causing death by negligence in the course of a misdemeanor or
civil wrong.[40] The code added cryptically, "When one in the execution of, or in
attempting to execute, an act made a felony by the penal law, shall kill another,
though without an apparent intention to kill, the offence does not come within
the definition of negligent homicide."[41] So the only possible category for such
unintentional killings was murder based on implied malice. Finally, the code
included a provision transferring intent among felonies: "If one intending to
commit a felony, and in the act of preparing for or executing the same, shall,
through mistake or accident, do another act, which, if voluntarily done, would
be a felony, he shall receive the punishment affixed by law to the offence actually committed."[42]

The concepts of express and implied malice were defined in the important 1860 case of *McCoy v. State*,[43] which relied on Blackstone and on Hale's
discussion of *Salisbury*. The court defined express malice as the intent to kill
or seriously injure the victim or *any person opposing a felony*; or to commit *an
unlawful act likely to kill the victim*. Implied malice was simply the transferring
of any of these intentions to a victim outside of the class of intended victims.[44]
Thus defined, malice excludes any general rule imposing murder liability for
accidental killings in the course of felonies. If the risk of harm intended to be-
fall one victim is misdirected onto another victim, a resulting death is not accidental: only the identity of the victim is an accident. The *McCoy* court seemed
willing to transfer the intent to commit a felony to the death of a victim only if
the felony involved violence or great risk.

The 1879 case of *Pharr v. State*[45] reasserted the independent significance of
the malice requirement. Pharr shot his victim in the head and took his effects,
but claimed to have shot him in self-defense. The Texas Court of Appeals overturned his first-degree murder conviction, complaining that

> the court charged, in effect, that if the jury believed that the . . . killing was
> unlawful . . . and was committed in the perpetration or in the attempt at the
> perpetration of robbery . . . then the jury were instructed to find the defendant
> guilty of murder in the first degree. The defect in this portion of the charge is
> that it ignores malice, the indispensable requisite in all murder; without malice,
> either express or implied, there can be no murder.[46]

The 1895 case of *Richards v. State*[47] established that non-enumerated felonies could support second-degree felony murder, and that the felony murder rule was based on the intent-transferring provision. Richards unintentionally shot and killed his victim while attempting to murder her husband. Since murder is not one of the enumerated felonies supporting first-degree felony murder, Richards was charged with and convicted of second-degree murder. The court reasoned that the common law concept of malice included transferred intent to kill,[48] so the Texas penal code provision transferring intent from one felony to another could support murder liability.[49] The court added that it was a "well settled" rule that "where a party, in attempting to commit a felony, kills another, whether by accident or intention, with malice aforethought, nothing less than murder could be the result."[50] Thus if and only if the predicate felony involved malice towards someone, that malice could transfer to a different victim killed unintentionally.

While malice remained an independent element of felony murder, a felonious purpose could make a killing malicious that would not be otherwise. In the 1899 case of *Hedrick v. State*,[51] the defendant was convicted of first-degree murder when he killed a resisting victim during a burglary. The defendant shot blindly when the victim attempted to wrest his gun away from him. The court rejected the defendant's requested instruction that to be convicted of first-degree murder, he must have committed what would be at least second-degree murder absent the burglary.[52] Yet the court reiterated that "a party could commit a homicide in the perpetration of burglary, and not be guilty of either [first- or second-degree] murder."[53] The *Hedrick* court reaffirmed the holding of *McCoy* that an unlawful act likely to kill—a reckless act—would supply the requisite malice.

Texas felony murder cases reflected these limits. Every reported conviction was predicated on an enumerated felony except for *Richards*, which was predicated on murder. Moreover, almost all of the cases involved the deliberate infliction of violence. One defendant slashed his robbery victim's throat and shot him in the head.[54] Another bound his robbery victim and shot him in the head.[55] Yet another shot two robbery victims repeatedly at point-blank range.[56] In *Wilkins v. State*,[57] the defendant shot his robbery victim with both a pistol and a shotgun, and boarded up the victim's house to conceal the body. In *Elizando v. State*,[58] the defendant beat a feeble elderly robbery victim and then shot him in the back of the head. Three other defendants shot their robbery victims.[59] One burglar deliberately split a victim's head open with an axe.[60] Another burglar robbed and raped the victim and then slashed her throat from ear to ear.[61] In *Cook v. State*,[62] the defendant instead strangled his rape victim. Several robbers bludgeoned their victims to death.[63] Three of these defendants concealed or burned the body.[64]

In four Texas cases robbers were held liable for murder without having had the intent to injure or kill. One of these was a train robbery where the robbers deliberately wrecked the train, with predictable, albeit unintended, loss of life.[65] The other three cases involved shootings where robbers were liable although physically remote from the scene of the killing.[66] In *Darlington v. State*, for example, the court held accomplices responsible for killings that were "natural and probable consequences likely to result" from a robbery.[67]

FELONY MURDER STATUTES WITHOUT MALICE

Statutes in four states—New York, Mississippi, Missouri, and Oregon—identified unintended killings in the course of felonies as first- or second-degree murder.

In 1829, New York adopted a provision defining the killing of a human being, without the authority of law, as murder "[w]hen perpetrated without any design to effect death, by a person engaged in the commission of any felony."[68] In 1860, New York divided murder into degrees, along the lines of the Pennsylvania statute.[69] Eventually, in 1873, New York expanded first-degree felony murder to include killing in the course of any felony.[70]

Early cases suggested a very broad felony murder rule. In 1834, an appellate panel of the New York Supreme Court argued that, rather than creating a new crime, the felony murder provision reduced the scope of the unlawful act murder doctrine Coke had attributed to the common law.[71] On further appeal, the Court for the Correction of Errors commented that

> [m]alice was implied in many cases at the common law, where it was evident that the offenders could not have had any intention of destroying human life, merely on the ground that the homicide was committed while the person who did the act was engaged in the commission of some other felony, or in an attempt to perpetrate some offence of that grade . . . [N]early all [felonies] were punishable with death . . . . In such cases, therefore, the malicious and premeditated intent to perpetrate one kind of felony, was, by implication of law, transferred from such offense to the homicide which was actually committed, so as to make the latter offence a killing with malice aforethought, contrary to the real fact of the case as it appeared in evidence. This principle is still retained in the law of homicide . . . [72]

Thus the court adopted an account of the felony murder rule that accorded with Hawkins' "general rule" of transferred culpability among felonies.

Yet the New York courts did impose some limits on this broad rule, beginning with the 1838 case of *People v. Rector*, which embraced Hawkins' merger limitation.[73] This required that the predicate felony have some purpose independent of the victim's death or serious injury. Absent this limitation, all manslaughters would be automatically aggravated to murders. The court upheld a murder conviction, on grounds that a fatal assault with a heavy iron bar reflected depraved indifference to human life. Yet the court rejected a felony murder theory, dismissing the argument "that the blow cannot be a misdemeanor when it results in death, because the act is then a felony, to wit, manslaughter, ergo it is murder."[74]

A second area of limitation was accomplice liability. An 1845 decision, *People v. Van Steenburgh*,[75] recorded the murder conviction of two men for killing a sheriff "without design to effect death," in the perpetration of the felony of riot or resistance to legal process while being armed or disguised. The defendants were participants in a mob of about 150 men who assembled to prevent the sale of a tenant farmer's personal property to pay back rent. Several of these men followed the order of a leader to fire at the horses of those conducting the sale. The sheriff was wounded and died. While some fifty participants were convicted of varying crimes, only two were convicted of murder, apparently because they were seen firing their guns. The restriction of murder liability to identified shooters, but without proof that they shot the fatal bullets, suggests that murder liability hinged on aiding or encouraging the shooting, and not just joining the underlying felony.

An 1871 case, *Ruloff v. People*,[76] involved an intentional killing of a resisting store clerk during a burglary. The court held that all three burglars were liable for the killing "[i]f . . . committed . . . in the prosecution of an unlawful purpose or common design" and "[i]f there was a general resolution against all opposers, and to resist to the utmost all attempts to detain or hold in custody any of the parties."[77] Yet in the 1895 case *People v. Wilson*, the court rejected an instruction that one burglar who assaulted an arresting officer was not guilty of his partner's killing of the same officer unless he had agreed to it.[78]

The New York felony murder rule was broad in two ways. First, it was applied to felonies beyond the usual quartet of burglary, robbery, rape, and arson. Reported murder convictions were predicated on such felonies as grand larceny,[79] assault or unauthorized entry by a "tramp,"[80] attempted murder of another victim,[81] and escape.[82]

New York law also expanded the category of killing beyond simply shooting or stabbing. In two cases felons clubbed victims with iron bars.[83] In *Buel v. People*,[84] where the defendant strangled a rape victim, the court affirmed an instruction that the defendant was guilty of murder even if he had put the rope around the victim's neck only in order to silence or restrain rather than kill her. In *Cox v. People*,[85] the victim died in a struggle with a burglar, perhaps of a heart attack. The court commented, "If his violence so excited the terror of the deceased that she died from the fright, and she would not have died except for the assault, then the prisoner's act was in law the cause of her death."[86] Even this heart attack case—unique in nineteenth-century American felony murder law—still was predicated on an act of violence.

In 1839, Mississippi adopted New York's murder definition, imposing murder liability for unintended killings in the course of any felony.[87] Then, in 1857, the Mississippi legislature limited felony murder to unintended killings in the course of the enumerated felonies of rape, burglary, arson, and robbery.[88] The 1858 case of *Mask v. State*[89] involved a shooting preceding this change. Mask went to the house of R. J. Smith to shoot him for having testified against Mask. Mask wounded Smith's son, William, and then killed Smith's daughter, Susan, when she told him to leave. The Mississippi Supreme Court upheld an instruction that the jury should convict for murder "if . . . the defendant was endeavoring to kill William Smith, or commit a felony upon him, and killed in that attempt the deceased, either accidentally or willfully."[90] The court treated this instruction as harmless error, because instructions were also given on a theory of intentional murder, which the court deemed proven beyond a reasonable doubt.[91] It seems the Mississippi court was reluctant to predicate felony murder on assault, because of the lack of a sufficiently independent felonious purpose.[92]

Missouri's first homicide statute, passed in 1825, simply punished murder without defining it.[93] Missouri adopted the Pennsylvania grading scheme in 1845, but added the phrase "or [any] other felony" to the Pennsylvania enumeration of felonies triggering first-degree murder liability.[94] Missouri's 1845 legislation also contained an implied felony murder provision in an elliptical definition of involuntary manslaughter:

> The killing of a human being, without a design to effect death, by the act, procurement or culpable negligence of another, while such other is engaged in the perpetration or attempt to perpetrate any crime or misdemeanor, not amounting to a felony, in cases when such killing would be murder at the common law, shall be deemed manslaughter in the first degree.[95]

The exclusion of felonies from the class of crimes supporting involuntary manslaughter implied murder liability for at least some unintended killings in the course of at least some felonies. Yet these would have been restricted to unintended killings that would have been murders at common law, arguably those involving intentional injuries or the use of violence.

Since both the Missouri and the New York statutes restricted unlawful act murder at common law to murders in the course of felonies, the two statutes posed similar interpretive problems, especially during the periods when each statute graded all murder in the course of felonies as murder in the first degree. In 1879, however, the Missouri legislature restricted first-degree felony murder to the enumerated felonies of arson, burglary, rape, robbery, and mayhem.[96]

The Missouri Supreme Court applied the 1845 murder statute in two first-degree murder cases in the 1850s involving the predicate felony of assault with intent to injure, *State v. Jennings* and *State v. Nueslein*.[97] The use of felony assault as a predicate felony in these two cases implied a rejection of New York's requirement of an independent felonious purpose.

Two Missouri Supreme Court cases from 1877 supported the view that all homicide in the course of felonies was murder. In *State v. Wieners*,[98] the court defined malice as the unlawful infliction of bodily harm[99] or the commission of a dangerous and unlawful act.[100] Yet the court then concluded that "[i]f one in perpetrating or attempting to perpetrate a felony, kill a human being, such killing is murder, although not specifically intended, for the law attaches the intent to commit the other felony to the homicide. The law conclusively presumes the intent to kill."[101] In *State v. Green*,[102] the court upheld a first-degree murder conviction based on the predicate felony of resisting arrest for a felony. The court cited *Jennings* and *Wieners* in support of the principle that homicide in the course of any felony was murder.[103]

These cases provoked a reassessment of the felony murder rule in Missouri. An 1878 article in Missouri's *Central Law Journal* invoked Wharton's then-recent critique of felony murder liability, condemned the *Wieners* decision, and insisted that the Missouri statute punished only malicious killings in the course of felonies as murder.[104] The author proposed a definition of malice as "a condition of the mind evidenced by the intentional doing of a wrongful act, not in the 'heat of passion,' which might reasonably be expected to result in death or bodily harm to some human being."[105]

Also in 1878, the Missouri Supreme Court embraced New York's requirement of an independent predicate felony, thereby overruling *Jennings*. In the case of *State v. Shock*, the court overturned a first-degree murder conviction for the killing of a child in a vicious beating.[106] The court held that the felony of inflicting great bodily harm could not support felony murder:

> [T]he words "other felony" used in the first section refer to some collateral felony, and not to those acts of personal violence to the deceased which are necessary and constituent elements of the homicide itself, and are, therefore, merged in it, and which do not, when consummated, constitute an offense distinct from the homicide.[107]

The court also implied that in future cases it would hold that only the traditional common law felonies would support felony murder liability.[108] The following year these views prevailed in the Missouri legislature, as the murder statute was revised to predicate first-degree murder only on arson, burglary, robbery, rape, and mayhem.[109] During the remainder of the nineteenth century, there were no reported convictions of second-degree felony murder, that is, murder predicated on non-enumerated felonies.

The Missouri Supreme Court temporarily restricted Missouri's felony murder rule even further. In the 1879 case of *State v. Earnest*,[110] the court upheld a first-degree murder conviction for the killing of a robbery victim, but rejected as harmless error the trial court's instruction that any homicide committed in the course of any felony was first-degree murder. By a 3–2 majority, the court held that "[t]he statute does not declare that every homicide committed in the perpetration, or attempt to perpetrate, any arson, rape, robbery, &c., shall be murder in the first degree, but that any murder, so committed, shall be deemed murder of the first degree."[111] The same justices reiterated this position in the 1880 case of *State v. Hopper*,[112] this time citing Wharton.[113]

By 1884, however, the makeup of the Missouri Supreme Court had changed. In *State v. Hopkirk*,[114] a 3–2 majority of the court rejected *Earnest* and *Hopper*. In affirming a first-degree murder conviction for the killing of a robbery victim, the court reasoned that while the grading provision made "no homicide murder that was not murder at common law," the common law had provided "that a homicide committed in the perpetration of a felony was murder . . . whether there was any precedent intention of doing the homicidal act or not."[115] Subsequent to this decision, there were five more reported felony murder convictions during the nineteenth century, all involving killings in the course of robberies.[116] The ultimate result, then, was a compromise between those who regarded the enumerated felonies merely as a grading element for intentional murders and those who saw unintended killings in the course of any felony as murder. Henceforth, murder liability for unintended killings would be conditioned only on enumerated felonies.

Oregon adopted a criminal code in 1864 with a grading provision[117] identical to the Ohio provision held to require purpose to kill in *Robbins*. Yet Oregon combined this first-degree murder provision with two provisions implying that purpose was not required for first-degree murder. One prescribed that "[t]here shall be some other evidence of malice than the mere proof of the killing, to constitute murder in the first degree, unless the killing was effected in the commission or attempt to commit a felony . . ."[118] The other was Oregon's second-degree murder provision: "If any person shall purposely and maliciously, but without deliberation and premeditation, or in the commission or attempt to commit any felony, other than rape, arson, robbery or burglary, kill another, such person shall be deemed guilty of murder in the second degree."[119] This implied that nonpurposeful killings would be second-degree murder if committed during non-enumerated felonies. In the 1879 case of *State v. Brown*, the defendants robbed a pawnshop, knocking the proprietor out cold.[120] A policeman pursued them for a few blocks, whereupon they stopped and Brown shot at him, killing a bystander. The court rejected the authority of *Robbins*,[121] and upheld an instruction that "it is not necessary to prove . . . a purpose to kill" which would be "implied" by a killing during robbery.[122] While Oregon's statute clearly imposed second-degree felony murder liability, Oregon had no reported second-degree felony murder cases during the nineteenth century.

THIRD-DEGREE FELONY MURDER STATUTES

Three states, Wisconsin, Florida, and Minnesota, graded killings "without design to effect death" in the course of any felony as third-degree murder. These statutes were rarely used.

Wisconsin's 1849 criminal code prescribed that "[t]he killing of a human being, without the authority of law . . . [w]hen perpetrated without any design to effect death, by a person engaged in the commission of any felony shall be murder in the third degree, and shall be punished by imprisonment . . . not more than fourteen years nor less than seven years."[123] Second-degree murder required killing by a dangerous act manifesting depraved indifference to human life, while first-degree murder required premeditated intent to kill.[124] One robber was convicted of third-degree murder when his co-felon shot a victim. The trial court instructed the jury that the defendant's participation in the robbery made her guilty of third-degree murder even if she had no expectation that her co-felon would kill.[125] Wisconsin rejected the merger doctrine, permitting assault[126] and maiming[127] as predicate felonies for third-degree murder. The Wisconsin Supreme Court reversed several third-degree murder convictions on the ground that the predicate felony had not been proven.[128] In another case, the court imposed a narrow time frame on the predicate felony, holding that an assault on one victim concluded the instant the defendant turned his attention to attacking the victim he killed.[129]

Minnesota adopted Wisconsin's three-degree scheme in 1853,[130] but did not apply the felony murder provision in any reported case. Florida, from the time of its admission to the Union until 1868, left the definition of murder to the common law.[131] In 1868, however, Florida adopted the Wisconsin statute.[132] Florida's only reported third-degree murder conviction during the nineteenth century was overturned.[133] One court suggested that dangerous felonies would give rise to second-degree murder liability because they inherently manifested depraved indifference to human life.[134] Finally, in 1892, unintended killings in the course of the traditional quartet of dangerous felonies—arson, rape, robbery, and burglary—were moved up to first-degree murder.[135]

DANGEROUS FELONIES STATUTES

In addition to Mississippi (after 1857), two other states adopted statutes conditioning murder liability on causing death in the course of particular dangerous felonies: New Jersey and Alabama. These two statutes were little used.

In 1829, New Jersey enacted a provision that conditioned murder liability on enumerated felonies or other unlawful acts dangerous to human life: "[I]f any person . . . in committing, or attempting to commit sodomy, rape, arson, robbery or burglary, or any unlawful act against the peace of this state, of which the probable consequence may be bloodshed, shall kill another, or if the death of any one shall ensue . . . such . . . persons . . . shall be adjudged guilty of murder, and shall suffer death."[136] The New Jersey Supreme Court applied this statute in the 1833 case of State v. Cooper, holding that a conviction for arson barred a subsequent conviction for murder resulting from the arson.[137] The court read the statute as an expression of the "well established principle of the common law, that if a person, whilst doing or attempting to do another act, undesignedly kill a man, if the act done or attempted, were a felony, the killing is murder; especially if death were a probable consequence of the act."[138] Thus the court inferred that those felonies enumerated by the statute were selected because of their dangerousness to human life. This understanding of the purpose of felony murder liability as punishment for the consequences of culpable risk explains the court's position on the double jeopardy question. The arson rendered the killing culpable because of its danger to life. Thus, to punish the killing on top of the arson would punish the same act of risk taking twice.[139] New Jersey had no reported felony murder convictions during the nineteenth century.

Alabama adopted the Pennsylvania grading language in 1841, although with two pertinent differences. First, rather than defining first-degree murder to include all *murder* committed in the perpetration or attempts to perpetrate enumerated felonies, the Alabama statute defined first degree to include all *homicide* committed under such circumstances.[140] In this way, Alabama implied that reckless or negligent killing in the course of enumerated felonies would be murder. Second, the Alabama statute defined second-degree murder as all other homicide constituting "murder at the common law."[141] This provision left open the question of second-degree felony murder for unintended killing in the course of non-enumerated felonies, although no second-degree felony murder convictions appear in the reported Alabama cases from the nineteenth century.

The Alabama felony murder provision was little applied, but Alabama courts explained felony murder liability as a form of transferred intent. The 1862 case of *Isham v. State*[142] concerned the offense of "voluntary manslaughter of a white man" by a slave, the races of the parties constituting an aggravating circumstance. The victim was a member of a slave patrol disguised in blackface. In holding that the race of the victim was a strict liability element, the court invoked the felony murder doctrine as evidence that the criminal law did not require a strict correlation between the wrong intended and the wrong punished.[143] Commenting on Bacon's principle of the transferability of intent to crimes of like grade, the court argued:

> If the maxim import that there must be a perfect correspondence between the intent and the act, it can not be harmonized with principles too well established to be controverted. A homicide, not intended, but committed, in the perpetration of burglary or arson, would be murder, notwithstanding the offenses intended are not, in our law, of as high a grade, or subject to as severe penalties, as murder.[144]

In *Kilgore v. State*,[145] a felony murder conviction based upon the repeated stabbing of a prostrate robbery victim, the court explained that the criminal intent involved in the statutorily enumerated felonies "determines the character of the unlawful killing perpetrated in their commission."[146]

While Mississippi restricted its New York–style felony murder statute to enumerated dangerous felonies after 1857, the revised statute yielded no reported convictions during the remainder of the century.[147]

ORIGINAL LIMITS OF AMERICAN FELONY MURDER RULES: PREDICATE FELONIES

Our review of applications of felony murder rules in nineteenth-century America shows that felony murder rules were usually limited in two ways: by predicate felony and by means of killing. Each of these limitations effectively conditioned felony murder on culpability and prevented imposition of strict liability for accidental death.

Many nineteenth-century American felony murder rules predicated murder liability on enumerated dangerous felonies. Of fourteen states applying enumerated felony aggravator statutes to impose felony murder liability,[148] ten did so only in cases predicated on enumerated felonies.[149] In all, twenty-three of twenty-nine felony murder convictions in states with felony aggravator statutes were first-degree felony murder convictions predicated on enumerated felonies. Six[150] of the eight[151] states with both felony murder statutes and grading based on enumerated felonies did not impose second-degree murder liability at all. In these eight graded felony murder states, there were thirty-four first-degree murder convictions predicated on enumerated felonies and just two second-degree murder convictions predicated on non-enumerated felonies.[152] Altogether, of twenty-two states that had felony aggravator grading statutes and also enacted felony murder rules (whether legislatively or judicially), sixteen restricted felony murder to enumerated felonies. Those states that did predicate second-degree felony murder on non-enumerated felonies did so rarely. Only eight of sixty-five reported felony murder convictions in states with enumerated felony aggravator provisions involved non-enumerated felonies.[153] The predicate felony in four of these cases was abortion,[154] and in one was theft under circumstances that could have been charged as robbery.[155] The other cases were based on the dangerous predicate felonies of murder[156] and robbery.[157]

Two explanations are possible for this pattern of disuse of second-degree felony murder liability. First, prosecutors and courts may have understood the statutory enumeration of predicate felonies to be exhaustive. In Indiana, for example, courts recognized only a first-degree felony murder rule, rejecting murder charges based on even the non-enumerated felony of murder.[158] Alabama's felony murder statute predicated felony murder liability only on enumerated felonies, as did Mississippi's after 1857.[159] Missouri's legislature restricted first-degree felony murder to enumerated felonies immediately after the Missouri Supreme Court suggested that only such felonies supplied the requisite malice for murder.[160]

Second, prosecutors and courts may have seen enumerations as illustrative of the type of dangerous felonies that merited felony murder liability. In Texas, for example, the penal code's provision on transferring intent among felonies clearly established second-degree felony murder liability for unintentional killing in the course of non-enumerated felonies. Yet the Texas code also required malice, which the case of *McCoy v. State*[161] defined as intent to kill, intent to injure, or recklessness. Texas courts required a knowing imposition of a probability of death in felony murder cases.[162] Of twenty-two Texas felony murder convictions during the nineteenth century, only one, *Richards v. State*,[163] was predicated on a non-enumerated felony, murder of another victim. This was also the only Texas felony murder case to specifically cite the intent-transferring provision. It seems that, outside the context of enumerated felonies, Texas courts construed the intent-transferring provision in the narrowest possible way, so as to conform to the requirement of malice.

Courts in other states connected malice with dangerousness as well. In Massachusetts, courts endorsed second-degree felony murder liability in the abstract,[164] but apparently never applied it. Here, too, they appeared to take the enumerated felonies as prototypes for the coercive and dangerous imposition of risk that implied malice.[165] In Pennsylvania, which reported no second-degree felony murder convictions during the nineteenth century, courts saw the special danger and moral "turpitude" attending the enumerated felonies as grounds for not requiring "intention."[166] In Michigan, which reported no second-degree felony murder convictions, one court reasoned that the predicate felony must display as much "malice" and "depravity" as murder to justify the transferring of intent.[167] In Connecticut, which reported no second-degree felony murder convictions during the nineteenth century, Justice Swift's influential treatise had argued that intent-transferring should be limited to capital crimes. In California, which reported no second-degree felony murder convictions until late in the nineteenth century, an early opinion conditioned intent-transferring on acts malum in se and dangerous to life.[168] So it appears that, across many states, courts took the enumerated aggravating felonies as models for the kind of morally reprehensible and dangerous felony that would support murder liability for unintended killing.

Where jurisdictions did not enumerate felonies, they still tended to require that predicate felonies be dangerous to life. New Jersey's felony murder statute did so explicitly.[169] Illinois construed its "abandoned and malignant heart" felony murder statute to require some degree of dangerousness to life.[170] Of twenty felony murder convictions in jurisdictions without enumerated predicate felonies, ten involved the traditional predicate felonies of arson, rape, robbery, and burglary.[171] Several others were predicated on felonies involving violence, such as the murder of another victim,[172] escape or resisting arrest,[173] and "inflicting great bodily harm."[174] Many of the remaining predicate offenses (e.g., riot,[175] assault by a tramp,[176] and suicide[177]) raise troubling issues, but are nevertheless violent felonies. One conviction was predicated on mere "theft."[178]

Overall, sixty-seven of our eighty-five nineteenth-century felony murder convictions were predicated on the traditional predicate felonies of robbery,[179] burglary,[180] rape,[181] and arson,[182] with more than half being predicated on robbery. An additional seven convictions were predicated on the clearly dangerous felonies of murder,[183] prison break or resisting arrest,[184] and inflicting grievous bodily injury.[185] The remaining eleven convictions were based on the more dubious predicates of riot,[186] theft, [187] assault by a tramp,[188] abortion,[189] and suicide.[190] Finally, two other limitations on predicate felonies were developed in the relatively few jurisdictions with felony murder statutes unrestricted by enumerated felonies or dangerousness limitations. One was the requirement of independent felonious purpose, developed in New York[191] and briefly applied in Missouri[192] and, possibly, Mississippi.[193] Any jurisdiction that restricts felony murder liability to the traditional enumerated felonies also thereby imposes a requirement of independent felonious purpose, as these all involve aims distinct from simply injuring or endangering the victim. Where jurisdictions did not require dangerousness, they sometimes limited the punishment imposed for felony murder. In Wisconsin, Minnesota, and Florida, felony murder was graded as murder in the third degree, subject to a minimum term of only seven years of incarceration, comparable to penalties for manslaughter in some other states.[194]

The limitation of predicate felonies to dangerous felonies ensures that felony murder is not a crime of strict liability with respect to the risk of death, but is instead conditioned on a form of per se gross negligence. To commit a dangerous felony is to create a particularly unjustifiable risk of death. The reasonable person is on notice that the felony is considered very dangerous because it is proscribed and severely punished. If the felony is an enumerated predicate for unintentional murder, this notice is even more explicit. The requirement of an independent felonious purpose, whether accomplished through a "merger" doctrine or an enumeration of predicate felonies, ensures that murder liability is also conditioned on an evil motive and not merely on a miscalculation of risks.

ORIGINAL LIMITS ON FELONY MURDER: MEANS OF KILLING

Perhaps the most important limitation on felony murder liability in nineteenth-century America is also the least apparent to modern observers. For modern lawyers, murder means causing death with one of a number of culpable mental states. By "causing death," the modern lawyer means committing an act or omission that is a necessary condition to a death. By contrast, lawyers in the seventeenth and eighteenth centuries conceived of murder as killing absent certain exculpatory or mitigating circumstances. Ordinarily, the malice characterizing murder was implicit in the act of killing, a hostile and dangerous attack on the person, which happened to prove fatal. The nineteenth-century statutes and cases defining felony murder marked an intermediate point between these two conceptions of murder. Legislators and judges struggled to define the mental element of murder, but they also retained an older conception of killing as an inherently malicious act. These statutes and cases narrowed the scope of common law murder not because they restricted a preexisting felony murder doctrine, but because they restricted a preexisting unintentional murder doctrine to killings in furtherance of certain felonies.

Nineteenth-century statutes and cases rarely conditioned murder liability merely on maliciously "causing death." They defined murder as malicious "killing," and felony murder as "killing" in the course of certain felonies. And the nineteenth-century usage of "killing" in felony murder cases shows that the term had a much narrower meaning than causing death or even causing death foreseeably. This narrower concept of "killing" is discernible in the 1864 English case of R. v. Lee: "[I]f a man in the committal of a felony uses violence to the person, which causes death, even although he did not intend it, he is guilty of murder . . . ."[195] The major late-nineteenth-century English cases on the felony murder rule, R. v. Desmond and R. v. Serné, expanded the category of killing beyond fatal battery to include causing death by recklessly subjecting others to the great dangers of explosives or fire.[196] We see a similar notion of killing in American felony murder cases in the nineteenth century. "Killing" usually referred to causing death by intentionally injuring another. In a much smaller number of cases, it referred to causing death by doing an unlawful act imposing obvious dangers of death. Conceived this narrowly, a "killing" was always a criminal offense, unless justified or excused. If so, a crime of "killing" in the attempt of a serious felony always involved a culpable attack on the victim.

The method of killing was described in seventy-nine of the eighty-five reported felony murder convictions we have reviewed.[197] A total of thirty-four cases involved causing death by intentionally shooting another person.[198] In an additional thirty cases, death resulted from some form of direct physical contact by the perpetrator, aimed at injuring, hurting, or physically controlling the victim. Five involved stabbing or slashing (although one was also a shooting case, counted previously),[199] six involved strangling or drowning,[200] and twelve involved blows to the head.[201] In eight cases, the victim died as a result of some other sort of battery. One of these was a prolonged whipping.[202] One was an undisclosed infliction of "great bodily harm,"[203] and another was a killing by some unstated "force and violence."[204] There were two other cases of beatings.[205] One victim died during a struggle with a burglar.[206] Two child rape victims died of various wounds and lacerations.[207] In addition to these sixty-four cases of shooting or direct battery, there were three cases of death from intentional battery by less direct means. One was an intentional burning: robbers beat their victim unconscious and set fire to the building in which they left him.[208] Another group of robbers forced their victim to leap from a speeding train, and he died on impact.[209] The third case was an intentional poisoning, although not intended to be fatal: a rapist deceived his victim into taking a knockout drug.[210] Like shooting, these three cases involve intentionally harming or incapacitating a victim through physically remote means. Accordingly, they should be seen as unproblematic applications of the concept of battery. Altogether, sixty-seven of the seventy-nine nineteenth-century American felony murder cases for which we know the cause of death involved death by intentional battery.

The remaining twelve cases involve metaphoric extensions of this core concept, some more defensible than others. In seven cases, the victims did not die from the direct effects of intentional battery. Instead, they died because the defendants recklessly subjected them to a substantial danger of death. In one case, the defendants deliberately wrecked a train in order to rob it.[211] Another set of train robbers knowingly forced a railroad employee into a crossfire between robbers and resisters.[212] In two other cases, arsonists unintentionally caused the deaths of residents of hotels they burned down.[213] One rapist attacked his victim in a rowboat, threatening to drown her; she fell overboard during the struggle and did drown.[214] One death resulted from bank robbers shooting at random in a town in order to create a diversion.[215] Another involved shooting at the victim's mount.[216] In all of these cases, the defendants at least should have been aware that they were subjecting others to a substantial risk of death. Because these defendants were very culpable regarding these deaths, it seems fair to regard them as "killers," even though they did not cause death by intentional battery.

But the five remaining cases seem further removed from the core concept of death-by-battery, and so are less appropriately called "killings." These involved a botched suicide[217] and four botched abortions.[218] None were intentional batteries, because they directed force at a consenting recipient. They may have involved danger, but lacked the hostility to the interests of others associated with malice. Of course, the analysis of abortion changes if we view abortion as an unjustified assault on the life of the fetus. I think we must assume that those courts that predicated felony murder on abortion did view abortion in this way. If abortion is taken as a form of intentional homicide that also poses inherent risks to the life of the mother, then the unintended death of the mother seems as much a "killing" as any other instance of killing the "wrong" victim. Thus construed, the abortion-murder cases support rather than disconfirm our account of killing as organized around the paradigm of death by intentional battery. But even on antiabortion premises, we should still be troubled by felony murder liability for an abortionist who "kills" the pregnant woman. If abortion is felonious homicide, the consenting mother is a co-felon. And we have seen no other cases in nineteenth-century America of felony murder liability for the death of a co-felon. When the victim consents to risk, it is hard to say that an unintended death expresses sufficient disrespect to warrant murder liability.

Indeed, in order to see how limited felony murder liability was in nineteenth-century America, it is worth pointing out some of the other fact patterns missing from our litany of nineteenth-century American felony murder cases. Not only are there no cases in which the victim was a co-felon, but there is only one case in which the act causing death may have been committed by someone other than a felon.[219] In this one case, liability was premised on the defendant knowingly forcing the victim into the path of gunfire. There are no cases of a victim voluntarily contributing to his or her own death. There are no suicides, no voluntary drug overdoses, no overzealous police officers plunging off roofs or into icy rivers or in front of carriages while pursuing felons. There are no cases of victims having heart attacks out of mere fright (although there is one case in which a victim died while struggling with an assailant).[220] There are no cases of victims maltreated at hospitals, or getting killed accidentally in traffic. Notably, there are no cases of feloniously shooting at livestock or game and unforeseeably hitting a man. The exception that proves this rule is the one case involving an animal as a target, the *Van Steenburgh* case, where the defendant recklessly shot at a mounted horse.[221]

By conditioning felony murder on "killing," nineteenth-century American law restricted it to nonconsensual contact intended to injure or compel, or the unlawful imposition of patent danger to life. This understanding of killing as causing death by violence or unlawful risk taking effectively built culpability into the *actus reus* element of felony murder.

NINETEENTH-CENTURY LIMITS ON COMPLICITY IN FELONY MURDER

A narrow conception of killing may ensure that principals convicted of felony murder acted with substantial culpability, but what about accomplices? If an accomplice in a felony did not share in the intent to injure or endanger a victim, could he or she still be liable for felony murder in nineteenth-century America? A partial answer to this question is provided by the limitation of predicate felonies. The requisite culpability inheres in felonies necessarily involving danger (arson, murder, perhaps burglary of a dwelling) or forcible compulsion (robbery, rape, resisting arrest, forcible escape). Participation in such felonies therefore inculpates accomplices as long as the death is within the scope of the danger ordinarily imposed by the predicate felony.

Few American jurisdictions clearly determined the scope of accomplice liability for felony murders during the nineteenth century. Courts or legislatures addressed the issue in only eleven jurisdictions.[222] These few jurisdictions articulated disparate and potentially conflicting standards. At least four different standards of accomplice liability for felony murder appeared in the American case law and treatise literature.

Collateral deaths. The most expansive standard of accomplice liability was Justice Story's proposal that all deaths occurring "collateral" to a federal felony would result in murder liability for all co-felons, a proposal later rejected in *U.S. v. Boyd.* Wharton endorsed Story's "collateral death" standard in the first edition of his homicide treatise, but later rejected felony murder liability altogether. The Iowa Supreme Court approved Story's standard in dictum in *Shelledy,*[223] but declined to follow it in the felony murder case of *Weems.*[224]

Killings in furtherance of the felony. Iowa's *Weems* case implicitly made complicity in felony murder hinge on whether the killing was in furtherance of the felonious aims agreed to.[225] Similar requirements that the killing be instrumental to the felony were also supported by the Pennsylvania grand juror's manual,[226] and by cases in Georgia, California, and New York.[227]

Foreseeable killings. Several courts required that co-felons complicit in felony murder be in a position to anticipate violence or the danger of death. Decisions in Illinois required that death be a "probable" result of the act agreed to[228] or that accomplices agreed to an act of violence.[229] A Texas case required that death be a "natural and probable consequence" of the act agreed to,[230] while a Utah case required that the accomplice share an intent to use force.[231] New York's *Van Steenburgh* case perhaps limited murder liability to those rioters who actually fired guns. On the other hand, several courts rejected a requirement that accomplices in a felony murder agree to or expect a killing.[232]

Resolutions to overcome resistance. Finally, several courts and commentators invoked the accessorial liability standard from *Lord Dacre*, which implicated all those accomplices who joined in a "resolution against opposers."[233] Supporters of this "resolution" test included Webb's treatise on colonial Virginia law,[234] Toulmin and Blair's official commentary on Kentucky law,[235] the Pennsylvania grand juror's manual,[236] Story's instructions in *United States v. Ross*,[237] and cases in California[238] and New York.[239]

Overall, it appears that Story's sweeping collateral-death standard was not accepted in nineteenth-century American law. Most jurisdictions that considered the question limited accomplice liability for felony murder to killings that were in furtherance of and foreseeable as a result of the predicate felony.

In assessing the application of felony murder rules to accomplices, it is useful to distinguish four types of cases on a spectrum of diminishing culpability: (1) some co-felons participate in fatal violence, but do not strike the fatal blow; (2) some co-felons participate in a felony necessarily involving violence or the imposition of risk, but do not personally participate in the fatal violence; (3) some co-felons participate in a crime that may necessitate violence, depending on the circumstances, but do not personally participate in the fatal violence; and (4) some co-felons participate in a crime that ordinarily does not necessitate violence or risk, and do not personally participate in any fatal violence. Most observers will probably find accomplice liability for murder acceptable in the first two situations and unacceptable in the fourth situation. In the third situation, they might condition murder liability on further proof that a particular accomplice encouraged, facilitated, or expected violence.

Among the eighty-five reported nineteenth-century American felony murder convictions I have discovered, seventeen appear to impose felony murder liability on co-felons who may not have struck the fatal blow. Nine of these cases are of type 1, in which the defendants participated in the fatal attack.[240] Notable among these is New York's *Van Steenburgh* case. An additional seven cases were of type 2, all predicated on the necessarily forcible felony of robbery.[241] In one such case, the defendant robbed a bank at gunpoint while his accomplices opened fire on a neighboring street to create a diversion, with fatal results.[242] In another, the defendant participated in a train robbery while his accomplices in another part of the train killed victims they were assigned to subdue at gunpoint.[243] The most troubling case was another fatal train robbery in which the defendant's participation was physically and temporally remote from the violence: he fraudulently insured packages of money and mailed them aboard the train in preparation for filing a false insurance claim, the ultimate purpose of the robbery.[244] Another case in which the defendant professed to have no expectation that a fellow robber might kill involved only third-degree murder liability.[245] One nineteenth-century case appears to be of type 3: in the California case of *People v. Olsen*,[246] at least one of the participants shot and killed a pursuer during a theft. There were no nineteenth-century cases of type 4.

Overall, accomplice liability appears to have conformed to the standards enunciated by some courts, requiring that vicarious felony murders be instrumental to and foreseeable as a result of the predicate felonies agreed to. With one exception, accomplice liability was limited to those actually participating in the fatal assault, or to participants in the inherently violent felony of robbery. In other words, the dangerous felony limitation and the requirement of causing death by violence restricted felony murder liability for accomplices as well as principals.

In sum, most American jurisdictions limited felony murder to (1) causing death through either violence or the reckless imposition of risk, in the course of inherently dangerous felonies; or (2) participating in felonies foreseeably involving acts of violence that resulted in death. In these ways, most American jurisdictions built culpability requirements into the *actus reus* of felony murder, and so avoided holding felons strictly liable for accidental death.

Part Three

RECONSTRUCTING
FELONY MURDER LAW

9 FELONY MURDER AS NEGLIGENT HOMICIDE

How well does contemporary felony murder law conform to the dual culpability principle? There can be no simple answer to this question because felony murder law varies considerably across different jurisdictions. Yet felony murder laws can satisfy the dual culpability principle in different ways: by requiring mental states, by restricting predicate felonies, or by cabining causation and complicity. Reviewing the use of these different devices, we will find that most felony murder laws accord with the principle of dual culpability in most respects. At the same time felony murder law falls short of this standard in different ways in different jurisdictions. Accordingly, the necessary reforms vary as well. Rather than proposing a uniform statute that would often fix what is not broken, I will offer jurisdictionally specific suggestions to satisfy justice while respecting the integrity of existing law.

Contemporary law uses various devices to condition felony murder liability on negligence. Lawmakers can insert a requirement of foreseeable danger into the definition of felony murder in at least three places: as a required mental element, as part of the felony, or as part of the homicide. A substantial minority of felony murder jurisdictions have required some form of culpability. A great majority have required a dangerous felony. A substantial majority have also conditioned homicide on a foreseeable danger of death. It would be best for all jurisdictions to condition causation on foreseeable danger of death in felony murder cases.

CULPABILITY REQUIREMENTS

Penal codes may condition felony murder liability on a culpable mental state in their definitions of murder or homicide, or in rules for constructing the mental elements of offenses. In addition, courts may add such a requirement to the offense elements set forth in the code. We will consider requirements of culpability imposed by any of these four means. Almost half of American jurisdictions require some form of culpable mental state for murder in the context of a felony. Several require too much culpability for the resulting homicide offenses to count as felony murders.

Hawaii and Kentucky attach no significance to a felonious context for murder. Their codes simply define murder as killing with certain culpable mental states.[1] Five other states condition felony murder on the culpability otherwise required for murder, and so lack true felony murder rules. Thus Michigan and Vermont use a felonious context as an aggravator, raising murder liability from second to first degree. In both states, courts have interpreted the statutory term "murder" as requiring at least reckless disregard of a probability of grievous injury, whether or not in the context of a felony.[2] Courts in a third state, New Mexico, have interpreted that state's felony murder rule similarly. New Mexico's code defines second-degree murder as killing with knowledge of "a strong probability of death or great bodily harm," and provides that second-degree murder is a lesser included offense of first-degree murder.[3] In *State v. Ortega*, the New Mexico Supreme Court read this mental state into first-degree murder, otherwise defined simply as killing in commission or attempt of any felony.[4] New Hampshire and Arkansas require extreme indifference to human life for felony murder by statute. New Hampshire makes causing death by using a deadly weapon in the commission of certain grave felonies the basis for a rebuttable presumption of such extreme indifference, giving rise to second-degree murder.[5] Arkansas predicates noncapital first-degree murder on causing death under circumstances manifesting extreme indifference in the commission of any felony.[6] Since second-degree murder also requires such circumstances,[7] a felony merely aggravates conduct that would otherwise be murder. Because the murder laws in these five states require so much cognitive culpability in the context of predicate felonies, they should not be classified as felony murder laws.

Two other states arguably condition felony murder on reckless killing. The Illinois code requires culpability with respect to every element unless a legislative purpose to impose strict liability is "clearly" expressed in the statute. Illinois requires recklessness for any element lacking a culpable mental state, absent such an expressed legislative intention. Illinois predicates felony murder on a "forcible felony,"[8] which includes any of an enumerated list of felonies, and any other felony attempted with the use or threat of violence.[9] It also punishes any other killing as "unmitigated" murder if the defendant had knowledge that his conduct created a "strong probability" of death.[10] The legislative drafting commission and Illinois courts have reasoned that the commission of a forcible felony entails knowledge of such a strong probability.[11]

The North Dakota code, based on a proposed federal code, provides that every act element requires an accompanying culpable mental state unless strict liability is explicitly imposed by requiring that the act element be achieved "in fact."[12] The default culpable mental state required when none is specified is recklessness.[13] Because North Dakota's felony murder rule contains neither a culpability term nor the phrase "in fact,"[14] it appears to require recklessness. On the other hand, the felony murder provision includes an affirmative defense for accomplices who participate in the felony without negligence toward death.[15] This defense seems superfluous if felony murder liability requires recklessness. A federal code drafting commission comment suggests that the felony murder provision covers accidental killings, but also implies that it serves only to aggravate reckless manslaughters to murder.[16]

At least six states define felony murder as requiring a form of negligence.[17] Delaware requires recklessness for first-degree murder in the course of any felony,[18] and negligence for second-degree murder in the course of any felony.[19] The Pennsylvania, Alabama, and Texas codes define murder as a form of homicide, and define homicide as requiring negligence. The Maine and New Jersey codes condition felony murder on foreseeable danger.

Pennsylvania's code requires proof of mental culpability with respect to every act element[20] and defines criminal homicide as causing death with a culpable mental state of at least negligence.[21] It defines second-degree murder as including criminal homicide in the perpetration of enumerated felonies.[22] A Pennsylvania court has approved a jury instruction requiring negligence for felony murder in language that tracks the statutory definition of criminal homicide.[23]

Alabama's code also defines homicide as causing death with a culpable mental state of at least negligence,[24] and conditions felony murder on any felony "clearly dangerous to human life."[25] An official commentary explains this language as a requirement of foreseeability and reasons that a felony murder rule punishing unforeseeable deaths would be indefensible.[26] Cases have invoked this requirement of foreseeability in holding that danger must have been apparent to the perpetrator.[27] Alabama's culpability default rules create a presumption against strict liability absent clear legislative intent and require culpability if the proscribed conduct (here causing death and committing a felony clearly dangerous to life) "necessarily involves" a culpable mental state.[28]

The Texas code, too, defines homicide as causing death with at least negligence.[29] In addition, the code contains a general rule of interpretation requiring a culpable mental state of at least negligence with respect to a conduct element.[30] The felony murder provision requires that the defendant cause death by means of an act "clearly dangerous to life" committed in the course and in furtherance of a felony. Since the danger must be apparent, but need not be actually known to the defendant, this provision would appear to require negligence. The 1980 decision of *State v. Kuykendall* embraced this interpretation, holding that negligent homicide is a lesser included offense of felony murder, noting that an act clearly dangerous to life implies negligence.[31] A later Texas decision concluded that no separate proof of culpability is required, but that the required act clearly dangerous to life entails "reckless and wanton disregard of an obvious risk to human life."[32]

Maine does not require separate proof of any culpable mental state but nevertheless requires proof that death be a "reasonably foreseeable consequence" of the predicate felony, which is tantamount to a negligence requirement.[33]

The New Jersey code requires that a culpable mental state accompany every offense element unless there is a clear legislative intent to impose strict liability.[34] While the New Jersey Supreme Court has found such a legislative intent, it has also read the code as requiring that strict liability result elements must be "probable" and "foreseeable" results of a defendant's conduct.[35] The court has admitted that this foreseeability standard is equivalent to a requirement of "negligence."[36] The court also requires that the result be "not too remote, accidental in its occurrence, or too dependent on another's volitional act to have a just bearing on the defendant's culpability," as the code requires for crimes of negligence.[37]

Another nine jurisdictions—California, Nevada, Idaho, South Carolina, Iowa, Mississippi, Rhode Island, Virginia, and the United States—condition felony murder on malice.[38] Courts have associated malice with the imposition of danger in the eight states, but not in the federal system.

The California courts have long viewed the felony murder doctrine as an artificial rule that should be confined by the purpose of deterring dangerous conduct in the commission of felonies.[39] The California Supreme Court has recently read the California code to base felony murder on "implied malice" or circumstances showing an "abandoned and malignant heart." In *People v. Chun*,[40] the court explained that implied malice requires both "an act the natural consequences of which are dangerous to life" and knowledge of this danger. The court reasoned that an inherently dangerous felony substitutes for this knowledge because "when society has declared certain inherently dangerous conduct to be felonious, . . . society has warned . . . [the defendant] of the risk involved."[41] In essence, the court treated notice of danger as the equivalent of awareness of danger, where the actor's motive is felonious. The court limited this claim to second-degree felony murder, but its reasoning would apply equally well to first-degree felony murder, predicated on enumerated felonies.

Although the Nevada murder statute was essentially borrowed from California, Nevada courts have characterized malice as a "legal fiction" in felony murder cases.[42] Like the California Supreme Court, however, the Nevada Supreme Court has identified the purpose of the felony murder doctrine as deterring dangerous conduct during the felony.[43] In the 1999 case of *Labastida v. State* the Nevada Supreme Court conditioned second-degree felony murder on an inherently dangerous felony foreseeably and directly causing death.[44] Presumably the requirements for first-degree felony murder are the same, with the only difference being that the legislative enumeration of predicate felonies obviates a determination of inherent danger.

Idaho courts have upheld an instruction that "[t]he term malice . . . signifies . . . a general malignant recklessness toward the lives and safety of others. Malice may be shown from the fact that an unlawful killing took place during the perpetration or attempted perpetration of the crime of robbery."[45] Perhaps the courts see the requirement of "malignant recklessness" as now limiting felony murder to first-degree murder predicated on enumerated felonies.

South Carolina's felony murder rule is judicially created. South Carolina case law holds that fact finders may, but need not, infer malice from participation in a felony.[46] In the 1973 case of *Gore v. Leeke*, the South Carolina Supreme Court upheld a felony murder conviction as consistent with a requirement of foreseeable danger to human life, because the felons were armed during a residential burglary.[47] In the 2007 case of *Lowry v. State*, the court overturned a conviction because the jury was wrongly instructed to presume malice if a defendant participated in an armed robbery. The court held that malice was a distinct offense element that the prosecution bears a burden to prove under the due process clause, and observed that the only evidence of malice was testimony that the defendant was prepared to use deadly force against anyone who interrupted the robbers.[48] The definition of malice offered to jurors in South Carolina's pattern jury instructions incorporates both the disregard of a risk to life and an unlawful purpose—but without clearly indicating whether these are conjunctive or disjunctive requirements.[49] The pattern jury instruction on felony murder imposes liability on co-felons for homicides that are "natural and probable consequences" of the "common design."[50]

The Iowa statute defines murder as killing with malice and defines first-degree murder as including killing in the course of enumerated "forcible felonies." Iowa case law permits but does not require an inference of malice from the commission of such a felony.[51] In the 1988 case of State v. Ragland[52] the Iowa Supreme Court held that malice was an independent element of felony murder. The court reasoned, however, that malice could be inferred from enumerated felonies because the legislature had determined that these felonies posed "a substantial risk of . . . injury and death."[53] The court further reasoned that the punishment imposed for first-degree murder was not disproportionate where the defendant had acted with reckless indifference to human life.[54] A later decision approved an instruction that malice could be implied from a forcible felony, when combined with another instruction defining "malice" as the purpose to "do a wrongful act to the injury of another out of actual hatred or with an evil or unlawful purpose" and "malice aforethought" as "a fixed purpose or design to do some physical harm to another which exists before the act is committed . . ."[55] In a 2006 decision the Iowa Supreme Court invoked the malice requirement in holding that willful injury could not serve as a predicate felony because it merged with the killing.[56] Thus Iowa courts require the conscious imposition of a risk of injury in pursuit of some other felonious aim.

The Mississippi code classifies unintended killing in the course of non-enumerated felonies as murder, but as only "felony manslaughter" if committed without malice. This implies that enumerated felonies are inherently malicious, and that some non-enumerated felonies might share this malicious quality. Case law does not explain this distinction, and second-degree felony murder cases are rare in Mississippi. Nevertheless, second-degree felony murder convictions have been predicated on the dangerous offenses of shooting from a car with depraved indifference to human life[57] and felonious drunk driving.[58]

Courts in Rhode Island base the felony murder rule on the common law, which they understand to provide that "[h]omicide is murder if the death results from the perpetration or attempted perpetration of an inherently dangerous felony."[59]

Virginia's code leaves murder undefined, grading murder in the course of enumerated felonies as first degree, and unintended killing in furtherance of a felony as second degree.[60] Virginia courts have interpreted the code as incorporating the common law's definition of murder as killing with malice.[61] The 2001 decision in *Cotton v. Commonwealth* upheld a second-degree felony murder conviction predicated on child abuse, against a claim that Virginia's felony murder rule created an unconstitutional presumption of malice. The court responded that Virginia's felony murder rule is restricted to felonies entailing malice, since second-degree felony murder requires proof of "a felony that involved substantial risk to human life" and "a felony of violence manifests a person-endangering frame of mind such that malice may be imputed to the act of killing."[62]

The malicious character of felony murder remains untheorized in federal criminal law. Federal courts have simply explained felony murder as a fictional transfer of intent from an intended felony to an unintended death, without specifying what features the felony must have to be malicious.[63] This is understandable, since the federal murder statute predicates first-degree felony murder on enumerated felonies and federal courts have not imposed second-degree felony murder liability on the basis of unenumerated felonies. Accordingly they have not been forced to define features that would render some, but not all, deaths caused in the perpetration of such felonies murder. Federal courts should follow the example of courts in states that define murder in terms of malice, and identify malice with the dangerousness of enumerated predicate felonies. They should then use the malice requirement as a basis for requiring that death result foreseeably from the felony.

DANGEROUS FELONY RULES

Jurisdictions can condition felony murder on apparently dangerous conduct in three ways. Legislatures can restrict felony murder to enumerated felonies deemed dangerous. Legislatures or courts can restrict predicate felonies to those deemed by courts to satisfy a standard of inherent danger or violence. Finally, legislatures or courts can restrict felony murder to fatal acts in furtherance of a felony found dangerous at trial. An advantage to both the first and second approaches is that insofar as they require that negligence with respect to a risk of death inheres in the predicate felony itself, they ensure that any accomplice in that felony will also be negligent. The third alternative leaves the culpability of accomplices undetermined.

ENUMERATED PREDICATE FELONIES

To what particular predicate felonies have jurisdictions limited felony murder? To what extent do these ostensibly dangerous enumerated predicate felonies in fact entail negligence with respect to a risk of death?

Among the forty-five jurisdictions imposing true felony murder liability, a total of twenty-five jurisdictions exhaustively enumerate predicate felonies.[64] An additional fourteen jurisdictions enumerate several predicate felonies, but also permit others.[65] These enumerated felonies are often assumed to be inherently violent or dangerous,[66] and in a few jurisdictions are labeled as such in the code.[67]

For the most part, these different jurisdictions are fairly consistent in the predicate felonies they enumerate. Of the thirty-nine jurisdictions, all but two list some form of arson, burglary, rape, robbery, and kidnapping.[68] A few jurisdictions list special variants of these offenses,[69] while twenty-one also list escape or flight from custody.[70] A majority of enumerated felony jurisdictions—twenty-nine—list at least one other type of felony. Other popular predicate felonies include child or elder abuse,[71] drug offenses of various kinds,[72] and such politically motivated offenses as terrorism, treason, or espionage.[73] Two jurisdictions list poisoning consumable products.[74] A number of jurisdictions list murder or manslaughter, presumably of a person other than the victim killed,[75] or various forms of assault.[76] Three list theft offenses.[77] Two list simple breaking and entering.[78] One lists forcible obstruction of justice[79] and two list resisting arrest.[80] One lists train wrecking.[81]

How well do these various predicate felonies meet the requirement of apparent danger to human life? That depends on what we mean by "apparent danger." A tempting approach to this problem measures apparent danger to human life in strictly quantitative terms, as a probability of death. However, there are three related difficulties with this approach.

First, it is hard to know how much danger of death should qualify as negligent. Surely negligence cannot require that death be "probable" in the sense of more likely than not. Federal statistics suggest that no more than about 20 percent of the injuries resulting from intentional shootings are fatal.[82] A study of drive-by shootings of minors in Los Angeles found that only 5 percent resulted in deaths.[83] Federal statistics indicate that assaults with intent to injure result in death only about 3 percent of the time.[84] Yet English law has long regarded intent to injure as a sufficient mental state for murder.[85] Thus we view risks of death much lower than 50 percent as intolerable and apparently base judgments of culpability on other factors beyond risk.

Second, the probability of death arising from a type of felony is not always determinate. Some felonies may not impose a very high risk of death taken in isolation, but they may be part of a pattern of activity that in the aggregate produces high risk. For example, robbery results in homicide only .6 percent of the time.[86] Yet a Rand study estimated that the 10 percent of incarcerated robbers who committed robbery most frequently committed an average of 87 robberies a year.[87] Such high-rate muggers should generate an average of one death every two years. Narcotic trafficking poses similar questions. A single use may pose little risk. Habitual use is more dangerous, and marketing large amounts more dangerous still.

Moreover, the danger imposed by crime depends on victim behavior. When robbery victims do not resist, the risk of death drops to 0.2 percent; but when robbery victims do resist, the risk of death rises to 3 percent—greater than the risk from assault with intent to injure.[88] It seems fair to view the robber as culpable for the danger he threatens to impose if the victim exercises her right to resist. On the other hand, voluntary victim participation in drug abuse seems to undercut the trafficker's liability.

Third, the culpability of imposing risk depends on the ends for which the risk is imposed. The Model Penal Code's popular definition of criminal negligence requires reasonable notice of a substantial and *unjustifiable* risk that a proscribed result will occur. We view fast driving as negligent only if the risks outweigh the expected benefit of time saved. The risk of death resulting from arson may be no more than 1 percent,[89] but even that "small" risk is unjustifiable because the commission of the crime is wholly without benefit. For a death to be caused negligently arguably requires only that net harm is expected as a consequence of the act causing death, not that death is probable. Assuming that a crime has no benefit, a very small apparent probability of death would arguably render the crime inherently negligent.[90]

In light of these difficulties, it seems we must find some nonquantitative way to assess apparent danger. The point of requiring a dangerous felony is to ensure the defendant's culpability, which can be identified only through the exercise of normative judgment, not precise measurement. In evaluating felonious conduct that leads to death, the most promising approach is to assess the normative meaning of the felony rather than its probable consequences. What attitude towards the lives of others is expressed by the felony? Arguably, a violent felony that aims at injury expresses a willingness to endanger life, even if the actual risk is low. Whether these assaultive felonies meet the independent felonious purpose requirement is another matter.

Two crimes of political motive, treason and espionage, could meet this test of willingness to inflict a risk of death even though they do not explicitly require intent to injure. Treason, which requires aid and loyalty to an enemy during war,[91] is a crime of accessorial participation in the killing inherent in war, by one who lacks combatant immunity. It implies a willingness to shed blood. Espionage may be viewed similarly when it involves an intention that defense information be communicated to an enemy in wartime.[92]

Other offenses expressing negligent indifference to human life include inherently coercive felonies, in which the felon coerces the will of a victim by threatening violence. Such offenses imply a willingness to cause injury or death, regardless of the likelihood of those results. On the basis of this reasoning, robbery, rape, and kidnapping are all appropriate predicate felonies. They express negligent indifference to human life even if they result in death in less than 1 percent of all cases. One inculpatory characteristic of these offenses is that they deliberately cultivate and use fear, which shows that the defendant certainly could have adverted to the dangers imposed. This is also a feature of "terrorism," defined by the "Patriot Act" as illegal acts that "appear to be intended to . . . intimidate or coerce a civilian population[;] . . . influence the policy of a government by intimidation or coercion; or . . . affect the conduct of a government."[93] The offense of consumer product tampering has this feature as well. Child abuse is sometimes motivated by an aim to intimidate and control and so may meet this coercion criterion for negligent indifference, depending on how it is defined. Obstruction of justice can meet this test if it is limited to crimes involving the use or threat of violence against witnesses or officials.

What about the other three most commonly enumerated felonies—escape, arson and burglary? All three can inspire great alarm in the public, but they do not inherently involve intimidation as an element or aim of the crime. Their designation as predicate felonies must rest on some other basis.

While escape is not coercive, it entails resisting lawful coercion. The escapee must plan either to overcome resistance or to try to evade it. In either case he must foresee violent confrontation with armed officers who have not only a right but also a duty to resist, thus expressing a sufficiently negligent indifference to human life. This reasoning does not apply with equal force to all situations of flight from police. Suspects are not subject to the same comprehensive loss of liberty as prisoners, and police are duty bound to exercise restraint in using force or otherwise endangering the public (and themselves) in pursuit of suspects who may be neither dangerous nor guilty of anything, who may be heedless juveniles, or who may reasonably fear police mistreatment.

Arson—traditionally defined as maliciously burning a dwelling[94] or setting a fire with intent to destroy a building[95]—has been an enumerated predicate for felony murder in the United States since the early nineteenth century. Yet British juries were reluctant to convict arsonists of murder during the nineteenth century, when homicide was still conceptualized as fatal wounding. Today, in an era of pervasive fire safety codes, however, the public is highly sensitive to the dangers of fire. Fatal arson provides a kind of paradigm of the modern conception of homicide as causing death by wrongly exposing a victim to risk. The mortality of arson—approximately one death per hundred cases—is roughly comparable to the mortality of robbery and assault with intent to injure.

While few will disagree that arson entails culpability with respect to a risk of death, arson-murder convictions have sometimes provoked controversy. Recall Janet Danahey, who pled guilty to the felony murder of four victims who died in a fire she started by burning a bag of party decorations outside her ex-boyfriend's door. This result is undeserved, but *not* because her state's felony murder rule did not require sufficient culpability. North Carolina requires that death be caused by an act in furtherance of an enumerated felony or one involving the use of a deadly weapon, from which death is reasonably foreseeable.[96] Arson is defined in North Carolina by the common law, and requires the willful and malicious burning of the dwelling house of another.[97] If indeed Danahey set fire to debris outside of the building, with no expectation that the building would burn, she did not commit arson. Arson is suitable as an enumerated predicate felony for felony murder only if it requires the purpose of burning a potentially occupied building. This gives it an independent felonious purpose, and makes death a reasonably foreseeable consequence.

Burglary has also long been designated as a predicate felony. One could argue that residential burglaries are likely to provoke violent confrontations since victims of such burglaries generally have a right to resist with deadly force and no duty to retreat. Thus a home invasion, when victims are known to be present, *can* be seen as a coercive crime closely related to robbery. Yet most burglaries are planned to avoid encountering witnesses. As a result, the mortality rate for burglary is surprisingly low, no more than 0.02 percent.[98] Burglary is typically defined as entering a building without permission with the intent to commit another felony. Thus, when burglary does result in death, some other felony can often be used as a predicate. For example, where thieves expect to encounter victims in a residence, they intend a robbery. Where an individual burglar uses force to effectuate a theft, he commits robbery and is negligent with respect to death.

Given the scarcity of fatal burglaries, nonviolent fatal burglaries are bound to be rare indeed. In the *Ingram* case, mentioned in Chapter 1, the victim surprised and captured the burglar before suffering a heart attack. The burglar could hardly have expected such a result. In the Nebraska case of *State v. Dixon* the victim apparently suffered a heart attack when the defendant broke down her door. The court treated the break-in as the cause of the victim's heart attack. It is hard to see how such causation could have been proven. The defendant testified that the victim was already down when he entered, and there was no evidence that he touched her.[99] Had these courts properly defined causation, the defendants would not have been convicted without some showing of violence or foreseeable danger. Yet results like this could also be avoided if legislatures acknowledged that nonviolent burglaries are not inherently dangerous.

Conviction of a nonculpable defendant is also possible when several persons collaborate in a burglary, hoping and expecting not to encounter any victims or witnesses. If one thief encounters resistance and overcomes it with force, he becomes a robber, but his accomplices may not. In such cases, use of burglary as a predicate felony can inculpate accomplices in deaths that they had little reason to expect. Most jurisdictions solve this problem by limiting accomplice liability to deaths foreseeably resulting from an act in furtherance of the common plan.

A second problematic scenario arises when the fatal events occur during flight from a burglary. The California case of *People v. Fuller*[100] illustrates this problem. Defendants were interrupted by a police officer while breaking into cars in a parking lot. Fleeing from the pursuing officer at high speed, they ran a red light and struck another car, killing the driver. An appellate court reluctantly upheld a first-degree murder conviction. The court expressed regret for this result, noting that burglary was limited to nighttime break-ins to occupied structures at the time the felony murder provision was added to the California code and that first-degree burglary was still so limited. Thus the court called on the California Supreme Court to construe the code as predicating first-degree felony murder only on such aggravated burglaries. The court also argued that the defendants' reckless driving in flight from the burglary should not be seen as a danger inhering in burglary, because dangerous flight was a possibility in any crime. Most jurisdictions would avoid such a result by applying a causal test requiring that death be within the scope of the risk inhering in the felony.

Another illustrative flight case is *State v. Chambers*,[101] in which a Wisconsin court held a burglar liable for his accomplice's killing of a pursuing police officer during the accomplice's separate flight. The defendant, who had set out with his co-felon to commit a robbery, conceded his complicity in the predicate felony of armed burglary. Nevertheless, he denied responsibility for his part-ner's killing of the police officer. It can be argued that where, as here, a burglar knows his co-felons are armed, he accepts that they will use deadly force at least if necessary to defend themselves and make good their escape.

The *Chambers* case may be contrasted favorably with the famous Illinois case of *People v. Hickman*, in which one police officer shot another whom he took for an armed felon in flight from a burglary.[102] While it appears likely that one of Hickman's accomplices brought a gun, there was no evidence that either Hickman or the errant officer was aware of it. The court offered the following astonishing argument that death was indeed foreseeable as a consequence of their burglary: "There should be no doubt about the 'justice' of holding a felon guilty of murder who engages in a robbery followed by an attempted escape and thereby inevita-bly calls into action defensive forces against him, the activity of which results in the death of an innocent human being."[103] Since Hickman neither robbed nor threatened anyone, he did nothing to provoke defense. Where the felony is not inherently dangerous, causal responsibility for death cannot simply be presumed.

The *Chambers* case illustrates how foreseeable danger can be required by predicating felony murder on burglary aggravated by some dangerous circum-stance such as the use of arms or the presence of victims. Wisconsin is one of fif-teen enumerated felony jurisdictions that limit predicate burglaries in this way.[104]

The most common aggravating factors are that the burglary is committed in a dwelling or with a person present; that the felon is armed; or that the felon commits assault or causes injury.

These aggravating circumstances establish dangerousness, but they establish a burglar's negligence only if he or she is aware of these circumstances. In the Ohio case of *State v. Kimble*[105] the defendant induced a prostitute to bring a cus-tomer to the scene of a planned robbery, where a co-felon shot him. She was held to be an accomplice in the predicate felony of armed robbery, despite her claim that she did not know her co-felons were armed. The court considered the stat-utory element of possession or use of a weapon to be a strict liability element, reasoning that possession is typically a strict liability element. This is particu-larly troubling because Ohio's statutory default rules require recklessness unless a purpose to impose strict liability is clearly indicated.[106] Moreover, these de-fault rules require a voluntary act and provide that possession constitutes a vol-untary act only if the possessor knowingly procured, received, or controlled.[107] Finally, the code provides that offense definitions "shall be strictly construed against the state."[108] There is a danger that similar reasoning could be employed in a felony murder case predicated on armed burglary, holding a co-felon liable when a burglar unexpectedly brings a weapon. Such reasoning would be even more perverse in a burglary case because unlike simple robbery, simple burglary is not inherently violent. Moreover, if the aggravating result of injury during a burglary is treated as a strict liability element, there is a danger that an unforeseeable death could be counted twice, as the aggravating circumstance rendering the burglary dangerous, and as murder predicated on the dangerous burglary.

A further difficulty with the use of burglary as a predicate felony arises because burglary is an inchoate crime, depending on a possibly unexecuted intent to commit a further felony. Where a defendant aids in an unlawful entry that ultimately leads to a violent killing, prosecutors and juries may be tempted to overascribe the requisite felonious intent so as to impute complicity.[109] Thus, in the Colorado case of *Auman v. People*,[110] the defendant broke into a locked room in an apartment she had shared and retrieved her own belongings, while her codefendants apparently helped themselves to other property. One of these codefendants fatally shot a police officer in flight from this theft. The defendant's convictions for burglary and felony murder were ultimately overturned for failure to consider her claim that she had no felonious intent to take the property of another. A less careful result was reached in *Commonwealth v. Lambert*.[111] Lambert drove a friend to the home of the friend's girlfriend, and her mother, whom the friend claimed owed him money. The friend broke in and fatally shot the mother. In upholding Lambert's felony murder conviction, the court reasoned that the illegal entry justified an inference that the friend intended some undetermined illegal act within; the fact that Lambert observed the illegal entry justified an inference that he knew his friend had such an intention. The fact that he remained available to give his friend a ride implied the required "intent to promote or facilitate the offense."[112]

Unfortunately, it is unlikely that legislatures will abandon a two-hundred-year-old tradition of predicating felony murder on burglary. Yet there is little justification for viewing burglary as inherently dangerous, and there is some risk of wrongly convicting nonculpable accomplices. It would be best to remove burglary from enumerations of predicate felonies. As a second best alternative, predicate burglaries should be limited to aggravated burglary. Jurisdictions that now retain simple burglary as a predicate felony[113] should narrow it to aggravated burglary. Courts in such jurisdictions may achieve a similar effect by interpreting causation standards to prevent the ascription of death to the burglary unless the burglary is committed in a dangerous way. They should also carefully define criteria of accessorial responsibility for death, so as to ensure that participants in burglary are not punished for felony murder when they lacked awareness of circumstances rendering death foreseeable. Six states that predicate felony murder on simple burglary provide an affirmative defense for accomplices who had no reason to expect a killing and no knowledge that any participant was armed.[114] Of course it would be best for the prosecution to bear the burden to disprove this defense beyond a reasonable doubt.

Other non-forcible property offenses like theft are neither dangerous nor traditionally seen to be so. Because these offenses rarely lead to death, they rarely result in felony murder charges. Where they do, courts are rightly reluctant to attribute those deaths to the felonies. In the Tennessee case of *State v. Pierce*[115] a fifteen-year-old youth drove a car several weeks after its misappropriation by the owner's daughter. He lost control of the wheel at a police roadblock when he saw an officer aiming a gun at him. The resulting collision killed the officer. A Tennessee appellate court reversed the youth's felony murder conviction on the ground that the act causing death was "collateral to not in pursuance of the felony of theft." In another Tennessee case, the killing of a thief's accomplice by a resisting victim was held not to be in furtherance of the felony.[116] Commendable as these decisions were, it would be better to purge non-forcible property crimes from the list of enumerated predicate felonies.

Drug offenses are popular predicates despite the fact that they involve neither force nor coercion. Yet drugs are regulated primarily because of their dangers to health, so it may seem to follow that drug trafficking is inherently dangerous. There are two difficulties with this conclusion, however. First, the causal responsibility of drug traffickers for drug-related deaths is often undermined by the contribution of uncoerced victim behavior. Thus, in the case of *State v. Mauldin* the Kansas Supreme Court upheld a trial judge's dismissal of a felony murder charge based on a self-administered drug overdose.[117] The trial judge reasoned that

> the defendant's only connection with the homicide was that he sold a quantity of heroin to the deceased who some time later, voluntarily and out of the presence of the defendant, injected himself with an overdose and died as a result. This is not a case where the defendant injected the heroin into the deceased, or otherwise determined the amount of the dose, or assisted in administering the dosage . . .[118]

Unlike rape or robbery victims who resist, drug users have no legal right to endanger themselves. Voluntary drug users are arguably partners in crime rather than victims.

Second, the overall fatality of drug trafficking appears much lower than the fatality of paradigmatic predicate felonies like robbery and arson. At the high end, as many as 0.5 percent of heroin users have suffered a fatal overdose in some years.[119] By contrast, in 1998 approximately 0.05 percent of cocaine users died of overdoses.[120] And of course there are illegal drugs like marijuana that pose virtually no risk of overdose.

Nevertheless, there are countervailing considerations that militate in favor of felony murder liability for some drug offenses. First, drug users who overdose are disproportionately likely to be addicts, with an arguably compromised will. Second, the dangers of wholesale drug trafficking may greatly exceed the dangers of individual drug use. So it may be reasonable to use trafficking in narcotics as a predicate felony when the amount is very large. But if so, it may seem arbitrary and formalistic to focus on the scale of a single transaction that may be part of an ongoing business. An alternative approach is to distinguish between trafficking for profit and sharing drugs socially. Where companions are sharing the risks of drug use it seems morally arbitrary to hold the survivor liable for an unlikely misfortune that could as easily have fallen on him.

The West Virginia case of *People v. Rodoussakis*[121] offers a fact scenario supporting felony murder liability for a retail drug dealer. Prosecution witnesses testified that the defendant habitually dealt morphine, that he had recently witnessed another customer become ill from three doses of morphine and refused to render aid, and that he injected the victim three times on the day of his death, despite the fact that the victim became ill after the second injection and a witness urged him not to administer the third dose. Yet these facts are compelling because they include evidence that death was foreseeable, and the victim did not self-administer. This is circumstantial danger, not inherent danger.

A contrasting case mentioned in Chapter 1 illustrates the impropriety of predicating murder liability on social drug use. In *Hickman v. Commonwealth*[122] a Virginia court upheld the conviction of a defendant who jointly possessed a small amount of cocaine with the victim. Hickman sat with the victim in the victim's truck and helped him prepare an injection of cocaine which the victim self-administered and which proved fatal. Because the victim self-administered, Hickman did not directly cause the death. Because the ex ante risk of fatal overdose associated with the possession of a small amount for recreational use is low, proximate causation and negligence appear to be missing as well.

In sum, large-scale trafficking in dangerous, addictive drugs for profit may be sufficiently dangerous to justify felony murder liability. On the other hand, trafficking in less-dangerous, less-addictive drugs is not. Nor is small-scale possession of even dangerous and addictive drugs for personal use or social sharing. Because drug offenses do not inherently involve violence, coercion, or destruction, and because their dangers are so variable and context specific, they should not be viewed as inherently dangerous. Jurisdictions that enumerate predicate offenses should avoid including drug offenses among them.

DANGEROUSNESS STANDARDS

A total of twenty jurisdictions impose either first- or second-degree felony murder liability without exhaustively enumerating predicate felonies.[123] Six of these states do not enumerate at all.[124]

The great majority of these twenty jurisdictions condition felony murder liability on dangerous conduct in the commission or attempt of the felony. Standards requiring dangerous conduct may focus on risk, force, or the use of a weapon, and can be imposed by statute or by judicial decision. A requirement that dangerous conduct be a defining element of the predicate felony is a requirement of *inherent* danger. Such standards give courts the role of determining which felonies can be predicates for murders. If requirements of force or danger apply to the felons' conduct in committing any felony, they can be applied by properly instructed juries evaluating the facts of the case. Such case-specific requirements are usually called requirements of *foreseeable* danger, or of danger under the *circumstances*. Of the twenty states that do not exhaustively enumerate predicate felonies, only four—California, Nevada, Minnesota and Massachusetts—require an inherently dangerous predicate felony.

California's penal code defines second-degree felony murder obliquely, defining involuntary manslaughter as unlawful killing without malice in the commission of an unlawful act not amounting to felony.[125] The California courts have long predicated second-degree murder on non-enumerated felonies but limit predicate felonies to those determined by the court to be inherently dangerous.[126] The California Supreme Court reasoned that if felons had no reason to anticipate a danger of death, they could not be deterred by the threat of felony murder liability.[127] A 1989 case, *People v. Patterson*, remanded a felony murder conviction predicated on distribution of cocaine, for the court to determine whether there is always a "high probability" that the distribution of cocaine will result in death.[128]

Nevada's felony murder statute closely parallels that of its neighbor California.[129] In a 1983 case the Nevada Supreme Court recognized second-degree felony murder for the first time, upholding a conviction predicated on the distribution of barbiturates.[130] Relying on California cases, the court limited predicate felonies to those inherently dangerous in the abstract, to ensure that the felon could foresee the possibility of death or injury and so be deterred by the threat of murder liability.

Minnesota's code punishes causing death without intent in the attempt or commission of any non-enumerated felony as second-degree murder.[131] Minnesota courts formerly required only that the predicate felony involve danger,[132] but since 2003 they have required inherent danger.[133]

The Massachusetts criminal code grades murder predicated on the most severely punished felonies as first degree, without defining murder itself.[134] Massachusetts courts have recognized second-degree murder predicated on non-enumerated felonies since the nineteenth century.[135] In the 1982 case of *Commonwealth v. Matchett*, the Supreme Judicial Court held that when the felony is not inherently dangerous, the jury must find "circumstances showing conscious disregard of human life, and a heart regardless of social duty" to find second-degree murder. The court reasoned that "criminal liability for causing a particular result is not justified in the absence of some culpable mental state in respect to that result."[136] This requirement of inherent danger or gross recklessness applies to both first- and second-degree felony murder.[137]

Six states—Alabama, Texas, Illinois, Montana, North Carolina, and Delaware—restrict non-enumerated predicate felonies by statute to those involving danger or violence as committed.

Alabama predicates felony murder on enumerated felonies or "any other felony clearly dangerous to human life."[138] In 2006 an Alabama court upheld an indictment charging felony murder predicated on the felony of distributing marijuana, where one of the defendants shot a customer who attempted to rob them. The court rejected an inherent danger test and viewed circumstantial danger as a question of fact for the jury.[139]

The Texas criminal code predicates felony murder on "an act clearly dangerous to human life that causes the death of an individual" in the course of "a felony other than manslaughter."[140] Felony murder was predicated on an auto theft where the defendant dangerously drove the car away at night without headlights, while drunk.[141] The risks imposed by the defendant, while not in-hering in auto theft, were instrumental to this particular theft.

The Illinois code predicates first-degree murder on any forcible felony other than second-degree murder. It defines forcible felonies as those enumerated or "any other felony which involves the use or threat of force or violence."[142] Any felony can be deemed forcible if committed with violence.[143] The use or threat of violence must be intentional, however: reckless driving is not force, and can-not turn auto theft into a forcible felony.[144] Illinois courts have held that a forc-ible felony must also be foreseeably dangerous.[145] Nevertheless, the requirement of force can leave the bar to conviction quite low, as illustrated by the case of *People v. Jenkins*,[146] mentioned in Chapter 1. The defendant's "forcible" felony was simple battery of a police officer, consisting of elbowing him in the chest, with the obvious intent to escape rather than to inflict injury. That the offi-cer would react to this by shooting his partner was hardly foreseeable, but the jury was never told that it had to find that the defendant foreseeably caused the death. A federal court subsequently found this failure to instruct on causation erroneous, but—astonishingly—deemed the error harmless.[147]

The Montana criminal code predicates felony murder on enumerated fel-onies or any other forcible felony involving the threat or use of physical force or violence.[148] Forcible felonies need not require force or threat as offense el-ements. Thus witness tampering is a forcible felony if committed by coercion but not if committed by bribery.[149]

North Carolina case law previously conditioned first-degree murder on felonies involving either inherent danger or foreseeable danger as committed, but these cases have now been superseded by a statute predicating first-degree murder on any felony "committed or attempted with the use of a deadly weapon."[150] Accordingly, "there is no second degree felony murder" in North Carolina.[151] Unfortunately, North Carolina decisions have weakened the stat-utory requirement of a deadly weapon in two ways. First, the deadly weapon need only be brought along on the crime; it need not cause the death.[152] Sec-ond, a deadly weapon can be any implement capable of causing death, such as a car, if it has been used negligently.[153] A principled interpretation of the statute would require that the use of the weapon in furtherance of the crime cause the death.

Finally, Delaware case law formerly required a dangerously committed fel-ony,[154] but this requirement has now been subsumed within the statutory re-quirement that death be caused negligently or recklessly in the commission or attempt of any felony.[155] These mental states presuppose perpetrating the felony dangerously.

Six additional states appear to have adopted requirements of dangerousness under the circumstances by judicial decision: Georgia, Maryland, Oklahoma, Rhode Island, South Carolina, and Virginia.

Georgia's code does not enumerate predicate felonies at all, but simply provides that a person commits murder "when, in the commission of a felony, he causes the death of a human being, irrespective of malice."[156] A 1992 decision held that the predicate felony must be either inherently dangerous to life or dangerous under circumstances.[157] Georgia courts have found circumstantial danger in cases involving gun possession by a felon, possession of a weapon at school, and methadone distribution.[158] One court ascribed inherent danger to the felony of reckless driving in flight from police.[159]

The Georgia case of *Miller v. State*[160] featured in Chapter 1, illustrates the risk that courts will find danger whenever a fatality occurs, however improbably. Fifteen-year-old Miller was sentenced to life in prison for fatally punching a thirteen-year-old in the back of the head. His murder conviction was predicated on one of two offenses, aggravated assault and aggravated battery. Aggravated assault consists of intentionally striking someone with a weapon causing or likely to cause serious injury. Such a weapon includes hands when they cause actual injury.[161] Aggravated battery consists of disabling a body part "maliciously," which the trial court did not define in instructing the jury.[162] Both felonies *sound* inherently dangerous because they entail injury—but because the court treated both as strict liability offenses with respect to the required injury,[163] neither is foreseeably dangerous. In treating aggravated assault as a strict liability offense, the court ignored prior precedent requiring an attempt or threat to injure, or a likelihood of injury.[164] Without the aggravating deadly weapon element, simple assault is not a felony and could not trigger felony murder.

A federal district court ruled this to be harmless error in a habeas corpus review on the theory that the jury could have based felony murder on aggravated battery, and that Miller met the mental element for this offense because he intentionally punched the victim.[165] In failing to require *any* expectation of injury as an element of aggravated battery, however, the court effaced the statutory requirement of *malicious* injury and ignored prior precedent.[166] Moreover, if intentionally punching suffices, the aggravating injury adds no culpability to a simple non-felonious battery. Acknowledging that "the sentence of life with the possibility of parole . . . would be grossly disproportionate to the conduct and intent involved," the reviewing federal judge offered the anguished conclusion that "the charges on which Miller was convicted did not require any finding of serious moral culpability . . . ."[167] This result was possible because the trial court never instructed the jury that they had to find foreseeable danger, presumably on the assumption that aggravated assault and aggravated battery are *inherently* dangerous as a matter of law. But if these offenses impose strict liability for the injury, they are not inherently dangerous when viewed ex ante and their treatment as such was erroneous.

Rhode Island's code grades murder in the course of enumerated felonies as first-degree murder and leaves second-degree murder as a residual category.[168] The 1980 decision in *In re Leon* upheld a finding of guilt for second-degree felony murder predicated on unlawful burning. The court purported to derive a second-degree felony murder rule from the common law and conditioned it on an inherently dangerous felony.[169] A subsequent decision permitted second-degree felony murder predicated on felonies dangerous to life under the circumstances.[170]

Maryland's code leaves murder undefined, grading it as first degree if committed in the course of enumerated felonies. Courts read a felony murder rule into the first-degree murder provision during the twentieth century,[171] but did not establish a second-degree felony murder rule until a 2001 decision upholding a conviction predicated on child abuse.[172] The court traced both first- and second-degree felony murder rules to a supposed common law rule predicating murder on felonies foreseeably dangerous to life as committed.[173] The court invoked Stephen's nineteenth-century opinion in *Serné*, as well as recent cases from Delaware, Rhode Island, Massachusetts, Georgia, North Carolina, and Virginia, in support of a foreseeably dangerous felony rule.[174]

The Oklahoma criminal code defines second-degree murder as including homicide in the commission of any unenumerated felony. The 1978 decision in *Wade v. State*[175] upheld a second-degree murder conviction predicated on unlawfully possessing a firearm in a bar, where the defendant fatally shot the victim from seven feet away. The court required either inherent danger or danger under the circumstances.[176] This dangerous felony requirement should have precluded murder liability in the *Malaske* case from Chapter 1. The case is troubling for three reasons. First, murder liability was predicated on a regulatory offense, committed routinely by millions, and not punished as a felony in most states. Second, because the regulation of juvenile alcohol consumption is primarily concerned with safety, and the defendant did not profit in any way, there was no discernibly independent felonious purpose. Third, however, the offense is not ordinarily very dangerous—perhaps less dangerous than distributing alcohol legally to adults of driving age. In finding causation, the jury did determine that Malaske's conduct was a "substantial factor in bringing about the death and the conduct is dangerous and threatens *or destroys* life."[177] Yet this instruction allowed the jury to determine that the conduct was dangerous because death resulted, rather than determining that the conduct caused death because it was foreseeably dangerous. On appeal, the majority finessed the requirement of foreseeability by ruling the felony *inherently* dangerous to human life as a matter of law, without discussing any empirical evidence. Like Georgia's *Miller* case, the *Malaske* case illustrates the paradox that a requirement of inherent danger can be easier to satisfy than a requirement of foreseeable danger, because it does not require proof beyond a reasonable doubt.

In the 1984 case of *Heacock v. Commonwealth* the Virginia Supreme Court rejected a requirement of inherent danger in upholding a second-degree felony murder conviction predicated on cocaine distribution. The court nevertheless found the offense in fact dangerous to life.[178] In the 1990 case of *Hickman v. Commonwealth*, described in Chapter 1, the defendant and the victim together brought cocaine to the victim's truck. The defendant placed some of the cocaine on a mirror. The victim took some of that cocaine, injected himself "three or four times," and then died. It was not proven who had acquired or provided the cocaine. Citing *Heacock*, the court upheld a second-degree murder conviction based on the theory that the defendant had jointly possessed the cocaine and had aided the victim in possessing the cocaine.[179] Because Hickman did not impose a significant risk on an unwilling victim, there was no moral basis for murder liability.

Yet Virginia law has long required an adequate causal connection between the felony and the resulting death.[180] On this basis, Virginia courts have refused to treat fatal collisions in stolen cars as felony murder, even when the car thief drives recklessly to avoid the police.[181] They have similarly declined to impose felony murder liability based on a plane crash during a drug distribution offense.[182] The court reasoned that there was no justification for imputing malice unless an "increased risk of death or serious harm occasioned by the commission of the felony demonstrated the felon's lack of concern for human life."[183] A 2000 decision overturned a second-degree felony murder conviction for an accidental shooting involving the felony of "use of a firearm by a felon" because the felony did not "dictate conduct which led to the homicide," and death did not result from an act integral to or in furtherance of the felony.[184] Finally, Virginia adopted a requirement of foreseeable danger with the 2001 decision in *Cotton v. Commonwealth.*[185] In light of these developments it appears that *Hickman* is no longer good law.

South Carolina's felony murder rule is judicially developed and received little definition until the 1973 case of *Gore v. Leeke*, which endorsed a requirement of danger as committed. The court upheld Gore's murder conviction for a cofelon's fatal shooting of a police officer during their flight with the proceeds of a daytime residential burglary. The court endorsed a jury instruction holding accomplices responsible for acts of violence that are the "probable or natural consequence" and "in furtherance of the common design." Rejecting a requirement of inherent danger, the court preferred the majority rule that unenumerated felonies must be foreseeably dangerous to life as committed and approvingly quoted from a North Carolina opinion adopting this test.[186]

In three states courts have not directly addressed the question as to whether predicate felonies must be foreseeably dangerous. Florida decisions explain felony murder rules as protecting "the public from *inherently dangerous* situations caused by the commission of the felony."[187] Florida courts have therefore required a causal relationship between the felony and the death,[188] overturning felony murder convictions predicated on auto theft and drug possession where the act causing death was not instrumental to the felony.[189] A 1929 Washington decision overturned a murder conviction predicated on theft where a defendant ran over a child while trying to return a stolen car. Liability required that "death must have been the probable consequence of the unlawful act."[190] A 1974 decision justified the felony murder doctrine on the ground that one attempting "an inherently dangerous felony possesses a malevolent state of mind which the law calls malice . . . ."[191] Finally, Mississippi's code conditions murder, "done without any design to effect death . . . in the commission of any" unenumerated felony, on *malice.*[192] In all three states lawyers can draw on the consensus in other states to argue that death should be attributed to the felony only insofar as death resulted from a foreseeably dangerous act in furtherance of the felony.

Missouri alone, of all the states, has some authority explicitly *rejecting* a requirement of dangerousness. Yet Missouri also has adopted a causation standard that *requires* foreseeable danger. Missouri restricts felony murder to second-degree murder, which it defines as the commission or attempt of any felony "as a result of" the commission or attempt of which, or the flight from which, a person is killed.[193] The 1932 case of *State v. Glover* upheld a murder conviction predicated on arson because death was a reasonably foreseeable danger of the crime under the circumstances.[194] The 1975 case of *State v. Chambers* ignored *Glover*'s requirement of foreseeable danger, however. A drunken Chambers drove a stolen vehicle at night, without lights, into oncoming traffic. While the court observed that Chambers' conduct was foreseeably dangerous, it rejected requirements of both inherent and foreseeable danger.[195]

While a requirement of foreseeable danger would not have changed the result in *Chambers*, it would have prevented the grotesque result in another car-theft case, *State v. Colenburg*, also featured in Chapter 1.[196] Colenburg was convicted of murder because an unsupervised two-year-old darted into the street while he was driving a vehicle stolen seven months previously. He may have been driving over the speed limit, but if so there was no indication that driving at the speed limit would have enabled him to avoid the child. The prosecution initially charged him with involuntary manslaughter, but then charged him with second-degree felony murder when he refused to concede that he had killed recklessly.

The predicate felony in *Colenburg* was not theft per se but "tampering with a motor vehicle," which embraces merely possessing a vehicle without the owner's permission. Thus, one factor producing the unjust result in *Colenburg*, as in *Malaske*, was the unusual legislative choice to punish a relatively minor offense as a felony. Moreover, because Colenburg's offense was not required to be foreseeably dangerous, he was not required to have been culpable for the death at all. The court did not cite *Chambers* or distinguish *Glover*, but nevertheless rejected the defendant's argument that he could not be convicted because he "could not reasonably foresee the death."[197] The *Colenburg* majority offered no reason for rejecting a requirement of foreseeability apart from characterizing felony murder generally as a strict liability offense.[198] The court ignored the statutory requirement of a causal relationship between the felony and the resulting death. Nor did it require that the risk be imposed in furtherance of the theft—as was the reckless driving in *Chambers*.[199] Finally, in order to find even a temporal connection between the felony and the death, the court had to reject the common view of theft offenses as episodic crimes in favor of a conception of tampering as a crime that can continue indefinitely.[200]

But was *Colenburg* correctly decided from the standpoint of Missouri law prevailing in 1989? It was not. *Glover*'s requirement of a foreseeable danger of death remained authoritative. The *Chambers* court did not repudiate *Glover*, but simply failed to recognize its requirement of foreseeable danger. That requirement was reconfirmed in the 1979 case of *State v. Moore*.[201] Here the court upheld the first-degree felony murder conviction of a robber for an unintended killing by a resisting witness, on the ground that such defensive fire was foreseeable. Although Moore's conviction was ultimately overturned by a federal court, that court still required that the killing be a "natural and proximate result of the felony."[202] A foreseeability standard was again endorsed in the 1980 case of *State v. Baker*,[203] and reconfirmed in the 1993 case of *State v. Blunt*.[204]

Not only must a Missouri felon foreseeably cause the death, he arguably must do so in furtherance of the felony. In the 1936 case of *State v. Adams*[205] the court upheld a felony murder conviction for an armed burglar, whose accomplice fatally shot a pursuer during their flight. The court held that it was irrelevant that the burglary had ended, because the killing was "closely connected in time, place *and causal relation*" to the felony. Thus, a killing was attributable to the felony if committed "to prevent detection, or promote escape." Since Colenburg's fatal collision with the toddler was not motivated or caused by his aim of misappropriating the vehicle, the required linkage between the felony and the death seems absent—as the dissent argued. *Colenburg* was not only a very unjust decision. It was also illegal.

Our survey of dangerousness standards has revealed that many jurisdictions limit felony murder to enumerated felonies, most of which are inherently dangerous or violent. Almost all of the remaining felony murder jurisdictions require that the felony be committed in a way foreseeably dangerous to human life. No jurisdiction has clearly repudiated a requirement of danger, and there is a compelling argument for it in those few jurisdictions that have not yet decided the question.

CAUSATION STANDARDS

Two closely related issues arise concerning the causal responsibility of felons for deaths in the commission or attempt of a felony. One is the causal link between a felon's act and the resulting death. The other is the causal link between the felony and the resulting death. If either causal link requires foreseeable danger of death, the felon whose act caused the result must have negligently imposed a risk of death.

Lawyers conceptualize "legal causation" as a normative filter that assigns responsibility for a subset of those acts that contribute to a result "in fact." Such "factual causation" requires only that the offender's act be one of several qualifying causal conditions—usually that it be a necessary condition for the harmful result. It is tempting to require nothing more than this, so as to keep the concept of causation morally neutral. We could then confine the moral assessment of the defendant's conduct entirely to the mental element of the offense.

Yet it seems unfair to attribute a result to an actor's choice unless her reasons for action serve to *explain* the result. Suppose an arsonist is on his way to start a fire. A robber demands his wallet, shooting a gun to frighten him, and inadvertently kills a bystander. Surely the arsonist's recklessness of life does not make him causally responsible for the bystander's death. It was not within the risk of which he was reckless. It seems we cannot exorcise normative judgment from the attribution of causal responsibility. "Legal causation" is this necessarily normative attribution of responsibility for a result.

Causal attribution is normative because it depends on the values expressed by action. Recall that we punish harmful results in order to vindicate the equal status of those harmed. This purpose is served only when injury implies disrespect. When the arsonist walks to the site of his crime, he expresses no disrespect to his fellow pedestrians because he does not endanger them. The robber firing a gun on a public street, however, disrespects them by knowingly endangering them for a bad end. Because causal responsibility in criminal law is about the insult implied by injury, it depends on the offender's expectations and ends.

Thus "legal causation" has traditionally been defined in terms of fault. The first common law treatise to analyze causation in homicide, Matthew Hale's, focused exclusively on acts of violence. Seventeenth- and eighteenth-century English law defined killing in such a way as to entail a hostile motive and an expectation of injury. More recently, Hart and Honoré's influential study of causation defined a legal cause (in part) as an abnormal act necessary to a result, and associated with such a result in normal experience. "Abnormality" here connotes not just rarity but illegitimacy. Wayne LaFave's influential treatise follows this approach to legal causation.[206] The Model Penal Code makes defendants causally responsible only for results of the kind they intended, or culpably risked. The code conditions causation on apparent danger even for strict liability offenses, requiring that the results were "probable consequence[s]" of defendant's conduct.[207]

How do these principles apply in the case of felony murder? Does felony murder require a violent or dangerous act from which death is reasonably foreseeable? Or does it simply require factual causation—that is, an act necessary to the resulting death? LaFave rejects the latter view as an analytic mistake, observing that the same principles of legal causation apply in felony murder cases as in other homicides.[208] Even when homicide requires no separate proof of a culpable mental state, causal responsibility still requires a death within the scope of a culpably imposed risk. As we shall see, LaFave's analysis accords with prevailing law.

Litigation concerning causation in felony murder is often framed as a choice between an "agency" test that restricts liability to deaths directly caused by felons and a "proximate cause" test that includes all deaths foreseeably resulting from the felons' acts. Yet LaFave argues persuasively that the proximate cause and agency limitations address two different issues. Foreseeability is a test of causal responsibility, while agency is a test for determining whether the act causing death is sufficiently related to the felony.[209] In fact, most agency rule jurisdictions *also* require foreseeability. While fifteen felony murder jurisdictions have adopted an agency test,[210] twelve of these require foreseeability for all predicate felonies,[211] and one more requires foreseeability for predicate felonies not deemed inherently dangerous.[212] An additional nineteen jurisdictions without an agency rule also require that death result foreseeably.[213] Thus a substantial majority of felony murder jurisdictions—at least thirty-two out of forty-five—condition felony murder liability on the foreseeability of death, as a result of either a felon's act or the felony itself. Significantly, the great majority of those jurisdictions that exhaustively enumerate predicate felonies—sixteen out of twenty-five—also require that the felons foreseeably cause death.[214]

Several jurisdictions have neither adopted nor rejected a foreseeability standard. All of these have other limits that tend to ensure some measure of apparent danger. Iowa, South Carolina, and Mississippi require separate proof of malice. Colorado, Iowa, Oregon, South Dakota, Wyoming, and the United States limit felony murder to enumerated predicate felonies. Florida courts tend to view deaths in the course of such non-dangerous felonies as auto theft as unrelated to the felony.

Only four jurisdictions explicitly reject a requirement of foreseeability for causal responsibility, and these also may achieve a similar effect in most cases through other doctrinal devices.[215] Minnesota restricts predicate felonies to those that are inherently dangerous to human life, while Wisconsin, Alaska, and North Dakota limit predicate felonies to enumerated felonies. The Wisconsin Supreme Court saw a foreseeability standard as unnecessary because the legislature had restricted predicate felonies to those it regarded as inherently dangerous to human life. The Alaska courts have substituted a requirement of unlawful force for a foreseeability standard. Finally, North Dakota's culpability default rules may condition felony murder on recklessness.

Nevertheless, it would be far better for these jurisdictions to join the majority and require foreseeable danger as a criterion of causal responsibility. The failure to require that death result from a foreseeably dangerous act can lead to unwarranted convictions, even in cases involving dangerous predicate felonies. In the infamous 1967 California case of *People v. Stamp*, described in Chapter 1, the defendant was convicted of felony murder when a robbery victim suffered a fatal heart attack shortly after the robbery. The trial court refused the defendant's requested instruction on foreseeability and an appellate court upheld his conviction, insisting that even an accidental death in the course of a robbery sufficed for murder.[216]

Today, California requires foreseeability, at least in cases, like *Stamp*, where no battery is committed and no injury is inflicted. Thus California's pattern jury instructions now require that if there is more than one cause of death, as in heart attack cases, the felony must be a "substantial factor in *causing*" the death.[217] Causation in turn requires that death be "the direct, *natural, and probable consequence* of the act . . . ."[218] The instruction adds that "a natural and probable consequence is one that *a reasonable person would know is likely to happen* if nothing unusual intervenes."[219] These instructions are consistent with the requirement of an act naturally dangerous to life recognized in the *Patterson* and *Chun* cases.[220] If the *Stamp* fact pattern were to occur in California today, the defendant would be entitled to an instruction requiring proof that the heart attack would have appeared probable to a reasonable person as a result of the stickup.

A foreseeability standard is not the only way to condition causation on danger, however. *Stamp* is usefully contrasted with the Alaska case of *Phillips v. State*.[221] Here a police officer suffered a fatal heart attack while struggling with the defendant, who was resisting arrest. Although the Alaska court rejected a foreseeability test, it required that death result from the felon's unlawful use of force, and suggested that if the heart attack had occurred during a strenuous chase rather than a violent struggle there would be no liability.[222]

Nevertheless, not every use of unlawful force renders death foreseeable. Thus, in *State v. Gorman*, the Minnesota Supreme Court upheld a second-degree murder conviction predicated on felony assault, where the defendant merely punched the victim, who died as a result of his head striking the floor.[223] In a similar Illinois case from the 1920s, a murder conviction was overturned on the ground that death was not a "reasonable and probable consequence" of a blow with a fist.[224] The *Gorman* decision is particularly disturbing because the predicate felony did not require any culpability with respect to the physical injury that rendered it felonious. Such a strict liability assault-with-injury offense may be inherently dangerous ex post, but the danger is not necessarily apparent ex ante. The *Gorman* case is further troubling because assault offenses lack any independent felonious purpose. Thus the *Gorman* case fulfills neither branch of the dual culpability requirement.

Like the *Gorman* decision, Georgia's controversial *Miller* decision also resulted in large part from the misguided decision to define aggravated assault as a strict liability offense. Georgia compounded this mistake by dropping its foreseeability standard for predicate felonies deemed inherently dangerous, such as aggravated assaults. In *Durden v. State*, a Georgia court imposed liability for a burglary victim's heart attack after the defendant fired a gun at him.[225] The court rejected the traditional requirement of physical injury as archaic, but did not replace it with a requirement of foreseeability. A jury might well have found such foreseeability on these facts but was never given the chance.

Indeed, we cannot be sure that a foreseeability standard would prevent conviction on facts like those in *Stamp*. First, there is the danger that courts will simply ignore the legal limits on causal responsibility. New York's *Ingram* case illustrates this risk.[226] Recall that the hapless Ingram's captor died of a heart attack without a physical struggle. Prior case law in New York conditioned causation of death on (1) a physical interaction between defendant and victim directly causing death as (2) a foreseeable consequence of the defendant's act.[227]

The court gave no instruction on these two elements of causation, but the defense attorney never requested one. The New York Court of Appeals upheld Ingram's conviction for felony murder because the error had not been preserved. Ingram—as unlucky in law as in life—was unjustly convicted not because of New York's definition of causation but in spite of it.[228]

Second, even properly instructed juries may be influenced by hindsight bias to blame a felon for the unexpected death of a frail victim. Thus in the Maine case of *State v. Reardon*, the victim of a mugging suffered a heart attack while reporting the incident to the police. Acting as the fact finder in the case, the trial judge found that it was reasonably foreseeable that a sixty-seven-year-old victim would have heart disease and that robbing him would cause him to have a heart attack and die.[229] Recall the *Dixon* case, where a burglar kicked in the door of an elderly woman's home and cut the phone cord, but apparently never touched her. The Nebraska court upheld Dixon's conviction on the ground that the victim's heart attack was foreseeable under the circumstances.[230] In *People v. Matos*, described in Chapter 1, a police officer fell off a roof while pursuing a robber. The trial court reasoned that the officer's death was foreseeable as a result of the robber's flight across a roof and rejected any requirement of a direct physical interaction between defendant and victim.[231] It justified these conclusions by relying on the *result* in *People v. Ingram*,[232] even though the *reasoning* in that case never reached the questions of direct causation and foreseeability because they were not raised below.

Death from a heart attack seems more foreseeable, where the defendant inflicts physical injuries especially to an obviously frail victim or the victim shows physical distress during the crime. Thus murder liability was defensible in the Connecticut case of *State v. Spates*,[233] where defendants left a robbery victim bound despite his asking for doctor and telling robbers he was having heart attack; and in the North Carolina case of *State v. Atkinson*,[234] where a victim with heart disease was beaten with a baseball bat during a robbery. A conviction was also warranted in the Kansas case of *State v. Shaw*,[235] where an eight-six-year-old victim of a robbery/burglary was found bound and gagged, with bruises and abrasions, dead of heart attack likely caused by her struggles to breathe and to free herself.[236] The same reasoning could apply to other unexpected complications from physical injury to an elderly victim.[237] Assuming that a defendant should have foreseen death occurring in some simpler way, the victim's death would arguably meet the Model Penal Code's standard for negligent causation. The code imposes causal responsibility for a death outside the risk of which the actor should have been aware, if it was not "not too remote or accidental in its occurrence to have a just bearing on the actor's liability."[238]

Almost all felony murder jurisdictions condition felony murder on dangerous conduct, at least in theory. Yet most of these enumerate at least some predicate felonies that are not in fact very dangerous. Fortunately, a majority of jurisdictions also require foreseeable causation. Together, these two requirements effectively condition felony murder liability on negligence in most jurisdictions.

10 COMPLICITY AND COLLECTIVE LIABILITY

THE PROBLEM OF COMPLICITY IN FELONY MURDER

If a killer must cause death negligently to be liable for felony murder, an accomplice in felony murder should be no less culpable. Yet critics have contended that the felony murder doctrine holds accomplices in predicate felonies strictly liable for their co-felons' unexpected killings. A *New York Times* story on felony murder liability dramatized this claim with a detailed discussion of the Ryan Holle case.[1]

Assessing the *Holle* case requires that we clarify the concept of complicity in a predicate felony. Complicity requires aiding or encouraging a principal in committing an offense. Because the accomplice's conduct is different from the perpetrator's conduct, the accomplice's mental state must differ as well. Most jurisdictions require intent to aid, which they interpret as a purpose of making the crime succeed.[2] These jurisdictions include Florida, where the *Holle* case was decided.

Holle, who routinely shared the use of his car with a cohabitant, should not have been convicted of burglary without proof that he provided the car on this occasion for the purpose of—not just with the expectation of—facilitating the burglary. Holle testified that he heard one of the burglars say that it might be necessary to knock out the victim.[3] So he had reason to foresee that she would be clubbed fatally. If Holle accepted this risk as a means to the end of stealing, he arguably deserved murder liability. But if stealing was never his goal and he was merely fulfilling his household obligations by sharing use of his possessions, he deserved liability for neither the murder nor the predicate felony of burglary. Accordingly, the injustice of Holle's *murder* conviction resulted from his *undeserved accomplice liability for the burglary* rather than any undeserved attribution of the killing to the burglary. Unjust convictions of complicity in felony murder often result from misattributions of complicity in the predicate felony.[4]

The general problem of accomplice liability for felony murder can be illustrated with two hypothetical scenarios.

First, imagine that Armory plans the armed robbery of a bank with Rob and Driver. Armory supplies a loaded gun for Rob to use in sticking up a teller, while Driver waits outside in a getaway car. A security guard, Vigilant, opens fire on Rob during the robbery. Rob returns fire, killing Vigilant. Rob exits the bank and flees with Driver in the getaway car. Police pursue them in a high-speed chase. Driver eventually runs a stoplight and collides with another vehicle, killing Passenger. Armory and Driver are certainly liable as accomplices in Rob's bank robbery. They purposely aided it. Rob is liable for the felony murder of Vigilant in any felony murder jurisdiction, and Driver is liable for the felony murder of Passenger in most such jurisdictions. But is Armory liable for Rob's felony murder of Vigilant? Is he liable for Driver's felony murder of Passenger?

Second, imagine that Cat asks Buddy to drive him to and from a warehouse at night and wait for him while he burglarizes it. Buddy asks if anyone will get hurt. Cat replies that the warehouse is unguarded, he is not expecting any trouble, and he is not bringing a gun. Buddy agrees to drive and wait. In fact, Cat is interrupted by Watchman, an armed security guard. Cat attempts to disarm Watchman and shoots him with Watchman's own gun in the ensuing struggle. Buddy will certainly be liable as an accomplice in Cat's burglary, which he intentionally aided. Cat will be guilty of felony murder. Although he did not expect resistance in advance and did not bring a gun, his felony became foreseeably dangerous once he decided to struggle with an armed victim. The presence of a victim and the use of a gun would aggravate the burglary sufficiently to meet requirements for a predicate burglary in almost all jurisdictions. But what about Buddy? Does his complicity in Cat's burglary also implicate him in the death of Watchman?

There are three possible answers to such questions, depending on whether accomplices in predicate felonies are held liable for all killings by their co-felons, for killings they intend, or for killings they should foresee. If accomplices in the predicate felony are strictly liable for their co-felon's killings, Armory must be liable for the death of Passenger and Buddy must be liable for the death of Watchman. This would make Buddy liable with *less* culpability than would be required to convict the actual killer of felony murder. On the other hand, if complicity in felony murder requires the intent to promote that crime, Armory may not even be liable for the foreseeable but undesired death of Vigilant. This test requires *more* culpability to convict an accomplice of felony murder than to convict an actual killer. Intermediate between these extremes is the answer given by the principle of dual culpability, punishing negligent killing in the pursuit of a felonious purpose. This test permits Armory's liability for Vigilant's death, which was foreseeable to Armory as a result of supplying a gun for use in robbing a defended target. The same test may or may not convict him for Passenger's death, depending on whether it was foreseeable to him. This foreseeability test acquits Buddy, who never became aware of the armed guard and so had no reason to foresee a fatal struggle. This foreseeability test requires the same culpability, negligence, to convict both perpetrator and accomplice.

The question of accomplice liability for felony murder is one example of a larger problem with complicity. How does the required purpose of promoting the offense apply to crimes involving the careless rather than intentional infliction of harm? Must the accomplice in an unintentional crime be more culpable than the perpetrator? The Model Penal Code and several state codes solve this problem by distinguishing between conduct elements and result elements. Thus, the accomplice must purposely aid or encourage the perpetrator in committing proscribed conduct. However, the accomplice need only have the same culpable mental state with respect to a result as the perpetrator.[5]

Accordingly, if a perpetrator must cause death negligently by means of certain conduct, the accomplice must purposely aid or encourage that conduct, with negligence toward the resulting risk of death. If felony murder were defined as negligently causing death by means of certain felonies, an accomplice in felony murder would have to purposely promote the predicate felony, with negligence toward the risk of death. This mental element would satisfy the principle of dual culpability.

The difficulty is that felony murder definitions rarely spell out the requirement of negligence this straightforwardly. Felony murder rules often require negligence obliquely, by requiring conduct that is negligent per se. Such per se negligent conduct includes inherently dangerous predicate felonies, foreseeably dangerous commission of the predicate felony, or foreseeable causation of death. How can we apply the Model Penal Code standard for complicity in crimes of unintended results, to crimes requiring no explicit culpable mental state? The problem disappears when the predicate felony is inherently dangerous: intentionally promoting the felony automatically entails negligence with respect to the risk of death. Yet most states predicate felony murder on at least some felonies that are *not* inherently dangerous. Accomplices in these felonies might not be in a position to foresee danger. Thus, the aims of the Model Penal Code complicity scheme are best fulfilled by holding accomplices in predicate felonies complicit in only those deaths they are in a position to foresee.

Such a foreseeability standard comports with traditional tests of accomplice responsibility for felony murder. Collective liability for crimes of violence long preceded the attachment of any significance to felonious motive. Recall that the *Lord Dacre's Case* in 1535 held that when a group embarks on a crime, resolving to kill resisters, all are liable for a killing by any.[6] The 1558 case of *Mansell & Herbert* extended this ruling to make all collaborators in a violent assault liable for a killing by any, on the ground that intent to injure or wound supplied the malice required for murder liability.[7] In first proposing a felony murder rule in 1700, Justice Holt reasoned that complicity should transfer from the predicate offense to the killing only if four conditions were met: (1) the predicate offense must be "deliberate" rather than careless; (2) "the killing must be in pursuance of that unlawful act, and not collateral to it"; (3) the predicate offense must "tend to the hurt of another either immediately, or by necessary consequence"; and (4) the accomplice "must know of the malicious design of the party killing."[8] Holt's rule limits accomplice liability to deaths caused in furtherance of felonies involving a substantial danger of injury, known to the accomplice. Blackstone restricted accomplice liability for murder to those anticipating violence: "[I]f two or more come together to do an unlawful act against the king's peace, of which the probable consequence might be bloodshed . . . and one of them kills a man; it is murder in them all . . . ."[9] Where they considered accomplice liability for felony murder, nineteenth-century American cases and treatises generally followed this English literature.

Today, many jurisdictions address the problem of complicity in felony murder with a two-part test that Professor LaFave traces back to Holt. This test holds a participant in a predicate felony responsible for fatal acts of co-felons in furtherance of the felony, and foreseeable as a result of the felony.[10] A majority of felony murder jurisdictions require that death be caused by an act in furtherance of the felony. A dozen states' codes mention such a requirement,[11] and a number of other jurisdictions have adopted similar tests by judicial decision.[12]

In addition, a majority of felony murder jurisdictions have required that death or a fatal act should be foreseeable as a result of the felony.[13] This two-part test reflects the two dimensions of culpability recognized by the principle of dual culpability: negligence of death in the pursuit of a felonious motive. It resonates with traditional understandings of collective liability for felony murder and is compatible with the Model Penal Code's approach to complicity in crimes of inadvertent harm.

INDIVIDUAL FELONY MURDER LIABILITY JURISDICTIONS

Most jurisdictions define felony murder individually, as causing death in perpetrating a predicate felony.[14] Wyoming, for example, imposes first-degree murder liability on "whoever . . . in the perpetration or attempt to perpetrate" various felonies "kills any human being."[15] In these jurisdictions, one who does not personally cause death can be liable for felony murder only as an accomplice to one who does. Yet ordinarily, one is liable as an accomplice only insofar as one intentionally aids or encourages the conduct constituting the crime. Typically an accomplice in an offense must intend to promote it.[16] A few jurisdictions provide that co-felons are liable for any act in furtherance and foreseeable as a result of the offense, but this is the exception.[17] Yet the fact that one knowingly aided or encouraged a predicate felony does not entail that one also knowingly aided or encouraged a killing.

Thus in individual felony murder liability jurisdictions, accomplices in the predicate felony are liable for a killing only if they meet general criteria of accomplice liability for homicide, or satisfy special rules for complicity in felony murder developed by courts. If courts *choose* to impose felony murder liability on co-felons who do not intentionally aid or encourage a killing, *without statutory authorization*, they need some principled rationale. In the case of *Mares v. State*[18] the Wyoming Supreme Court rejected a burglar's proposed affirmative defense that he did not know a weapon would be present and had no reason to expect a killing. The court rested this decision entirely on grounds of institutional competence, reasoning that the creation of such a defense was a legislative function. Yet on such reasoning there should have been no need for an affirmative defense. Wyoming's code imposes no murder liability on non-killers unless they knowingly aid or encourage a killing. The Wyoming code provides that one who "knowingly aids or abets in the commission of a felony" is liable as an accessory before the fact in that felony.[19] Thus the Wyoming court acted without legislative authorization in imposing accomplice liability for killings on co-felons without intent to kill. The court might have reasoned that Mares knowingly aided an act proximately causing death if he knew that the burglary was foreseeably dangerous. But the burden to prove that foreseeability should then have logically fallen on the prosecution. *There is no statutory basis for accomplice strict liability in the thirty jurisdictions imposing individual felony murder liability.*

There is arguably no need to prove that death was foreseeable to the accomplice when the felony he aided or encouraged is inherently dangerous to human life. Individual liability jurisdictions use one of two approaches to ensure that the felony is dangerous. About half of these jurisdictions restrict predicate offenses to an enumerated list of felonies. The remaining jurisdictions restrict predicate felonies to those found by courts or juries to be dangerous or violent. We will examine accomplice liability for felony murder in each group.

INDIVIDUAL LIABILITY JURISDICTIONS WITH EXHAUSTIVE ENUMERATION

Fifteen individual liability jurisdictions enumerate exhaustively.[20] If we assume that all of these predicate felonies are inherently dangerous, participants in these felonies are at least negligent with respect to a risk of death. Thus the Pennsylvania pattern jury instructions reason that "[b]ecause [robbery] . . . is a crime inherently dangerous to human life, there does not have to be any other proof of malice."[21] Similarly, a District of Columbia court explained the imposition of accomplice liability for a "reasonably foreseeable killing" on the ground that "malice may be presumed from the commission of certain 'dangerous' or 'violent' felonies that 'generally involve a risk that . . . someone might be killed.'"[22] Courts in Kansas and Wisconsin have offered similar arguments.[23]

Unfortunately, every jurisdiction with individualized liability and exhaustive enumeration has at least one predicate felony that is *not* inherently dangerous. Almost all of these jurisdictions—including Wyoming—predicate felony murder on unaggravated burglary.[24] Six of these jurisdictions predicate felony murder on drug offenses, and three predicate felony murder liability on theft.[25]

The Kansas code makes accomplices liable for all foreseeable secondary crimes,[26] and Kansas courts have long justified felony murder liability on the basis that dangerous felonies foreseeably risked death.[27] However, Kansas courts have held that a foreseeability instruction is unnecessary because predicate felonies are limited to those designated inherently dangerous.[28] Yet Kansas predicates felony murder on unaggravated burglary, drug offenses, and theft. Thus Kansas could impose felony murder liability for an unforeseeable killing on an accomplice like Buddy. The court's reasoning conflates notice that the legislature *considers* an offense dangerous with notice of actual danger.

Tennessee courts have taken a similar approach. Tennessee generally holds accomplices responsible for secondary crimes natural and probable as a result of their primary crimes.[29] Like Kansas courts, however, Tennessee courts have held that this requirement of foreseeability does not apply to felony murder.[30] Indeed, in *State v. Mickens*, an intermediate appellate court held the requirement of foreseeability inapplicable to felony murder, quoting a passage from LaFave's treatise that precisely contradicted the court's position.[31]

While Tennessee generally restricts predicate felonies to genuinely dangerous ones—the predicate felony in *Mickens* was kidnapping—it is one of the few states conditioning felony murder on simple theft. As noted earlier, Tennessee courts have managed to avoid holding thieves liable for unexpected deaths by holding these deaths causally unrelated to the felony. A similar expedient is available in Kansas, which limits accomplice liability to killings in furtherance of the felony.[32] Pennsylvania courts have also insulated accomplices from liability for unexpected killings by treating such killings as unrelated to the felony.[33] A conclusion that death is unrelated to the felony is almost always available when death results in an improbable way. Yet a jury instruction that death must be foreseeable to the accomplice as a result of the felony is a more reliable and intellectually honest way to restrict liability to those who are culpable.

A number of other individualized liability/enumerated felony jurisdictions *do* require that death be foreseeable as a result of the felony. These include the District of Columbia, Idaho, Indiana, Iowa, Louisiana, and South Dakota.[34] Nebraska, Pennsylvania, Utah, and West Virginia have conditioned causation on foreseeability of death to the killer without addressing the responsibility of co-felons. They should be presumed to condition complicity in murder on foreseeability of death to the co-felons. Kansas and Tennessee should also extend their foreseeability requirements from killers to co-felons. Finally, the United States, Wisconsin, and Wyoming should join other states in conditioning causation on foreseeability.

Because non-dangerous predicate felonies necessarily do not generate a lot of felony murder cases, the problem of non-negligent accomplices arises infrequently. Nevertheless, complicity statutes require culpability and courts should routinely instruct juries to condition complicity in felony murder on foreseeability, even for murders predicated on enumerated felonies.

INDIVIDUAL LIABILITY WITH DANGEROUS FELONY RULES

Fifteen jurisdictions impose individual felony murder liability predicated on dangerous felony rules.[35] Of these, California, Massachusetts, Minnesota, and Nevada restrict predicates to those that are inherently dangerous. This precludes felony murder liability for non-negligent accomplices in non-enumerated felonies. Massachusetts requires either inherent danger or recklessness for all felony murders, including those predicated on enumerated felonies.[36] Minnesota enumerates only dangerous offenses, while providing that accomplices are always responsible for additional crimes "committed in pursuance of" and "reasonably foreseeable as a probable consequence of" the intended crime.[37] California and Nevada enumerate only violent predicate felonies, except for non-aggravated forms of burglary. California imposes liability on co-felons for killings "logically related" to the felony,[38] but also instructs juries that death must be the "natural and probable consequence" of the felony.[39] This instruction comports with California's general rule that "the liability of an aider and abettor extends . . . to the natural and reasonable consequences of the acts he knowingly and intentionally aids and encourages."[40] The question of accomplice liability for felony murder predicated on burglary does not appear to have been decided in Nevada, but Nevada courts often follow California precedent in interpreting Nevada's very similar code.

Eleven other states predicate individual felony murder on non-enumerated felonies committed in foreseeably dangerous ways.[41] These jurisdictions therefore must confront the problem of liability for accomplices to whom death was not foreseeable. Only five of these jurisdictions also predicate individual felony murder liability on any non-dangerous enumerated felonies: Illinois, Maryland, Mississippi, and North Carolina predicate felony murder on simple burglary, while Rhode Island predicates felony murder on drug offenses.[42] Almost all of these jurisdictions set high standards of culpability for accomplice liability, requiring intent to aid, or sharing in the principal's intent.[43]

Almost all of these jurisdictions also condition accomplice liability for felony murder on the foreseeability of death as a result of the predicate felony. Delaware, which conditions felony murder on killing recklessly or negligently in the course of a felony, holds co-felons liable only if the killing was a "foreseeable consequence" of the felony.[44] This is also Delaware's general standard concerning the liability of accomplices for secondary crimes. Illinois holds co-felons responsible for any killing "reasonably or probably necessary to accomplish the objects of the felony" or that is a "direct and foreseeable consequence" of the felony.[45] South Carolina holds co-felons liable for any homicide that is the "probable or natural consequence of the acts done in pursuance of the common design."[46] Virginia holds accomplices liable for the "probable consequences" of concerted action,[47] including killings that "should have been within [their] contemplation as the probable result" of the felony.[48] North Carolina also holds felons responsible for any crimes, including killings, in furtherance of, and foreseeable as a consequence of, the felony.[49] Rhode Island courts have held that an accomplice in burglary is liable for all further crimes "naturally and foreseeably" resulting.[50] Because the Texas code requires that felony murderers cause death by means of an act clearly dangerous to life, an accomplice arguably cannot "intend to promote" the offense without aiding or encouraging the clearly dangerous act. Moreover, the Texas code provides that conspirators to commit a felony are guilty of any felony that should have been anticipated as a result of and in furtherance of the conspiracy.[51] Mississippi conditions accomplice liability for a secondary homicide on "a common design" to commit a "crime of violence."[52] Oklahoma has traditionally held co-conspirators liable for fatal acts perpetrated in felonies that involve some danger of death,[53] while its pattern jury instructions hold co-felons liable only for secondary crimes "necessary in order to complete" the felony or flight from the felony.[54]

Courts have weakened requirements of foreseeability of death for co-felons in two states. Georgia conditions complicity in felony murder on foreseeability in principle, but in the 2003 case of *Williams v. State*, the Georgia Supreme Court upheld an instruction that when a victim is killed in furtherance of a conspiracy to rob, "such killing is the probable consequence of the unlawful design to rob."[55] This instruction appears to be an unconstitutional presumption, requiring the jury to infer foreseeable danger from felonious motive. Such a presumption is defensible only if confined to felonies that are, like robbery, inherently dangerous. Maryland pattern jury instructions hold accomplices liable only for "acts that naturally and necessarily flow from the common design . . . ."[56] The 1974 decision of an intermediate court required that death must be "a natural probable consequence" of the intended felony,[57] but a 1999 decision of the same court required only that the killing be in furtherance of the felony.[58] The Maryland Court of Appeals should reconfirm that foreseeability is required, as well as felonious motive.

COLLECTIVE LIABILITY JURISDICTIONS

A substantial minority of jurisdictions have sought to avoid the complicity problem by defining felony murder collectively, as a crime of participation in a felony that causes death. Such statutes treat all participants as principals.

Collective liability felony murder statutes take two quite different forms. One defines felony murder as causing death *by means of* certain felonies. We may call this *direct collective liability*. Direct collective felony murder liability logically requires that non-killers be just as culpable for the death as the killer. The other form conditions felony murder on participating in a felony in which *another person* causes death. We may call this *vicarious collective liability*. Vicarious collective liability may permit liability for participants who cannot foresee the dangers imposed by the killer.

Ohio, Maine, and Missouri employ direct collective liability for all felony murders,[59] while Oklahoma employs it for first-degree felony murder liability only.[60] Ohio defines felony murder as causing the death of a person as a proximate result of the commission or attempt of a violent felony of sufficiently high grade. Ohio's code enumerates several violent felonies and also defines a violent felony as an offense committed purposely or knowingly and involving injury or a risk of serious injury or death.[61] Given the use of violent felonies as predicates for felony murder, it seems most reasonable to construe such felonies as requiring knowledge of the circumstances that create the risk of serious injury or death. To be liable as an accomplice in Ohio, one must aid or abet another in committing the offense with the kind of culpability required for the commission of the offense.[62] Thus an accomplice in an aggravated burglary should be as aware of the aggravating circumstance creating a risk of death or serious injury as would the perpetrator. On this reasoning, Buddy would be guilty of neither aggravated burglary nor felony murder. Unfortunately, a mid-level Ohio court eschewed this approach in the troubling case of *State v. Kimble*.[63] As argued earlier, the decision is not authorized by the language or structure of the code and it should be corrected by Ohio's highest court.

Maine, Missouri, and Oklahoma define felony murder as including participation in a felony in which death is caused by the commission, attempt, or *flight from* a predicate felony.[64] The inclusion of flight within the felony is analytically unsound, as it is not an offense element. Participation in a felony does not entail participation in, or anticipation of, flight. Could these provisions implicate Armory for the unexpected felony murder of Passenger during reckless flight from the felony?

The Maine statute limits predicate felonies to the traditional five plus escape and murder of a different victim.[65] It requires that death be "a reasonably foreseeable consequence of such commission, attempt or flight." Because the Maine statute makes all participants potentially liable for such deaths, it would seem that death must be foreseeable to each participant. This interpretation is consistent with Maine's general provision on complicity, implicating one in any crime reasonably foreseeable as a result of her conduct.[66] A Maine standard jury instruction provides that one is guilty of murder if "commission of the crime of murder by . . . [another] person was a reasonably foreseeable consequence of *participation by the accused* in the robbery."[67] Finally, Maine provides an apparently redundant affirmative defense for accomplices like Buddy who do not kill, are not armed, are not aware that a co-felon is armed, and do not expect the co-felon to kill.[68]

While Missouri does not limit predicate felonies to enumerated or inherently dangerous offenses, it conditions causation of death on foreseeable danger. Missouri requires that accomplices have "the required culpable mental state" for the offense[69] and attempt to aid "with the purpose of promoting the offense."[70] Missouri courts hold co-felons responsible for deaths foreseeable as a result of the felony.[71]

Oklahoma's convoluted statute imposes first-degree felony murder liability on those who participate in an enumerated felony that results in death or in the commission of which a participant causes death.[72] Oklahoma's enumerated felonies are all dangerous except for drug offenses. Its jury instructions provide that "[a] death is caused by . . . conduct if the conduct is a substantial factor in bringing about the death and the conduct is dangerous and threatens or destroys life."[73] The jury instructions make participants liable for deaths caused by the conduct of another participant that is "inseparable from" or "necessary to" the offense, or flight from the offense.[74] The statute would be clearer if it simply required participation in an enumerated felony causing death.

A dozen states employ vicarious collective liability rules. Of these, only Florida, Alaska, and possibly Colorado have not required foreseeability. Seven jurisdictions—Alabama, Connecticut, Montana, New York, North Dakota, Oregon, and Washington—define felony murder as participation in a felony in which any participant causes death.[75] In all of these states but Alabama, the felony includes flight.[76] All require that accomplices have the intention to promote the offense, the mental culpability required for the offense, or both.[77] All appear to require that death be caused in furtherance of the felony.[78] Thus, for the most part, these states require that the accomplice share in the felonious aim that motivates the act causing death.

To what extent do these seven states also condition the felony-murder liability of non-triggermen on negligence? As noted above, the North Dakota Code's default rules appear to condition felony murder on recklessness. Alabama's definition of homicide requires a culpable mental state of at least negligence for felony murder. Connecticut, New York, North Dakota, Oregon and Washington have an affirmative defense for non-triggermen who were not armed, and had no reason to know their co-felons were armed or would kill.[79] Such a defense would acquit Buddy. Unfortunately, it shifts the burden onto the defendant to disprove negligence.[80]

Previous analysis showed that Oregon restricts predicates to inherently dangerous enumerated felonies. Alabama, North Dakota, and Washington predicate felony murder on non-enumerated foreseeably dangerous felonies as well as traditional dangerous felonies. Of these, Alabama limits predicate burglaries to aggravated ones, and limits non-enumerated felonies to those "clearly" dangerous to human life.[81] This requirement comports with the official commentary on the felony murder provision, characterizing felony murder liability as justifiable only if restricted to foreseeable deaths. Thus Oregon and Alabama limit felony murder liability to participation in felonies implying negligence.

Courts in four other states—Connecticut, Washington, Montana, and New York—appear to base felony murder liability on the foreseeability of death to each participant. Connecticut courts have interpreted the requirement that death be caused "in furtherance" of the felony to mean that death must result from circumstances foreseen as part of the common plan.[82] A Washington court upheld a felony murder conviction based on evidence that a child's death was "a natural and probable consequence" of defendant's "actions as an accomplice" in an assault.[83] The Montana Supreme Court overturned a conviction for complicity in a felony murder predicated on attempted aggravated assault because of a failure to prove that the defendant could foresee death or knew the killer had a gun.[84] Another Montana decision justified accomplice liability for felony murder as imposing responsibility on "people who engage in dangerous acts likely to result in death."[85] New York long used the same foreseeability standard in assessing the responsibility of killers and other participants,[86] and appears to have continued to do so after adopting its collective liability statute.[87]

It appears that all seven states conditioning felony murder on participating in a felony in which another participant causes death effectively require that all felony murderers exhibit at least negligence toward death. Buddy should not be liable in any of these states.

An additional five states—Alaska, Arizona, Colorado, Florida, and New Jersey—condition liability on participating in an enumerated predicate felony in which death is caused by any person.[88] Non-inherently dangerous predicate felonies include drug offenses in Alaska, Florida, and Arizona; and simple burglary in Arizona, Colorado, Florida, and New Jersey.[89] All of these states except Florida include flight in the felony. All provide, either by statute or in pattern jury instructions, that accomplices must purposely or knowingly promote the offense.[90]

Of these five states, New Jersey, Arizona, and possibly Colorado require that the felony cause death in a way foreseeable to the accomplice. The New Jersey pattern instruction requires the prosecution to prove that "death was a probable consequence" of the commission, attempt, or flight from the predicate felony. In addition, New Jersey has the affirmative defense for unarmed non-triggermen who do not know their co-felons are armed and do not have reason to expect they will kill and—unlike other states—places the burden on the prosecution to disprove it beyond a reasonable doubt.[91] Arizona holds participants in a felony liable for deaths that are the "natural and proximate result thereof,"[92] or that are naturally and foreseeably caused by acts in furtherance of the felony.[93] It has approved an instruction saying "A person whose deliberate acts in perpetrating" a predicate felony have "set in motion a chain of events which cause the death of another person, which was a risk reasonably to be foreseen, is guilty of first degree murder."[94] A Colorado decision implied—but did not directly hold—that felons are responsible for killings they have reason to foresee. The court argued that the defendant's knowledge that the killer was armed and posed a danger to the victim would have inculpated her, if she had been complicit in the predicate burglary.[95]

Finally, Alaska and Florida have not adopted foreseeability standards for causation or complicity. They could well convict Buddy of felony murder even though he had no reason to anticipate Cat's fatal struggle with the armed security guard. Although Florida law was misapplied in the *Holle* case, Florida law does currently permit conviction for complicity in felony murder on the basis of strict liability. Yet this is unusual among collective felony murder liability jurisdictions. Florida and Alaska courts should determine that a person is not killed in the perpetration of a felony unless such a death is a foreseeable consequence of the felony. Until then, their felony murder laws will remain proverbial exceptions proving the rule of foreseeability.

Yet even if these five states instruct on foreseeability, their statutes—imposing vicarious collective liability for killings by nonparticipants in the felony—are wrong in principle. They are obviously designed to inculpate felons for defensive killings by precluding any requirement of direct causation. The end is legitimate but the means chosen—absolving the prosecution of proving causation altogether—is not. No one can deserve blame for homicide without either causing death or aiding one who did.

11 FELONIOUS PURPOSE

The dual culpability principle conditions felony murder liability on culpable indifference to a risk of death combined with felonious purpose. We have seen that most felony murder jurisdictions limit felony murder liability to deaths caused negligently. We will now consider the normative dimension of dual culpability, the requirement of felonious purpose.

All felony murder jurisdictions require felonious purpose in one important way: they limit felony murder liability to those who have committed, attempted, or promoted certain felonies. In most jurisdictions one cannot attempt or participate in a felony without having a wrongful purpose. Traditional predicate felonies—arson, burglary, robbery, rape, and kidnapping—all involve wrongful purposes. Traditional accounts of felony murder liability as transferring of intent from an intended wrong to an unintended injury also presume that the predicate felony involves a wrongful purpose.

Most jurisdictions require felonious purpose by means of a second device as well—requiring that the act causing death be committed in furtherance of the felony. As noted earlier, more than thirty jurisdictions require an instrumental or causal relationship between the felony and the act causing death.

In this chapter, we will focus on a third important device for conditioning felony murder liability on felonious purpose: merger limitations. These rules require that predicate felonies endanger some interest other than the health of the victim. Our review the development of the merger doctrine will show that merger limitations are integral and traditional features of felony murder law, widely adhered to in contemporary law. Where applicable, the merger doctrine is best understood as an independent felonious purpose requirement. Yet we should view an independent felonious purpose requirement as merely one means of realizing the dual culpability principle, rather than an end in itself. While some commonly enumerated predicate felonies lack an independent felonious purpose, these usually entail extreme indifference to human life. Thus most exceptions to the merger doctrine are nevertheless compatible with the principle of dual culpability that underlies it.

THE MERGER PROBLEM

A felony murder rule aggravates an unintended killing to murder on the basis of committing or attempting a felony. To aggravate the unintended killing to murder, the felony must be distinct from the killing. Yet felonies include some unintended killings punished less severely than murder. It would subvert any effort to grade homicide if every felonious homicide aggravated itself to murder. Some criterion is therefore needed to distinguish predicate felonies from the homicides they aggravate. This is the merger problem.

It may seem that we could solve this problem by simply excluding homicide offenses as predicate felonies. Yet a nonfatal felony may involve the same conduct and culpability required for a lesser homicide offense such as manslaughter. If death results, the perpetrator could be guilty of murder for conduct that the legislature graded as a lesser form of homicide. Indeed, a felony might involve less culpability than a lesser homicide offense. Thus most jurisdictions punish intentional killing as voluntary manslaughter if committed with provocation or extreme emotional disturbance. If a similarly aroused defendant struck a blow with intent to injure, or with a deadly weapon, he would likely be guilty of a felonious assault. If the victim died, the assailant might not be guilty even of voluntary manslaughter if he lacked intent to kill; yet he might be guilty of felony murder. The assailant might be guilty of involuntary manslaughter based on reckless disregard of a risk of death. Yet if felonious assault could serve as a predicate felony, the assailant would be guilty of murder rather than manslaughter.

The Miller and Jenkins cases from Chapter 1 illustrate the potential injustice of predicating felony murder on assault. Miller's only intentional act was punching another teen with his fist. His assault was aggravated to a felony only because of the fatal result. Jenkins merely struggled to shake free of a pursuing police officer. His offense was a felony only because the victim was an officer, not because of any felonious motive. An unexpected death from an unarmed physical altercation would not have been murder at common law, and might not even have been manslaughter.[1] Thus, predicating felony murder on felonious assault would frustrate the grading schemes typically found in American homicide statutes. Adding conduct or culpability not included in homicide offenses requires a predicate felony that attacks some interest other than the health of the victim.

Merger limitations may take at least five forms. A *homicide test* simply excludes all statutory homicide offenses punished less severely than felony murder. A *lesser included offense test* excludes predicate felonies unless they have statutory offense elements not included in lesser homicide offenses. An *independent act test* excludes predicate felonies unless they involve some act beyond that required for the homicide. An *independent interest test* excludes predicate felonies unless they endanger some interest other than the life or health of the victim. An *independent culpability test* excludes predicate felonies unless they involve culpability with respect to harming an interest other than the life or health of the victim. The most prevalent formulation of this test requires an independent *purpose*, but less demanding versions might require only knowing acceptance of, or reckless indifference toward, an independent harm.

Which of these tests is best? The oft-stated purpose of a merger rule is to maintain the coherence of a scheme for grading homicide offenses. Thus a merger limitation requires that a predicate felony have some feature that appropriately aggravates a homicide and *relevantly* distinguishes it from homicides graded below murder. We cannot assess the coherence of a grading scheme without choosing a normative criterion for distributing punishment.

Merger tests have often been justified by one of three purposes: deterring dangerous felonies, deterring dangerous acts by those engaged in felonies, or transferring culpability from an intended felonious result to an unintended homicide. I have argued that a felony murder rule is not an effective method of deterring dangerous conduct. If a felony murder rule is justifiable it must be on the basis of desert. Desert is conventionally understood to be a function of wrongdoing and culpability, where wrongdoing is injuring or endangering some legal interest.[2] Assuming that all homicides are equally wrongful injuries to life, differences in punishment should depend on differences in culpability. Thus the merger test most relevant to desert is the independent culpability test; and the most persuasive traditional rationale for a merger standard is the aim of transferring culpability from the felony to the wrongful killing.

Because legal scholars generally disapprove of felony murder liability itself, they have offered little guidance to courts on how to solve the merger problem. Herbert Wechsler and Jerome Michael's influential "Rationale of Homicide" article dismissed New York's merger doctrine as a "less sensible" substitute for a dangerous felony requirement, rather than evaluating it as an additional limitation ensuring additional culpability.[3]

One of the few contemporary criminal law theorists to address the issue is

Claire Finkelstein. Finkelstein assumes that felony murder requires two separate acts: an act that constitutes a felony and a distinct act committed in the course of the felony that causes death.[4] On this basis she argues that the traditional predicate felony of arson should be deemed to merge with any resulting homicide, since the homicide would result from the same act as that intended to destroy the building.[5] Yet Finkelstein's independent act test has further counterintuitive implications. If a sexual assailant inflicts a fatal injury by sodomizing a victim with a broom handle, the act causing death is an element of the forcible sodomy. If a robber fatally shoots the driver of an armored car and takes money from the truck, the fatal shooting supplies the element of force required for robbery. Thus Finkelstein's requirement of an independent act causing death would exclude paradigmatic felony murder scenarios. Moreover, Finkelstein's independent act test is subject to a more fundamental objection: she offers no moral reason why two *acts* are necessary for the felon to deserve murder liability for causing death. This is for the sensible reason that—like most contemporary scholars—she doubts that felony murder liability *is* deserved.[6] Thus she endorses an independent act standard only as a logical implication of what she sees as a morally arbitrary rule.

Yet the felony murder doctrine is not a morally arbitrary rule. Instead, it imposes deserved punishment for those who kill with a combination of two forms of culpability: bad expectations and bad purposes. Rather than viewing felony murder as a combination of *two acts*, the principle of dual culpability explains the merger doctrine as a requirement that the fatal felony combines *two culpable mental states*: indifference to a risk of death and an independent felonious purpose. To be sure, felony murder requires a dangerous and therefore negligent act causing death *and* an act aimed at some other wrongful end. These two acts may be the same, as long as the defendant is culpable with respect to two different results.

This independent culpability test explains why arson has been a traditional predicate for felony murder, and why courts do not see it as merging with the resulting homicide. Thus the purpose of destroying a building is the additional bad end that makes fatal arson worse than reckless manslaughter. Such an independent felonious purpose renders the felon who negligently or recklessly causes death culpable enough to deserve murder liability. Her culpability for causing death carelessly is aggravated by the bad end she seeks.

Therefore, a merger doctrine enhances the coherence of a grading scheme by ensuring that a predicate felony sufficiently aggravates a killer's culpability to justify murder liability. If the cognitive dimension of culpability is greater, however, the normative dimension of culpability need not be as great to merit murder liability. Accordingly, where a felony entails depraved indifference to human life, a merger limitation is no longer needed.

Which predicate felonies violate the requirement of dual culpability? Clearly felony murder should not be predicated on manslaughter of the deceased, or assault with recklessness of human life. Should it be predicated on manslaughter or felonious assault of another victim? Arguably the answer may depend on the circumstances. If the assailant misses the intended victim and fatally hits someone else, it seems sensible simply to transfer manslaughter liability. If the assailant knowingly endangers multiple victims in attacking one intended victim, however, he acts with depraved indifference to human life rather than merely recklessness. If a victim is killed, murder liability seems warranted. On similar reasoning, a drive-by shooting might be an acceptable predicate felony, where the offense involves intent to kill or endangers multiple victims.

Suppose there are special circumstances aggravating a fatal and otherwise felonious assault. Murder liability might be justified if these additional wrongs are sufficiently substantial and independent. We might ask if the aggravating circumstance entails a purpose sufficiently malign to warrant felony liability by itself. Suppose an assailant breaks into a building to commit an injurious assault, or shoots into a dwelling. Both of these felonies involve unlawful purposes independent of physical injury to the victim, but the intended trespasses against property are not by themselves felonious. These considerations suggest that murder liability is not deserved.

An alternative analysis considers whether the aggravating circumstance adds *enough* culpability to the felonious assault to warrant murder liability. A felonious assault entailing recklessness of death needs less additional culpability to justify murder liability than does a felony entailing negligence. Perhaps an antisocial but not necessarily felonious purpose, or a willingness to endanger additional victims, will suffice. If burglary for purposes of an aggravated assault is reckless with regard to life and purposely violates a property interest in habitation, perhaps it reflects extreme indifference to human life. If additional victims are likely to be present, the case for extreme indifference murder is strengthened further. Intentionally shooting into an occupied dwelling could also be a justifiable predicate, assuming the assailant must be aware of the danger to human life. Such an offense is more justifiable as a predicate felony if it requires shooting with intent to injure, or knowledge that victims are present. If an aggravated assault is particularly cruel—involving torture or mutilation, for example—this additional malign purpose arguably aggravates recklessness to depraved indifference to human life. Thus mayhem should be acceptable as a predicate felony.

Child abuse is another common predicate felony that can embody a particularly aggravated form of assault. Aggravating factors might include such wrongful desiderative attitudes as (1) indifference to the physical and emotional vulnerability of a youthful victim, (2) willful violation of a duty of care toward the child, or (3) a purpose to degrade. These attitudes are not felonious purposes, but choosing to act on the basis of such values can nevertheless aggravate an assailant's culpability from recklessness to depraved indifference. A sadistic purpose to torture or enslave is an independent felonious purpose that can aggravate a merely negligent rather than a reckless act. Thus child abuse is a potentially defensible predicate felony, provided it is defined in such a way as to require reckless endangerment of the child's life or negligent endangerment for a sadistic purpose. Similar arguments would apply to elder abuse.

Another problematic set of offenses are those we criminalize not because they aim at an injury but because they carelessly impose a risk to life. One example would be drunk driving, which can become a felony in some jurisdictions if the offense is repeated. While drunk driving may be considered reckless, there is no additional culpability to aggravate the reckless killing to murder. Many jurisdictions do predicate felony murder on drug trafficking, criminalized primarily because of the health risks of drug use. Moreover, the risk imposed by drug trafficking is well below that imposed by drunk driving. When a drug customer dies of an overdose, is there any additional wrong that aggravates the dealer's culpability? Arguably there is: the dealer profits by exploiting the drug user's addictive or otherwise irrational desire for a product that society has proscribed on paternalistic grounds. On this analysis, drug profits are misappropriated property, and their pursuit can count as an independent felonious purpose, analogous to theft. While drug trafficking is not usually sufficiently dangerous to qualify as a predicate felony, it may be sufficiently independent on these paternalistic premises.

EMERGENCE OF THE MERGER PROBLEM

The merger problem was recognized as soon as felony murder rules were first proposed. In his 1716 treatise William Hawkins held that "[s]uch killing shall be adjudged murder which happens in the execution of an unlawful action principally intended for some other purpose, and not to do a personal injury to him in particular who happens to be slain."[7]

When felony murder liability developed in nineteenth-century American states, most jurisdictions avoided the merger problem by limiting predicate felonies. As we have seen, second-degree felony murder liability predicated on non-enumerated felonies was rare. My research revealed no second-degree murder cases predicated on assault of the deceased. The merger problem instead emerged in the minority of jurisdictions that had categorical felony murder rules. These were ungraded felony murder statutes, third-degree felony murder statutes, or common law felony murder rules.[8] A merger limitation was first developed in New York. The 1838 case of *People v. Rector* concerned a murder conviction for a fatal beating with a heavy iron bar. Although upholding the conviction on the extreme indifference theory, the court rejected a felony murder theory. The court considered fallacious the argument "that the blow cannot be a misdemeanor when it results in death, because the act is then a felony, to wit, manslaughter, ergo it is murder."[9] Manslaughter could not be a predicate felony because it "merged" with the homicide. The 1872 decision in *Foster v. People* extended this logic to exclude felonious assault as a predicate felony for felony murder, on grounds that it, too, merged with the homicide.[10] An 1879 case rejected this analysis for the predicate felony of rape, however. Even if the fatal assault supplied the force traditionally required as an element of rape, rape involved a felonious purpose independent of that assault.[11]

Later New York cases predicated murder on "illegal entry or assault by a tramp," and murder of a different victim.[12] Nevertheless, in the 1906 case of *People v. Hüter* the New York Court of Appeals reaffirmed that assault of the deceased merged. The key requisite for a predicate felony was a *purpose* independent of the homicide, rather than a second *act*: "By the same act one may commit two crimes . . . [and so] it is not necessary that there should be an act collateral to or independent of that which causes the death; but if the act causing the death be committed with a collateral and independent felonious design it is sufficient."[13] This holding was reaffirmed repeatedly throughout the first half of the twentieth century.[14]

Another state that developed a merger doctrine in the nineteenth century was Missouri. In 1845 Missouri adopted a felony aggravator statute conditioning first-degree murder on any felony. In applying this statute, the Missouri Supreme Court initially rejected New York's merger doctrine, upholding first-degree murder convictions for beating deaths predicated on the felony of "inflicting great bodily harm."[15] In the 1878 case of *State v. Shock*, however, the court overruled these cases and embraced the merger doctrine formulated in *Rector*.[16] Overturning the first-degree murder conviction of a defendant who had viciously beaten a small child to death, the court held that "inflicting great bodily harm" could not be a predicate for felony murder:

> [T]he words "other felony" used in the first section refer to some collateral felony, and not to those acts of personal violence to the deceased which are necessary and constituent elements of the homicide itself, and are, therefore, merged in it, and which do not, when consummated, constitute an offense distinct from the homicide.[17]

The court restricted the phrase "other felony" to traditional common law felonies.[18] The following year, the Missouri legislature codified the court's position by limiting predicate felonies for first-degree murder to arson, burglary, robbery, rape, and mayhem.[19]

At least four other courts touched on the problem during the nineteenth century. A Mississippi court disapproved an instruction predicating murder of one victim on assault of another.[20] By contrast, an 1889 South Carolina decision approved an instruction predicating felony murder on assault and battery of the victim.[21] Finally, Wisconsin and Florida permitted third-degree murder to be predicated on assault or mayhem of the deceased.[22] This is not surprising, since the punishment for this offense was comparable to that imposed for manslaughter in other states.

In the early twentieth century North Carolina and Kansas took opposing positions on the merger question. North Carolina adopted a categorical felony aggravator statute in 1893 and soon applied it in imposing felony murder liability.[23] In the 1904 case of *State v. Capps*[24] the North Carolina Supreme Court rejected the merger doctrine in upholding a first-degree felony murder conviction predicated on the felony of firing into occupied property. Kansas courts appear not to have imposed felony murder liability under the state's categorical felony aggravator statute until 1921.[25] Soon thereafter, the Kansas Supreme Court considered the merger problem in the 1926 case of *State v. Fisher*. The defendant shot at the tires of a car trespassing on his land and fatally hit a passenger. Convicted of first-degree murder predicated on assault with a deadly weapon, he appealed successfully. The court held that assault with a deadly weapon merged because its elements were "ingredients" of the homicide.[26] In 1944 the Kansas court again struck down a first-degree murder conviction predicated on assault, citing the holding in *Fisher*.[27]

Litigation of the merger issue became more widespread in the 1960s, after the Model Penal Code brought the felony murder doctrine under increasing critical scrutiny and before legislatures responded with code revisions. Courts in Oklahoma, Kansas, Arizona, Oregon, and California applied merger limitations, while courts in Florida, Washington, and Maine rejected such limitations. During this period Oklahoma's code defined murder as including unintended homicide in the commission of any felony. In a 1961 case the Oklahoma Supreme Court held that manslaughter and assault merged with the resultant homicide, citing Kansas and New York cases with approval.[28] Kansas reiterated its merger limitation in a 1967 case upholding a murder conviction predicated on gun possession by an ex-felon, arguing that possession and use of a gun are distinct acts.[29] This two-act test implied that assault continued to merge with the resulting homicide, as a 1969 case confirmed.[30]

Arizona had a graded felony murder statute similar to California's until 1978. In 1965, the Arizona Supreme Court also ruled that assault with a deadly weapon merged with a resulting homicide, so that no second-degree felony murder instruction was necessary in a case where first-degree murder was charged.[31] The court argued that predicating felony murder on assault would transform manslaughters into murders. Later cases declined to apply this doctrine to two enumerated felonies: burglary for the purpose of assault on a different victim and arson.[32]

Oregon had a graded felony murder statute providing second-degree felony murder liability for unintended killings in non-enumerated killings.[33] The Oregon Supreme Court allowed assault of one victim to be used as a predicate for felony murder of another in a 1957 case,[34] but held in 1966 that assault of the deceased could not serve as a predicate for felony murder.[35] Nevertheless, the Oregon court permitted burglary for the purpose of assault to be used as a predicate for felony murder.[36]

The California courts initially rejected the merger doctrine. Between 1951 and 1966 California decisions predicated second-degree felony murder on felonious assault[37] and possession of a gun by a felon,[38] and predicated first-degree murder on burglary for the purpose of murder.[39] In 1969, however, the California Supreme Court embraced a merger limitation in the pivotal case of *People v. Ireland*, holding that the felony assault with a deadly weapon was an "integral part of the homicide, included in fact."[40]

Over the next two years, California courts decided several merger cases. In *People v. Wilson* the California Supreme Court took the surprising step of barring felony murder liability predicated on burglary for the purposes of assault. The court viewed the requisite element of intent to commit assault as "integral to the homicide," even though the act of unauthorized entry obviously is not.[41] With this decision, the court transformed the "integral to the homicide" test into a requirement of independent felonious purpose. Soon the court further extended this rule to hold that burglary predicated on assault of one victim merged with the killing of a second victim.[42] An appellate court held that the felony of firing into an occupied dwelling lacked an independent felonious purpose.[43] The 1971 decision in *People v. Burton* confirmed the authority of the independent felonious purpose test and rejected a "same act" test. The court denied that robbery merges even though it "includes" assault as a necessary element, instead emphasizing that robbery has a purpose independent of assault.[44] Eventually, the California Supreme Court would apply the independent felonious purpose test to preclude predicating felony murder on child abuse, whether in the form of assault or neglect.[45]

California courts also applied the independent felonious purpose test to permit predicating felony murder on the sale of dangerous drugs, including heroin[46] and methyl alcohol.[47] Arguing that felony murder liability serves to deter negligent and reckless killing during predicate felonies, the California Supreme Court reasoned that such deterrence presupposed a felonious aim independent of endangering the victim. Presumably the independent felonious purpose of distributing drugs is illicit profit.

Other state courts rejected the merger doctrine during this period. The Florida Supreme Court declined to apply it to a burglary committed for the purpose of assault in a 1966 case. The court reasoned that the merger doctrine was unnecessary in a state that enumerated all predicate felonies.[48] The Washington Supreme Court declined to adopt New York's merger rule, on the ground that Washington graded felony murder predicated on non-enumerated felonies as second-degree murder rather than first.[49] The court also noted that fatal assaults had been punished as murder in the common law.[50] The Maine Supreme Court upheld an instruction predicating felony murder on assault, a few years before the legislature adopted a new code limiting predicate felonies to those enumerated.[51]

MERGER IN THE ERA OF NEW CODES

Many states adopted new criminal codes in response to the promulgation of the Model Penal Code, but continued to impose felony murder liability. A majority of these new felony murder provisions limited predicate felonies to those enumerated, and so limited the potential scope of any merger limitation.[52] This included four states (Arizona, Kansas, New York, and Oregon) with prior merger limits, and one state (Maine) that had previously rejected merger. Kansas continued to apply a merger doctrine, and Iowa, another enumerated felony state, eventually adopted one. In addition, a substantial minority of new codes defined predicate felonies categorically.[53] This included Florida, which had deemed a merger limitation unnecessary when it enumerated all predicate felonies. A few of these categorical codes excluded murder and manslaughter as predicates.[54] Courts examined the merger question under almost all of these new categorical codes, although not always very conclusively. Courts in several categorical jurisdictions with older codes, notably California, Maryland, Massachusetts, Mississippi, North Carolina, and Oklahoma, have also considered merger questions in recent decades. Categorical jurisdictions have divided fairly evenly as to whether felony murder can be predicated on assault of the deceased.

Oklahoma, California, and Kansas have retained their merger doctrines. All three have invoked these doctrines in precluding felony murder predicated on child abuse.[55] In the 1995 case of *People v. Hansen*, the California Supreme Court narrowed its merger rule in upholding a conviction predicated on the felony of firing a gun in a dwelling. The court construed the independent felonious purpose as permitting any inherently dangerous predicate felony other than an assault.[56] Subsequent decisions criticized this analysis[57] and the 2009 case of *People v. Chun* overruled *Hansen* and barred felony murder predicated on shooting into an occupied vehicle.[58] Other California decisions first narrowed,[59] and then overruled the *Wilson* decision by permitting felony murder predicated on burglary for purposes of assault.[60] The court reasoned that a merger doctrine should not limit a legislatively enumerated predicate felony, and emphasized the added danger of assaults in the home.[61] In 2009, the Kansas legislature narrowed that state's merger limitation by dividing its enumeration of inherently dangerous felonies into those that can and cannot merge with a resulting homicide. Felonies that can merge include various homicide and assault offenses. Those that cannot merge include child abuse and burglary offenses.[62]

Courts in Massachusetts, Alabama, North Carolina, and arguably Mississippi have joined the jurisdictions barring felony murder predicated on assault. In Massachusetts, a 1984 case relied on Professor LaFave's treatise in finding that a predicate felony must be "separate from the acts of personal violence which constitute a necessary part of the homicide itself."[63] In Alabama, which predicates felony murder on any felony dangerous to life, an appeals court excluded assault as a predicate felony on the grounds that it merges with a resulting homicide.[64] In North Carolina, which predicates felony murder on any felony committed with a deadly weapon, courts have repeatedly predicated felony murder on the felony of shooting into a house.[65] In 2000, however, the North Carolina Supreme Court barred felony murder predicated on assault of the deceased with a deadly weapon.[66] "Otherwise," the court reasoned, "virtually all felonious assaults on a single victim that result in his or her death would be first-degree murders via felony murder, thereby negating lesser homicide charges such as second-degree murder and manslaughter."[67] Mississippi courts have implicitly retained a merger doctrine by virtue of applying an independent interest test to permit child abuse and burglary as predicate felonies.[68] To be sure, the court failed to distinguish the interest protected by punishing child abuse from the interest protected by punishing fatal child abuse.[69] Nevertheless, the court's futile struggle to identify an independent interest bespoke the continuing authority of a merger limitation.

After initially rejecting the merger limits, Iowa and Illinois subsequently adopted them. The 1962 Illinois code predicated murder on any forcible felony, including an aggravated battery. In 1975 the Illinois Supreme Court placed weight on the legislature's enumeration of aggravated battery in arguing that a merger limitation would violate legislative intent. The court also argued that fatal aggravated battery had been murder at common law, and that the purpose of conditioning felony murder on forcible felonies is to deter such felonies, not to deter dangerous acts in furtherance of such felonies.[70] A 2001 decision reversed this position and precluded felony murder charges based on aggravated battery of or aggravated shooting at the deceased. The court concluded that "when the acts constituting forcible felonies arise from and are included in the act of murder itself these forcible felonies cannot be predicates for felony murder."[71] Subsequent Illinois cases have continued to permit felony murder charges predicated on assaults against victims other than the deceased.[72] Iowa's 1978 code included a provision predicating felony murder on enumerated forcible felonies including assaults. In a 1982 case, the Iowa Supreme Court held that the "forcible felony" of willful injury could support felony murder.[73] The court viewed the legislature's mention of assault as evidence of an intention to reject a merger limitation.[74] In 2006, however, the Iowa Supreme Court overruled this decision, holding that an assault causing the death of the victim cannot be a predicate for felony murder.[75]

By contrast, courts in Missouri and Texas have moved away from merger doctrines after initially adopting them. Between 1978 and 1983 Missouri conditioned second-degree murder on extreme indifference to human life manifested by the commission of any felony. In applying this statute a Missouri court held that such murder could not be predicated on assault, because a fatal assault was either manslaughter or murder, depending on whether it was accompanied by intent to kill. Thus it was "included" within homicide.[76] The 1998 decision of an intermediate appellate court, although endorsing the merger doctrine, offered an almost comically strained rationale to avoid applying it to assault with a deadly weapon where the defendant fired two shots.[77] A later decision of a different appellate court permitting felony murder on the basis of child abuse rejected the merger doctrine for predicate felonies other than manslaughter.[78] Thus it is unclear whether or not Missouri retains a merger doctrine.

In 1974 Texas adopted a new criminal code defining murder as including causing death by means of an act clearly dangerous to life in the course of any felony other than manslaughter. In the 1978 case of *Garrett v. State*, however, a Texas criminal appeals court expanded this modest statutory merger limitation to also bar felony murder predicated on aggravated assault.[79] The court argued that the statutory requirement of a fatal dangerous act in the course of a felony implied that the clearly dangerous act causing death must be distinct from the predicate felony. Another decision applied this test to permit felony murder predicated on aggravated assault of another victim.[80] In the 1983 case of *Murphy v. State*, a Texas court curiously invoked *Garrett's* independent act test in predicating murder on arson, even though homicide does not require any act independent of arson. Yet the court properly emphasized that the defendant's purpose—to destroy a building and fraudulently collect insurance—was independent of the homicide and threatened property rather than life.[81] In 1987, a Texas court used an independent interest test to permit a felony murder charge predicated on shooting into a building.[82] Two subsequent decisions predicating murder on child abuse ignored *Garrett's* independent act test and instead reasoned that child abuse was not a "lesser included offense" of murder or manslaughter.[83] In 1997 the Texas Supreme Court criticized the *Garrett* decision as judicial legislation and rejected its independent act test in favor of this independent offense test.[84] In a later case, a Texas criminal appeals court applied this standard to permit felony murder predicated on assault with intent to injure.[85] These decisions are unfortunate. Applying a merger limitation is not an act of judicial legislation in Texas, because the code requires an apparently dangerous act in furtherance of a felony other than manslaughter. This does not require an act independent of homicide, but it does require that the act causing death "further" a felonious purpose other than the reckless endangerment of life required for manslaughter. The *Murphy* decision, requiring a purpose to endanger some interest other than the health of the victim, provides an appropriate interpretation of the statute.

Courts in two more states, Delaware and Washington, attempted to impose merger limitations but were checked by legislatures. Both states required that death be caused in furtherance of the predicate felony. In its 1992 decision in *Chao v. State*, upholding an arson-murder conviction, the Delaware Supreme Court sensibly denied that a killing in furtherance of the felony must be an *act* independent of the felony.[86] In the 2002 case of *Williams v. State* the court reached the equally plausible conclusion that the "in furtherance" requirement precluded predicating felony murder on burglary for the purpose of assault.[87] Both results are compatible with a requirement of independent felonious purpose. Yet the court unnecessarily based the *Williams* decision on an independent act test, overturning *Chao* and concluding that its merger rule would preclude felony murder liability predicated on arson. The legislature responded to this clumsy reasoning by eliminating the "in furtherance" language.[88] If this is taken to express an intention to restore the law of the *Chao* case, there is still room to advocate an independent felonious purpose test, as compatible with the result and reasoning in *Chao*. Yet the new statute may also be interpreted as overturning *Chao*'s merger doctrine. In the 2002 case of *In re Andress* the Washington Supreme Court held that Washington's "in furtherance" requirement incorporated a merger rule, precluding second-degree felony murder liability predicated on assault.[89] A 2003 statute, however, specifically included assault among the predicate crimes and was accompanied by a statement repudiating *Andress*.[90] This outcome was unfortunate, since as the *Andress* court pointed out, assault in Washington includes negligent injury.[91] Thus defined, assault does not entail any felonious purpose, let alone an independent one.

Courts in Georgia, Minnesota, Maryland, and Montana have all permitted felony murder predicated on assault. Georgia's 1969 code defined murder as including causing death in the commission of any felony, "irrespective of malice."[92] It defined involuntary manslaughter only as causing death by means of unlawful acts other than felonies, or committing lawful acts likely to cause death. In the 1970s, Georgia courts held that voluntary and involuntary manslaughter would merge with the resulting homicide,[93] but assault would not.[94]

The Georgia Supreme Court reasoned that it was necessary to grade fatal assaults as murder because they could not be punished as involuntary manslaughter under the Georgia code, which excluded dangerous acts during felonies.[95] Georgia courts have expressed dissatisfaction with this statutory scheme, urging the legislature to add reckless homicide to the code and exclude fatal assaults from felony murder.[96] The legislature's failure to heed this advice eventually led to the infamous result in the *Miller* case.[97] Because Georgia courts permit predicating felony murder on assault, they have also approved predicating felony murder on child abuse.[98]

In Maryland, first-degree felony murder requires enumerated felonies, while second-degree murder is undefined. Maryland first recognized second-degree felony murder in 2001, in a murder conviction predicated on child abuse.[99] The decision was surprising: assuming that child abuse could not serve as a predicate for felony murder, the legislature had instead defined fatal child abuse as an aggravated child abuse offense. Yet the court found both that second-degree murder could be predicated on non-enumerated felonies and that child abuse did not merge. It offered the theory that child abuse harms an interest distinct from the victim's health, a relationship of custodial trust. A subsequent case rejected the merger doctrine altogether, finding that assault could serve as a predicate for felony murder on the rationale that the felony murder doctrine serves simply to deter dangerous felonies.[100] This unprincipled expansion of felony murder beyond the limits prevailing in other jurisdictions was not authorized by the Maryland legislature.

Minnesota's 1963 code predicated second-degree murder on unintended killing in the course of any felony.[101] The code graded negligent killings as first-degree manslaughter if committed pursuant to a misdemeanor and second-degree manslaughter otherwise, but graded extreme indifference murder as third-degree murder. Minnesota's courts have repeatedly imposed murder liability predicated on felonious assaults without addressing a merger challenge.[102] In Montana, the crime of "deliberate homicide" includes causing death in the course of any "forcible felony." A 2004 case permitted deliberate homicide to be predicated on aggravated assault.[103]

Courts in remaining categorical jurisdictions have not resolved the question of predicating felony murder on assault. A Virginia court has declined to impose a merger limit in upholding a second-degree murder conviction predicated on child abuse.[104] The court used a lesser included offense test, noting that felony child abuse includes the independent circumstance element of having a duty to care for the child.[105] This reasoning leaves open the possibility that other types of assault offenses might merge. Courts in Florida, Nevada, Rhode Island, and South Carolina have not addressed the question at all.

Apart from assault, two other kinds of predicate felony have been the focus of controversy. As we have seen, several courts have considered merger arguments in felony murder cases predicated on child abuse during this period. As noted, courts accepted such arguments in Oklahoma, Kansas, and California, and rejected such arguments in Georgia, South Dakota, Mississippi, Missouri, Texas, and Maryland. In addition, South Dakota formerly applied a now defunct categorical felony murder statute to fatal child abuse.[106]

Controversy also focused on the predicate felony of burglary for the purpose of assault or murder. Courts rejected arguments that such felonies merged in California, Oregon, New York, Arizona, The District of Columbia, Kansas, and Mississippi. Courts expressed reluctance to bar a statutorily enumerated felony,[107] noted the danger of assaults in the home,[108] and sometimes argued that burglary threatens an independent property interest.[109] Only Arkansas, which lacks a true felony murder rule, bars burglary with intent to assault as a predicate felony.[110] A few courts considered and rejected challenges to other traditionally enumerated felonies such as robbery[111] and rape,[112] as well as arson.[113]

OVERT AND COVERT MERGER LIMITATIONS IN CONTEMPORARY LAW

Our history of the merger doctrine has revealed persistent controversy in the courts. Yet greater consensus becomes apparent when we include legislation in the picture and view the resulting pattern through the lens of the principle of dual culpability.

An explicit merger limitation is best understood as just one means of enforcing the principle of dual culpability. This principle permits murder liability for unintended killing in the course of felonies only when the felony adds enough culpability to the assailant's expectation of causing death. The higher the assailant's expectation of death, the less additional culpability the felony must supply. When the killing is negligent, the felony must supply an independent felonious purpose. When the killing is reckless, however, the felony need only establish enough additional culpability to aggravate that recklessness to depraved indifference. A reckless homicide may manifest depraved indifference if it involves a cruel or spiteful motive for endangering another, a willingness to harm some other legal interest in endangering another, or a willingness to endanger many people.

Conditioning murder on aggravated assault or battery violates the principle of dual culpability. Yet other assaultive felonies are permissible predicate felonies if defined so as to entail depraved indifference per se. Burglary for the purpose of aggravated assault or homicide always meets this test, because it is at least reckless of life and involves purposeful violation of an independent property interest. Intentionally shooting into a home or a vehicle in use arguably meets this test, on the assumption that it entails knowingly endangering victims and purposefully violating an independent property interest. Shooting *from* a car does not meet this test. Fatal child abuse often involves recklessness of death combined with a purpose to degrade and a violation of custodial responsibility. Intentional injury of a child victim arguably involves an aggravated form of reckless indifference. If a child abuse predicate felony is defined simply as battery of a child that in fact results in death, however, the result could be undeserved murder liability.

Not every felony murder jurisdiction has explicitly adopted a merger doctrine. Nevertheless, the vast majority have avoiding predicating felony murder on aggravated assault or battery. In so doing, they have covertly observed merger limitations. Many legislatures have obviated a merger doctrine by predicating felony murder only on enumerated felonies involving either an independent felonious purpose or depraved indifference to human life. Recall that twenty-five of the forty-five felony murder jurisdictions enumerate exhaustively.[114] Of these twenty-five, only two jurisdictions violate the principle of dual culpability by predicating felony murder on assault of the deceased.[115] Wisconsin imposes a penalty enhancement of up to fifteen years when death results from various assault offenses. At least one scholar considers this relatively low penalty a form of manslaughter liability, despite Wisconsin's use of the term "felony murder."[116] Ohio predicates felony murder on "violent" felonies of the first or second degree, which include an assault requiring knowing infliction of serious physical harm.[117] As of this writing, Ohio courts have not considered a merger challenge to this predicate felony.[118] In addition to these jurisdictions predicating felony murder on aggravated assault, Louisiana predicates felony murder on "assault by drive-by-shooting"[119] without conditioning this offense on intent to injure or exposure of multiple victims.[120]

Ten of these twenty-five jurisdictions predicate felony murder on child abuse offenses.[121] These offenses are defined quite variably, however. Some are clearly defensible as predicate felonies. Thus, the Kansas child abuse predicate felony requires a sadistic motive, supplying an independent felonious purpose, and arguably depraved indifference as well: "intentionally torturing, cruelly beating . . . or inflicting cruel and inhuman corporal punishment."[122] The federal child abuse defense requires "a pattern or practice of assault or torture against a child or children."[123] Such a pattern arguably implies an assailant with custodial obligations toward the child and a malign purpose to torture or degrade. Oregon's aggravated child abuse felony requires, at a minimum, that the assailant intentionally inflict an injury to a victim under fourteen.[124] Tennessee's child abuse predicate felony requires either intentional injury, like Oregon, or knowingly harming the child's welfare through neglect of a custodial duty.[125]

Some enumerated child abuse defenses are debatable as predicate felonies. The Washington, D.C. code predicates felony murder on an offense requiring reckless infliction of an injury on a minor.[126] If death is the recklessly inflicted injury, the youth of the victim may suffice to aggravate the offense to depraved indifference murder; if, however, the assailant is merely reckless as to a non-fatal injury, the assailant lacks the culpability required for murder. The Wyoming statute is similar, requiring recklessly causing physical or mental injury to a child under the age of sixteen.[127] The Ohio child abuse predicate felony requires causing injury by means of abuse, torture, excessive punishment, unwarranted discipline, or a drug offense.[128] No culpable mental state is assigned to the injury element, but if recklessness—Ohio's default culpability standard[129]— is required, murder liability *might sometimes* be warranted. Torture adds a substantial malign purpose independent of injury. Excessive punishment, unwarranted discipline, and drug dealing are independent malign purposes, but not necessarily very weighty. The vague term "abuse" does not add any culpability to a reckless injury. Utah's code predicates murder on killing a domestic partner at least negligently in the presence of a child.[130] The resulting emotional harm to a child toward whom the assailant bears some custodial responsibility is an independent wrong, but probably insufficient to aggravate a merely negligent killing to murder.

Finally, some enumerated child abuse offenses are clearly insufficient as predicate felonies. Thus predicate child abuse offenses in Idaho and Louisiana appear to require nothing more than causing death or injury negligently or foreseeably. Idaho predicates felony murder on aggravated battery on a child under the age of twelve.[131] Aggravated battery is defined as an intentional blow or act of violence that causes "great bodily harm, permanent disability, or permanent disfigurement" with no further culpability required.[132] Louisiana requires only negligent mistreatment causing "unjustifiable pain and suffering."[133] These predicate offenses violate the dual culpability principle and should be either redefined or eliminated as predicates for felony murder.

An additional fourteen jurisdictions partially enumerate predicate felonies while also permitting felony murder predicated on unenumerated felonies. Most have avoided enumerating assault offenses or have enumerated only assaults sufficiently aggravated to entail depraved indifference. California and Maryland predicate felony murder on mayhem, which manifests depraved indifference.[134] California also predicates felony murder on the defensible predicate felonies of torture and drive-by shooting with intent to kill.[135] Illinois enumerates the offense of aggravated battery resulting in injury, but by court decision precludes its use in cases where the assault is committed against the deceased.[136] Minnesota and Oklahoma have each enumerated some assault-type felonies that may fall short of the recklessness toward death required for depraved indifference. Minnesota enumerates a drive-by-shooting offense predicated on recklessly shooting toward persons or buildings or vehicles.[137] Oklahoma enumerates intentionally shooting into a building (not necessarily a dwelling), with no requirement of knowingly endangering anyone.[138]

Courts in five of these states—Alabama, California, Illinois, North Carolina, and Oklahoma—have adopted merger rules barring felony murder predicated on assault of the deceased.[139] Illinois courts have permitted felony murder predicated on assault of another, and would likely permit predicate felonies combining assault with violation of a property interest. North Carolina courts have permitted intentionally shooting into an occupied dwelling as a predicate felony.[140] We have seen that a sixth state, Mississippi, has upheld felony murder predicated on child abuse using an independent interest test, which should preclude predicating liability on assault.[141]

Four other states have clearly rejected merger altogether: Maryland, Minnesota, Montana, and Washington.[142] These states permit felony murder liability predicated on aggravated assault.

The law is less clear in four other states. Virginia courts have used a lesser included offense test in predicating felony murder on a child abuse offense requiring violation of a custodial duty.[143] Nevada has upheld a felony murder conviction predicated on intentionally shooting into a dwelling, without considering a merger argument.[144] The court relied on a later overruled California case, involving a similar crime, which nevertheless acknowledged California's merger rule.[145] As of this writing, the question of felony murder predicated on assault has not yet been decided in Florida[146] and Rhode Island.

Six of the fourteen partial enumeration states predicate felony murder on child abuse offenses. Most of these child abuse predicate felonies arguably satisfy our dual culpability test by involving either depraved indifference toward human life or an attack on an independent legal interest. The Mississippi child abuse predicate requires intent to injure.[147] The child abuse predicate approved by the Virginia courts involves intentional injury in violation of a custodial duty.[148] The Maryland child abuse predicate felony requires that the custodian of a minor cause physical injury to the child by a cruel, inhumane, or malicious act.[149] The North Carolina child abuse predicate requires an injurious assault on a child victim with a deadly weapon.[150] The Florida predicate felony of aggravated child abuse requires intentional injury, willful torture, or malicious punishment of a child.[151] More dubiously, the Nevada predicate felony involves the intentional infliction of pain or suffering on a child. The mere infliction of pain on a child does not seem a very great harm, but it is an independent purpose that the Nevada legislature has deemed felonious. Both Florida and Nevada have elder abuse predicates similar to their child abuse predicates.[152]

Six states predicate felony murder only on unenumerated felonies: Delaware, Georgia, Massachusetts, Missouri, South Carolina, and Texas. These are the jurisdictions in which an explicit merger doctrine is most needed. Indeed, the Georgia, Missouri, and Texas legislatures acknowledged the merger problem by excluding homicide offenses as predicate felonies.[153] Unfortunately, a merger doctrine is firmly established only in Massachusetts.[154] Georgia has rejected a merger limitation for assault offenses, while Delaware, Missouri, and Texas have retreated from previously established merger rules. South Carolina courts have not considered the problem.

Of these six purely categorical jurisdictions, only Georgia and Texas have endorsed child abuse as a predicate felony.[155] The Georgia offense requires merely negligent infliction of pain.[156] The Texas offense appears to require only negligent injury.[157] Neither offense meets the dual culpability test.

The authority of the merger doctrine in contemporary law depends on how we pose the question. If we simply ask how many jurisdictions have overtly adopted the merger doctrine and how many have overtly rejected it, we will find the merger doctrine deeply controversial. Courts actively employ a merger doctrine in only eight or nine states: Alabama, California, Kansas, Iowa, Illinois, Massachusetts, North Carolina, Oklahoma, and possibly Mississippi. Courts or legislatures have unambiguously rejected merger limitations in seven states: Georgia, Wisconsin, Maryland, Minnesota, Montana, Texas, and Washington.

The situation remains unclear in several states: Missouri, Delaware, Nevada, Rhode Island. and Virginia.

Yet we have instead assessed the authority of the merger doctrine only after asking what its purpose is. We have identified that purpose as ensuring that persons convicted of felony murder are sufficiently culpable to deserve murder liability. An independent felonious purpose ensures that the predicate felony combines enough culpability with criminal negligence to merit murder liability. However, felonies entailing depraved indifference to human life do not need an independent felonious purpose to justify murder liability. Predicate felonies requiring intent to injure or recklessness toward life satisfy the dual culpability principle if they also require either knowing violation of an independent interest, a depraved motive, or a danger to multiple potential victims. The merger doctrine achieves its purpose by requiring an independent felonious purpose for negligent killings, not for all felonious killings.

We have also assessed the authority of the merger doctrine in light of the fact that predicate felonies are determined more often by legislatures than by courts. Legislatures apply a covert merger limitation when they predicate felony murder only on felonies entailing sufficient culpability to satisfy the principle of dual culpability. Measured by this standard, the overwhelming majority of felony murder jurisdictions have limited felony murder liability, whether overtly or covertly, in conformity with the principle of dual culpability. To be sure, seven jurisdictions have clearly decided that a fatal aggravated assault or battery suffices for murder. In addition, Ohio's code predicates felony murder on aggravated battery, and Louisiana predicates felony murder on a merely reckless drive-by-shooting offense. Yet remarkably, the remaining thirty-six felony murder jurisdictions, four-fifths of the total, have not predicated felony murder on assault of the deceased.

Although many jurisdictions predicate felony murder on child abuse, these offenses usually entail either depraved indifference or an independent felonious purpose. Child abuse predicate felonies often involve knowing harm to child welfare and violation of custodial duties and sometimes require an independent purpose such as torture or unwarranted discipline. They are usually defined to require at least reckless injury. Predicating felony murder on such offenses does not violate the principle of dual culpability. The same is true of compound felonies like shooting into a dwelling or burglary for purposes of aggravated assault or homicide. These felonies involve an expectation rather than a purpose of harming an independent property interest. If they also involve recklessness toward life, however, they arguably involve enough combined culpability to warrant murder liability.

A merger test therefore satisfies the principle of dual culpability if it takes the form of a flexible standard, requiring an independent felonious purpose when the predicate felony entails only negligence toward death. Such a flexible merger limitation is consistent with the judgment of almost all those legislatures that have fully enumerated predicate felonies. Legislatures leaving the class of predicate felonies partially or completely unenumerated have not thereby rejected a merger limitation but have instead invited courts to exercise principled judgment in determining which felonies can serve as predicates. Courts should decide that question in conformity with the principle of dual culpability by adopting a flexible standard requiring either negligence in pursuit of an independent felonious purpose or depraved indifference to human life.

12 A PRINCIPLED LAW OF FELONY MURDER

Constructive interpretation of a body of law identifies a just principle that explains as much as possible of the law as it is and has been. This principle in turn provides a criterion to guide reform toward a law that is defensible as both coherent and just. By maintaining continuity with existing law, constructive interpretation respects the processes by which law has been developed and enacted, and the investment that legal actors have made in developing routines of compliance. Constructive interpretation therefore offers a particularly democratic method for critique and reform of law made by elected legislatures and enforced primarily through the voluntary compliance of law-abiding citizens. Accordingly, it is an appropriate method for critique and reform of American criminal law.

The felony murder doctrine, though widely criticized by legal theorists, persists as law in most American jurisdictions. It is therefore important that criminal law theory acknowledge and articulate its normative appeal. To dismiss felony murder liability as inherently irrational—as most criminal law scholars have done—insults the democratic public that supports it and frees legislators, judges, and prosecutors to pander by enacting and applying it without reason or restraint. If felony murder liability is going to be part of our law, we must be prepared to justify it, and to confine it to its justifying principles.

To that end, we have here developed a constructive interpretation of the felony murder doctrine in American law, justifying felony murder liability as sometimes deserved on the basis of an expressive theory of culpability. This theory explains punishment as serving to motivate popular support for the rule of law by vindicating the equal status of all legal subjects. Punishment rebukes those who demean others by harming them for unworthy ends. Such punishment is properly assessed on the basis of the dignitary injury done to victims by the offense. This dignitary injury is a function of both the harm done and the culpability with which it is done. That culpability, in turn, has two dimensions: a cognitive dimension, concerned with the harm expected, and a normative dimension, concerned with the moral worth of the ends for which that risk was imposed.

Because culpability has two dimensions, killers may deserve murder liability for killing with a variety of different culpable mental states. Murder liability may be warranted for causing death certainly or purposefully and for no good reason, or for causing death recklessly and with an antisocial purpose or attitude, or for causing death negligently with a felonious purpose. The first form of murder is intentional murder; the second form is depraved indifference murder; and the third form is felony murder. Thus felony murder liability is justifiable insofar as we understand culpability for killing as the product of two dimensions of culpability that can vary in gravity. This dual culpability principle justifies felony murder liability but restricts it to negligent killings for an independent felonious purpose. It also permits definitions of murder embracing both negligent killings for an independent felonious purpose and grossly reckless killings.

We began by acknowledging the importance of defending felony murder liability as just rather than merely expedient. The deterrence rationales routinely invoked by courts are not persuasive. They are supported neither by empirical evidence of deterrent effect, nor by theoretical intuitions. From the standpoint of deterrence theory, a felony murder rule is an inefficient punishment lottery, increasing the severity rather than the certainty of punishment. In any case, criminal law is more likely to induce compliance by appealing to a sense of justice than by threatening to impose undeserved punishment.

Rather than evading the charge that felony murder rules impose undeserved strict liability, Part I proceeded to confront it by recognizing that the charge depends on two assumptions: (1) a formalist conception of strict liability as any conduct, circumstance, or result element unaccompanied by a corresponding mental element and (2) a purely cognitive conception of culpability as expected harm.

Next, a critique of the formalist conception of strict liability showed that culpability can be required in a variety of ways, including by proscribing conduct deemed culpable per se. We characterized prevailing formulations of felony murder as per se negligence rules, and speculated that constitutional due process may require conditioning murder liability on at least negligence with respect to death.

We critiqued a purely cognitive conception of culpability, which we associated with a view of the liberal state as a neutral arbiter among competing values, incompetent to evaluate and punish actor's ends. We then demonstrated the impossibility of a value-neutral attribution of responsibility for harmful results. We therefore concluded that a cognitivist critique of felony murder liability "proves too much": it rejects not just felony murder liability specifically but homicide liability of any kind. Any theory of culpability for homicide must assess the offender's aims as well as expectations. It must then determine if the fatal result sufficiently expresses the values on which she acted to warrant attributing that result to her choice. This inherently evaluative question is unavoidable in any criminal justice system that punishes for actual harm.

Moving beyond a purely cognitive conception of culpability, we next developed an expressive account of culpability that assesses ends as well as expectations. Rather than presuming an instrumental account of rationality as preference satisfaction, we proceeded from an expressive account of rational action as aimed at identifying the actor with values. Expressively rational action often involves carrying out the responsibilities of a role within a normative social practice. We reasoned that action becomes culpable by virtue of the normative meaning that it expresses in relation to this world of social practice. Thus culpability has a normative as well as a cognitive dimension. Punishment, which communicates blame, is an expressive response to expressive action.

Punishing for felony murder involves attributing a death to the actor's felonious aim. When a felon compels another by force to acquiesce in the violation of an important right, the felon thereby denies the victim's autonomy and equality by asserting mastery over him or her. The death of a victim under the offender's dominion and as a result of the offender's coercion typifies the wrongfulness of assuming power over the fate of another in order to wrong her. Felony murder rules appropriately impose liability for negligently causing death for a very malign motive, as long as the predicate felony involves coercion or destruction and a felonious purpose of sufficient gravity, that is independent of the fatal injury. In evaluating the offender's motives, felony murder rules are compatible with other rules of American criminal law.

Finally, we saw that a frankly evaluative assessment of the ends for which violence is deployed is well within the competence of an appropriately conceived liberal state. Such a state authorizes the use of violence exclusively to foster and protect the good of a liberal society. It defends equality, autonomy, and democracy because it properly values them, and it permissibly punishes violent expressions of disrespect for those values.

After identifying a principle justifying murder liability for negligent killing in pursuit of a felonious motive, we proceeded to test the authority of that principle against past and current law—and to test the legitimacy of past and current law against that principle. We reexamined the origins of felony murder law, rebutting the prevailing view that American felony murder laws descended from a common law rule holding felons strictly liable for all deaths caused in the course of all felonies. According to this conventional wisdom, an unlimited felony murder rule is pervasively authoritative in default of legislative or judicial reform.

Our investigation exposed the received account of the origins of felony murder liability as a myth. First, we saw that English common law had no felony murder rule at the time of the American Revolution. If Coke proposed a general rule of murder liability for deaths resulting accidentally from unlawful acts (itself a dubious proposition), such a rule was emphatically rejected by English courts and commentators. While a rule that any felony resulting in death was murder was proposed in eighteenth-century opinions and treatises, such a rule does not appear to have been applied by any English court. Prior to the American Revolution, English law (1) denied the excuses of self-defense and provocation to those who killed in overcoming resistance to crime, (2) equated the intention to wound and the intention to kill, (3) transferred the intention to kill or wound from one victim to another, and (4) attributed the act of each accomplice to others who shared the same culpable intent. But it did not equate the intent to commit a felony with the intent to murder.

Next, we saw that English rules of criminal law were authoritative in the United States only insofar as they were enacted by legislatures and courts. English constitutional law denied the automatic authority of the common law in the colonies, so the reception of any particular rule of English law depended on enactment by competent local authorities. After independence, Americans typically recognized the continuing authority of the common law only as developed in their own states. While learned American lawyers were familiar with the English treatise literature, there is little evidence that felony murder liability was actually imposed in any American colony. Some Americans were particularly critical of English criminal law, which they saw as unduly punitive and as undemocratic in origin and content. Americans were generally opposed to judicial definition of crimes in the early nineteenth century, and they quickly set about enacting codes of criminal legislation.

Felony murder rules developed in the United States only after this process of codification was under way. Felony aggravator statutes began to spread in the 1790s, and felony murder statutes proliferated beginning in the 1810s. Yet the first American felony murder convictions were not reported until the 1840s. Indeed, reported felony murder convictions were quite rare until the last three decades of the nineteenth century, by which time the vast majority of jurisdictions had passed felony aggravator or felony murder statutes. A majority of reported nineteenth-century felony murder convictions took place in states with felony murder statutes. In jurisdictions with felony aggravator statutes only, felony murder liability was usually confined to killings in the course of statutorily enumerated felonies, suggesting that the courts considered the statutes to be the source of felony murder liability. Only three felony murder convictions were reported in jurisdictions with neither felony murder nor felony aggravator statutes—all at the end of the nineteenth century, after statutory felony murder liability had become widespread. In short, Americans created their felony murder rules primarily by statute rather than by common law adjudication.

These statutorily based felony murder rules had a much narrower scope than the "common law felony murder rule" is supposed to have had. In the great bulk of jurisdictions and cases, felony murder liability was predicated on the dangerous felonies of robbery, burglary, rape, arson, and murder. Except for one case predicated on a bungled suicide and four cases predicated on consensual abortions, none of the known felony murders punished in nineteenth-century America could plausibly be described as accidental. In almost all of these cases, death resulted from the deliberate infliction of violence. In a few cases defendants knowingly imposed a great risk of death on their victims in pursuit of their criminal ends. As a practical matter, vicarious liability for co-felons was restricted to those who had participated in or agreed to violence. In the rare cases where courts defined complicity in felony murder, they often restricted it to killings in furtherance and foreseeable as a result of their felony.

In short, nineteenth-century felony murder rules required culpability indirectly, by requiring menacing predicate felonies and retaining a traditionally restrictive conception of killing as fatal violence. While there are a handful of troubling cases that depart from this prevailing pattern, those cases cannot be taken as indications of the scope of "*the* felony murder rule," because there was no general rule with interjurisdictional authority. Since each jurisdiction enacted its own rule, decisions were of precedential value only where they were decided. We can criticize particular felony murder rules as unjustly defined and applied, but that does not condemn other felony murder rules defined more narrowly and applied more justly.

Criticism of felony murder liability has long practiced the rhetoric of guilt by association, linking the limited felony murder rules actually in force to a sweeping and morally primitive principle of strict liability. Critics have dismissed these limitations as incoherent compromises, bespeaking lawmakers' lack of conviction in an archaic doctrine. Thus critics have viewed the limits of felony murder as evidence of the superiority of a rigorously formalist and cognitivist system of culpability.

This rhetoric of guilt by association has been underwritten by two oft-repeated but seldom examined assumptions. One such assumption is that no rational principle could justify a limited felony murder rule. We have refuted that assumption by defending an expressive theory of culpability and deriving the principle of dual culpability from that theory. The second assumption is that the limited felony murder rules in current force are legacies of injustice because descended from a despotically imposed harsh rule. We have refuted that assumption as well, by showing that no such rule ever existed. No felony murder rules were inherited from our colonial masters. American felony murder rules were enacted after independence, by statute or statutory construction, as part of a distinctively American project of codifying criminal law. Although rarely defined with great precision before the twentieth century, these felony murder rules were applied reasonably in most jurisdictions.

Because felony murder rules were enacted independently in different jurisdictions and at different times, we cannot attribute every detail of nineteenth-century American felony murder law to a single coherent theory. Nevertheless, nineteenth-century American explanations of felony murder law lend some authority to the principle of dual culpability. In explaining why some felonies rendered unintended killings malicious, some courts emphasized the wickedness of the felonious purpose.[1] Other courts emphasized the dangerousness of certain felonies.[2] The most cogent explanations emphasized both, as in the Massachusetts case *Commonwealth v. Pemberton*:

> If the purpose of the defendant was to commit robbery, and if in the execution of that purpose, and in order to overcome the resistance and silence the outcries of the victim, he made use of violence that caused her death, no further proof of premeditation or of wilful intent to kill is necessary. Robbery committed by force and violence, and in spite of all resistance, is of course malicious, and if in the perpetration of that crime the person robbed is killed, it is a killing with malice aforethought . . .[3]

Here we see the twin themes of wicked motives and dangerous acts linked—the felony murderer is malicious because he is determined to achieve wicked aims by force, regardless of the inevitable danger to others. That, in a nutshell, is the principle of dual culpability.

We initially established that the dual culpability principle provides a morally plausible and historically authentic rationale for felony murder liability, and then showed that existing felony murder law accords with the dual culpability principle on most issues in most jurisdictions. Taken together, these three claims support the dual culpability principle as a constructive interpretation of the felony murder doctrine. While the dual culpability principle justifies much existing law, it also justifies reforms in many jurisdictions.

Our analysis of contemporary felony murder law focused on three issues: requirements of cognitive culpability, dangerousness, and causal responsibility that condition killing on negligence; standards of complicity and collective liability that determine the culpability required for non-killing participants in felonies; and requirements of an independent predicate felony. This analysis set aside seven jurisdictions that require intent to kill or depraved indifference to human life for all murders, and focused on forty-five jurisdictions imposing true felony murder liability. It also set aside the problem of capital punishment, which should be irrelevant for killings without intent to kill or depraved indifference to human life.

A third of felony murder jurisdictions explicitly condition felony murder on the culpable mental states of negligence[4] or malice.[5] With the exception of the federal system, all the jurisdictions conditioning felony murder on malice have interpreted it to require apparently dangerous conduct. Courts should interpret the federal statute similarly. Two additional jurisdictions, Illinois and North Dakota, have default culpability standards apparently requiring reckless indifference to human life for felony murder. Illinois can best harmonize this requirement with the rest of its law by interpreting the category of "forcible felonies" as those involving not only violence but also a "strong probability" of death. North Dakota's code predicates felony murder only on enumerated felonies, which except for burglary are all inherently dangerous. North Dakota should apply the recklessness default rule to require that death be foreseen as a result of the felony, limit predicate burglaries to those aggravated by dangerous circumstances, or shift the burden onto the prosecution to disprove the affirmative defense for non-negligent co-felons.

We established that almost all felony murder jurisdictions condition the offense on per se negligent conduct by requiring a dangerous felony. A requirement of an inherently dangerous felony ensures that all participants in the felony are negligent with respect to death. A requirement of foreseeable danger ensures that at least one participant, usually the actual killer, acted negligently.

Twenty felony murder jurisdictions predicate felony murder on unenumerated felonies in at least some cases. Few of these, if any, convict participants in unenumerated felonies of murder for killing accidentally. Thus, four jurisdictions restrict unenumerated felonies to those that are inherently dangerous.[6] Another thirteen restrict unenumerated felonies to those foreseeably dangerous as committed.[7] Only Florida, Mississippi, and Washington have not clearly required foreseeably dangerous felonies. Of these, Mississippi has defined malice, and Washington has defined causation of death, in ways that seem to require dangerous conduct. Florida, Mississippi, and Washington courts should bring their states in line with the consensus by explicitly requiring a felony inherently or foreseeably dangerous.

Finally, we showed that most felony murder convictions are predicated on enumerated felonies. Twenty-five jurisdictions restrict predicate felonies to enumerated felonies,[8] and another fourteen predicate felony murder on both enumerated and unenumerated felonies.[9] Although most enumerated felonies are inherently negligent, some are not. While killing in the course of burglary is almost always negligent, mere participation in a burglary does not entail negligence toward a risk of death, particularly if the burglary is unaggravated. Drug crimes can involve culpability towards death but need not. In all, twenty-six jurisdictions enumerate unaggravated burglary or simple breaking and entering,[10] twelve enumerate drug offenses,[11] and three enumerate theft.[12] None of these should be enumerated felonies. Moreover, courts have sometimes frustrated legislative intent to condition felony murder on inherent danger. When codes classify predicate felonies as dangerous or violent because of aggravating elements such as injuries, weapons, or victims present, courts must require culpability with respect to those elements.

Most felony murder jurisdictions—thirty-two out of forty-five—require negligence indirectly by defining homicide as the foreseeable causation of death.[13] This includes twenty-two of the thirty-two jurisdictions enumerating felonies that are not inherently dangerous.[14] Only Alaska, Minnesota, North Dakota, and Wisconsin have explicitly rejected a requirement of foreseeability. Yet Alaska substitutes a requirement of violent physical contact, Minnesota permits only inherently dangerous predicate felonies, and Wisconsin uses the homicide only as a moderately severe penalty enhancement for the underlying felony. The remaining jurisdictions have not clearly defined causation.[15] Four of these undecided jurisdictions—Iowa, Mississippi, South Carolina, and the federal system—can invoke requirements of malice in support of foreseeability requirements, as some states have done in requiring dangerous felonies. Foreseeability is less necessary in Oregon, which—like Minnesota—uses only inherently dangerous predicate felonies. Nevertheless, it would be best for the four dissenters and nine undecided jurisdictions to join the majority by adopting foreseeability as a causation standard. All courts and fact finders must resist the temptation to overattribute foreseeability on the basis of hindsight. Heart attacks, self-administered overdoses, and reckless police work are rarely predictable.

We also demonstrated that most felony murder jurisdictions condition vicarious felony murder liability on negligence, although they use a variety of doctrinal devices to achieve this. Three jurisdictions[16] completely restrict predicate felonies to inherently dangerous crimes. Four jurisdictions define felony murder simply as participation in a felony foreseeably causing death.[17] At least twenty-seven jurisdictions condition complicity in felony murder on foreseeable or inherent danger, or expected violence.[18] Eight felony murder jurisdictions provide an affirmative defense for accomplices without notice of danger.[19] In most of these jurisdictions, the defense is redundant with other requirements of foreseeability or inherent danger, but it could make a difference in Colorado and North Dakota. Jurisdictions requiring foreseeability for killers should make clear that the same requirement applies to their accomplices.[20] Courts rejecting a foreseeability requirement for accomplices, such as Maryland, Tennessee, and Kansas—or for all felons, such as Wisconsin and Alaska—should reconsider. Jurisdictions that have not yet adopted foreseeability requirements for perpetrators or accomplices—such as Florida and Wyoming—should follow the majority rule on both questions.

We also established two more general points. First, in the thirty jurisdictions that impose individual felony murder liability, co-felons who do not kill are liable for murder only insofar as they meet judicially established criteria of complicity in the killing. Judges are not authorized by statute to impose strict murder liability on co-felons, and have no principled justification for doing so. Second, the five statutes[21] imposing collective liability on felons for deaths caused by nonfelons are unjustifiable. No one should be liable for homicide without participating in an act that causes death. Courts should read these statutes as conditioning liability on the foreseeability to the defendant of death.

Felony murder jurisdictions have usually conditioned causal responsibility and complicity on normative as well as cognitive culpability. Two-thirds of the jurisdictions require an instrumental or causal relationship between the felony and the death,[22] while only seven have rejected such a requirement.[23] The required linkage between the felony and the fatality implies that culpability is being transferred from the felony to the killing. Thus, felonious motive is part of the culpability required for felony murder in most jurisdictions. Negligence toward death and felonious motive combine to justify murder liability as deserved.

The dual culpability required for felony murder—negligence and felonious motive—explains the purpose and the contours of the otherwise puzzling merger doctrine. Felonies aimed at injuring some interest other than the health of the victim—such as rape, robbery, arson, or aggravated burglary for purposes of theft—supply the normative culpability needed to aggravate a negligent homicide to murder. Yet courts need not require an independent felonious purpose if legislatures enumerate only predicate felonies with such purposes. Because judicial application of a merger doctrine is primarily helpful in limiting unenumerated felonies, it is not necessary in most jurisdictions. Moreover, the principle of dual culpability does not require that every predicate felony have an independent felonious purpose. Murder liability is also deserved when death is caused by a felony entailing depraved indifference to human life. Although the dual culpability principle precludes murder predicated on simple aggravated assaults, it may permit murder predicated on a property offense committed for the purpose of an aggravated assault, an aggravated assault on a vulnerable dependent, or a particularly cruel and demeaning assault, such as mayhem. A legislature may rationally conclude that these predicate felonies express depraved indifference to human life.

Most jurisdictions have limited predicate felonies in conformity with these principles. To be sure, only eight or nine jurisdictions have adopted the merger doctrine,[24] while seven have rejected it.[25] Yet few other jurisdictions have violated the principles underlying the merger doctrine, and these violations are easily fixed.[26] Courts that have rejected the merger doctrine should reconsider. Properly understood, the doctrine is not very restrictive, but those few restrictions are integral to the principles that justify felony murder liability.

In sum, most felony murder jurisdictions condition the offense on negligence through a combination of culpability requirements, enumerations of predicate felonies, dangerous felony limits, foreseeable causation requirements, and complicity rules. In addition, most jurisdictions condition the offense on felonious motive through a combination of enumerated felonies, causal linkage requirements, and merger limitations. Thus, felony murder law conforms to the principle of dual culpability in most respects in most jurisdictions. It should be brought into conformity where it falls short.

Because felony murder laws generally conform to just principles, the ten unjust cases presented at the outset of this book are anomalous rather than typical. These ten decisions all violated the principle of dual culpability. None of the defendants could reasonably have foreseen that death would result from their actions. In addition, Miller, Jenkins, and (arguably) Malaske lacked an independent felonious purpose, while Colenburg, Holle, and Danahey lacked any felonious purpose at all. These cases effectively illustrate why the felony murder doctrine needs limits, but they do not show that felony murder law has no such limits. Some of these cases are no longer good law. The rest were misapplications of existing law when they were decided.

Stamp's jury convicted him for fatally frightening a robbery victim without any instruction on foreseeability. California law no longer permits this. Hickman's murder conviction for sharing cocaine with a friend resulted from Virginia's failure to require foreseeability. Since foreseeability is now required, the case is no longer good law.

Colenburg's murder conviction for driving a car stolen months before resulted in part from the trial court's failure to apply Missouri's requirements that death result foreseeably from and in furtherance of the felony. Jenkins was convicted for being tackled by a trigger-happy officer partly because Illinois had not yet adopted its current merger rule. His conviction also resulted from the trial court's erroneous failure to instruct on the requirement of foreseeability. Ingram, the New York burglar convicted of causing his captor's heart attack, acquiesced in the trial court's erroneous failure to instruct the jury on the requirements of foreseeability and a physical interaction. The case has no authority as precedent. Matos was convicted of provoking an officer to jump off a roof because a New York court wrongly treated the result in *Ingram* as authoritative precedent.

Malaske's murder conviction for supplying his younger sister with alcohol was obtained on the basis of a jury instruction that failed to require foreseeability. An appellate court justified this oversight on the dubious ground that his felony was inherently dangerous to human life, and was never asked to apply Oklahoma's merger doctrine. Miller's murder conviction for punching his schoolmate resulted in large measure from Georgia's rejection of a merger limitation. Yet Miller's trial court also erroneously instructed his jury that assault with a deadly weapon required no knowledge of the deadly potential of a fist; ignored precedent requiring an expectation of injury for aggravated battery; and failed to instruct on foreseeability on the ground that these strict liability offenses were nevertheless inherently dangerous.

Holle's unjust conviction for felony murder resulted from his wrongful conviction as an accomplice in burglary. No proof was offered that he provided transportation with the intent to further burglary. Danahey's prosecutors somehow persuaded her to plead guilty to felony murder with no proof that she intended the predicate felony of arson.

These results are not representative of prevailing felony murder law even in the jurisdictions where they were decided. Yet it should be no surprise to find the law misapplied to the defendant's detriment in felony murder cases. After all, lawyers are taught to expect that felony murder rules will yield unjust results. Their teachers tell them that felony murder rules are inherently irrational and unfair. On the basis of this training, judges must assume that legislatures can have no other purpose in enacting felony murder rules than to help the prosecution win convictions without proving guilt. Prosecutors must assume that in convicting the blameless they are only taking advantages to which they are entitled. Lawyers in both roles have been taught they need not—and indeed cannot—defend felony murder liability as deserved. In proclaiming that popular felony murder rules are rationally indefensible, academic critics foment cynicism among those charged with enforcing those rules.

In opposition to such cynicism, this book has argued that the felony murder doctrine is not a presumption, not a legal fiction, not a trick or weapon or device: it is a principle of *justice*. Properly applied, felony murder rules should impose deserved punishment for very culpable killing. Prosecutors are obliged to justify convictions as deserved by proving that culpability; and judges are obliged to instruct juries to require such proof. Felony murder rules do not govern felons only. They are rules of *law*, by which those who stand in judgment must also be judged.

NOTES

Chapter 1

1. Commonwealth v. Hanlon, 3 Brewster's Rep. 461, 470–76 (Pa. Ct. Oyer & Terminer 1870).

2. Slater v. State, 316 So. 2d 539, 540 (Fla. 1975).

3. People v. Goldvarg, 178 N.E. 892 (Ill. 1931).

4. Model Penal Code § 210.2 cmt. 6, 31–32 (Official Draft and Revised Comments 1985); Pillsbury, 1998, 106–08; Crum, 1952, 203–10; Fletcher, 1981, 415–16; Gardner, 1993, 706–08; Kadish, 1994, 695–97; Packer, 1973, 3–4; Roth & Sundby, 1985, 490–91; Schulhofer, 1974, 1498–99.

5. Roth & Sundby, 1985.

6. Many student texts make this claim. See Loewy, 2003, 42; Dressler, 2001, 515; Kadish & Schulhofer, 1989, 514; Robinson, 1997, 726.

7. But see Cole, 1990 (defending a limited felony murder rule on utilitarian grounds); Crump & Crump, 1985 (defending felony murder liability as deserved based on harm alone, regardless of culpability); Simons, 1997, 1121–24 (defending felony murder liability as a form of negligence when predicated on inherently dangerous felonies); Tomkovicz, 1994 (acknowledging the persistent legislative popularity of felony murder).

8. Kadish, 1994, 695–96.

9. Model Penal Code § 210.2 cmt. 6, 37 (Official Draft and Revised Comments 1985).

10. State v. Colenburg, 773 S.W.2d 184, 185 (Mo. Ct. App. 1989).

11. Miller v. State, 571 S.E.2d 788, 792 (Ga. 2002).

12. People v. Jenkins, 545 N.E.2d 986, 990–91 (Ill. App. Ct. 1989).

13. People v. Stamp, 82 Cal. Rptr. 598, 601 (Cal. Ct. App. 1969).

14. People v. Ingram, 67 N.Y.2d 897, 898 (N.Y. 1986).

15. People v. Matos, 568 N.Y.S.2d 683 (1991), aff'd 83 N.Y.2d 509, 510–11 (N.Y. 1994).

16. Hickman v. Com., 398 S.E.2d 698, 699 (Va. Ct. App. 1990).

17. Malaske v. State, 89 P.3d 1116, 1117 n.1 (Okla. Crim. App. 2004).

18. Liptak, 2007.

19. North Carolina Citizens for Felony Murder Rule Change, http://www.ncfelony murder.org/Janet%20Danahey/janet.html (last visited Nov. 12, 2010).

20. Liptak, 2007.

21. Kadish, Schulhofer & Steiker, 2007, 438; Dressler, 2007, 312; Boyce, Dripps & Perkins, 2010, 547–50; Harris & Lee, 2005, 432–35; Weinreb, 2003, 156–59; Cloud & Johnson, 2002, 254.

22. Enmund v. Florida, 458 U.S. 782 (1982) and Tison v. Arizona, 481 U.S. 137 (1987). *Tison* attributes gross recklessness to a hypothetical robber who intentionally shoots a victim, and appears to justify death eligibility on that basis.

23. Binder, Felony Murder and Mens Rea Default Rules, 2000, 400–401.

24. Stuntz, 2001, 530; Barkow, 2006, 1718; Simon, 2007, 34–35.

25. Robinson & Darley, 1995, 169–81.

26. Dworkin, 1986, 5–15.

27. Id., 53.

28. Binder & Weisberg, 2001, 47–50, 84–85, 188–95; Lieber, 1880; Eskridge, 1994; Hart & Sacks, 1957; Radin, 1942; Sutherland, 1943.

29. Dworkin, 1986, 211, 213, 225.

30. Id., 52–53, 225.

31. Id., 53.

32. Dworkin, 1978; Dworkin, 1986, 4–6.

33. Dworkin, 1986, 48.

34. Id., 49–51, 228–38; Dworkin, 1985, 167–77.

35. Dworkin, 1986, 178–84.

36. For previous works recognizing the expressive dimension of culpability, see Gross, 1979, 103–06; Binder, Rhetoric of Motive and Intent, 2002, 56–59; Finkelstein, 1995, 270–75; Gardner, 1998, 575; Hampton, 1990, 1–2; Hampton, 1984, 238; Huigens, 1995, 1424; Kahan & Nussbaum, 1996, 273; Michaels, 1998; Simons, 1992, 495–522; Binder, Meaning and Motive in the Law of Homicide, 2000, 761–66; Nourse, 1998, 1456–57.

37. Commonwealth v. Twitchell, 617 N.E.2d 609, 612–13 (Mass. 1993).

38. Block, 1977, 83; Zimring & Zuehl, 1986, 8 tbl.1 (5.2 killings per 1,000 robberies), 18 (resistance in 8% of robberies, but 55% of robbery killings). Together, these statistics indicate 2.2 deaths per 1,000 unresisted robberies, and 30 deaths per 1,000 resisted robberies.

39. People v. Washington, 62 Cal. 2d 777 (1965); Jenkins v. State, 230 A.2d 262 (Del. 1967).

40. Moynihan v. State, 70 Ind. 126, 130 (1880); People v. Scott, 6 Mich. 287, 293 (1859); Com. v. Flanagan, 7 Watts & Serg. 415 (Pa. 1844); Simpson v. Com., 293 Ky. 831 (1943).

41. Robinson & Darley, 1995, 169–81. The 22–27-year penalty was just for the homicide, not the separately punishable robbery. Very little punishment was imposed, however, when the victim was a co-felon and the shooter was a robbery victim. Id., 179. See also Finkel, 1995, 164–71. Finkel's results are harder to interpret because he put his subjects in the role of jurors instructed to apply a particular legal standard. One of his two felony murder scenarios would not be felony murder in most jurisdictions.

42. Robinson & Darley, 1995, 176–78.

43. Id., 169–81.

44. Binder, 2007.

45. Clark & Marshall, 1900, 514–16; Dressler, 2006, 556–57; LaFave, 2003, 744; Loewy, 2003, 45.

46. Clark & Marshall, 1900, 514–16.

47. LaFave, 2003, 744–45.

48. Binder, 2007, 93.

49. Id., 95–101.

50. Id., 97–101.

51. Id., 101–06.

52. Id., 95–101.

53. Mansell & Herbert's Case, (1558) 2 Dy. 128b, 128b, 73 Eng. Rep. 279, 279–80 (K.B.); Lord Dacre's Case, (1535) Moo. K.B. 86, 86, 72 Eng. Rep. 458, 458.

54. See R. v. Plummer, (1701) Kel. J. 109, 112–18, 84 Eng. Rep. 1103, 1105–07 (K.B.).

55. Banner, 2002, 89–100.

56. Act of Apr. 22, 1794, ch. 1766, 1794 Pa. Laws 186.

57. Act of Apr. 22, 1794, § 2, 1794 Pa. Laws, 187.

58. State v. Shock, 68 Mo. 552, 556 (1878); People v. Rector, 19 Wend. 569, 605 (N.Y. Sup. Ct. 1838).

59. R. v. Lee, (1864) 4 F. & F. 63, 66–67, 176 Eng. Rep. 468, 469–70 (Q.B.); R. v. Collison, (1831) 4 Car. & P. 565, 565–66, 172 Eng. Rep. 827, 827–28 (K.B.); Duffey's & Hunt's Case, (1830) 1 Lewin. 194, 194–95, 168 Eng. Rep. 1009, 1009 (K.B.).

Chapter 2

1. People v. Washington, 402 P.2d 130, 133 (Cal. 1965) (en banc); Baker v. State, 377 So. 2d 17, 19–20 (Fla. 1979); State v. Allen, 875 A.2d 724, 729–30 (Md. 2005); State v. Maldonado, 645 A.2d 1165, 1172 (N.J. 1994); State v. Martin, 573 A.2d 1359, 1368 (N.J. 1990); State v. Ervin, 577 A.2d 1273, 1277 (N.J. Super. Ct. App. Div. 1990).

2. Malani, 2002.

3. See, e.g., People v. Patterson, 778 P.2d 549, 558 (Cal. 1989); Linehan v. State, 442 So. 2d 244, 254 (Fla. Dist. Ct. App. 1983); State v. Goodseal, 553 P.2d 279, 286 (Kan. 1976), overruled by State v. Underwood, 615 P.2d 153, 163 (Kan. 1980); Martin, 573 A.2d, 1368.

4. Holmes, 1982, 48; Macaulay, 1890, 313; Wharton, 1875, 39 n.3; Roth & Sundby, 1985, 452.

5. Radzinowicz, 1957, 452–56; Schulhofer, 1974, 1546; Andenaes, 1952, 192 ("[M]aximum deterrence does not follow from the severest punishment. . . ."); Doob & Webster, 2003, 143 ("[V]ariation in the severity of sanctions is unrelated to levels of crime."); Ehrlich, 1973, 544–47 (probability of punishment negatively correlated with crime rate more than the severity of punishment for murder, rape, and robbery, although not necessarily for burglary).

6. Schulhofer, 1974, 1540.

7. Coffee, 1980, 432.

8. Darley, 2005, 201–02.

9. Block & Lind, 1975, 481; Harel & Segal, 1999, 280, 296–97; Polinsky & Shavell, 1999, 12.

10. Seidman, 1984, 347–48.

11. Polinsky & Shavell, 1979, 883–85.

12. Cole, 1990, 113–15.

13. Sunstein & Vermeule, 2005, 713.

14. Tobias, 1979, 139–47; Donohue & Wolfers, 2005, 841–45; Schulhofer, 1974, 1536.

15. People v. Smith, 678 P.2d 886, 891–92 (Cal. 1984) (en banc); People v. Washington, 402 P.2d 130, 133 (Cal. 1965) (en banc); People v. Hernandez, 215 Cal. Rptr. 166, 168 (Ct. App. 1985).

16. Cole, 1990, 94–95.

17. Mannheimer, 2011.

18. See, e.g., State v. Martin, 573 A.2d 1359, 1368 (N.J. 1990); Cole, 1990, 89, 96–97.

19. See generally Wechsler & Michael, 1937, 730–61 (providing a normative analysis of homicide law based on considerations of deterrence). This article is generally seen as the origin of the culpability scheme incorporated into the Model Penal Code.

20. Kahan, 1999; Harcourt, 1999.

21. Packer, 1968, 62–66; Ross, 1975, 37–38; Andenaes, 1966, 950; Hart, 1958, 409–13; Robinson & Darley, 1997, 468–70; Seidman, 1984, 333–36.

22. Seidman, 1984, 333.

23. Id., 334–35.

24. See, e.g., Sinclair, 1962, 220–41 (criminogenic effect of prohibition).

25. Goodin, 1995, 70; Hart, 1968, 181–82; Rawls, 1972.

26. Binder & Smith, 2000, 174–76.

27. Id., 211–12; Binder, Punishment Theory, 2002, 325–27.

28. Kelman, 1983, 1512.

29. Model Penal Code § 1.13(9).

30. Model Penal Code § 2.02(1) (1962).

31. Id., §§ 2.02(1), 2.05(2)(a) (using the phrase "absolute liability" rather than "strict liability").

32. Simons, 1997, 1085–88.

33. Id.

34. Kelman, 1983, 1516–18.

35. Simons, 1997, 1085–88.

36. Model Penal Code § 2.02(2)(d).

37. Alexander, 1990, 84, 101; Hall, 1963, 634–37.

38. Ferzan, 2001, 600; Garvey, 2006, 335–38.

39. Katz, 1988, 164.

40. See, e.g., Gardner, 1998, 593–98; Horder, 1997, 514–15; Huigens, 1995, 1475.

41. Duff offers such a view in Intention, Agency, and Criminal Liability. See Duff, 1990, 121–34, 158–63.

42. Roth & Sundby, 1985.

43. 3 Stephen, 1883, 80–81.

44. Id.

45. See State v. Moffitt, 199 Kan. 513 (1967); Simpson v. Com., 293 Ky. 831 (1943); State v. Glover, 330 Mo. 709, 718 (1932).

46. E.g., State v. Oliver, 341 N.W.2d 744 (Iowa 1983).

47. People v. Aaron, 299 N.W.2d 304 (Mich. 1980); State v. Ortega, 817 P.2d 1196 (N.M. 1991).

48. Lowry v. State, 657 S.E.2d 760 (S.C. 2008).

49. State v. Judge, 38 S.E.2d 715, 719 (S.C. 1946).

50. State v. Kinard, 646 S.E.2d 168, 170 (S.C. 2007).

51. People v. Chun, 203 P.3d 425 (Cal. 2009); People v. Dillon, 668 P.2d 697 (Cal. 1983); State v. Ragland, 420 N.W.2d 791 (Iowa 1988) (overruled on other grounds); State v. Cox, 879 P.2d 662 (Mont. 1994); State v. Nichols, 734 P.2d 170, 176 (Mont. 1987); Cotton v. Commonwealth, 546 S.E.2d 241 (Va. Ct. App. 2001).

52. Cotton, 546 S.E.2d, 243.

53. Roth & Sundby, 1985.

54. Solem v. Helm, 463 U.S. 277 (1983).

55. Gregg v. Georgia, 428 U.S. 153 (1976).

56. See Atkins v. United States, 536 U.S. 304 (2002); Roper v. Simmons, 543 U.S. 551 (2005).

57. Lee, 2009.

58. Ewing v. California, 538 U.S. 11 (2002); Harmelin v. Michigan, 501 U.S. 957 (1991); Rummel v. Estelle, 445 U.S. 263 (1980).

59. Graham v. Florida, 130 S. Ct. 2011 (2010) (no life without parole for juvenile offender committing non-homicide offense).

60. State v. Ragland, 420 N.W.2d 791 (Iowa 1988) (overruled on other grounds).

61. 255 U.S. 224 (1921).

62. 258 U.S. 250 (1922).

63. 342 U.S. 246 (1952).

64. U.S. v. Wulff, 758 F.2d 1121 (6th Cir. 1985); Holdridge v. U.S., 282 F.2d 302 (8th Cir. 1960); cf. U.S. v. Engler, 806 F.2d 425, 434 (3d Cir. 1986).

65. Lambert v. California, 355 U.S. 225 (1957).

66. U.S. v. X-Citement Video, Inc., 513 U.S. 64 (1994); Smith v. Cal., 361 U.S. 147 (1959).

67. Michaels, 1999, 836.

266 NOTES TO CHAPTER 3

Chapter 3

1. Bentham, 1970, 100.

2. Mill, 1947; Harcourt, 1999, 120–21.

3. Fletcher, 1978, 396.

4. Id., 397–98.

5. Id., 400–401.

6. Locke, 1988, 142–43.

7. For the influence of this conception of rights in nineteenth-century legal thought, see generally Singer, 1982; Gordon, 1983.

8. Mill, 1947, 9–10.

9. Harcourt, 1999, 131–38.

10. 539 U.S. 558 (2003); see Haque, 2007.

11. Wisconsin v. Mitchell, 508 U.S. 476 (1993); Ohio v. Wyant, 508 U.S. 969 (1993).

12. Moore, 1997, 405.

13. Id., 405–06.

14. Alexander, 2000.

15. Id., 931–32.

16. Id., 933.

17. Id., 934–35.

18. Id., 942–43. Alexander concedes that under prevailing law the justifiability of that harm by expected countervailing benefits is considered separately, as part of the issue of wrongdoing, rather than as part of the calculus of culpability. See id., 943.

19. See id., 943.

20. Id.

21. Id., 942–44.

22. Id., 936.

23. Alexander, 1994, 28; Alexander & Kessler, 1997, 1174–78; Alexander, 1990, 101–03.

24. Alexander, 2000, 946–47 ("[B]ecause I would not distinguish between 'attempts' and 'successes' [in complicity cases] . . . all that would matter is what harms the defendant unjustifiably risked."); Alexander & Kessler, 1997, 1176–78 (saying that recklessness should suffice for attempt liability "regardless of the mens rea required" for the completed crime).

25. Ferzan, 2002, 209.

26. Moore, 1997, 405–06.

27. Ferzan, 2002, 210.

28. Id., 209–12. Stephen Morse agrees that "affect and emotion" are "not intentional and simply happen to us" and that "[t]houghts, desires, and character are not primarily a product of our reason." Morse, 2004, 369. He would limit culpability to the intent to do an act that unreasonably places another at risk, but surprisingly holds that purposeful is worse than knowing endangerment even though he regards desires as unchosen. Id., 376.

29. Hurd, 2001, 216.

30. Id., 223–24.

31. Id., 224–26.

32. Id., 229.

33. Id., 230.

34. Moore and Hurd see a purpose of causing harm as culpable, but only because it implies an expectation of causing harm. See Moore, 1997, 408–09; Hurd, 2001, 218, 223.

35. Duff, 1990, 75–76, 109 (attributing this view of homicide to utilitarianism and similar consequentialist views); Alexander, 2000, 939–44; Ferzan, 2002, 208–12.

36. Binder, Rhetoric of Motive and Intent, 2002, 28; Binder & Smith, 2000, 176–82.

37. Binder, Rhetoric of Motive and Intent, 2002, 28.

38. Binder & Smith, 2000, 156.

39. Helvetius, 1970, 229–35.

40. Id., 7, 10, 29, 39, 124–25.

41. Binder, Rhetoric of Motive and Intent, 2002, 29.

42. Bentham, 1970, 97.

43. Id., 101.

44. Id., 100.

45. Id., 161.

46. Id., 143.

47. Id., 92.

48. Austin, 1885, 407–24.

49. Id., 414–15.

50. Id., 414.

51. Id., 421.

52. Id., 419.

53. Id.

54. Id., 418–19.

55. Id., 423.

56. Id., 418–24.

57. Id., 459.

58. Id., 425–34.

59. Id., 424.

60. Id., 496–98.

61. Wechsler, 1952, 1105, 1108 (describing deterrence as the essential purpose of the Model Penal Code and its requirement of culpability); Wechsler & Michael, 1937, 730–61.

62. Model Penal Code § 1.02(1)(a) (1962); Harcourt, 1999, 136 (discussing the influence of the harm principle on the Model Penal Code); Wechsler, 1968, 1432 (harm prevention the purpose of the Model Penal Code).

63. Model Penal Code § 2.02; Simons, 1992, 466, 468–71.

64. Model Penal Code §§ 2.02(1), 2.05(1)(2)(a).

65. Id., § 210.2 cmt. 6, 29 (Official Draft and Revised Comments 1985).

66. Id., § 2.02(4) (1962).

67. Id., §§ 2.03(2), 2.08(2), 210.2(1), 220.2(1).

68. Id., § 2.02(7).

69. Id., § 5.01(1)(b)–(c).

70. Id., § 5.05(1).

71. Id., § 2.03.

72. Brandt, 1992, 158–75.

73. Id., 159; Hausman & McPherson, 1996, 73; Hurley, 1989, 55.

74. Hausman & McPherson, 1996, 72.

75. Id., 72–73.

76. Id., 77, 80 (showing how the possibility of changing preferences threatens the idea of rational self-interest with incoherence). See Arrow, 1963, 9–11; Hausman & McPherson, 1996, 27–28 (formal conditions for stability of preferences).

77. Bentham, 1970, 143.

78. Model Penal Code § 2.03 (1962).

79. Hurley, 1989, 314.

80. Id., 14.

81. Id., 24, 102.

82. Schick, 1991, 107.

83. Hurley, 1989, 20–28, 55–83.

84. Blumenthal, 2005, 165–81; Kelman, 2005, 394–95; Loewenstein & Schkade, 1999, 85–105.

85. Schick, 1991, 87.

86. Id., 2–8.

87. E.g., State v. Hall, 722 N.W.2d 472, 477 (Minn. 2006).

88. Model Penal Code § 2.03.

89. Hart & Honoré, 1985, 13–22 (discussing causal theories of Hume and Mill); Hume, 2000, 37–39.

90. Hart & Honoré, 1985, 256–57; Moore, 1997, 363–99; Kelman, 1981, 595–96, 640–42; Morris, 1952, 198.

91. Hausman & McPherson, 1996, 75–77.

92. Id., 77–80.

93. Dworkin, Taking Rights Seriously, 1978, 234–38 (sadistic and other external preferences); Herzog, 1989, 2–3 (consent to oppression); Scarre, 1996, 155–62; Elster, 1999, 25–45 (addictive preferences).

94. Hausman & McPherson, 1996, 80.

95. Nagel, 1986, 166–71.

96. Arrow, 1963, 59 (explicating the General Possibility Theorem).

97. Seidman, 1984, 319–34.

98. Ross, 2002, 38 (claiming that the utilitarian calculus is indeterminate because the consequences are infinite); Kelman, 1987, 579–80, 618–19.

99. Wechsler, 1952, 1106.

100. Model Penal Code § 210.2 cmt. 6, 36 (Official Draft and Revised Comments 1985).

101. Id., § 5.05(1) (1962).

102. Hart, 1967, 5.

103. Schulhofer, 1974, 1533–57.

104. Beccaria, 1986, 48–50; Bentham, 1970, 170, 183, 288.

105. Schulhofer, 1974, 1565–69.

106. Kadish, 1994, 681, 686, 698.

107. Hart, 1960, 1–26; Packer, 1968, 39–57; Hart, 1958, 409–11, 413.

108. Kadish, 1994, 680.

109. Id., 697–99.

110. Id., 684–88, 697–99.

111. Id., 680–84.

112. Id., 682. For explanations of the problem of moral luck, see Nagel, 1979, 24–38; Williams, 1982, 20–39.

113. Hart & Honoré, 1985, 13–22.

114. Zimmerman, 1987, 385.

115. Feinberg, 1965, 25, 33.

116. Kadish, 1994, 695–97.

117. Kelman, 1987, 581–87.

118. Coase, 1960, 1–8.

119. Kelman, 1987, 595–96, 600–601.

120. Id., 579, 581–86.

121. Id., 580.

122. Id., 608 (probabilistic conception of causation unsuited to determining causal responsibility for particular injuries).

123. Thode, 1968, 431–33.

124. Baumeister & Capone, 2003, 1027–30 (describing causation burdens facing toxic tort plaintiffs).

125. Kelman, 1987, 598–99.

126. Wechsler, 1952, 1106.

127. Brandt, 1979, 276; Murphy, Liam, 2000, 3–25; Brink, 1986, 431–38; Railton, 1984, 138–46, 160–63.

128. For defenses of utilitarianism as a policy standard rather than an ethical standard, see generally Goodin, 1995, 3–27; Binder & Smith, 2000, 174–84.

129. Hart & Honoré, 1985, 68–70.

130. Id., 70, 106–07, 257, 259–75. They prefer a different test, however, that focuses on the intervention of abnormal events.

131. Model Penal Code § 2.03 (1962); Hart & Honoré, 1985, 257–58; Moore, 1997, 395–96.

132. Hohfeld, 1913, 28–32 (arguing that rights and duties are jural correlatives).

133. Rawls, 2005, 22–29, 259–88; Rawls, 1999, 3–29, 130–56, 496–511; Kant, 1999 (contractarian theories). Bargain and contract often play prominent roles in libertarian theories as well. See, e.g., Gauthier, 1986, 113–56; Nozick, 1974, 297–334. The difference is that libertarian theories distribute natural rights in advance of the contracting process and allow them to be modified only through voluntary transactions. By contrast, Rawls' contractarianism derives rights from a hypothetical contract among featureless persons in order to ensure that the process of defining rights is impartial among persons holding different values. See Rawls, 2005, 271–81.

134. Mill, 1947, 9.

135. Coase, 1960, 1–8; see also Singer, 1982, 984–89, 993–98, 1021–24 (arguing that there is a necessary indeterminacy of liberty rights because of the inevitability of mutual interference).

136. Mill, 1947, 9–12.

137. Id., 10–11, 95–104; Harcourt, 1999, 120–22, 185–89.

138. Rawls, 1999, 28.

139. Rawls, 2005, 16–35.

140. Murphy, 1994; Rawls, 1999, 239–41; Rosen, 1996, 33–34.

141. Kant, 1999, 116, 139, 142; Murphy, 1979, 77–92; Binder, Punishment Theory, 2002, 350–53; Davis, 1993, 141–43; Davis, 1983, 736–46; Galligan, 1981, 152–63; Greenawalt, 1983, 1336, 1339; Morris, 1976, 31–58.

142. Kant, 1999, 137–38 (distinguishing between private and public crimes).

143. Id., 46–47.

144. Id., 116, 166–67.

145. Id., 118.

146. Id., 180–82.

147. Id., 116–17.

148. Id., 30–32.

149. Ashworth, 1978, 94; Dillof, 1998, 503, 507–08, 520–22. Dillof rejects intent-transferring among victims because he sees duties as running only to individual rights holders, and so rejects the idea of public duties to cooperative institutions. See id.

150. Dillof, 1998, 514.

151. Dressler, 2006, 133–34 (arguing that the legally relevant intention is to cause a proscribed type of injury rather than to injure a particular person); Moore, 1997, 474–75 (same).

152. E.g., Hall, 1963, 637–38.

153. Alexander, 1990, 101–03; Hall, 1963, 638–39; id., 643–44.

154. Dillof, 1998, 506–07 (treating felony murder liability as a special case of trans-

ferred intent, and condemning felony murder for "permitting punishment disproportionate to culpability").

155. Coase, 1960.

156. Huigens, 1995, 1429–37 (arguing that the conflict of rights can be resolved only
by the theory of the good).

157. Eskridge, 1994, 13–47.

158. Id., 23–34 (tendency of legislatures to compromise on controversial issues by
adopting equivocal language). Balkin, 1986, 4–13; Kennedy, 1991, 75–76, 90–104 (adjudication often preserves rather than resolves intractable conflicts of principle).

159. Hart & Honoré, 1985, 62 (distinguishing causes from necessary conditions by
their abnormality).

160. Id., 41–44, 136–62, 326–40.

161. Id., 109–14.

162. Id., 39–41.

163. Id., 44–49.

164. Id., 162–85, 340–51.

165. Compare Office of Applied Studies, Substance Abuse and Mental Health Admin., U.S. Dept. of H. H. S., Summary of Findings from the Nat'l Survey on Drug Abuse
(1999) http://www.oas.samhsa.gov/nhsda/98summHtml/NHSDA98SummTbl-06.htm
#P2065_18890 (3,811,000 cocaine users in 1998), and CDC Mortality Query Results,
http://www.briancbennett.com/charts/death/cdc/cocaine-yr.htm (1,802 cocaine-induced
deaths in 1998), with Bureau of Transp. Statistics Table 1–11 http://www.bts,gov/publica
tions/national_transportation_statistics/2005/html/table_01_11.html (5,780,870 motorcycles in 2004), and Nat'l Highway Traffic Safety Admin., Traffic Safety Facts 1 tbl. 1
(July 2007), http://www-nrd.nhtsa.dot.gov/Pubs/810791.pdf (4,576 motorcyclists killed
in 2005) (0.05% mortality for cocaine and 0.08% for motorcycles).

166. E.g., Kan. Stat. Ann. § 21–3436 (1996 & Supp. 2006) ("inherently dangerous
felon[ies]" include manufacturing and possession of cocaine); Hindelang et al., 1975.

167. Kelman, 1987, 586 (concluding that the Hart and Honoré test requires value
judgments).

168. Hart & Honoré, 1985, 62; see also Duff, 1990, 65 ("[Causation is] a normative,
not a purely factual issue . . . we select A, from the whole range of causal factors which
were involved, as 'the cause' of B.").

169. This hypothetical is loosely based on People v. Newton, 87 Cal. Rptr. 394, 397–
401 (Ct. App. 1970).

170. Model Penal Code § 2.03(3)(a)–(b) (1962).

171. Duff, 1990, 156, 159, 166.

172. See Moore, 1997, 192.

173. Id., 48.

174. Id., 49.

175. Id., 232–46.

176. Id., 225–33.

177. Robinson & Darley, 1995, 13–28, 74–79.

178. Duff, 1990, 189–90.

179. Id., 189.

180. Moore, 1997, 231.

181. Duff, Criminal Attempts, 1996, 345; Duff, 1990, 191–92; Duff, Subjectivism, Objectivism, 1996, 37–39.

182. Kant, 2002.

183. Id., 55–62.

184. Binder, Punishment Theory, 2002, 352–55.

185. Davis, 1986, 28–29.

186. Hart, 1968, 131.

187. Kessler, 1994, 2219.

188. Ashworth, 1988, 746.

189. Morse, 2004, 427.

190. Kant, 1999, 138–39.

191. Id., 36.

192. E.g., Mayes v. People, 106 Ill. 306, 308–09, 311 (1883) (affirming a conviction for murder of a man who threw a beer glass in anger at his wife who was carrying an oil lamp and failed to aid her after she ignited); Commonwealth v. Malone, 47 A.2d 445, 447 (Pa. 1946) (affirming the murder conviction of a teen who bullied a younger child into shooting himself).

193. Katz, 1988, 164–236.

194. Brownmiller, 1993, 194–97.

195. See Hampton, 2007, 116–42; Hampton, 1984, 208, 217, 227; Hampton, 1988, 111–61.

196. See McAdams, 1992, 31–48 (explanatory power of status-maintenance as source of motivation).

197. Abbott, 1981, 75–76 (discussing social pressures on prison inmates to avenge insults and injuries).

198. See Miller, 1990, 179–220 (defining and explaining the retributive practices of feuding and vengeance); Wyatt-Brown, 1982, 262–434 (study of vengeance in an honor-based society).

199. E.g., Miller, 1983, 159–60.

200. Hampton, 1988, 124–30.

201. Moore, 1997, 207–08; Kessler, 1994, 2216.

Chapter 4

1. Raz, 1986, 288–320.

2. Id., 300–313.

3. Schick, 1991.

4. Anderson, 1993, 6–7, 11–15.

5. Raz, 1986, 307–13.

6. Anderson, 1993, 17–43.

7. Hampton, 2007, 102–06.

8. Id.

9. Id., 134–50.

10. Id., 120–34.

11. 102 Ala. 25 (1894).

12. Kutz, 2000, 116–24.

13. Dan-Cohen, 2002, 183–85.

14. Id.

15. Just as I can be harmed by tangible injuries I don't know about. Id., 174–78; Hampton, 2007, 120.

16. Dan-Cohen, 2002, 178; Feinberg, 1984, 83–91.

17. Dan-Cohen, 2002, 185–86.

18. Searle, 1995, 27 (defining institutional facts as those that can exist only by virtue of institutions); id., 40–47 (describing statuses as institutional facts).

19. Id., 31–58.

20. Brownmiller, 1993, 15; Hampton, 2007, 131; MacKinnon, 1987, 7.

21. Hampton, 2007, 131.

22. Brownmiller, 1993, 257–68; Eigenberg, 1994, 145–61; Lockwood, 1994, 97–102.

23. Askin, 1997, 261–82; Brownmiller, 1993, 31–113.

24. Katz, 1988, 176–78.

25. Id.

26. Id.

27. Id., 164.

28. Id., 215–18.

29. Id., 164–65.

30. Id., 191–92.

31. Id., 187–89.

32. Id., 178–87.

33. Id., 185–87.

34. Id., 218–36.

35. Schick, 1997, 19.

36. Tadros, 2005, 44.

37. Duff, 1990, 47–51; Tadros, 2005, 31–34.

38. E.g., Moore, 1997, 405–06; Ferzan, 2002, 209–12.

39. Hurd & Moore, 2004, 1105, 1128–29.

40. Id., 1118–29.

41. Id., 1121–29; Hurd, 2001, 223–26.

42. Kahan & Nussbaum, 1996, 285–97.

43. Id., 285–90.

44. Id., 305–21.

45. Hurd, 2001, 224–25.

46. Id., 225–26. See also Hurd & Moore, 2004, 1129–31.

47. Binder & Weisberg, 1997, 1155–65 (discussing identity as role performance).

48. Hampton, 2007, 77–78.

49. Id.

50. Kant, 2002, 37.

51. Hampton, 2007, 85–101.

52. Horder, 1997, 514–17.

53. Hampton, 2007, 80.

54. Id., 105–06; also Huigens, 1998, 447–55 (discussing a character theory of negligence).

55. E.g., People v. Burton, 491 P.2d 793, 801–02 (Cal. 1971) (en banc).

56. People v. Ireland, 450 P.2d 580, 589–91 (Cal. 1969) (en banc); State v. Heemstra, 721 N.W.2d 549, 556 (Iowa 2006); State v. Lucas, 759 P.2d 90, 95 (Kan. 1988); State v. Shock, 68 Mo. 552, 555 (1878); People v. Moran, 158 N.E. 35, 36–37 (N.Y. 1927); People v. Rector, 19 Wend. 569, 605 (N.Y. Sup. Ct. 1838).

57. Finkelstein, 2005, 218–40.

58. Hurd & Moore, 2004, 1118, 1122–23, 1133–38.

59. Id., 1130–31.

60. Huigens, 1995, 1429–30.

61. Finkelstein, 2002, 344–55 (arguing that offenses should be excused if motivated by "rational" dispositions that would usually yield the best outcome).

62. Model Penal Code § 2.09(1) (1962).

63. Finkelstein, 1995, 269–70.

64. Model Penal Code § 2.09(2).

65. Lee, 2003, 230–35.

66. Id.

67. Id. Kahan & Nussbaum, 1996, 305–21; Nourse, 1997, 1392–94.

68. Commonwealth v. Twitchell, 446 Mass. 114 (1993); Lambert v. California, 355 U.S. 225 (1957); Long v. State, 44 Del. 262 (1949); Kahan, 1997.

69. E.g., Ala. Code § 13A-4-2 (LexisNexis 2005); Cal. Penal Code § 653F (West 1999); Tex. Penal Code Ann. § 15.03 (Vernon 2003).

70. E.g., State v. Lyerla, 424 N.W.2d 908, 912–13 (S.D. 1988).

71. See generally Zaibert, 2005, 33–66 (arguing that purposeful wrongdoing was the paradigm of culpability in many different ethical and legal systems across history).

72. Michaels, 1998, 960–70.

73. Simons, 1992, 486–90 (discussing the indifference conception of recklessness).

74. Model Penal Code § 2.02(2)(d) (1962).

75. Simons, 1997, 1123–25.

76. Id., 1121–24 (arguing that a smaller risk of harm suffices for negligence if the purpose of a risky activity is worse).

77. Pillsbury, 1998, 161–79; Nourse, 2002, 366–79.

78. State v. Joy, 452 A.2d 408, 410 (Me. 1982).

79. State v. McCrary, 675 P.2d 120, 121 (N.M. 1984).

80. Commonwealth v. Malone, 47 A.2d 445, 446–47 (Pa. 1946).

81. People v. Protopappas, 246 Cal. Rptr. 915, 918 (Ct. App. 1988).

82. E.g., People v. Thomas, 261 P.2d 1, 7 (Cal. 1953) (en banc); Protopappas, 261 Cal. Rptr., 920.

83. LaFave, 2003, 1017.

84. Id., § 20.3, 996–97.

85. Id., § 19.8, 975–77; see also Smith v. United States, 291 F.2d 220, 221–22 (9th Cir. 1961).

86. 18 U.S.C. § 1512(2) (Supp. IV 2004).

87. Id., § 201(b)(1) (2000).

88. Id., § 1091(a).

89. London Agreement 1945 (defining crimes against humanity as "persecutions on political, racial, or religious grounds").

90. Cal. Penal Code § 422.6(a) (West Supp. 2007) ("No person . . . shall by force or threat of force, willfully injure, intimidate, interfere with, oppress, or threaten any other person in the free exercise or enjoyment of any right or privilege secured . . . by the Constitution or laws of this state. . . .").

91. USA PATRIOT Act of 2001, Pub. L. No. 107–56, § 802, 115 Stat. 272, 376 (codified at 18 U.S.C. §§ 2331, 3077 (Supp. IV 2004) (defining domestic terrorism as an illegal act intended to "influence the policy of a government by intimidation or coercion" or by "affect[ing] the conduct of a government by mass destruction, assassination, or kidnapping").

92. Fletcher, 1978, 205–17 (adherence to the enemy required for commission of treason).

93. McKinsey, Kitty, Mass Rape in Bosnia, Southam News, Jan. 23, 1993, http://www .peacewomen.org/news/BosniaHerzegovina/newsarchive/massrape/html.

94. This scenario is based on Hodges v. United States, 203 U.S. 1, 2–4 (1906).

95. Dominic Bailey, Spain Votes Under a Shadow, BBC News, Mar. 14, 2004, http:// news.bbc.co.uk/2/hi/europe/3509744.stm.

96. Chechen Gunmen Seize Moscow Theater, CNN.com, Oct. 24, 2002, http:// archives.cnn.com/2002/World/europe/10/23/russia.siege/.

97. E.g., Cal. Penal Code § 422.7 (West Supp. 2007); N.Y. Penal Law § 240.31 (McKinney Supp. 2007).

98. Binder, 1989, 1330–34.

99. Restatement (Third) of Foreign Relations § 404 (1987) (recognizing universal jurisdiction to punish the slave trade, genocide, war crimes, and certain acts of terrorism).

100. Hampton, 2007, 149–50.

101. Gardbaum, 1991, 1356, 1359.

102. Almond & Verba, 1963, 5–10.

103. Galston, 1991, 165.

104. Id., 165–90.

105. Id.; Galston, 1982, 627–29.

106. Macedo, 1990.

107. Id., 51–52.

108. Id., 69.

109. Id., 70.

110. Id.

111. Id., 55.

112. Id., 72.

113. Id., 53–59, 69–73.

114. Id., 240–51.

115. Raz, 1986, 132–33, 407, 424–25; Gardbaum, 1996, 400–401, 405–06.

116. Raz, 1986, 407–08.

117. Id., 148–57, 198–207.

118. Id., 148–62.

119. Id., 156–57.

120. Id., 378.

121. Id., 415–18.

122. Id., 124–33.

123. Binder, 2001, 1533.

124. Neal, 1985, 671–74.

125. Id., 673–74.

126. Id., 674.

127. Id.

128. Ackerman, 1980, 4.

129. Id., 11.

Chapter 5

1. Clark & Marshall, 1900, 514–16.

2. LaFave, 2000, 671.

3. Model Penal Code § 210.2 cmt. 6, 31 nn.73–74.

4. Id., 30–31.

5. Dressler, 2001, 515.

6. Loewy, 2003, 42.

7. Kadish & Schulhofer, 1989, 514; 1 Michie, 1914, 112; Robinson, 1997, 726; 2 Torcia, 1994, § 147.

8. See, e.g., State v. Lucas, 794 P.2d 1353, 1367 (Ariz. Ct. App. 1990) (Gerber, J., concurring); People v. Dekens, 695 N.E.2d 474, 480 (Ill. 1998) (Heiple, J., dissenting); Commonwealth v. Prater, 725 N.E.2d 233, 241–42 (Mass. 2000); Commonwealth v. Balliro, 209 N.E.2d 308, 312–13 (Mass. 1965); State v. Branson, 487 N.W.2d 880, 881–82 (Minn. 1992); State v. Harrison, 564 P.2d 1321, 1323 (N.M. 1977); People v. Topino, 573 N.Y.S.2d 848, 850 (Sup. Ct. 1991); Rodriguez v. State, 953 S.W.2d 342, 345–46 (Tex. Ct. App. 1997); State v. Doucette, 470 A.2d 676, 679–80 (Vt. 1983); State v. Thompson, 558 P.2d 202, 206–07 (Wash. 1977) (Utter, J., dissenting); State v. Sims, 248 S.E.2d 834, 839, 843 (W. Va. 1978).

9. Adlerstein, 1975–76, 249–50, 19 n.22; Cole, 2002; Dickey et al., 1989, 1365; Gerber, 1999, 764–66; Hancock, 1979, 856; Michaels, 1999, 838; Simon, 1994, 226–27; Marcus, Book Review, 1982, 823–24; cf. Tomkovicz, 1994, 1443.

10. See, e.g., Anooshian, 1988, 454–57; Baier, 1994, 703–04; Bailey, 1998, 237–39; Note, 1986, 1919; Hoecker, 1974, 685–86; Holcomb, 2000, 571; Houck, 1999, 360–63; Sachs, 1990, 634–38.

11. See, e.g., Model Penal Code § 210.2 cmt. 6, 31–32 (1980); People v. Aaron, 299 N.W.2d 304, 307 (Mich. 1980); Crum, 1952, 210; Roy Moreland, 1962, 82; Note, 1957, 427.

12. For earlier expressions of like suspicions, see Arent & MacDonald, 1934, 288 ("[T]he decisions, whether in New York or elsewhere, except in dicta, have never supported [defining all homicides committed in the perpetration of a felony as murders]; if a rule were to be extracted from the actual holdings of the cases, it would be confined within much narrower boundaries."); Wharton, 1875, 39.

13. See Frankowski, 1986, 412; Gardner, 1993, 656; Sayre, 1932, 984–85.

14. See Augustine, 1861, 187.

15. 38 Aquinas (1975), II-II, q. 64, art. 8, 44–45, citing Gratian, 1959, pt. 1, dist. 50, chs. 4–8 (c. 1140), 178–80.

16. 38 Aquinas, 1975, II-II, q. 64, art. 8, 44–47 (footnotes omitted, citing Gregory, 1959, bk. 5, tit. 12, ch. 23, 803).

17. Hurnard, 1969, 68–69.

18. Id., 76.

19. 2 Bracton, 1968, 341.

20. Id., 384.

21. Id., 340 (footnote omitted).

22. Id., 341 (footnote omitted).

23. See Hurnard, 1969, 70.

24. 2 Pollock & Maitland, 1898, 485–86; Hurnard, 1969, 7–9; Green, 1976, 416–19; Green, 1985, 30.

25. 2 Pollock & Maitland, 1898, 479–81.

26. Statutes of Gloucester, 1278, 6 Edw. 1, c. 9 (Eng.), reprinted in 1 The Statutes of the Realm 45, 49 (photo. reprint 1963); see also 3 Stephen, 1883, 38.

27. Hurnard, 1969, 99–108; 2 Pollock & Maitland, 1898, 483; Green, 1976, 420, 444. Indeed, by the later fourteenth century, truly faultless deaths often led to verdicts of acquittal rather than misadventure. Hurnard, 1969, 100–102; Green, 1976, 444–45.

28. Green, 1985, 70; Green, 1976, 426–27, 457.

29. Green, 1985, 70–74; Kaye, 1967, 380.

30. Statute the Second, 1389–90, 13 Rich. 2, c. 1 (Eng.), reprinted in 2 The Statutes of the Realm, supra note 46, 68–69.

31. Compare Kaye, 1967, 369, 391–92 with Green, 1976, 462–69.

32. Green, 1985, 10, 33; 2 Pollock & Maitland, 1898, 466; Green, 1976, 470; Kaye, 1967, Part 1, 387–88.

33. 1 Stephen, 1883, 461; Gabel, 1928, 68–70.

34. Green, 1976, 469; Kaye, 1967, Part 2, 569–70.

35. See 3 Stephen, 1883, 44–45.

36. See, e.g., Fitzherbert, 1541, fol. cxxiiia; Fitzherbert, 1510 fol. 4a–b; Marowe, 1503, 378.

37. 72 Eng. Rep. 458 (K.B. 1535).

38. Mansell & Herbert's Case, 73 Eng. Rep. 279 (K.B. 1558); Dallison, n.d.

39. See, e.g., Dallison, n.d.; Kaye, 1967, Part 2, 579. Kaye suggests as a possible basis for this holding a 1330 case reported at Plees del Corone No. 314 (Iter Northampton 1330), in Anthony Fitzherbert, La Graunde Abridgement fol. 256a (1565)).

40. R. v. Saunders, 75 Eng. Rep. 706 (Q.B. 1576); accord Agnes Gore's Case, 77 Eng. Rep. 853 (K.B. 1612).

41. Kaye, 1967, 580. Kaye argues that Staundford's 1557 treatise Plees del Corone took a similar position. Id., 582–83.

42. Edmund Plowden, Les Comentaries, ou les Reportes de Edmund Plowden, fol. 100 (1571); Kaye, 1967, 585–86.

43. Kaye, 1967, 585–86 (discussing Salisbury).

44. Richard Crompton, 1587; see also Kaye, 1967, 589.

45. Lambarde, 1588, 251.

46. Id., 243–44.

47. Green, 1976, 460–61, 472, 479 (enduring association of the term "murder" with criminally motivated homicide).

48. Bacon, 1596, 55.

49. Id., 55–56.

50. Dalton, 1619, 225. A later edition approved the statement that in such cases "if a man intend to doe any unlawfull act, & in doing thereof another hurt ensueth, not intended, but by chance cleane beyond all expectation, or desire, yet shall he be said the author of that act not intended. . . ."; Dalton, 1635, 241.

51. Dalton, 1619, 226.

52. Id., 220.

53. Id., 218.

54. Coke, 1644.

55. Id., 54–55.

56. Id., 47.

57. Id., 51.

58. Id., 52.

59. Fletcher, 1978, 280.

60. Coke, 1644, 57.

61. Lanham, 1983, 94.

62. Fletcher, 1978, 278.

63. Id., 278–79.

64. Coke, 1644, 56.

65. Bracton, 1235, 341; see also 3 Stephen, 1883, 58 (pointing out the discrepancy between Bracton and Coke).

66. Plees del Corone No. 354 (Iter Northampton 1330), in Anthony Fitzherbert, La Graunde Abridgement, fol. 257a (1565); Y.B. 2 Hen. 4, fol. 18 (1400).

67. Y.B. 11 Hen. 7, fol. 23a (1496).

68. 3 Stephen, 1883, 57.

69. Sir John Chichester's Case, 82 Eng. Rep. 888 (K.B. 1647).

70. R. v. Hull, 84 Eng. Rep. 1072, 1072–73 (K.B. 1664).

71. Sir Charles Stanley's Case, 84 Eng. Rep. 1094 (K.B. 1663).

72. Id.

73. Hobbes, 1840, 87.

74. Hale, 1678, 31–32; Lanham, 1983, 95–96.

75. Hale, 1678, 44–45.

76. Id., 49.

77. Id., 46; see also 1 Hale, 1736, 465.

78. Hale, 1678, 50.

79. Id., 47; see also 1 Hale, 1736, 465 (citing Lord Dacre).

80. 1 Hale, 1736, 429–30.

81. Id., 432–33.

82. Id., 426.

83. Id., 429.

84. Fletcher, 1978, 280.

85. R. v. Plummer, 84 Eng. Rep. 1103, 1105–07 (K.B. 1701).

86. Id., 1107.

87. 1 Hawkins, 1716, 86.

88. Even theft of fowl. See id.

89. Id., 100.

90. Id., 87.

91. 2 Pollock & Maitland, 1898 464–66.

92. See 1 Stephen, 1883, 463 (discussing Coke).

93. Fletcher, 1976, 469; LaFave, 2000, 791.

94. 1 Hawkins, 1716, 81–82.

95. Id., 80.

96. 1 Stephen, 1883, 470–71. See Hall, 1935, 3–36; Hay, 1975.

97. See Tomkovicz, 1994, 1446.

98. 1 Stephen, 1883, 467.

99. 1 Radzinowicz, 1968, 151, 153, 159; Hay, 1975, 22–23, 43–49.

100. Fletcher, 1978, 132–35. R. v. Scofield, Cald. 397 (1784) (attempt of any crime also a crime).

101. Fletcher, 1978, 132–35.

102. 4 Blackstone, 1769, 196.

103. 16 St. Trials 53 (Suffolk Assizes 1722).

104. Id., 79–80 (footnote omitted).

105. Based on review of 376 murder convictions reported in the Proceedings at the Old Bailey between 1674 and 1799, available at http://www.oldbaileyonline.org.

106. R. v. Price (Old Bailey Apr. 23, 1718), http:// www.oldbaileyonline.org/html_units /1710s/t17180423-24.html.

107. Foster, 1776 258–59.

108. Id., 256.

109. Id., 257.

110. Mueller, 1966, 19.

111. 4 Blackstone, 1769, 21.

112. Id., 26–27 (citing 1 Hale, 1736, 39).

113. Id., 198–99.

114. Id., 199.

115. Id., 192–93.

116. Id., 200.

117. Id., 201 (footnote omitted).

118. Lanham, 1983, 97–99.

119. See generally Binder, 2007.

120. 168 Eng. Rep. 150, 150 (K.B. 1773).

121. Lanham, 1983, 100.

122. See R. v. Balfe, Nos. 108–09 (Old Bailey Jan. 12, 1769), http://www.oldbaileyon line.org/html_units/1760s/t17690112-22.html (conviction of thugs hired to beat voters as accomplices of unidentified killer of one such voter). In considering an evidentiary issue, one of three judges argued that if persons were "assembled upon an unlawful

occasion . . . and any act was done by any one that terminated in murder, all persons concerned in the prosecution of that unlawful design or purpose, will be answerable for it, if they were present, aiding and abetting it. . . ."

123. R. v. Walker, No. 1 (Old Bailey Dec. 15, 1786), http:// www.oldbaileyonline.org/ html_units/1780s/t17861215–1.html.

124. R. v. Gray, No. 622 (Old Bailey Oct. 16, 1782), http://www.oldbaileyonline.org/ html_units/1780s/t17821016–11.html (emphasis omitted). R. v. Carty, No. 103 (Old Bailey Jan. 14, 1789), http:// www.oldbaileyonline.org/html_units/1780s/t17890114–6.html.

125. R. v. Borthwick, 99 Eng. Rep. 136 (K.B. 1779); see also Crum, 1952, 194 (viewing Borthwick as inconsistent with a felony murder rule); R. v. Hubbard, No. 184 (Old Bailey Mar. 29, 1792), http:// hri.shef.ac.uk/luceneweb/bailey/highlight.jsp?ref=t17920329–26.

126. 1 East, 1806, 255.

127. Id.

128. 1 Russell, 1819, 660–61.

129. First Report from His Majesty's Commissioners on Criminal Law 29 (1834).

130. Wechsler & Michael, 1937 (citing Commission reports from 1839, 1843, and 1846); see also Glazebrook, 2002, 400, 405, 408.

131. 172 Eng. Rep. 999 (Old Bailey 1832).

132. Id.

133. 172 Eng. Rep. 827 (Maidstone Assizes 1831).

134. 168 Eng. Rep. 1009, 1009 (Lancaster Assizes 1830); see also R. v. Holloway, 1806–07 Proc. Old Bailey 131 (1807); R. v. Hawkins, 172 Eng. Rep. 470 (Worcester Assizes 1828) (holding that poachers who assaulted a gamekeeper were not responsible for the later robbery of the gamekeeper by one of their number). But see R. v. Eyres, No. 84 (Old Bailey Jan. 9, 1799), http:// www.oldbaileyonline.org/html_units/1790s/t17990109–5.html (instigator of riot held liable for death of bystander shot by undetermined assailant).

135. 174 Eng. Rep. 313 (Liverpool Assizes 1841).

136. Id., 313.

137. Id.

138. 7 Cox's Crim. L. Cas. 404 (Liverpool Assizes 1857).

139. Id., 404.

140. 175 Eng. Rep. 1195 (Croydon Assizes 1861).

141. Id., 1196.

142. Id.

143. Id., 1197.

144. R. v. Horsey, 176 Eng. Rep. 129, 130–31 (Kent Assizes 1862).

145. Id., 131.

146. 176 Eng. Rep. 468 (Kent Assizes 1864).

147. Id., 469–70.

148. 11 Cox's Crim. L. Cas. 146 (Cent. Crim. Ct. 1868).

149. See Wharton, 1875, 39–43 & 39 n.3; Wechsler & Michael, 1937, 701, 703 n.8, 713 n.47.

150. See Wharton, 1875, 39–43 n.3.

151. 1 Russell & Prentice, 1877, 761 n.(w).

152. Communication of the Law Revision Commission to the Legislature Relating to Homicide, in State of N.Y. Law Revision Comm'n, Report of the Law Revision Commission for 1937, 517, 670 (1937); 3 Stephen, 1883, 80–81.

153. 16 Cox's Crim. L. Cas. 311, 313 (Cent. Crim. Ct. 1887).

154. 62 J.P.R. 711, 712 (Cent. Crim. Ct. 1898).

155. 4 Stephen, 1914, 62.

156. 1920 App. Cas. 479 (H.L. 1920); accord R. v. Betts, 22 Crim. App. R. 148 (1930).

157. 9 Halsbury's Laws of England 437 (2d ed. 1933).

158. Homicide Act, 1957, 5 & 6 Eliz. 2, c. 11, § 1 (Eng.).

Chapter 6

1. Mueller, 1966, 10 (citing, with disapproval, Clark & Marshall, 1958, 23; see also Haskins, 1960, 56, 186 (discussing the hostility of Massachusetts settlers toward common law).

2. 77 Eng. Rep. 377 (Ex. Ch. 1608).

3. Blankard v. Galdy, 91 Eng. Rep. 356, 356–57 (K.B. 1693); see also Brown, 1964, 12–13.

4. Smith v. Brown, 91 Eng. Rep. 566 (K.B. 1705).

5. 1 Blackstone, 2002, 104–05.

6. Brown, 1964, 6.

7. See Charter to Sir William Raleigh (1584), reprinted in 1 Thorpe, 1909, 55; The Second Charter of Virginia (1609), reprinted in 7 Thorpe, 1909, 3790, 3801; The Charter of New England (1620), reprinted in 3 Thorpe, 1909, 1827, 1833; The Charter of Maryland (1632), reprinted in 3 Thorpe, 1909, 1677, 1680; Grant of the Province of Maine (1639), reprinted in 3 Thorpe, 1909, 1625, 1628; Charter of Carolina (1663), reprinted in 5 Thorpe, 1909, 2743, 2746; Charter of Rhode Island and Providence Plantations (1663), reprinted in 6 Thorpe, 1909, 3211, 3215; Charter for the Province of Pennsylvania (1681), reprinted in 5 Thorpe, 1909, 3035, 3038. But see The Charter of Massachusetts Bay (1629), reprinted in 3 Thorpe, 1909, 1846, 1853 (omitting convenience clause). Some required royal approval of local laws. See Charter for the Province of Pennsylvania (1681), reprinted in 5 Thorpe, 1909, 3035, 3039; The Charter of Massachusetts Bay (1691), reprinted in 3 Thorpe, 1909, 1846, 1857; Charter of Georgia (1732), reprinted in 2 Thorpe, 1909, 765, 772.

8. Vidmar & Hans, 2007, 45.

9. Id., 51–52.

10. Brown, 1964, 19–21.

11. See, e.g., Act of Dec. 12, 1712, no. 322, reprinted in 2 The Statutes at Large of South Carolina 401 (Thomas Cooper ed., 1837); An Act for the More Effectual Observing of

the Queen's Peace, and Establishing a Good and Lasting Foundation of Government in North-Carolina (1715), reprinted in Laws of the State of North-Carolina 17 (James Iredell ed., 1791).

12. See, e.g., Horwitz, 1977, 6.

13. Mueller, 1966, 13.

14. Hall, 1951, 794–95.

15. Nelson, 1994, 23–30; Vidmar & Hans, 2007, 49–50.

16. Mueller, 1966, 1415; Hall, 1951, 794, 797; Reinsch, 1907, 367.

17. Brown, 1964, 20.

18. Articles, Laws, and Orders, Divine, Politique, and Martiall for the Colony in Virginea, para. 8 (1611), reprinted in For the Colony in Virginea Britannia: Laws Divine, Morall and Martiall, etc. 9, 12 (David H. Flaherty ed., Univ. Press of Va. 1969) (William Strachey ed., 1612); The Book of the General Lauues and Libertyes Concerning &c (1648), reprinted in 1 The Laws and Liberties of Massachusetts, 1641–91, 7, 11 (John D. Cushing ed., 1976); An Act for Punishing Criminal Offences, para. 5 (1662), reprinted in The Earliest Acts and Laws of the Colony of Rhode Island and Providence Plantations, 1647–1719, 140, (John D. Cushing ed., 1977); The General Laws and Liberties of New-Plimouth Colony, ch. 2, para. 5 (1671), reprinted in The Laws of the Pilgrims 5, 8 (John D. Cushing ed., 1977); The Duke of York's Laws, para. 2 (1675), reprinted in State of N.Y. Law Revision Comm'n, report of the Law Revision Commission for 1937, 839 (1937).

19. The Great Law, ch. 7 (1682), reprinted in The Statutes at Large of Pennsylvania in the Time of William Penn 128, 129 (Gail McKnight Beckman ed., 1976).

20. Keedy, 1949, 760–61.

21. An Act Against Murder and Man-slaughter (1705), reprinted in The Earliest Printed Laws of Pennsylvania, 1681–1713, 36, 36–37 (John D. Cushing ed., 1978).

22. Keedy, 1949, 760–61; see also Geimer, 1983, 343; Felony Murder as a First Degree Offense, 1957, 431.

23. An Act Against Murder (1697), reprinted in Massachusetts Province Laws, 1692–99, 114 (John D. Cushing ed., 1978); The General Laws and Liberties of New-Plimouth Colony, ch. 2, para. 5 (1671), reprinted in The Laws of the Pilgrims 5, 8 (John D. Cushing ed., 1977); An Act Against Murder, &c., para. 1 (1716), reprinted in Acts and Laws of New Hampshire, 1680–1726, 140 (John D. Cushing ed., 1978); Act of Mar. 19, 1774, ch. 31, para. 2, reprinted in Laws of the State of North-Carolina, (James Iredell, ed. 1791), 274.

24. Acts of Aug. 19–21, 1647, "Murder," para. 1, reprinted in The Earliest Acts and Laws of the Colony of Rhode Island and Providence Plantations, 1647–1719 (John D. Cushing ed., 1977), 5, 19 (emphasis added).

25. Chapin, 1983, 6.

26. Plymouth v. Arthur Peach (New Plymouth Gen. Ct. Sept. 4, 1638), reported in 1 Records of the Colony of New Plymouth in New England 96 (Nathanial B. Shurtleff & David Pulsifier eds., 1855); see Chapin, 1983, 111–17.

27. Webb, 1969, 231–32.

28. Id., 232.

29. Id., 233.

30. Id., 234.

31. Starke, 1774, 196.

32. Id.

33. Id., 197.

34. Vidmar & Hans, 2007, 51; Blinka, 2003.

35. Act of Sept. 16, 1777, no. 236, reprinted in 1 A Digest of the Laws of the State of Georgia 202 (Robert Watkins & George Watkins eds., 1800).

36. Act of May 2, 1778, ch. 5, reprinted in Laws of the State of North-Carolina, 353 (James Iredell, ed. 1791).

37. An Ordinance to Enable the Present Magistrates and Officers to Continue the Administration of Justice, and for Settling the General Mode of Proceedings in Criminal and Other Cases Till the Same Can Be More Amply Provided For, para. 6 (1776), in 9 The Statutes at Large; Being a Collection of All the Laws of Virginia 126, 127 (William Walter Hening ed., 1821).

38. 5 Blackstone's Commentaries, 1803, n.1.

39. Brown, 1964, 129.

40. Id., 158, 159, 162, 165.

41. See, e.g., Mass. Const. of 1780, ch. 6, art. 6, reprinted in 3 Thorpe, 1909, 1888, 1910; N.H. Const. of 1784, pt. 2, reprinted in 4 Thorpe, 1909, 2453, 2469; S.C. Const. of 1790, art. 7, reprinted in 6 Thorpe, 1909, 3258, 3264.

42. Del. Const. of 1776, art. 25, reprinted in 1 Thorpe, 1909, 562, 566–67; Md. Const. of 1776, Declaration of Rights art. 3, reprinted in 3 Thorpe, 1909, 1686, 1686–87; N.J. Const. of 1776, art. 22, reprinted in 5 Thorpe, 1909, 2594, 2598; N.Y. Const. of 1777, art. 35, reprinted in 5 Thorpe, 1909, 2623, 2635; Act of May 2, 1778, ch. 5 (North Carolina); Act of Jan. 28, 1777, ch. 63, § 2, reprinted in The General Laws of Pennsylvania 119, 119 (James Dunlop ed., 2d ed. 1849); see also Act of Jan. 29, 1798, § 5, 1798 R.I. Laws 75, 78 (continuing in force British statutes "introduced into practice" in Rhode Island).

43. An Act for Securing the General Privileges of the People, and Establishing Common Law and the Constitution, as Part of the Laws of This State (1779), reprinted in Vermont State Papers 287, 288 (William Slade ed., 1823).

44. Act of Nov. 4, 1797, ch. 2, § 1, 1798 Vt. Laws 71, 71 (1797).

45. Hall, 1951, 800.

46. See Conn. Const. of 1818, art. 10, § 3, reprinted in 1 Thorpe, supra, note 218, 536, 546.

47. Act of Feb. 14, 1805, ch. 55, § 1, 1804–05 Ohio Laws 248, 248 (1805); Act of Jan. 2, 1806, § 1, 1805–06 Ohio Laws 38, 38 (1806).

48. Brackenridge, 1972, 37.

49. Marks v. Morris, 14 Va. (4 Hen. & M.) 463 (Va. Super. Ct. Ch. 1809).

50. See Brown, 1964, note 214, 41; Hall, 1951, note 223, 806; Pound, 1914, 676, 686.

51. 5 Blackstone, 1803, n.1.

52. Id., app. 8–9 (quoting approvingly from Justice Chase's opinion in United States v. Worrall, 2 U.S. (2 Dall.) 384 (C.C.D. Pa. 1798)).

53. James Madison, Report to the General Assembly of Virginia (1800), reprinted in The Kentucky-Virginia Resolutions and Mr. Madison's Report of 1799, 15, 46–48 (Va. Comm'n on Constitutional Gov't ed., 1960); see also 1 Goebel, 1971, 296 (quoting Letter from James Madison to George Washington (Oct. 18, 1787), reprinted in 4 Documentary History of the Constitution of the United States of America, 1786–1890, 334 (Bureau of Rolls and Library, U.S. Dep't of State ed., 1905)). James Madison, Report to the General Assembly of Virginia (1800), reprinted in The Kentucky-Virginia Resolutions and Mr. Madison's Report of 1799, 15, 46–48 (Va. Comm'n on Constitutional Gov't ed., 1960); see also 1 Julius Goebel, 1971, 296 (quoting Letter from James Madison to George Washington (Oct. 18, 1787), reprinted in 4 Documentary History of the Constitution of the United States of America, 1786–1890, 334 (Bureau of Rolls and Library, U.S. Dep't of State ed., 1905)).

54. 1 Swift, 1795, 43–45 (citing Wilford v. Grant, 1 Kirby 114 (Conn. Super. Ct. 1786)).

55. Preyer, 1986, 223. The same was true of federal law. Presser, 1991, 81–83.

56. 1 Blackstone's Commentaries, 1803, app. 430.

57. Id., app. 438–39 (quoting a Virginia resolution of Jan. 11, 1800, calling the common law of crimes a "code of sanguinary criminal law, both obsolete and unknown, and either wholly rejected or essentially modified in almost all it's parts by state institutions"); James Madison, Report to the General Assembly of Virginia (1800), reprinted in The Kentucky-Virginia Resolutions and Mr. Madison's Report of 1799, 15, 46–48 (Va. Comm'n on Constitutional Gov't ed., 1960), 53; see also Keedy, 1949, 764–70.

58. Thomas Jefferson, A Bill for Proportioning Crimes and Punishments § 11 (1779), http://etext.virginia.edu/etcbin/ot2wwwsingleauthor?specfile=/web/data/jefferson/texts/jefall.o2w&act=text&offset=7504163&textreg=1&query=proportioning+ crimes. On the legislative fate of Jefferson's proposed code, see Beckman, 1966, 148, 155–59; Preyer, 1983, 68–70.

59. Horwitz, 1977, 10; Letter from Thomas Jefferson to Gideon Granger (Aug. 13, 1800), reprinted in 7 The Writings of Thomas Jefferson 450, 451 (Paul Leicester Ford ed., 1896); see also Thomas Jefferson, Kentucky Resolution of 1798, para. 2, reprinted in 4 The Debates in the Several State Conventions on the Adoption of the Federal Constitution 540 (Jonathan Elliot ed., 1876); 1 Blackstone's Commentaries, 1803, note 254, app. 438–39 (quoting Virginia resolution of Jan. 11, 1800).

60. Presser, 1991, 79–80, 98.

61. Id., 79.

62. 2 U.S. (2 Dall.) 384 (C.C.D. Pa. 1798).

63. Compare Presser, 1991, 95–96, and 1 Warren, 1947, 159n. (most early Supreme Court justices supported federal common law crimes), with Palmer, 1986, 267, and

Preyer, 1986 (most early Supreme Court justices doubted the Constitution incorporated the common law).

64. Levy, 1963, xv–xvi; Presser, 1991, 95–96.

65. Presser, 1991, 98.

66. 11 U.S. (7 Cranch) 32 (1812).

67. See United States v. Coolidge, 25 F. Cas. 619 (C.C.D. Mass. 1813) (No. 14,857).

68. Trial of William Butler for Piracy 21–29 (1813) (original pamphlet in Buffalo & Erie County Public Library).

69. See, e.g., United States v. Bevans, 16 U.S. (3 Wheat.) 336 (1818); United States v. Wiltberger, 18 U.S. (5 Wheat.) 76 (1820).

70. Chipman, 1793, 134.

71. 2 Swift, 1795, 365.

72. Id.

73. Id., 366–67.

74. Goodenow, 1819; see also Goodenow, 1817, 13–21.

75. Livingston, 1833, 7–9, 54–59; see also Beckman, 1966, 159–68.

76. Rantoul, 1836, 472, 473–74.

77. Act of Apr. 30, 1790, § 3, reprinted in 2 Annals of Cong. 2273, 2274 (1790).

78. Act of Feb. 14, 1787, ch. 22, §§ 1–3, 1785–88 N.Y. Laws 391, 391–92; Act of Feb. 28, 1785, ch. 2, para. 1, reprinted in The perpetual Laws of the Commonwealth of Massachusetts 249, 249 (1788); An Act for the Punishment of Murder (n.d.), reprinted in Acts and Laws of the State of Connecticut, in America 162 (1784); Act of Feb. 15, 1779, reprinted in 1 Laws of Vermont, 1770–80, 154 (Allen Soule ed., 1964).

79. Keedy, 1949, 764–70.

80. Id., 770 (quoting Bradford, 1793, 35).

81. Id., 771 (quoting 4 Journal of the Senate 38 (Pa. 1793)).

82. Id., 772–73 (quoting 4 Journal of the Senate 242 (Pa. 1794)).

83. Act of Apr. 22, 1794, ch. 1766, § 2, 1794 Pa. Laws 186, 187 (emphasis added).

84. Date of enactment of or admission with Pennsylvania grading statute in parentheses: VA (1796), KY (from 1798 to 1801), MD (1810), LA (from 1812 to 1855), TN (1829), MI (1838), AR (1838), NH (1842), CT (1846), DE (1852), MA (1858), WV (1863).

85. Date of enactment of or admission with modified grading statute in parentheses: OH (1815), ME (1840), AL (1841), MO (1845), IA (1851), IN (1852), CA (1856), TX (1858), NY (1860), KS (1861), OR (1864), NV (1864), NE (1873), MT (1889), WA (1889), ID (1890), WY (1890), NC (1893), UT (1896).

86. Ga. L. 1811, 28, 32–33.

87. Ga. L. 1817, 95.

88. Ga. L. 1817, 96.

89. Ill. Rev. Code, Crim. Code, §§ 22, 24, 28 (1827).

90. Act of Feb. 17, 1829, § 66, 1828–29 N.J. Acts 109, 128.

91. N.Y. Rev. Stat. pt. 4, ch. 1, tit. 1, § 5 (1829).

92. Date of enactment of or admission with felony murder laws in parentheses: GA (1817), IL (1827), NJ (1829), NY (1829), MS (1839), AL (1841), MO (1845), WI (1849), CA (1850), TX (1857), MN (1858), NV (1864), OR (1864), NE (1866 to repeal in 1873), FL (1868), CO (1876), ID (1889), MT (1889), UT (1896).

93. Mueller, 1966, 18–25.

94. 2 Swift, 1795, 300.

95. Id., 306.

96. 1 Toulmin & Blair, 1804, 3–4 (emphasis added).

97. Id., 46.

98. Id., 47.

99. Id., 48.

100. Id., 4.

101. Id., 48.

102. Id., 20, 48.

103. Id., 20.

104. Id., 50–51.

105. Id., 51.

106. 2 Bishop, 1858, § 627, 405–06 (1858) (footnotes omitted).

107. 32 Me. 369 (1851).

108. 1 Bishop, 1858, §§ 251–60, 220–29.

109. Wharton, 1855, 46.

110. Id.; see also id., 345–46.

111. Id., 346 (citing the federal cases of United States v. Ross, 27 F. Cas. 899 (C.C.D.R.I. 1813) (No. 16,196) and United States v. Travers, 28 F. Cas. 204 (C.C.D. Miss. 1814) (No. 16,537), both discussed below).

112. Id.

113. Id., 348–50.

114. Wharton, 1875, iii–iv.

115. Id., 39.

116. Id., 153.

117. Id., 44–45.

118. Id., 43–45 n.3 (quoting Macaulay, 1837).

119. Id., 154.

120. Holmes, 1881, 48.

121. Id., 49.

122. Id., 49–50.

123. The first federal statutory definition of murder appears in Act of Mar. 4, 1909, ch. 321, § 273, 35 Stat. 1088, 1143.

124. S.C. Rev. Stat. ch. 128, § 1 (1873) ("Murder is the killing of any person with mal-

ice aforethought, either express or implied."); 2 S.C. Rev. Stat. pt. 5, § 108 (1894) (same); State v. Coleman, 8 S.C. 237 (1876) (interpreting statute as incorporating common law definition of murder).

125. An Act in Amendment of an Act, Entitled "An Act to Reform the Penal Laws," 1814 R.I. Laws 22, 22–23. But see William R. Staples, History of the Criminal Law of Rhode Island (1854), in 1854 R.I. Acts app. 1, 9 (showing that the 1647 laws remained in force except where modified by subsequent statutes).

126. Vt. Rev. Stat. ch. 94, § 1 (1840).

127. NC (until 1893); MA (until 1858); DE (until 1852); CT (until 1846); NH (until 1842); NY (until 1829); NJ (until 1829); GA (until 1817); MD (until 1810); VA (until 1796); PA (until 1794); TN (from 1792 to 1829); KY (after 1801); OH (1803 to 1817); IN (1816 to 1852); MS (1817 to 1839); IL (1818 to 1827); AL (1819 to 1841); ME (1820 to 1840); MO (1821 to 1845); FL (1845 to 1868); TX (1845 to 1856); IA (1846 to 1851); LA (after 1855); OR (1859 to 1864); ND (after 1889); SD (after 1889).

128. Commonwealth v. Flanagan, 7 Watts & Serg. 415 (Pa. 1844); People v. Van Steenburgh, 1 Parker's Crim. Rep. 39 (N.Y. Ct. Oyer & Terminer 1845); Bratton v. State, 29 Tenn. (10 Hum.) 103 (1849); State v. Smith, 32 Me. 369 (1851); State v. Jennings, 18 Mo. 435 (1853); Stocking v. State, 7 Ind. 326 (1855); State v. Nueslein, 25 Mo. 111 (1857); McGinnis v. State, 31 Ga. 236 (1860); Commonwealth v. Miller, 4 Phila. Rep. 195 (Pa. Ct. Oyer & Terminer 1860); People v. Pool, 27 Cal. 572 (1865); State v. Pike, 49 N.H. 399 (1869); Miller v. State, 25 Wis. 384 (1870); Commonwealth v. Hanlon, 3 Brewster's Rep. 461 (Pa. Ct. Oyer & Terminer 1870); State v. Boice, 1 Houst. Crim. Cas. 355 (Del. Ct. Oyer & Terminer 1871); Brown v. Commonwealth, 76 Pa. 319 (1874); People v. Vasquez, 49 Cal. 560 (1875); Commonwealth v. Pemberton, 118 Mass. 36 (1875); Dolan v. People, 64 N.Y. 485 (1876); Bissot v. State, 53 Ind. 408 (1876); Singleton v. State, 1 Tex. Ct. App. 501 (1877); State v. Green, 66 Mo. 631 (1877); State v. Brown, 7 Or. 186 (1879); Buel v. People, 78 N.Y. 492 (1879); State v. Wiese, 4 N.W. 827 (Iowa 1880); Cox v. People, 80 N.Y. 500 (1880); Moynihan v. State, 70 Ind. 126 (1880); Poe v. State, 78 Tenn. 673 (1882); Duran v. State, 14 Tex. Ct. App. 195 (1883); Stanley v. State, 14 Tex. Ct. App. 315 (1883); Kilgore v. State, 74 Ala. 1 (1883); Adams v. People, 109 Ill. 444 (1884); State v. Hopkirk, 84 Mo. 278 (1884); Sharpe v. State, 17 Tex. App. 486 (Ct. App. 1885); State v. Gray, 8 P. 456 (Nev. 1885); Gonzales v. State, 19 Tex. Ct. App. 394 (1885); People v. Willett, 6 N.E. 301 (N.Y. 1886); State v. Leeper, 30 N.W. 501 (Iowa 1886); Giles v. State, 4 S.W. 886 (Tex. Ct. App. 1887); State v. Johnson, 34 N.W. 177 (Iowa 1887); Washington v. State, 8 S.W. 642 (Tex. Ct. App. 1888); People v. Deacons, 16 N.E. 676 (N.Y. 1888); People v. Johnson, 17 N.E. 684 (N.Y. 1888); People v. Olsen, 22 P. 125 (Cal. 1889); People v. Greenwall, 22 N.E. 180 (N.Y. 1889); State v. Deschamps, 7 So. 703 (La. 1890); State v. Levelle, 13 S.E. 319 (S.C. 1891); Mendez v. State, 16 S.W. 766 (Tex. Ct. App. 1891); Williams v. State, 17 S.W. 408 (Tex. Ct. App. 1891); State v. Lodge, 33 A. 312 (Del. Ct. Oyer & Terminer 1892); Cook v. State, 18 S.W. 412 (Tex. Ct. App. 1892); Smith v. State, 19 S.W. 252 (Tex. Ct. App. 1892); Elizando v. State, 20 S.W. 560 (Tex. Crim. App. 1892); State v. Avery, 21 S.W.

193 (Mo. 1893); Commonwealth v. Manfredi, 29 A. 404 (Pa. 1894); People v. Miles, 38 N.E. 456 (N.Y. 1894); Robertson v. Commonwealth, 20 S.E. 362 (Va. 1894); People v. Wilson, 40 N.E. 392 (N.Y. 1895); Richards v. State, 30 S.W. 805 (Tex. Crim. App. 1895); People v. Willett, 62 N.W. 1115 (Mich. 1895); State v. Myers, 40 P. 626 (Wash. 1895); State v. Donnelly, 32 S.W. 1124 (Mo. 1895); Commonwealth v. Gilbert, 165 Mass. 45 (1895); State v. Covington, 23 S.E. 337 (N.C. 1895); State v. Minard, 65 N.W. 147 (Iowa 1895); State v. Weems, 65 N.W. 387 (Iowa 1895); Reddick v. Commonwealth, 33 S.W. 416 (Ky. 1895); Wilkins v. State, 34 S.W. 627 (Tex. Crim. App. 1896); Isaacs v. State, 38 S.W. 40 (Tex. Crim. App. 1896); State v. Schmidt, 38 S.W. 719 (Mo. 1897); State v. Foster, 38 S.W. 721 (Mo. 1897); Morgan v. State, 71 N.W. 788 (Neb. 1897); Garza v. State, 46 S.W. 242 (Tex. Crim. App. 1898); People v. Miller, 53 P. 816 (Cal. 1898); Little v. State, 47 S.W. 984 (Tex. Crim. App. 1898); State v. Sexton, 48 S.W. 452 (Mo. 1898); Parker v. State, 49 S.W. 80 (Tex. Crim. App. 1899); Commonwealth v. Eagan, 42 A. 374 (Pa. 1899); Darlington v. State, 50 S.W. 375 (Tex. Crim. App. 1899); Hedrick v. State, 51 S.W. 252 (Tex. Crim. App. 1899); Commonwealth v. Epps, 44 A. 570 (Pa. 1899); Nite v. State, 54 S.W. 763 (Tex. Crim. App. 1899); People v. Meyer, 56 N.E. 758 (N.Y. 1900); Keaton v. State, 57 S.W. 1125 (Tex. Crim. App. 1900); State v. Cross, 46 A. 148 (Conn. 1900); State v. Morgan, 61 P. 527 (Utah 1900).

129. Deschamps, 7 So. 703 (Louisiana); Levelle, 13 S.E. 319 (South Carolina); Reddick, 33 S.W. 416 (Kentucky).

130. State v. Norris, 2 N.C. (1 Hayw.) 429 (Super. Ct. Law & Eq. 1796).

131. Id., 445.

132. Id.

133. 27 F. Cas. 899 (C.C.D.R.I. 1813) (No. 16,196).

134. Id., 901.

135. 84 Eng. Rep. 1103, 1105 (K.B. 1708).

136. 28 F. Cas. 204 (C.C.D. Mass. 1814) (No. 16,537).

137. Id., 209.

138. 45 F. 851 (C.C.W.D. Ark. 1890), rev'd on other grounds, Boyd v. United States, 142 U.S. 450 (1892).

139. Id., 860–63.

140. Id., 861, 865–66.

141. Id., 864–65 (citing Lamb v. People, 96 Ill. 73 (1880)).

142. Act of Dec. 19, 1801, ch. 67, § 1, 1801 Ky. Acts 116, 116–17.

143. Act of Dec. 22, 1802, ch. 53, § 17, 1802 Ky. Acts 107, 116.

144. Act of Jan. 12, 1825, ch. 203, § 3, 1824–25 Ky. Acts 190, 190.

145. Act of Jan. 22, 1827, ch. 68, § 1, 1826–27 Ky. Acts 74, 74.

146. Ky. Gen. Stat. ch. 29, art. 3, § 3 (1873).

147. 72 Ky. (9 Bush) 669, 672 (1873) (citing 2 Francis Wharton, A Treatise on the Criminal Law of the United States § 1004 (1846)).

148. 72 Ky. (9 Bush) 593, 596 (1873).

149. 9 S.W. 509, 511 (Ky. 1888) (manslaughter for recklessly causing death of a pregnant woman by means of illegal but nonfelonious abortion).

150. 33 S.W. 416 (Ky. 1895).

151. Id., 417.

152. 7 So. 703 (La. 1890).

153. Id., 705.

154. 48 S.C.L. (14 Rich.) 215, 225 (Ct. App. Law 1867).

155. 8 S.E. 440, 441 (S.C. 1889).

156. Id., 442.

157. Id., 441 (citing Blackstone).

158. 13 S.E. 319 (S.C. 1891).

159. Id., 321.

160. Id.

Chapter 7

1. AR, CT, DE, IN, IA, KS, KY (briefly), LA (until the 1850s), ME, MD, MA, MI, NE, NH, NC, OH, PA, TN, VA, WA, WV, and WY.

2. Pa. Legislature, Addendum to Act of April 5, 1790 (1810), in 2 The Laws of the Commonwealth of Pennsylvania 542, 562 (1810) (citations omitted).

3. Id., 564 (citations omitted).

4. Id., 566–67 (citations omitted).

5. Id., 573.

6. 1 Ashmead 289 (Pa. Ct. Oyer & Terminer 1826).

7. Id., 298–99.

8. 24 Pa. 386 (1855).

9. 4 Pa. L.J. 257 (1844).

10. See Charge of Judge King, on the Trial of John Daley for Murder (1844), reprinted in Wharton, 1855, 466, 474.

11. See Wharton, 1855, 46.

12. Brooks v. Commonwealth, 61 Pa. 352 (1869) (defendants intentionally killed victim in resisting lawful citizen's arrest for theft, precluding self-defense or provocation. First-degree murder conviction based on premeditated intent to kill upheld).

13. 7 Watts & Serg. 415 (Pa. 1844).

14. Id., 418.

15. Kelly v. Commonwealth, 1 Grant 484, 487–88 (Pa. 1858); Rhodes v. Commonwealth, 48 Pa. 396, 399–400 (1864).

16. 4 Pa. 195, 196 (Pa. Ct. Oyer & Terminer 1860).

17. 3 Brewster's Rep. 461 (Pa. Ct. Oyer & Terminer 1870).

18. 76 Pa. 319, 330 (1874).

19. 29 A. 404 (Pa. 1894).

20. 42 A. 374 (Pa. 1899).

21. 44 A. 570, 571 (Pa. 1899).

22. Thomas Jefferson, A Bill for Proportioning Crimes and Punishments § 11 (1779), http://etext.virginia.edu/etcbin/ot2wwwsingleauthor?specfile=/web/data/jefferson/texts/jefall.o2w&act=text&offset=7504163&textreg=1&query=proportioning+ crimes. On the legislative fate of Jefferson's proposed code, see Beckman, 1966, 148, 155–59; Preyer, 1983, 68–70.

23. Act of Dec. 15, 1796, reprinted in 2 The Statutes at Large of Virginia, 1792–1806, 5 (AMS Press 1970) (Samuel Shepherd ed., 1835); see also Beckman, 1966, 149–59 (discussing the Virginia legislation).

24. Act of Feb. 10, 1798, ch. 4, § 2, 1798 Ky. Acts 11, 12; Act of Dec. 19, 1801, ch. 67, 1801 Ky. Acts 116. Act of Jan. 6, 1810, ch. 138, art. 3, 1809–10 Md. Laws. Act of July 3, 1805, ch. 4, § 1, 1805 Terr. of Orleans Acts 36, 36–37 (also providing that the definition of all offenses, including murder, is given by the common law of England). The division of murder into degrees was repealed in 1855. Act of Mar. 14, 1855, no. 120, 1855 La. Acts 130. Mich. Rev. Stat. pt. 4, tit. 1, ch. 3, § 1 (1838). Act of Dec. 17, 1838, § 1, 1838 Ark. Acts 121, 121–22; see also Bivens v. State, 11 Ark. 455, 458 (1850). N.H. Rev. Stat. ch. 214, § 1 (1843). Act of June 18, 1846, ch. 16, 1846 Conn. Acts 13. Prior to this statute, Connecticut had left murder undefined. See Conn. Stat. Laws tit. 22, § 3 (1821).

25. The Virginia provision appeared in West Virginia's first compiled code. W. Va. Code ch. 144, § 1 (1868).

26. Act of Dec. 9, 1829, ch. 23, §§ 2–3, 1829 Tenn. Acts 27, 27–28. Del. Rev. Stat. ch. 127, §§ 1, 2 (1852). Until 1858, Massachusetts simply criminalized "wilful murder." See, e.g., Mass. Rev. Stat. ch. 125, § 1 (1836). In 1858, Massachusetts divided murder into two degrees. Act of Mar. 27, 1858, ch. 154, §§ 1, 2, 1858 Mass. Acts 126, 126; Mass. Gen. Stat. ch. 160, §§ 1–2 (1860).

27. See Act of Feb. 3, 1859, ch. 28, §§ 1–2, 1859 Kan. Laws 231, 231; Kan. Gen. Laws ch. 33, § 1 (1862). Kansas entered the Union in 1861. Act of Feb. 11, 1893, ch. 85, 1893 N.C. Laws 76; Act of Mar. 4, 1893, ch. 281, 1893 N.C. Laws 228. Earlier law left murder undefined. See, e.g., Act of Dec. 23, 1817, ch. 18, 1817 N.C. Laws 18, 18–19.

28. Whiteford v. Commonwealth, 27 Va. (6 Rand.) 721, 723 (1828); Commonwealth v. Jones, 28 Va. (1 Leigh) 598, 610–12 (1829); Bratton v. State, 29 Tenn. (10 Hum.) 103, 109 (1849); State v. McNab, 20 N.H. 160 (1849); Bivens v. State, 11 Ark. 455, 459 (1850) People v. Potter, 5 Mich. 1 (1858); People v. Scott, 6 Mich. 287, 293 (1859) Commonwealth v. Jackson, 81 Mass. (15 Gray) 187 (1860) Bratton v. State, 29 Tenn. (10 Hum) 103, 109 (1849); People v. Potter, 5 Mich. 1 (1858); People v. Scott, 6 Mich. 287, 293 (1859); Commonwealth v. Jackson, 81 Mass. (15 Gray) 187 (1860).

29. State v. Pike, 49 N.H. 399 (1869); State v. Boice, 1 Houst. Crim. Cas. 355 (Del. Ct. Oyer & Terminer 1871); Commonwealth v. Pemberton, 118 Mass. 36, 43–44 (1875); Robertson v. Commonwealth, 20 S.E. 362 (Va. 1894); People v. Willett, 62 N.W. 1115 (Mich.

1895); State v. Covington, 23 S.E. 337 (N.C. 1895); see also State v. Gadberry, 23 S.E. 477 (N.C. 1895)(first-degree murder conviction overturned on procedural grounds); State v. Cross, 46 A. 148 (Conn. 1900).

30. Bratton v. State, 29 Tenn. (10 Hum.) 103, 109 (1849); State v. Pike, 49 N.H. 399 (1869); State v. Boice, 1 Houst. Crim. Cas. 355 (Del. Ct. Oyer & Terminer 1871); Commonwealth v. Pemberton, 118 Mass. 36, 43–44 (1875); Poe v. State, 78 Tenn. 673 (1882); People v. Willett, 62 N.W. 1115 (Mich. 1895); State v. Lodge, 33 A. 312 (Del. Ct. Oyer & Terminer 1892); Robertson v. Commonwealth, 20 S.E. 362 (Va. 1894); Commonwealth v. Gilbert, 165 Mass. 45 (1895); State v. Covington, 23 S.E. 337 (N.C. 1895); State v. Cross, 46 A. 148 (Conn. 1900).

31. Pike, 49 N.H. 399; Pemberton, 118 Mass. 43–44; Poe, 78 Tenn. 673; Robertson, 20 S.E. 362 (Virginia).

32. Willett, 62 N.W. 1115 (Michigan); Gilbert, 165 Mass. 45; Cross, 46 A. 148 (Connecticut).

33. Covington, 23 S.E. 337–38 (North Carolina).

34. State v. Lodge, 33 A. 312 (Del. Ct. Oyer & Terminer 1892); Commonwealth v. Jackson, 81 Mass. (15 Gray) 187 (1860); Commonwealth v. Mink, 123 Mass. 422 (1877); People v. Potter, 5 Mich. 1 (1858); People v. Scott, 6 Mich. 287, 293 (1859); State v. McNab, 20 N.H. 160 (1849); Bratton v. State, 29 Tenn. (10 Hum.) 103, 109 (1849); Whiteford v. Commonwealth, 27 Va. (6 Rand.) 721, 723 (1828); Commonwealth v. Brown, 19 S.E. 447, 449 (Va. 1894).

35. Bratton, 29 Tenn. (10 Hum.) 103.

36. State v. Boice, 1 Houst. Crim. Cas. 355 (Del. Ct. Oyer & Terminer 1871).

37. State v. Lodge, 33 A. 312 (Del. Ct. Oyer & Terminer 1892).

38. 27 Va. (6 Rand.) 721.

39. 33 A. 312.

40. 20 N.H. 160 (1849).

41. 118 Mass. 36, 43–44 (1875) (quoting Hawkins).

42. 5 Mich. 1, 7 (1858).

43. 28 Va. (1 Leigh) 598 (1829).

44. 29 Tenn. (10 Hum.) 103, 109 (1849).

45. 11 Ark. 455, 459 (1850).

46. 50 Conn. 193, 197 (1882).

47. State v. Pike, 49 N.H. 399, 403 (1869); Commonwealth v. Chance, 54 N.E. 551, 552 (Mass. 1899).

48. People v. Scott, 6 Mich. 287, 293 (1859).

49. People v. Abbott, 74 N.W. 529, 530 (Mich. 1898).

50. 118 Mass. 36, 36 (1875).

51. 165 Mass. 45 (1895).

52. Id., 49–50.

53. Act of Jan. 27, 1815, ch. 28, §§ 2, 3, 1814–15 Ohio Acts 85, 86.

54. Act of Jan. 27, 1815, ch. 28, § 2.

55. Id., § 3. An 1835 revision of the first-degree murder statute added poisoning to the enumerated felonies and added the word "and" immediately before the phrase "of deliberate and premeditated malice." Act of Mar. 7, 1835, § 1, 1834–35 Ohio Acts 33, 33.

56. 8 Ohio St. 131 (1857).

57. Id., 176–77.

58. 2 Ind. Rev. Stat. pt. 3, ch. 5, §§ 2, 7 (1852).

59. Reed v. State, 8 Ind. 200, 200–201 (1856).

60. 7 Ind. 326, 331 (1855).

61. 53 Ind. 408 (1876).

62. Id., 412.

63. 70 Ind. 126 (1880).

64. Id., 127–28.

65. Id., 130.

66. See Neb. Gen. Stat. ch. 58, pt. 1, ch. 2, §§ 3–4 (1873).

67. 70 N.W. 924, 924 (Neb. 1897).

68. Morgan v. State, 71 N.W. 788 (Neb. 1897).

69. Id., 794.

70. Id.

71. Id., 794–95 (quoting R. v. Serné, 16 Cox's Crim. L. Cas. 311 (Cent. Crim. Ct. 1887)).

72. Act of Dec. 2, 1869, ch. 2, §§ 12, 13, 16, 1869 Wash. Terr. Laws 198, 200–201.

73. 40 P. 626 (Wash. 1895).

74. See Act of Mar. 14, 1890, ch. 73, §§ 13, 16, 1890 Wyo. Terr. Laws 127, 129 (containing no comma after "purposely"); see also id., § 17.

75. Me. Rev. Stat. ch. 154, § 1, 2 (1840).

76. 32 Me. 369 (1851).

77. Id., 373–74.

78. Iowa Code §§ 2569, 2570 (1851).

79. Id., § 2568.

80. State v. Wells, 17 N.W. 90 (Iowa 1883).

81. Id., 92.

82. State v. Wiese, 4 N.W. 827 (Iowa 1880); State v. Johnson, 34 N.W. 177 (Iowa 1887).

83. 8 Iowa 477, 505 (1859).

84. 65 N.W. 387, 394 (Iowa 1895).

85. Id.

86. 25 Iowa 128, 134 (1868).

87. State v. Leeper, 30 N.W. 501 (Iowa 1886); State v. Minard, 65 N.W. 147 (Iowa 1895).

88. AR, CT, DE, IN, IA, KS, KY, LA, ME, MD, MA, MI, NE, NH, NC, OH, PA, TN, VA, WA, WV, WY.

89. PA (1844), TN (1849), ME (1851), IN (1855), NH (1870), DE (1871), MA (1875), IA (1880), VA (1894), MI (1895), NC(1895), WA (1895), NE (1897), CT (1900). One additional jurisdiction, Arkansas, approved such liability in dictum, without ever applying it.

90. DE, IA, ME, TN.

91. Commonwealth v. Green, 1 Ashmead 289, 298–99 (Pa. Ct. Oyer & Terminer 1826); Commonwealth v. Jones, 28 Va. (1 Leigh) 598, 610–12 (1829); Commonwealth v. Flanagan, 7 Watts & Serg. 415, 418 (Pa. 1844); Bivens v. State, 11 Ark. 455, 459 (1850); State v. Pike, 49 N.H. 399, 403 (1869); Smith v. State, 50 Conn. 193, 197 (1882); Commonwealth v. Chance, 54 N.E. 551, 552 (Mass. 1899).

92. Flanagan, 7 Watts & Serg., 418 (Pennsylvania); People v. Scott, 6 Mich. 287, 293 (1859); Moynihan v. State, 70 Ind. 126, 130 (1880).

93. See, e.g., Commonwealth v. Pemberton, 118 Mass. 36, 43–44 (1875); Commonwealth v. Gilbert, 165 Mass. 45, 49–50 (1895); Morgan v. State, 71 N.W. 788, 794 (Neb. 1897).

94. See, e.g., Green, 1 Ashmead, 298–99 (Pennsylvania); Pemberton, 118 Mass., 43–44; State v. Wells, 17 N.W. 90, 92 (Iowa 1883).

95. State v. Shelledy, 8 Iowa 477, 505 (1859).

96. State v. Weems, 65 N.W. 387, 394 (Iowa 1895).

Chapter 8

1. Ga. L. 1817, 95.

2. Id., 96. In 1833 "a felonious intent" was changed to "a crime punishable by imprisonment or death." Act of Dec. 23, 1833, div. 4, § 9, 1833 Ga. Laws 143, 148–49. This language was substantially altered in 1895.

3. Ill. Rev. Code, Crim. Code, §§ 22, 24, 28 (1827).

4. See Neb. Rev. Stat. pt. 3, §§ 18–22 (1866). In 1873, Nebraska replaced these homicide provisions with those found in the Ohio penal code. Neb. Gen. Stat. ch. 58, pt. 1, §§ 3–5 (1873).

5. See Col. Rev. Stat. ch. 22, §§ 18–20, 24 (1868).

6. Colorado courts addressed felony murder only once, in a dictum stating that a felon killing a resister cannot plead self-defense. Boykin v. People, 45 P. 419, 423 (Colo. 1896).

7. 31 Ga. 236, 249 (1860). The latter point accords with the holding in McPherson v. State, 22 Ga. 478 (1857).

8. McGinnis, 31 Ga. 263.

9. But see Brennan v. People, 15 Ill. 511, 516–17 (1854) (intentionally encouraging or aiding an unlawful act causing death, though without intent to kill, is homicide; graded as implied malice murder where unlawful act is dangerous and violent, or involves intent to injure).

10. 96 Ill. 73, 82–83 (1879).

11. Id., 84.

12. 109 Ill. 444 (1884).

13. Id., 449.

14. Id., 449–50.

15. Act of Apr. 16, 1850, ch. 99, §§ 19–21, 25, 1849–50 Cal. Stat. 229, 231.

16. Act of Apr. 19, 1856, ch. 139, § 2, 1856 Cal. Stat. 219, 219. Act of Mar. 30, 1874, § 16, 1873–74 Cal. Acts 419, 427.

17. Act of Mar. 30, 1874, § 16, 1873–74 Cal. Acts 419, 427 (revising § 189 of the California penal code).

18. 17 Cal. 389, 399 (1861).

19. 25 Cal. 361, 366 (1864).

20. 34 Cal. 211, 213 (1867).

21. 27 Cal. 572 (1865).

22. Id., 581.

23. 48 Cal. 85, 94 (1874) (citations omitted).

24. 49 Cal. 560, 562–63 (1875). In fact, the evidence indicated that Vasquez had himself been the killer.

25. 22 P. 125 (Cal. 1889).

26. Id., 126.

27. Id.

28. Id., 126–27.

29. Act of Nov. 26, 1861, ch. 28, §§ 15–18, 21, 1861 Nev. Terr. Laws 56, 58–59.

30. State v. Lopez, 15 Nev. 407, 413 (1880).

31. 8 P. 456 (Nev. 1885).

32. See An Act Concerning Crimes and Punishments, ch. 4, §§ 15–17, 21 (1864), 1864 Mont. Laws 176, 178–80; Territory v. McAndrews, 3 Mont. 158, 161 (1878); People v. Mooney, 2 P. 876, 877 (Idaho Terr. 1882). Montana entered the Union with this law in 1889.

33. Idaho Rev. Stat. §§ 6560–62, 6565 (1887). Idaho entered the Union with these laws in 1889.

34. 2 Utah Comp. Laws §§ 4454, 4456 (1888). Utah entered the Union in 1896 and re-passed these provisions as Utah Rev. Stat. §§ 4161, 4163 (1898).

35. 61 P. 527 (Utah 1900).

36. Id., 530.

37. Act of Feb. 12, 1858, ch. 121, pt. 1, tit. 17, ch. 15, 1857–58 Tex. Laws 156, 173. The original language defined murder as: "voluntary homicide committed with deliberate design" and not included in other homicide offenses. Tex. Penal Code art. 607 (1857).

38. Act of Feb. 12, 1858, ch. 121, pt. 1, tit. 17, ch. 15.

39. Tex. Penal Code art. 595.

40. Id., arts. 577, 578, 587, 589.

41. Id., art. 590.

42. Id., art. 49.

43. 25 Tex. 33 (1860).

44. Id., 39–41.

45. 7 Tex. Ct. App. 472 (1879).

46. Id., 477.

47. 30 S.W. 805 (Tex. Crim. App. 1895).

48. Id.

49. Id., 806.

50. Id.

51. 51 S.W. 252 (Tex. Crim. App. 1899).

52. Id., 254.

53. Id., 255.

54. Singleton v. State, 1 Tex. Ct. App. 501 (1877).

55. Gonzales v. State, 19 Tex. Ct. App. 394 (1885).

56. Mendez v. State, 16 S.W. 766 (Tex. Ct. App. 1891).

57. 34 S.W. 627 (Tex. Crim. App. 1896).

58. 20 S.W. 560 (Tex. Crim. App. 1892).

59. Sharpe v. State, 17 Tex. Ct. App. 486 (1885); Smith v. State, 19 S.W. 252 (Tex. Ct. App. 1892); Parker v. State, 49 S.W. 80 (Tex. Crim. App. 1899).

60. Stanley v. State, 14 Tex. Ct. App. 315 (1883).

61. Washington v. State, 8 S.W. 642 (Tex. Ct. App. 1888).

62. 18 S.W. 412 (Tex. Ct. App. 1892).

63. Duran v. State, 14 Tex. Ct. App. 195 (1883); Giles v. State, 4 S.W. 886 (Tex. Ct. App. 1887); Little v. State, 47 S.W. 984 (Tex. Crim. App. 1898); Garza v. State, 46 S.W. 242 (Tex. Crim. App. 1898).

64. Duran, 14 Tex. Ct. App. 195; Giles, 4 S.W. 886; Little, 47 S.W. 984.

65. Williams v. State, 17 S.W. 408 (Tex. Ct. App. 1891).

66. Isaacs v. State, 38 S.W. 40 (Tex. Crim. App. 1896); Darlington v. State, 50 S.W. 375 (Tex. Crim. App. 1899); Nite v. State, 54 S.W. 763 (Tex. Crim. App. 1899).

67. Darlington, 50 S.W. 376.

68. N.Y. Rev. Stat. pt. 4, ch. 1, tit. 1, § 5 (1829).

69. Act of Apr. 14, 1860, ch. 410, § 2, 1860 N.Y. Laws 712, 712–13. Shortly thereafter, New York briefly limited first-degree felony murder to killing in the course of arson. Act of Apr. 12, 1862, ch. 197, sec. 6, § 5, 1862 N.Y. Laws 368, 369.

70. Act of May 29, 1873, ch. 644, 1873 N.Y. Laws 1014. An 1876 statute removed the phrase "without design to effect death," so as to include intentional as well as unintentional felony murders. Act of May 15, 1876, ch. 333, 1876 N.Y. Laws 317.

71. People v. Enoch, 13 Wend. 159, 165 (N.Y. 1834) (quoting unreported opinion of Supreme Court below).

72. Id., 174–75.

73. 19 Wend. 569, 593 (N.Y. 1838).

74. Id., 592. But see Act of July 26, 1881, ch. 676, § 183, 3 1881 N.Y. Laws 1, 44 (murder includes killing in the attempt or commission of a felony "either upon or affecting the person killed or otherwise").

75. 1 Parker's Crim. Rep. 39 (N.Y. Ct. Oyer & Terminer 1845).

76. 45 N.Y. 213 (1871).

77. Id., 216–17.

78. 40 N.E. 392, 394–95 (N.Y. 1895).

79. People v. Willett, 6 N.E. 301 (N.Y. 1886). The opinion does not say how the defendant killed the victim.

80. People v. Deacons, 16 N.E. 676 (N.Y. 1888).

81. People v. Miles, 38 N.E. 456 (N.Y. 1894).

82. People v. Johnson, 17 N.E. 684 (N.Y. 1888).

83. Id.; Dolan v. People, 64 N.Y. 485 (1876).

84. 78 N.Y. 492 (1879).

85. 80 N.Y. 500 (1880).

86. Id., 516.

87. Act of Feb. 15, 1839, ch. 66, tit. 2, § 4, 1839 Miss. Laws 102, 105–06. Mississippi's first murder statute did not define the offense. Miss. Rev. Code ch. 54, § 2 (1824).

88. Miss. Rev. Code ch. 64, art. 165 (1857).

89. 36 Miss. 77 (1858).

90. Id., 92.

91. Id., 92–93.

92. But see People v. Miles, 38 N.E. 456 (N.Y. 1894)(felony murder predicated on assault of a different victim).

93. Act of July 4, 1825, ch. 1, § 3, 1825 Mo. Laws 281, 282.

94. Mo. Rev. Stat. ch. 47, art. 2, § 1 (1845).

95. Id., § 7 (emphasis added).

96. Mo. Rev. Stat. § 1232 (1879).

97. State v. Jennings, 18 Mo. 435 (1853); State v. Nueslein, 25 Mo. 111, 125–26 (1857).

98. 66 Mo. 13 (1877). Note that Wieners is not a felony murder case.

99. Id., 20 (citing 1 Hale, 1736, 450).

100. Id., 15 (citing 1 East, 1806, 231); id., 17 (citing 2 Bishop, 1858, § 617).

101. Id., 22 (citing 1 East, 1806, 231).

102. 66 Mo. 631 (1877).

103. Id., 647, 649.

104. J.H.S.,1878, 225; see also J.H.S., 1880, 37.

105. J.H.S., 1878, 225.

106. 68 Mo. 552 (1878).

107. Id., 556 (citing Wharton, 1875, 38–46); see also id., 557 (citing People v. Rector, 19 Wend. 569, 605 (N.Y. 1838)).

108. Id., 562. The court also asserted that there could be no second-degree felony murder. Id., 560.

109. Mo. Rev. Stat. § 1232 (1879).

110. 70 Mo. 520 (1879).

111. Id., 522.

112. 71 Mo. 425 (1880).

113. Id., 429.

114. 84 Mo. 278 (1884).

115. Id., 287.

116. State v. Avery, 21 S.W. 193 (Mo. 1893) (shooting); State v. Donnelly, 32 S.W. 1124 (Mo. 1895) (bludgeoning); State v. Schmidt, 38 S.W. 719 (Mo. 1897) (shooting); State v. Foster, 38 S.W. 721 (Mo. 1897) (shooting); State v. Sexton, 48 S.W. 452 (Mo. 1898) (shooting).

117. See Or. Laws, Crim. Code, tit. 2, ch. 2, § 506 (1874) (noting that this and related sections were passed on Oct. 19, 1864).

118. Or. Laws, Crim. Code, tit. 2, ch. 2, § 519 (1874).

119. Id., § 507 (footnote omitted).

120. 7 Or. 186 (1879).

121. Id., 197–98.

122. Id., 204.

123. Wis. Rev. Stat. ch. 133, §§ 1–2 (1849).

124. Id.

125. Miller v. State, 25 Wis. 384, 388–89 (1870).

126. See Boyle v. State, 15 N.W. 827 (Wis. 1883) (reversing second-degree murder conviction, but stating that a killing with intent to do great bodily harm is done in the course of felony assault and therefore is murder in the third degree); Terrill v. State, 42 N.W. 243 (Wis. 1889) (reversing third-degree murder conviction on other grounds); Hoffman v. State, 59 N.W. 588 (Wis. 1894) (reversing third-degree murder conviction on other grounds).

127. See State v. Hammond, 35 Wis. 315 (1874) (reversing third-degree murder conviction on other grounds).

128. Hammond, 35 Wis. 315 (maiming); Terrill, 42 N.W. 243 (felony assault); Pliemling v. State, 1 N.W. 278 (Wis. 1879) (intentional killing during rape, but killer's identity not proven).

129. Hoffman, 59 N.W., 592–93.

130. Act of Mar. 5, 1853, ch. 2, § 7, 1853 Minn. Laws 5, 7. Minnesota entered the Union in 1858.

131. Act of Feb. 10, 1832, no. 55, § 1, 1832 Fla. Terr. Laws 63, 63 (providing that the common law of crimes was in force except as modified by legislation); id., § 2 (providing capital punishment for murder without defining the offense).

132. Act of Aug. 6, 1868, no. 13, ch. 3, §§ 1–2, 1868 Fla. Laws 61, 63.

133. Collins v. State, 12 So. 906 (Fla. 1893).

134. Johnson v. State, 4 So. 535, 538 (Fla. 1888).

135. Fla. Rev. Stat. § 2380 (1892).

136. Act of Feb. 17, 1829, § 66, 1828–29 N.J. Laws 109, 128.

137. 13 N.J.L. 361, 370 (1833).

138. Id., 370.

139. Id., 371–72.

140. Act of Jan. 9, 1841, ch. 3, § 1, 1840–41 Ala. Acts 103, 122.

141. Id., § 2.

142. 38 Ala. 213 (1862).

143. Isham, 38 Ala. 219.

144. Id., 220.

145. 74 Ala. 1 (1883).

146. Id., 8–9.

147. Miss. Rev. Code ch. 64, art. 165 (1857); see also Hoffheimer, 2001, 57–74.

148. CT, DE, IN, IA, ME, MA, MI, NE, NH, NC, PA, TN, VA, WA.

149. The exceptions were DE, IA, ME, TN.

150. AL, ID, MO (after 1879), NE, OR, UT.

151. AL, CA, ID, MO (after 1879), NV, OR, TX, UT.

152. People v. Olsen, 22 P. 125 (Cal. 1889); Richards v. State, 30 S.W. 805 (Tex. Crim. App. 1895).

153. Bratton v. State, 29 Tenn. (10 Hum.) 103, 109 (1849); State v. Smith, 32 Me. 369 (1851); State v. Boice, 1 Houst. Crim. Cas. 355 (Del. Ct. Oyer & Terminer 1871); State v. Leeper, 30 N.W. 501 (Iowa 1886); Olsen, 22 P. 125 (California); State v. Lodge, 33 A. 312 (Del. Ct. Oyer & Terminer 1892); State v. Minard, 65 N.W. 147 (Iowa 1895); Richards, 30 S.W. 805 (Texas).

154. Smith, 32 Me. 369; Leeper, 30 N.W. 501 (Iowa); Lodge, 33 A. 312 (Delaware); Minard, 65 N.W. 147 (Iowa).

155. Olsen, 22 P. 125 (California).

156. Bratton, 29 Tenn. (10 Hum.) 103; Richards, 30 S.W. 805 (Texas).

157. Boice, 1 Houst. Crim. Cas. 355 (Delaware).

158. Reed v. State, 8 Ind. 200, 200–201 (1856).

159. Act of Jan. 9, 1841, ch. 3, § 1, 1840–41 Ala. Acts 103, 122. Miss. Rev. Code ch. 64, art. 165 (1857).

160. Van Steenburgh, 1 Parker's Crim. Rep. 39 (New York); Lamb, 96 Ill. 82; cf. Wilson, 40 N.E. 392 (New York).

161. People v. Van Steenburgh, 1 Parker's Crim. Rep. 39 (N.Y. Ct. Oyer & Terminer 1845); Ruloff v. People, 45 N.Y. 213, 216–17 (1871); People v. Wilson, 40 N.E. 392 (N.Y. 1895).

162. Williams v. State, 17 S.W. 408 (Tex. Ct. App. 1891); Keaton v. State, 57 S.W. 1125 (Tex. Crim. App. 1900).

163. 30 S.W. 805 (Tex. Crim. App. 1895).

164. Commonwealth v. Jackson, 81 Mass. (15 Gray) 187 (1860); Commonwealth v. Mink, 123 Mass. 422 (1877).

165. Commonwealth v. Pemberton, 118 Mass. 36, 43–44 (1875); Commonwealth v. Gilbert, 165 Mass. 45, 49–50 (1895).

166. Commonwealth v. Flanagan, 7 Watts & Serg. 415, 418 (Pa. 1844).

167. People v. Scott, 6 Mich. 287, 293 (1859).

168. People v. Foren, 25 Cal. 361, 364 (1864).

169. Act of Feb. 17, 1829, § 66, 1828–29 N.J. Laws 109, 128.

170. Lamb v. People, 96 Ill. 73 (1880); Adams v. People, 109 Ill. 444 (1884).

171. Miller v. State, 25 Wis. 384, 388–89 (1870) (robbery); Dolan v. People, 64 N.Y. 485 (1876) (burglary); Buel v. People, 78 N.Y. 492 (1879) (rape); Cox v. People, 80 N.Y. 500 (1880) (burglary); Adams, 109 Ill. 444 (robbery); People v. Greenwall, 22 N.E. 180 (N.Y. 1889) (burglary); State v. Deschamps, 7 So. 703 (La. 1890) (rape); People v. Wilson, 40 N.E. 392 (N.Y. 1895) (burglary); Reddick v. Commonwealth, 33 S.W. 416 (Ky. 1895) (arson); People v. Meyer, 56 N.E. 758 (N.Y. 1900) (burglary).

172. People v. Miles, 38 N.E. 456 (N.Y. 1894).

173. State v. Green, 66 Mo. 631 (1877); People v. Johnson, 17 N.E. 684 (N.Y. 1888).

174. State v. Nueslein, 25 Mo. 111, 125–26 (1857); State v. Jennings, 18 Mo. 435, 435 (1853).

175. People v. Van Steenburgh, 1 Parker's Crim. Rep. 39 (N.Y. Ct. Oyer & Terminer 1845); McGinnis v. State, 31 Ga. 236 (1860).

176. People v. Deacons, 16 N.E. 676 (N.Y. 1888).

177. State v. Levelle, 13 S.E. 319 (S.C. 1891).

178. People v. Willett, 6 N.E. 301 (N.Y. 1886).

179. Stocking v. State, 7 Ind. 326 (1855); Commonwealth v. Miller, 4 Phila. Rep. 195 (Pa. Ct. Oyer & Terminer 1860); People v. Pool, 27 Cal. 572 (1865); State v. Pike, 49 N.H. 399 (1869); Miller v. State, 25 Wis. 384 (1870); State v. Boice, 1 Houst. Crim. Cas. 355 (Del. Ct. Oyer & Terminer 1871); Brown v. Commonwealth, 76 Pa. 319 (1874); People v. Vasquez, 49 Cal. 560 (1875); Commonwealth v. Pemberton, 118 Mass. 36 (1875); Singleton v. State, 1 Tex. Ct. App. 501 (1877); State v. Brown, 7 Or. 186 (1879); State v. Wiese, 4 N.W. 827 (Iowa 1880); Moynihan v. State, 70 Ind. 126 (1880); Poe v. State, 78 Tenn. 673 (1882); Duran v. State, 14 Tex. Ct. App. 195 (1883); Kilgore v. State, 74 Ala. 1 (1883); Adams v. People, 109 Ill. 444 (1884); State v. Hopkirk, 84 Mo. 278 (1884); Sharpe v. State, 17 Tex. Ct. App. 486 (1885); State v. Gray, 8 P. 456 (Nev. 1885); Gonzales v. State, 19 Tex. Ct. App. 394 (1885); Giles v. State, 4 S.W. 886 (Tex. Ct. App. 1887); State v. Johnson, 34 N.W. 177 (Iowa 1887); Washington v. State, 8 S.W. 642 (Tex. Ct. App. 1888); Mendez v. State, 16 S.W. 766 (Tex. Ct. App. 1891); Williams v. State, 17 S.W. 408 (Tex. Ct. App. 1891); Smith v. State, 19 S.W. 252 (Tex. Ct. App. 1892); Elizando v. State, 20 S.W. 560 (Tex. Crim. App. 1892); State v. Avery, 21 S.W. 193 (Mo. 1893); Robertson v. Commonwealth, 20 S.E. 362 (Va. 1894); State v. Donnelly, 32 S.W. 1124 (Mo. 1895); State v. Weems, 65 N.W. 387 (Iowa 1895); Wilkins v. State, 34 S.W. 627 (Tex. Crim. App. 1896); Isaacs v. State, 38 S.W. 40 (Tex.

Crim. App. 1896); State v. Schmidt, 38 S.W. 719 (Mo. 1897); State v. Foster, 38 S.W. 721 (Mo. 1897); Garza v. State, 46 S.W. 242 (Tex. Crim. App. 1898); Little v. State, 47 S.W. 984 (Tex. Crim. App. 1898); State v. Sexton, 48 S.W. 452 (Mo. 1898); Parker v. State, 49 S.W. 80 (Tex. Crim. App. 1899); Commonwealth v. Eagan, 42 A. 374 (Pa. 1899); Darlington v. State, 50 S.W. 375 (Tex. Crim. App. 1899); Commonwealth v. Epps, 44 A. 570 (Pa. 1899); Nite v. State, 54 S.W. 763 (Tex. Crim. App. 1899); Keaton v. State, 57 S.W. 1125 (Tex. Crim. App. 1900); State v. Morgan, 61 P. 527 (Utah 1900).

180. Commonwealth v. Flanagan, 7 Watts & Serg. 415 (Pa. 1844); Dolan v. People, 64 N.Y. 485 (1876); Bissot v. State, 53 Ind. 408 (1876); Cox v. People, 80 N.Y. 500 (1880); Stanley v. State, 14 Tex. Ct. App. 315 (1883); Gray, 8 P. 456 (Nevada); Washington, 8 S.W. 642 (Texas); People v. Greenwall, 22 N.E. 180 (N.Y. 1889); Commonwealth v. Manfredi, 29 A. 404 (Pa. 1894); People v. Wilson, 40 N.E. 392 (N.Y. 1895); People v. Miller, 53 P. 816 (Cal. 1898); Eagan, 42 A. 374 (Pennsylvania); Hedrick v. State, 51 S.W. 252 (Tex. Crim. App. 1899); People v. Meyer, 56 N.E. 758 (N.Y. 1900).

181. Commonwealth v. Hanlon, 3 Brewster's Rep. 461 (Pa. Ct. Oyer & Terminer 1870); Buel v. People, 78 N.Y. 492 (1879); Washington, 8 S.W. 642 (Texas); State v. Deschamps, 7 So. 703 (La. 1890); Cook v. State, 18 S.W. 412 (Tex. Ct. App. 1892); People v. Willett, 62 N.W. 1115 (Mich. 1895); Commonwealth v. Gilbert, 165 Mass. 45 (1895); Morgan v. State, 71 N.W. 788 (Neb. 1897); State v. Cross, 46 A. 148 (Conn. 1900).

182. Stocking, 7 Ind. 326; State v. Myers, 40 P. 626 (Wash. 1895); Reddick v. Commonwealth, 33 S.W. 416 (Ky. 1895).

183. Bratton v. State, 29 Tenn. (10 Hum.) 103 (1849); People v. Miles, 38 N.E. 456 (N.Y. 1894); Richards v. State, 30 S.W. 805 (Tex. Crim. App. 1895).

184. State v. Green, 66 Mo. 631 (1877) (resisting arrest); People v. Johnson, 17 N.E. 684 (N.Y. 1888) (escape).

185. State v. Jennings, 18 Mo. 435 (1853); State v. Nueslein, 25 Mo. 111 (1857).

186. People v. Van Steenburgh, 1 Parker's Crim. Rep. 39 (N.Y. Ct. Oyer & Terminer 1845) (riot in disguise); McGinnis v. State, 31 Ga. 236 (1860) (riot).

187. People v. Willett, 6 N.E. 301 (N.Y. 1886); People v. Olsen, 22 P. 125 (Cal. 1889); State v. Covington, 23 S.E. 337 (S.C. 1895).

188. People v. Deacons, 16 N.E. 676 (N.Y. 1888).

189. State v. Smith, 32 Me. 369 (1851); State v. Leeper, 30 N.W. 501 (Iowa 1886); State v. Lodge, 33 A. 312 (Del. Ct. Oyer & Terminer 1892); State v. Minard, 65 N.W. 147 (Iowa 1895).

190. State v. Levelle, 13 S.E. 319 (S.C. 1891).

191. People v. Rector, 19 Wend. 569, 592–93 (N.Y. Sup. Ct. 1838).

192. State v. Shock, 68 Mo. 552, 559–63 (1878).

193. Mask v. State, 36 Miss. 77 (1858).

194. See Act of Dec. 15, 1796, ch. 2, § 11, reprinted in 2 The Statutes at Large of Virginia, 1792–1806, 5 (AMS Press 1970) (Samuel Shepherd ed., 1835), 7 (voluntary manslaughter punishable by two to ten years' incarceration, and six to fourteen years for a

second offense); Mass. Rev. Stat. ch. 125, § 9 (1836) (manslaughter punishable by up to twenty years' incarceration); Act of Apr. 19, 1856, ch. 139, § 3, 1856 Cal. Stat. 219, 219 (manslaughter punishable by up to ten years' incarceration); N.H. Gen. Laws ch. 282, § 10 (1878) (up to thirty-year penalty for first-degree manslaughter; up to ten-year penalty for second-degree manslaughter); Act of July 26, 1881, ch. 676, § 192, 3 1881 N.Y. Laws 1, 46 (first-degree manslaughter punishable with five to twenty years' incarceration).

195. 176 Eng. Rep. 468, 469–70 (Kent Assizes 1864).

196. R. v. Desmond, 11 Cox's Crim. Cas. 146 (1868); R. v. Serné, 16 Cox's Crim. Cas. 311 (1887).

197. Reported convictions with no reported means of killing include Commonwealth v. Flanagan, 7 Watts & Serg. 415 (Pa. 1844); State v. Pike, 49 N.H. 399 (1869); State v. Wiese, 4 N.W. 827 (Iowa 1880); State v. Hopkirk, 84 Mo. 278 (1884); People v. Willett, 6 N.E. 301 (N.Y. 1886); and People v. Olsen, 22 P. 125 (Cal. 1889).

198. Bratton v. State, 29 Tenn. (10 Hum.) 103 (1849); People v. Pool, 27 Cal. 572 (1865); People v. Vasquez, 49 Cal. 560 (1875); Bissot v. State, 53 Ind. 408 (1876); Singleton v. State, 1 Tex. Ct. App. 501 (1877) (defendant also slashed victim's throat); State v. Green, 66 Mo. 631 (1877); State v. Brown, 7 Or. 186 (1879); Poe v. State, 78 Tenn. 673 (1882); Sharpe v. State, 17 Tex. Ct. App. 486 (1885); State v. Gray, 8 P. 456 (Nev. 1885); Gonzales v. State, 19 Tex. Ct. App. 394 (1885); People v. Greenwall, 22 N.E. 180 (N.Y. 1889); Mendez v. State, 16 S.W. 766 (Tex. Ct. App. 1891); Smith v. State, 19 S.W. 252 (Tex. Ct. App. 1892); Elizando v. State, 20 S.W. 560 (Tex. Crim. App. 1892); State v. Avery, 21 S.W. 193 (Mo. 1893); Commonwealth v. Manfredi, 29 A. 404 (Pa. 1894); People v. Miles, 38 N.E. 456 (N.Y. 1894); Robertson v. Commonwealth, 20 S.E. 362 (Va. 1894); People v. Wilson, 40 N.E. 392 (N.Y. 1895); Richards v. State, 30 S.W. 805 (Tex. Crim. App. 1895); State v. Covington, 23 S.E. 337 (N.C. 1895); State v. Weems, 65 N.W. 387 (Iowa 1895); Wilkins v. State, 34 S.W. 627 (Tex. Crim. App. 1896); Isaacs v. State, 38 S.W. 40 (Tex. Crim. App. 1896); State v. Schmidt, 38 S.W. 719 (Mo. 1897); State v. Foster, 38 S.W. 721 (Mo. 1897); People v. Miller, 53 P. 816 (Cal. 1898); State v. Sexton, 48 S.W. 452 (Mo. 1898); Parker v. State, 49 S.W. 80 (Tex. Crim. App. 1899); Darlington v. State, 50 S.W. 375 (Tex. Crim. App. 1899); Hedrick v. State, 51 S.W. 252 (Tex. Crim. App. 1899); People v. Meyer, 56 N.E. 758 (N.Y. 1900); State v. Morgan, 61 P. 527 (Utah 1900).

199. McGinnis v. State, 31 Ga. 236 (1860) (multiple stab wounds); Miller v. State, 25 Wis. 384 (1870) (stabbing and bludgeoning with soldering iron); Singleton v. State, 1 Tex. Ct. App. 501 (1877) (throat slashing with shooting); Kilgore v. State, 74 Ala. 1 (1883) (repeated stabbing of prostrate victim); Washington v. State, 8 S.W. 642 (Tex. Ct. App. 1888) (throat slashing).

200. Commonwealth v. Miller, 4 Phila. Rep. 195 (Pa. Ct. Oyer & Terminer 1860) (drowning in a stream); Commonwealth v. Hanlon, 3 Brewster's Rep. 461 (Pa. Ct. Oyer & Terminer 1870) (strangling six-year-old during rape); Buel v. People, 78 N.Y. 492 (1879) (strangling with rope during rape); People v. Deacons, 16 N.E. 676 (N.Y. 1888) (clubbing and then strangling prostrate victim); Cook v. State, 18 S.W. 412 (Tex. Ct. App. 1892)

(strangling rape victim); Commonwealth v. Epps, 44 A. 570 (Pa. 1899) (strangling robbery victim).

201. State v. Boice, 1 Hous. Crim. Cas. 355 (Del. Ct. Oyer & Terminer 1871) (punching elderly man); Brown v. Commonwealth, 76 Pa. 319 (1874) (bludgeoning); Dolan v. People, 64 N.Y. 485 (1876) (clubbing with piece of iron); Duran v. State, 14 Tex. Ct. App. 195 (1883) (clubbing with pistol); Stanley v. State, 14 Tex. Ct. App. 315 (1883) (axe murder); Giles v. State, 4 S.W. 886 (Tex. Ct. App. 1887) (clubbing with axe handle); State v. Johnson, 34 N.W. 177 (Iowa 1887) (blow on head); People v. Johnson, 17 N.E. 684 (N.Y. 1888) (clubbing with piece of iron); State v. Donnelly, 32 S.W. 1124 (Mo. 1895) (fracturing skull); Garza v. State, 46 S.W. 242 (Tex. Crim. App. 1898) (clubbing with log); Little v. State, 47 S.W. 984 (Tex. Crim. App. 1898) (clubbing with iron bar); State v. Cross, 46 A. 148 (Conn. 1900) (repeated punching of head on floor).

202. State v. Jennings, 18 Mo. 435 (1853).

203. State v. Nueslein, 25 Mo. 111 (1857).

204. Commonwealth v. Pemberton, 118 Mass. 36 (1875).

205. Moynihan v. State, 70 Ind. 126 (1880); Commonwealth v. Eagan, 42 A. 374 (Pa. 1899).

206. Cox v. People, 80 N.Y. 500 (1880).

207. Commonwealth v. Gilbert, 165 Mass. 45 (1895); Morgan v. State, 71 N.W. 788 (Neb. 1897).

208. Stocking v. State, 7 Ind. 326 (1855).

209. Adams v. People, 109 Ill. 444 (1884).

210. State v. Deschamps, 7 So. 703 (La. 1890).

211. Williams v. State, 17 S.W. 408 (Tex. Ct. App. 1891).

212. Keaton v. State, 57 S.W. 1125 (Tex. Crim. App. 1900).

213. State v. Myers, 40 P. 626 (Wash. 1895); Reddick v. Commonwealth, 33 S.W. 416 (Ky. 1895).

214. People v. Willett, 62 N.W. 1115 (Mich. 1895).

215. Nite v. State, 54 S.W. 763 (Tex. Crim. App. 1899).

216. People v. Van Steenburgh, 1 Parker's Crim. Rep. 39 (N.Y. Ct. Oyer & Terminer 1845).

217. State v. Levelle, 13 S.E. 319 (S.C. 1891).

218. State v. Smith, 32 Me. 369 (1851); State v. Leeper, 30 N.W. 501 (Iowa 1886); State v. Lodge, 33 A. 312 (Del. Ct. Oyer & Terminer 1892); State v. Minard, 65 N.W. 147 (Iowa 1895).

219. Keaton v. State, 57 S.W. 1125 (Tex. Crim. App. 1900).

220. Cox v. People, 80 N.Y. 500 (1880).

221. 1 Parker's Crim. Rep. 39 (N.Y. Ct. Oyer & Terminer 1845).

222. CA, GA, IL, IA, KY, NY, PA, TX, UT, WI, US.

223. 8 Iowa 477, 505 (1859).

224. 65 N.W. 387, 394 (Iowa 1895).

304 NOTES TO CHAPTER 8

225. Id.

226. Pa. Legislature Addendum to Act of April 5, 1790, in 2 The Laws of the Commonwealth of Pennsylvania 542, 562 (1810) (citations omitted), 566–67.

227. McGinnis v. State, 31 Ga. 236 (1860). People v. Pool, 27 Cal. 572, 580–82 (1865). People v. Vasquez, 49 Cal. 560, 562–63 (1875). Ruloff v. People, 45 N.Y. 213, 216–17 (1871).

228. Lamb v. People, 96 Ill. 73, 83–84 (1880).

229. Adams v. People, 109 Ill. 444, 449–50 (1884).

230. Darlington v. State, 50 S.W. 375, 376 (Tex. Crim. App. 1899).

231. State v. Morgan, 61 P. 527, 530 (Utah 1900).

232. Miller v. State, 25 Wis. 384, 388–89 (1870); People v. Olsen, 22 P. 125, 126–27 (Cal. 1889); People v. Wilson, 40 N.E. 392, 394–95 (N.Y. 1895). Consistent with this position is Mickey v. Commonwealth, 72 Ky. 593 (1873).

233. 72 Eng. Rep. 458, 458 (K.B. 1535).

234. Webb, 1736, 233.

235. 1 Toulmin & Blair, 1804, 51.

236. Pa. Legislature, Addendum to Act of April 5, 1790 (1810), in 2 The Laws of the Commonwealth of Pennsylvania 542, 562 (1810) (citations omitted, 566–67.

237. 27 F. Cas. 899, 901 (C.C.D.R.I. 1813) (No. 16,196).

238. People v. Pool, 27 Cal. 572, 581 (1865).

239. Ruloff v. People, 45 N.Y. 213, 217 (1871).

240. People v. Van Steenburgh, 1 Parker's Crim. Rep. 39 (N.Y. Ct. Oyer & Terminer 1845) (punishing shooters in the course of a riot); State v. Jennings, 18 Mo. 435 (1853) (punishing assailants who committed felony of grievous bodily injury); McGinnis v. State, 31 Ga. 236 (1860) (punishing participants in riot, defined as an act of violence); Bissot v. State, 53 Ind. 408 (1876) (punishing the shooter of a resisting watchman during burglary); Moynihan v. State, 70 Ind. 126 (1880) (punishing one who battered another during a robbery); Poe v. State, 78 Tenn. 673 (1882) (punishing shooters who committed "theft or robbery"); Adams v. People, 109 Ill. 444 (1884) (punishing a participant in a robbery who helped push a robbery victim off a moving train); People v. Wilson, 40 N.E. 392 (N.Y. 1895) (punishing the batterer of a policeman shot by an accomplice during escape); Commonwealth v. Eagan, 42 A. 374 (Pa. 1899) (punishing a batterer who attempted to commit robbery).

241. People v. Pool, 27 Cal. 572 (1865); Miller v. State, 25 Wis. 384 (1870) (third-degree murder); People v. Vasquez, 49 Cal. 560 (1875); Isaacs v. State, 38 S.W. 40 (Tex. Crim. App. 1896); State v. Schmidt, 38 S.W. 719 (Mo. 1897); Darlington v. State, 50 S.W. 375 (Tex. Crim. App. 1899); Nite v. State, 54 S.W. 763 (Tex. Crim. App. 1899).

242. Nite, 54 S.W. 763 (Texas).

243. Darlington, 50 S.W. 375 (Texas).

244. Isaacs, 38 S.W. 40 (Texas).

245. Miller, 25 Wis. 384.

246. 22 P. 125 (Cal. 1889). The opinion does not say whether the defendant knew his co-felons were armed, or whether he was aware of any danger of resistance or pursuit.

Chapter 9

1. Haw. Rev. Stat. § 707–701 (2006); Ky. Rev. Stat. Ann. § 507.020 (1984).

2. People v. Aaron, 409 Mich. 672, 708–09, 299 N.W.2d 304 (1980); State v. Doucette, 143 Vt. 573, 579, 470 A.2d 676, 680 (1983).

3. N.M. Stat. § 30–2–1 (1978).

4. State v. Ortega, 112 N.M. 554, 563, 817 P.2d 1196, 1205 (1991).

5. N.H. Rev. Stat. Ann. § 630:1–b (1974); N.H. Rev. Stat. Ann. § 626:7 (2) (1971).

6. Ark. Code Ann. § 5–10–102 (2006).

7. Ark. Code Ann. § 5–10–103 (2006).

8. 720 Ill. Comp. Stat. 5/9–1 (a) (3) (2010).

9. 720 Ill. Comp. Stat. 5/2–8 (1996).

10. 720 Ill. Comp. Stat. 5/9–1 (a) (2) (2010).

11. 720 Ill. Comp. Stat. 5/9–1 (1961), Illinois Laws 1961, 1983, § 9–1 (Criminal Code of 1961 committee comment at 15); People v. McEwen 157, 510 N.E.2d 74, 79 Ill. App. 3d 222, 228–29 (Ill. App. Ct. 1987); People v. Guest, 115 Ill.2d 72, 503 N.E.2d 255 (1986).

12. N.D. Cent. Code § 12.1–02–02.3 (1973).

13. N.D. Cent. Code § 12.1–02–02.1, 2.2 (1973).

14. N.D. Cent. Code § 12.1–16–01 (1993).

15. Id.

16. Final Report of the National Commission on Reform of Federal Criminal Laws § 1601, 174–75 (1971).

17. Although Oregon's code also defines homicide as requiring culpability in Or. Rev. Stat. § 163.005 (2007), Oregon's Supreme Court treats felony murder as requiring no culpable mental state beyond that required for the felony. (State v. Reams, 636 P.2d 913, 919–20, 292 Or. 1, 13 (1981) (en banc).

18. Del. Code Ann. tit. 11 § 636 (2009).

19. Del. Code Ann. tit. 11 § 635 (2004).

20. 18 Pa. Cons. Stat. § 302 (A) (1973).

21. 18 Pa. Cons. Stat. § 2501 (1973).

22. 18 Pa. Cons. Stat. § 2502 (1978).

23. Commonwealth v. Hassein, 490 A.2d 438, 454, 340 Pa. Super. 318, 348 (Pa. Super. Ct. 1985).

24. Ala. Code § 13A-6–1 (2006).

25. Ala. Code § 13A-6–2 (2006).

26. Ala. Code § 13A-6–2 (2006) (Official Commentary, 256).

27. Ex parte Mitchell, 936 So. 2d 1094 (Ala. Crim. App. 2006); Witherspoon v. State,

2009 WL 1164989 (Ala. Crim. App. 2009); Lewis v. State, 474 So. 2d 766 (Ala. Crim. App. 1985).

    28. Ala. Code § 13A-2-4 (b) (1977).

    29. Tex. Penal Code Ann. § 19.01 (1993).

    30. Tex. Penal Code Ann. § 6.02 (2005).

    31. State v. Kuykendall, 609 S.W.2d 791 (Tex. Crim App. 1980).

    32. State v. Rodriguez, 953 S.W.2d 342 (Tex. App. 1997).

    33. Me. Rev. Stat. Ann. tit. 17–A § 202 (1991).

    34. N.J. Stat. Ann. § 2C:2–2 (1981).

    35. N.J. Stat. Ann. § 2C:2–3 (1978).

    36. State v. Martin, 119 N.J. 2, 31, 573 A.2d 1359 (1990).

    37. Id., 32.

    38. Cal. Penal Code § 189 (2002); Idaho Code Ann. § 18–4001, 4003 (2002); Nev. Rev. Stat. § 200.010 (2005), 200.020; S.C. Code Ann. § 16–3–10 (1962); Iowa Code Ann. § 707.1; 18 U.S.C. § 1111 (2003); Miss. Code Ann. § 97–3–19(c) (2004), 97–3–27 (1994); R.I. Gen. Laws § 11–23–1 (2008).

    39. People v. Washington, 62 Cal. 2d 777 (1965).

    40. 45 Cal. 4th 1172, 203 P.3d 425 (2009).

    41. People v. Chun, 203 P.3d 425, 430 (Cal. 2009).

    42. Nay v. State. 123 Nev. 326, 332, 167 P.3d 430, 434 (2007).

    43. Id., 333.

    44. Labastida v. State, 986 P.2d 443, 115 Nev. 298 (1999).

    45. State v. Lankford, 781 P.2d 197, 116 Idaho 860, 866 (1989).

    46. State v. Norris, 328 S.E.2d 339, 285 S.C. 86, 91 (1985) (overruled on other grounds).

    47. Gore v. Leeke, 199 S.E.2d 755, 261 S.C. 308 (1973).

    48. Lowry v. State, 657 S.E.2d 760, 376 S.C. 499 (2008).

    49. S.C. Jury Instr.–Crim. § 2–1, SC JI CRIMINAL § 2–1 (Lexis 2007) (jury instructions on murder).

    50. S.C. Jury Instr.–Crim. § 2–3, SC JI CRIMINAL § 2–3 (Lexis 2007) (jury instructions on felony murder) (emphasis added).

    51. State v. Taylor, 287 N.W.2d 576, 577 (Iowa 1980).

    52. 420 N.W.2d 791 (Iowa 1988) (overruled on other grounds).

    53. Id., 794.

    54. Id., 795.

    55. State v. Bennet 503 N.W.2d 42, 45 (Iowa Ct. App. 1993).

    56. State v. Heemstra, 721 N.W.2d 554 (Iowa 2006).

    57. See Boyd v. State, 2006–KA-00562–SCT, 977 So. 2d 329 (Miss. 2008).

    58. Lee v. State, 98–CA-00015–SCT, 759 So. 2d 390 (Miss. 2000).

    59. In re Leon, 122 R.I. 548, 553, 410 A.2d 121, 124, quoting Perkins, Criminal Law 44 (2d ed. 1969).

60. Va. Code Ann. § 18.2–33 (1999).

61. Wooden v. Commonwealth, 284 S.E.2d 811, 814, 222 Va. 758, 762 (1981).

62. Cotton v. Commonwealth, 35 Va.App. 511, 515, 546 S.E.2d 241, 243 (Va. Ct. App. 2001) (quoting John L. Costello, Virginia Criminal Law and Procedure § 3.4–3, 33 (2d ed. 1995)); accord Kennemore v. Commonwealth, 653 S.E.2d 606, 50 Va. App. 703 (Va. Ct. App. 2007).

63. United States v. Shea, 211 F.3d 658 (1st Cir. 2000); United States v. Pearson, 159 F.3d 480, 485 (10th Cir. 1998).

64. Alaska Stat. § 11.41.110 (1999); Ariz. Rev. Stat. Ann. § 13–1105 (2009); Colo. Rev. Stat. Ann. § 18–3–102 (2000); Conn. Gen. Stat. Ann. § 53a–54c (1992); D.C. Code § 22–2401 (2001); Idaho Code Ann. § 18–4003 (2001); Ind. Code § 35–42–1–1 (2007); Iowa Code Ann. § 707.2 (2009); Kansas Stat. Ann. § 21–3401 (1993); LA. Rev. Stat. Ann. § 14:30 (2009); ME. Rev. Stat. Ann. tit. 17–A § 202 (1991); Neb. Rev. Stat. § 28–303 (2002); N.J. Stat. Ann. § 2C:11–3 (2007); N.Y. Penal Law § 125.25 (McKinney 2006); N.D. Cent. Code § 12.1–16–01 (1993); Ohio Rev. Code Ann. § 2903.02 (1998); Or. Rev. Stat. § 163.115 (2009); 18 PA. Cons. Stat. Ann. § 2502 (1978); S.D. Codified Laws § 22–16–4 (2005); Tenn. Code Ann. § 39–13–202 (2007); Utah Code Ann. § 76–5–203 (2009); W. Va. Code § 61–2–1 (1991); Wis. Stat. Ann. § 940.03 (2005); Wyo. Stat. Ann. § 6–2–101 (2007); 18 U.S.C. § 1111 (2003). Comber v. U.S., 584 A.2d 26, 40 (D.C. Cir. 1990); Kitt v. U.S., 904 A.2d 348, 356 (2006). There has been no reported case involving a federal charge of second-degree felony murder, but see U.S. v Pearson, 159 F.3d 480 (1998) (speculating that such a charge is possible).

65. Ala. Code § 13A-6–2 (2006); Cal. Penal Code § 189 (2002); Fla. Stat. § 782.04 (2010); 720 Ill. Comp. Stat. 5/9–1 (a) (3) (2010); Md. Code Ann., Crim. Law § 2–201(a) (4) (Lexis Nexis 2009); Minn. Stat. § 609.185 (2006); Miss. Code Ann. § 97–3–19 (2004); Mont. Code Ann. § 45–5–102 (1999); Nev. Rev. Stat. § 200.030 (2007); N.C. Gen. Stat. § 14–17 (2005); Okla. Stat. tit. 21, § 701.7 (2002); R.I. Gen. Laws § 11–23–1 (2010); VA. Code Ann. § 18.2–32 (1998); Wash. Rev. Code § 9A.32.030(1)(c) (2006).

66. LaFave, 2010, 788; Pa. Suggested Standard Jury Instr.- Crim. 15.2502B, Pa. SSJI (Crim) 15.2502B (Lexis 2008).

67. 720 Ill. Comp. Stat. 5/9–1 (a) (3) (2010), Iowa Code Ann. § 707.2 (2009) ("Forcible"); Ohio Rev. Code Ann. § 2903.02 (1998) ("Violent"); Kansas Stat. Ann. § 21–3401 (1993) ("Inherently Dangerous"); and Ala. Code § 13A-6–2 (2006) ("clearly dangerous to human life").

68. Conn. Gen. Stat. Ann. § 53a-54c (1992) (does not list arson); Minn. Stat. § 609.185 (2006) (does not list arson, burglary, robbery, or kidnapping).

69. Ind. Code § 35–42–1–1 (2007), Tenn. Code Ann. § 39–13–202 (2007), N.J. Stat. Ann. § 2C:11–3 (2007) and Wis. Stat. Ann. § 940.03 (2005) (hijacking); Fla. Stat. § 782.04 (2010), Idaho Code Ann. § 18–4003 (2001), Ind. Code § 35–42–1–1 (2007), Ohio Rev. Code Ann. § 2903.02 (1998), Or. Rev. Stat. § 163.115 (2009), S.D. Codified Laws § 22–16–4

(2005) (bombing); Ind. Code § 35–42–1–1 (2007), Or. Rev. Stat. § 163.115 (2009) (forced prostitution), and Ohio Rev. Code Ann. § 2903.02 (1998) (exposure to HIV).

70. Ala. Code § 13A-6–2 (2006); Alaska Stat. § 11.41.110 (1999); Ariz. Rev. Stat. Ann. § 13–1105 (2009); Colo. Rev. Stat. Ann. § 18–3–102 (2000); Conn. Gen. Stat. Ann. § 53a–54c (1992); Iowa Code Ann. § 707.2 (2009); Fla. Stat. § 782.04 (2010); La. Rev. Stat. Ann. § 14:30 (2009); Me. Rev. Stat. Ann. tit. 17–A § 202 (1991); Md. Code Ann., Crim. Law § 2–201(a)(4) (Lexis Nexis 2009); Mont. Code Ann. § 45–5–102 (1999); N.J. Stat. Ann. § 2C:11–3 (2007); N.Y. Penal Law § 125.25 (McKinney 2006); N.D. Cent. Code § 12.1–16–01 (1993); Ohio Rev. Code Ann. § 2903.02 (1998); Okla. Stat. tit. 21, § 701.7 (2002); Or. Rev. Stat. § 163.115 (2009); Utah Code Ann. § 76–5–203 (2009); W. Va. Code § 61–2–1 (1991); Wyo. Stat. Ann. § 6–2–101 (2007); 18 U.S.C. § 1111 (2003).

71. Fla. Stat. § 782.04 (2010); Idaho Code Ann. § 18–4003 (2001); Kansas Stat. Ann. § 21–3401 (1993); LA. Rev. Stat. Ann. § 14:30 (2009); Nev. Rev. Stat. § 200.030 (2007); Ohio Rev. Code Ann. § 2903.02 (1998); Or. Rev. Stat. § 163.115 (2009); Tenn. Code Ann. § 39–13–202 (2007); Utah Code Ann. § 76–5–203 (2009); Wyo. Stat. Ann. § 6–2–101 (2007); D.C. Code § 22–2401 (2001); 18 U.S.C. § 1111 (2003).

72. Alaska Stat. § 11.41.110 (1999); Ariz. Rev. Stat. Ann. § 13–1105 (2009); Fla. Stat. § 782.04 (2010); Ind. Code § 35–42–1–1 (2007); Kansas Stat. Ann. § 21–3401 (1993); LA. Rev. Stat. Ann. § 14:30 (2009); Ohio Rev. Code Ann. § 2903.02 (1998); Okla. Stat. tit. 21, § 701.7 (2002),; R.I. Gen. Laws § 11–23–1 (2010); Utah Code Ann. § 76–5–203 (2009); W. Va. Code § 61–2–1 (1991); D.C. Code § 22–2401 (2001). Some states also have separate drug distribution death offenses. See Col. Rev. Stat. 18–3–102 (e); N.J. Stat. Ann. § 2C:11–3 (2007); Nev. Rev. Stat. § 200.030 (2007); Minn. Stat. § 609.195 (b) (2006).

73. Ariz. Rev. Stat. Ann. § 13–1105 (2009), Fla. Stat. § 782.04 (2010); Idaho Code Ann. § 18–4003 (2001); Iowa Code Ann. § 707.2 (2009); 720 Ill. Comp. Stat. 5/9–1 (a) (3) (2010); Kansas Stat. Ann. § 21–3401 (1993); Nev. Rev. Stat. § 200.030 (2007); N.J. Stat. Ann. § 2C:11–3 (2007); N.D. Cent. Code § 12.1–16–01 (1993); Ohio Rev. Code Ann. § 2903.02 (1998); Tenn. Code Ann. § 39–13–202 (2007); 18 U.S.C. § 1111 (2003).

74. Ind. Code § 35–42–1–1 (2007); Kansas Stat. Ann. § 21–3401 (1993).

75. Fla. Stat. § 782.04 (2010); Kansas Stat. Ann. § 21–3401 (1993); 720 Ill. Comp. Stat. 5/9–1 (a) (3) (2010); ME. Rev. Stat. Ann. tit. 17–A § 202 (1991); Ohio Rev. Code Ann. § 2903.02 (1998); Okla. Stat. tit. 21, § 701.7 (2002); Tenn. Code Ann. § 39–13–202 (2007); 18 U.S.C. § 1111 (2003).

76. Cal. Penal Code § 189 (2002); D.C. Code § 22–2401 (2001); 720 Ill. Comp. Stat. 5/9–1 (a) (3) (2010); Iowa Code Ann. § 707.2 (2009); Kansas Stat. Ann. § 21–3401 (1993); LA. Rev. Stat. Ann. § 14:30 (2009); Md. Code Ann., Crim. Law 2–201(a)(4) (Lexis Nexis 2009); Minn. Stat. § 609.185 (2006); Ohio Rev. Code Ann. § 2903.02 (1998); Okla. Stat. tit. 21, § 701.7 (2002); Wis. Stat. Ann. § 940.03 (2005).

77. Kansas Stat. Ann. § 21–3401 (1993); Tenn. Code Ann. § 39–13–202 (2007); Wis. Stat. Ann. § 940.03 (2005).

78. W. Va. Code § 61–2–1 (1991); R.I. Gen. Laws § 11–23–1 (2010).

79. Wis. Stat. Ann. § 940.03 (2005).

80. Fla. Stat. § 782.04 (2010); R.I. Gen. Laws § 11–23–1 (2010).

81. Cal. Penal Code § 189 (2002).

82. Melonie Heron et al. "Deaths: Final Data for 2006," *National Vital Statistics Reports*, vol. 57, no. 14, April 17, 2009, p. 3, http://www.cdc.gov/nchs/data/nvsr/nvsr57/nvsr57_14.pdf (12,791 homicide deaths by firearm in 2006). Centers for Disease Control and Prevention: National Center for Injury Prevention and Control—Assault Firearm Gunshot Nonfatal Injuries and Rates per 100,000, http://webappa.cdc.gov/sasweb/ncipc/nfirates2001.html (52,748 intentional but nonfatal firearm injuries in 2006).

83. Hutson et al., 1994, 324–27.

84. Federal Bureau of Investigation, *Crime in the United States 2007, Uniform Crime Reports*, "Offense Definitions," http://www.fbi.gov/ucr/cius2007/about/index.html [hereafter FBI] (defining aggravated assault); FBI Table 16 (603,212 aggravated assaults in 2007). Centers for Disease Control and Prevention: National Center for Injury Prevention and Control—Homicide Injury Deaths and Rates per 100,000, available at http://webappa.cdc.gov/sasweb/ncipc/mortrate10_sy.html (18,361 homicide deaths due to injury in 2007).

85. Stephen, 1883, 3.

86. Zimring & Zuehl, 8, tbl. 1, 1986 (5.2 killings per 1,000 robberies); Wolfgang, 1958 (5.9 homicides per 1,000 robberies for Philadelphia, 1948–52).

87. Wilson & Abrahamse, 1992, 362.

88. Binder, Culpability, 2008, 968.

89. United States Fire Administration, *Intentionally Set Structure Fires*, Arson fire statistics, http://www.usfa.dhs.gov/statistics/arson/ (for 2005–08, 124,500 arson fires and 1,230 deaths).

90. See Simons, 1997, 1121–24.

91. 18 U.S.C. § 2381 (1994).

92. 18 U.S.C. § 794b (1996). However, federal criminal law defines several espionage offenses that do not require the occurrence or expectation of war. See, e.g., 18 U.S.C. § 793 (1996); 18 U.S.C. § 794 (1996).

93. 18 U.S.C.A. § 2331 (2001).

94. LaFave, 2010, 1089–90.

95. Model Penal Code § 220.1(1).

96. State v. Bonner, 330 N.C. 536, 546, 411 S.E.2d 598, 604 (1992).

97. State v. Allen, 322 N.C. 176, 196 (1988); State v. Vickers, 306 N.C. 90 (1982).

98. Zimring, 1997, 69 (two fatalities per 10,000 burglaries for New York City in 1992); Federal Bureau of Investigation, *Crime in the United States 2007, Uniform Crime Reports*, Burglary, Expanded Homicide Data, http://www.fbi.gov/ucr/cius2007/documents/

burglarymain.pdf and http://www.fbi.gov/ucr/cius2007/documents/expandedhomicide main.pdf (86 of 1,749,497 reported burglaries resulted in death in 2007).

99. State v. Dixon, 222 Neb. 787, 387 N.W.2d 682 (1986).

100. 150 Cal.Rptr. 515 (Cal. Ct. App. 1978).

101. 183 Wis. 2d 316, 515 N.W.2d 531 (Wis. Ct. App. 1994).

102. 12 Ill. App. 3d 412, 297 N.E.2d 582 (Ill. App. Ct. 1973).

103. Id., 417.

104. Ala. Code § 13A-6–2 (2006) (of a dwelling, or armed, or causes injury); Alaska Stat. § 11.41.110 (1999) (of a dwelling, armed, or attempts or causes injury); D.C. Code § 22–2401 (2001) (of a dwelling while armed); Iowa Code Ann. § 707.2 (2009) (occupied structure with persons present; and armed, recklessly injures, or sexually assaults); LA. Rev. Stat. Ann. § 14:30 (2009) (armed, or commits battery); Md. Code Ann., Crim. Law § 2–201(a)(4) (Lexis Nexis 2009) (of a dwelling or barn); Mass. Gen. Laws ch. 265, § 1 (2008) (of a dwelling, armed, or commits assault); N.C. Gen. Stat. § 14–17 (2005) (of a dwelling at night, according to case law); Ohio Rev. Code Ann. § 2903.02 (1998) (in an occupied structure with person present, or dwelling when person likely to be present); Okla. Stat. tit. 21, § 701.7 (2002) (of a dwelling with victim present); Or. Rev. Stat. § 163.115 (2009) (of a dwelling, or armed, or causes or attempts injury); R.I. Gen. Laws § 11–23–1 (2010) (of a dwelling at night, according to case law); VA. Code Ann. § 18.2–32 (1998) (of a dwelling at night); Wash. Rev. Code § 9A.32.030(1)(c) (2006) (armed, or commits assault); W. Va. Code § 61–2–1 (1991); Wis. Stat. Ann. § 940.03 (2005) (of a dwelling with persons present, armed, uses explosive, or commits battery).

105. Slip Copy, 2008 WL 852074, 2008 Ohio 1539 (Ohio Ct. App. 2008).

106. Ohio Rev. Code Ann. § 2901.21 (d) (1) (1972).

107. Ohio Rev. Code Ann. § 2901.21 (a) (1) (1972).

108. Ohio Rev. Code Ann. § 2901.04 (a) (2004).

109. Dripps, 2003; Lijtmaer, 2008.

110. 109 P.3d 647 (Colo. 2005).

111. 795 A.2d 1010 (Pa. Super. Ct. 2002).

112. 18 PA. Cons. Stat. Ann. § 306 (c) (1) (1998).

113. AZ, CA, CO, CT, FL, ID, IL, IN, KS, ME, MS, MT, NE, NV, NJ, NY, ND, PA, SD, TN, UT, WY, US.

114. Colo. Rev. Stat. Ann. § 18–3–102 (2000); Conn. Gen. Stat. Ann. § 53a–54c (1992); 17–A Me.Rev.Stat. § 202 (2009); N.Y. Penal Law § 125.25 (McKinney 2006); N.J. Stat. Ann. § 2C:11–3 (2007); N.D. Cent. Code § 12.1–16–01 (1993).

115. 23 S.W. 3d 289 (Tenn. 2000).

116. State v. Severs, 759 S.W.2d 935 (Tenn. Crim. App. 1988).

117. 529 P.2d 124 (Kan. 1974).

118. Id., 126.

119. United States Department of Health and Human Services, Substance Abuse

and Mental Health Services Administration, 2007 National Survey on Drug Use and Health, http://dx.doi.org/10.3886/ICPSR23782; Lois A. Fingerhut and Centers for Disease Control and Prevention, Increases in Poisoning and Methadone-Related Deaths: United States, 1999–2005, Health E-Stats, Feb. 2008, 4, http://www.cdc.gov/nchs/data/hestat/poisoning/poisoning.pdf

120. Binder, Culpability, 2008, 1023–24.

121. 511 S.E.2d 469 (W.Va. 1998).

122. 398 S.E.2d 698 (Va. Ct. App. 1990).

123. AL, CA, DE, FL, GA, IL, MD, MA, MN, MS, MO, MT, NV, NC, OK, RI, SC, TX, VA, WA (note that I am not including felony aggravator states that require gross recklessness).

124. DE, GA, MA, MO, SC, TX. Massachusetts permits felonies to serve as predicates for felony murder regardless of punishment, only if inherently dangerous. Massachusetts Superior Court Criminal Practice Jury Instructions § 2.2.

125. Cal. Penal Code § 192 (West 2008).

126. People v. Ford, 388 P.2d 892 (Cal. 1964); People v. Williams, 406 P.2d 647 (Cal. 1965); People v. Phillips, 414 P.2d 353 (Cal. 1966).

127. People v. Williams, 406 P.2d 647 (Cal. 1965).

128. 49 Cal.3d 615, 627, 778 P.2d 549 (1989).

129. Nev. Rev. Stat. § 200.030 (2007).

130. Sheriff of Clark County v. Morris, 99 Nev. 109, 118, 659 P.2d 852, 859 (1983).

131. Minn. Stat. § 609.19 (2010).

132. State v. Nunn, 297 N.W.2d 752 (Minn. 1980); State v. Back, 341 N.W.2d 273 (1983); accord State v. Cole, 542 N.W.2d 43 (Minn. 1996); accord State v. Gorman, 532 N.W.2d 229 (Minn. Ct. App. 1995).

133. State v. Anderson, 666 N.W.2d 696 (Minn. 2003); accord State v. Smoot, 737 N.W.2d 849 (Minn. Ct. App. 2006).

134. Mass. Gen. Laws ch. 265, § 1 (2008).

135. Commonwealth v. Jackson, 81 Mass. (15 Gray) 187, 1860 WL 6796 (1860); Commonwealth v. Mink, 123 Mass. 422, 1877 WL 10314 (1877) (dictum).

136. 386 Mass. 492, 436 N.E.2d 400 (1982); accord Commonwealth v. Moran, 387 Mass. 644 (1982); Commonwealth v. Ortiz, 408 Mass. 463, 560 N.E.2d 698 (1990); Comm. v. Chase, 42 Mass. App. Ct. 749, 679 N.E.2d 1021 (Mass App. Ct. 1997) (larceny, theft of truck).

137. Massachusetts Superior Court Criminal Practice Jury Instructions § 2.2; Commonwealth v. Garner; 59 Mass. App. Ct. 356, 357, 795 N.E.2d 1202, 1209 (Mass App. Ct. 2003).

138. Ala. Code § 13A–6–2 (2006).

139. Ex parte Mitchell, 936 So. 2d 1094 (Ala. Crim. App. 2006).

140. Tex. Penal Code Ann. § 19.02 (Vernon 2003).

141. In re E.B.M., 2005 WL 2100481 (Tex. App. 2005).

142. 720 Ill. Comp. Stat. 5/2–8 (1995).

143. People v. Golson, 207 N.E.2d 68 (Ill. 1965).

144. People v. Belk, 784 N.E.2d 825 (Ill. 2003); People v. McCarty, 785 N.E.2d 859 (Ill. 2003).

145. People v. Pugh, 634 N.E.2d 34, 35, 261 Ill. App. 3d 75, 77 (Ill. App. Ct. 1994).

146. 545 N.E.2d 986 (Ill. App. Ct. 1989).

147. Jenkins v. Nelson, 157 F.3d 485 (7th Cir. 1998).

148. Mont. Code Ann. § 45–5–102 (1999).

149. State ex rel. Murphy v. McKinnon, 556 P.2d 906 (Mont. 1976).

150. N.C. Gen. Stat. § 14–17 (2005).

151. State v. Vines, 345 S.E.2d 169, 175 (N.C. 1986); State v. Davis, 290 S.E.2d 574, 590–91 (N.C. 1982).

152. State v. Fields, 337 S.E.2d 518 (N.C. 1985).

153. State v. Jones, 538 S.E.2d 917 (N.C. 2000).

154. Jenkins v. State, 230 A.2d 262 (Del. 1967).

155. Del. Code Ann. tit. 11, § 636 (2009).

156. Ga. Code Ann. § 16–5–1 (West 2009).

157. Ford v. State 423 S.E.2d 255, 256 (Ga. 1992).

158. Metts v. State, 511 S.E.2d 508 (1999); Mosley v. State, 272 Ga. 881, 536 S.E.2d 150 (2000); Hulme v. State, 273 Ga. 676, 544 S.E.2d 138 (2001).

159. State v. Tiraboschi, 504 S.E.2d 689, 691 (Ga. 1998).

160. Miller v. State, 571 S.E.2d 788 (Ga. 2002).

161. Id., 793.

162. Id.

163. Id.

164. Smith v. Hardrick, 464 SE 2d 198, 266 Ga. 54 (1995).

165. Miller v. Martin, 2007 U.S. Dist. LEXIS 13112.

166. An earlier case approved an instruction requiring intentional injury. Wade v. State, 401 S.E.2d 701.

167. Miller v. Martin, 47–48.

168. R.I. Gen. Laws § 11–23–1 (2010).

169. 410 A.2d 121, 122 R.I. 548 (1980).

170. State v. Stewart, 663 A.2d 912 (R.I. 1995) (child neglect).

171. Wood v. State, 62 A.2d 576 (Md. 1948); Stansbury v. State, 146 A.2d 17, 218 Md. 255 (1958).

172. Fisher and Utley v. State, 786 A.2d 706, 367 Md. 218 (2001).

173. This rule is now also reflected in Maryland's pattern jury instructions. M.L. Crim. Pattern Jury Instr. 4:17.7.2, MPJI-Cr 4:17.7 (2007).

174. Fisher, 786 A.2d 706, 728–29.

175. 1978 OK CR 77, 581 P.2d 914 (Okl. Crim. App. 1978).

176. Id., 916.

177. Malaske v. State, 2004 OK CR 18, 89 P.3d 1116 (2004) (emphasis added).

178. 323 S.E.2d 90, 228 Va. 397 (1984).

179. 398 S.E.2d 698, 699–700 (Va. App. 1990).

180. Doane v. Commonwealth, 237 S.E.2d 797, 218 Va. 500 (1977); Haskell v. Commonwealth, 243 S.E.2d 477, 218 Va. 1033 (1978).

181. Doane, 237 S.E.2d 797; Commonwealth v. Montague, 536 S.E.2d 910, 260 Va. 697 (2000).

182. King v. Commonwealth, 368 S.E.2d 704, 6 Va. App. 351 (Va. Ct. App. 1988).

183. Id., 705.

184. Griffin v. Commonwealth, 533 S.E.2d 653 (Va. Ct. App. 2000).

185. 546 S.E.2d 241 (Va. Ct. App. 2001).

186. Gore v. Leeke, 199 S.E.2d 755, 758 (S.C. 1973), citing State v. Thompson, 185 S.E.2d 666, 280 N.C. 202 (1972).

187. State v. Hacker, 510 So. 2d 304, 306 (Fla. Dist. Ct. App. 1986) (emphasis added); Parker v. State, 570 So. 2d 1048, 1051 (Fla. Dist. Ct. App. 1990).

188. Santiago v. State, 874 So. 2d 617 (Fla. Dist. Ct. App. 2004); State v. Williams, 776 So. 2d 1066 (Fla. Dist. Ct. App. 2001).

189. Allen v. State, 690 So. 2d 1332 (Fla. Dist. Ct. App. 1997); State v. House, 831 So. 2d 1230 (Fla. Dist. Ct. App. 2002); Lester v. State, 737 So. 2d 1149 (Fla. Dist. Ct. App. 1999); State v. Williams, 776 So. 2d 1066 (Fla. Dist. Ct. App. 2001); Santiago v. State, 874 So. 2d 617 (Fla. Dist. Ct. App. 2004); cf. Baker v. State, 793 So. 2d 69 (Fla. Dist. Ct. App. 2001); Howard v. State, 545 So. 2d 352 (Fla. Dist. Ct. App. 1989).

190. State v. Diebold, 277 P. 394 (Wash. 1929).

191. State v. Lee, 538 P.2d 538 (Wash. Ct. App. 1974).

192. Miss. Code Ann. § 97–3–19, § 97–3–20 (2004).

193. Mo. Rev. Stat. § 565.021 (2009).

194. State v. Glover, 50 S.W.2d 1049, 1053 (Mo. 1932).

195. State v. Chambers, 524 S.W.2d 826 (Mo. 1975).

196. State v. Colenburg, 773 S.W.2d 184 (Mo. Ct. App. 1989).

197. Id., 187.

198. Id., 187–89.

199. Dissent, 189.

200. Id., 188.

201. 580 S.W.2d 747 (Mo. 1979).

202. Moore v. Wyrick, 766 F.2d 1253 (8th Cir. 1985).

203. 607 S.W.2d 153 (Mo. 1980).

204. 863 S.W.2d 370 (Mo. Ct. App. 1993).

205. 98 S.W.2d 632 (1936).

206. LaFave, 2010, 374.

207. Model Penal Code § 2.03(4) (1980).

208. LaFave, 2010, 376–78.

209. Id., 6.4(h) 374–75, 14.4(d) 795–96.

210. See People v. Washington, 402 P.2d 130 (Cal. 1965); Alvarez v. City of Denver, 525 P.2d 1131 (Colo. 1974); Comer v. State, 977 A.2d 334 (Del. 2009); State v. Pina, 2009 Ida. LEXIS 100 (2009); State v. Sophophone, 19 P.3d 70 (Kan. 2001); State v. Garner, 115, So. 2d 855 (La. 1959); State v. Myers, 99–1849 (La. 04/11/00); 760 So. 2d 310; Campbell v. State, 444 A.2d 1034 (Md. 1982); Commonwealth v. Balliro, 209 N.E.2d 308 (Mass. 1965); State v. Branson, 487 N.W.2d 880 (Minn. 1992); State v. Rust, 250 N.W.2d 867 (Neb. 1977); Sheriff v. Hicks, 506 P.2d 766 (Nev. 1973); State v. Oxendine, 122 S.E. 568 (N.C. 1924); State v. Bonner, 411 S.E.2d 598 (N.C. 1992); Commonwealth v. Redline, 137 A.2d 472 (Pa. 1958); Commonwealth *ex rel* Smith v. Myers, 261 A.2d 550 (Pa. 1970); State v. Severs, 759 S.W.2d 935 (Tenn. Crim. App. 1988); Wooden v. Commonwealth, 284 S.E.2d 811 (Va. 1981).

211. See Del. Code Ann. Tit. 11, §§ 261–64 (2010); 18 Pa. Cons. Sat. § 2501 (2010); 18. Pa. Cons. Sat § 2502(b) (2010); 18 Pa. Cons. Stat. § 303(c),(d); State v. Hokenson, 527 P.2d 487, 492 (Idaho, 1974); State v. Branch, 573 P.2d 1041, 1043 (Kan. 1978); State v. Kalathakis, 563 So. 2d 228 (La. 1990); Fisher v. State, 786 A.2d 706 (Md. 2001); Jackson v. State, 408 A.2d 711 (Md. 1979); State v. Dixon, 387 N.W.2d 682 (Neb. 1986); Sheriff v. Morris, 659 P.2d 852, 859 (Nev. 1983); State v. Bonner, 411 S.E.2d 598 (N.C. 1992); State v. Severs, 759 S.W.2d 935 (Tenn. 1988); State v. Mickens, 123 S.W.3d 355 (Tenn. Crim. App. 2003) (but see State v. Simerly, Lexis 230 (Tenn. Crim. App. Mar. 11, 2004) (no longer requires foreseeability of killing for accomplice liability)); Kennemore v. Commonwealth, 653 S.E.2d 606, 609 (Va. Ct. App. 2007); Cotton v. Commonwealth, 546 S.E.2d 241, 243–44 (Va. Ct. App. 2001); King v. Commonwealth, 368 S.E.2d 704, 706 (Va. Ct. App. 1988); Heacock v. Commonwealth, 323 S.E.2d 90, 94 (Va. 1984); 1–500 Judicial Council of Cal. Crim. Jury Inst. 540C. The exceptions are Colorado and Minnesota.

212. Commonwealth v. Baez, 694 N.E.2d 1269 (Mass. 1998).

213. Ala. Code § 13A-6–1 (2010); Ala. Code § 13A-2–5 (2010); 17–A Me. Rev. Stat. Ann. § 202 (2010); N.J. Stat. Ann. § 2C: 2–3 (West 2010); Tex. Penal Code § 19.01 (2010); Tex. Penal Code § 19.02 (b)(3) (2010); Witherspoon v. State, CR-07–1505 (Ala. Crim. App. May 1, 2009); Lewis v. State, 474 So. 2d 766 (Ala. Crim. App. 1985); State v. Lopez, 845 P.2d 478, 482 (Ariz. Ct. App. 1992); State v. Spates, 405 A.2d 656, 660 (Conn. 1978); Bonhart v. United States, 691 A.2d 160 (D.C. 1997); United States v. Heinlein, 490 F.2d 725 (D.C. 1973); Lee v. United States, 699 A.2d 373 (D.C. 1997); Wilson-Bey v. United States, 903 A.2d 818 (D.C. 2006); Hulme v. State, 544 S.E.2d 138 (Ga. 2001); People v. Jenkins, 545 N.E.2d 986 (Ill. App. Ct. 1989); People v. Smith, 307 N.E.2d 353 (Ill. 1974); People v. Brown, 388 N.E.2d 1256 (Ill. App. Ct. 1979); People v. Burke, 407 N.E.2d 728 (Ill. App. Ct. 1980); People v. Tillman, 388 N.E.2d 1253 (Ill. App. Ct. 1979); People v. Lowery, 687 N.E.2d 973 (Ill. 1997); Sheckles v. State, 684 N.E.2d 201, 204 (Ind. Ct. App. 1997); Moon v. State, 419 N.E.2d 740 (Ind. 1981); State v. Baker, 607 S.W.2d 153 (Mo. 1980); State v. Burrell, 160 S.W.3d 798, 803

(Mo. 2005); State v. Black, 50 S.W.3d 778 (Mo. 2001); State v. Blunt, 863 S.W.2d 370 (Mo. Ct. App. 1993); State v. Glover 50 S.W.2d 1049 (Mo. 1932); State v. Moore, 580 S.W.2d 747 (Mo. 1979); O'Neal v. State, 236 S.W.3d 91 (Mo. Ct. App. 2007); State v. Cole, 248 S.W.3d 91, 95 n.4 (Mo. Ct. App. 2008); State v. Weinberger, 671 P.2d 567 (Mont. 1983); Murphy v. McKinnon, 556 P.2d 906 (Mont. 1976); State v. Martin, 573 A.2d 1359 (N.J. 1990); People v. Flores, 476 N.Y.S. 2d 478 (N.Y. Sup. Ct. 1984); People v. Matos, 634 N.E.2d 157 (N.Y. 1994); State v. Franklin, 2008 Ohio 2264 (Ohio Ct. App. 2008); State v. Adams, 2004 Ohio 3510 (Ct. App. 2004); State v. Ervin, 2006 Ohio 4498 (Ct. App. 2006); State v. Dixon, 2002 Ohio 541, 17 (Ct. App. 2002); Kinchion v. State, 2003 OK CR 28, 81 P.3d 681 (Okla. Crim. App. 2003); Dickens v. State, 2005 OK CR 4, 106 P.3d 599 (Okla. Crim. App. 2005); Johnson v. State, 386 P.2d 336 (Okla. Crim. App. 1963); In re Leon, 410 A.2d 121 (R.I. 1980); State v. Dunn, 850 P.2d 1201, 1216 (Utah 1993) (causation of death requires foreseeability); State v. Jackson, 976 P.2d 1229, 1238 (Wash. 1999); State v. Diebold, 277 P. 394, 396 (Wash. 1929); State v. Weisengoff, 101 S.E. 450, 455 (W. Va. 1919); Ohio Jury Inst. 2–CR 417, CR 417.23; Okla. Jury Inst.-Crim. § 4–60 (200).

214. AZ, CT, DC, IA, ID, IN, KS, LA, ME, NE, NY, OH, PA, TN, UT, and WV.

215. N.D. Cent. Code § 12.1–02–05 (2010); Phillips v. State, 70 P.3d 1128 (Alaska 2003); State v. Gorman, 532 N.W.2d 229 (Minn. Ct. App. 1995); State v. Oimen, 184 Wis.2d 423, 516 N.W.2d 399 (1994).

216. People v. Stamp, 2 Cal. App. 3d 203, 209–10 (1969); see also People v. Hernandez, 169 Cal. App. 3d 282 (1985) (robber liable for heart attack of victim forced to crawl about strenuously).

217. 1–500 Judicial Council of Cal. Jury Inst. 540C (emphasis added).

218. Id. (emphasis added).

219. Id. (emphasis added).

220. People v. Patterson, 778 P.2d 549, 551 (Cal. 1989); People v. Chun, 203 P.3d 425, 429 (Cal. 2009).

221. Phillips v. Alaska, 70 P.3d 1128 (Alaska 2003).

222. Id., 1141.

223. State v. Gorman, 532 N.W.2d 229 (Minn. 1995).

224. People v. Crenshaw, 131 N.E. 576, 578 (Ill. 1921).

225. Durden v. State, 297 S.E.2d 237 (Ga. 1982).

226. People v. Ingram, 492 N.E.2d 1220 (N.Y. 1986).

227. People v. Kibbe, 321 N.E.2d 773, 776 (N.Y. 1974); People v. Flores, 476 N.Y.S.2d 478, 480 (Sup. Ct. 1984).

228. Cf. Howard v. Walker, 406 F.3d 114 (2d. Cir. 2005) (habeas decision overturning felony murder conviction based on admission of "unreasonable" medical testimony that burglary had caused elderly homeowner's heart attack).

229. State v. Reardon, 486 A.2d 112, 117 (Me. 1984).

230. State v. Dixon, 387 N.W.2d 682, 688 (Neb. 1986).

231. People v. Matos, 568 N.Y.S.2d 683 (1991), aff'd 634 N.E.2d 157, 158 (N.Y. 1994).

232. Id., 686.

233. State v. Spates, 405 A.2d 656 (Conn. 1978).

234. State v. Atkinson, 259 S.E.2d 858 (N.C. 1979).

235. State v. Shaw, 921 P.2d 779 (Kan. 1996).

236. See also People v. Cable, 96 A.D.2d 251 (N.Y. App. Div. 1983) (delayed death of elderly victim as a result of binding); In re Anthony M, 471 N.E.2d 447 (N.Y. 1984); People v. Brackett, 510 N.E.2d 877 (Ill. 1987) (delayed deaths of elderly victims following physical injury).

237. People v. Brackett, 510 N.E.2d 877, 882 (Ill. 1987); Commonwealth v. Tevlin, 741 N.E.2d 827 (Mass. 2001).

238. Model Penal Code § 2.03(3)(b) (1980).

Chapter 10

1. Liptak, 2007.

2. E.g., People v. Beeman, 35 Cal. 3d 547 (1984); Fla. Stan. Jury Inst. in Crim. Cases § 3.5(a) (1995) ("conscious intent that the criminal act be done"); 2 Ga. State Bar-Crim. Jury Inst. § 1.42.10; Md. Crim. Pattern Jury Inst. 6:01 (2007); N. J. Stan. Jury Inst. 2C:2–6; Pa. Suggested Stan. Crim. Jury Inst. 8.306(a)(1) (2008); 1–3 Tenn. Crim. Jury Inst. 3.01; 1–3 Crim. Jury Inst. for D.C. Inst. 3.200.

3. Liptak, 2007.

4. See, e.g., State v. Medeiros, 599 A.2d 723 (R.I. 1991); Commonwealth v. Lambert, 795 A.2d 1010, 1013–14 (Pa. Super. Ct. 2002).

5. Conn. Gen.Stat. § 53a–8 (2010); N.Y. Penal Law § 20.00 (2010): Model Penal Code 2.06 (3)(a)(ii), Model Penal Code 2.06 (4) (1980).

6. Lord Dacre's Case, (1535) 72 Eng. Rep. 458 (K.B.).

7. Mansell & Herbert's Case, (1558) 73 Eng. Rep. 279 (K.B.).

8. Rex v. Plummer, (1700) 84 Eng. Rep. 1103, 1105–07 (K.B.).

9. 4 Blackstone, 2002, 200.

10. LaFave, 2010, 789–90.

11. See Ala. Code § 13A-6–2 (2010); Alaska Stat. § 11.41.110 (2010); Ariz. Rev. Stat. § 13–1105 (LexisNexis, 2010); Colo. Rev. Stat. § 18–3–102 (2010); Conn. Gen. Stat. § 53a–54c (2010); N.Y. Penal Law § 125.25 (Consol. 2010); N.D. Cent. Code § 12.1–16–01 (2010); Or. Rev. Stat. § 163.115 (2009); Tex. Penal Code Ann. § 19.02 (2009); Wash. Rev. Code Ann. § 9A.32.030 (LexisNexis 2010); Iowa Code § 703.2 (2009); Minn. Stat. § 609.05, Subd 3 (2009).

12. United States v. Heinlein, 490 F.2d 725, 735 (D.C. 1973); Lee v. United States, 699 A.2d 373, 384 (D.C. 1997); People v. Bongiorno, 192 N.E. 856, 857–58 (Ill. 1934); Vance v. State, 620 N.E.2d 687, 690 (Ind. 1993); Mumford v. State, 313 A.2d 563, 566 (Md. Ct. Spec. App. 1974); Commonwealth v. Heinlein, 152 N.E. 380, 384 (Mass. 1926); Commonwealth v. Ortiz, 560 N.E.2d 698, 700 (Mass. 1990); State v. Day, No. A07–0455 (Minn. Ct. App. June

10, 2008); State v. Mahkuk, 736 N.W.2d 675, 682 (Minn. 2007); Romero v. State, 164 N.W. 554, 555 (Neb. 1917); People v. Hernandez, 624 N.E.2d 661, 665 (N.Y. 1993); State v. Bonner, 411 S.E.2d 598, 600 (N.C. 1992); Commonwealth v. Tate, 401 A.2d 353, 355 (Pa. 1979); Gore v. Leeke, 199 S.E.2d 755, 757–58 (S.C. 1973); D.C. Jury Ins. 3–200; Md. Crim. Pattern Jury Inst. 4:17.7 (2007); S.C. Requests to Charge-Crim. § 2–3; 1–3 Va. Model Jury Ins.– Crim. Ins. No. 3.160 (concert of action). See also Lester v. State, 737 So. 2d 1149 (Fla. Dist. Ct. App. 1999); Allen v. State, 690 So. 2d 1332 (Fla. Dist. Ct. App. 1997); State v. Hokenson, 527 P.2d 487 (Idaho 1974); State v. Campbell, 755 P.2d 7 (Kan. 1988); State v. Mauldin, 529 P.2d 124 (Kan. 1974); Commonwealth v. Christian, 722 N.E.2d 416, 423 (Mass. 2000); State v. Weinberger, 671 P.2d 567 (Mont. 1983); State v. Russell, 2008 MT 417, 347 Mont. 301, 198 P.3d 271 (2008); State ex rel. Murphy v. McKinnon, 556 P.2d 906 (Mont. 1976), but see State v. Cox, 879 P.2d 662 (Mont. 1994) (rejecting causal standard); Nay v. State, 167 P.3d 430 (Nev. 2007); State v. Buggs, 995 S.W.2d 102 (Tenn. 1999); State v. Pierce, 23 S.W.3d 289 (Tenn. 2000); 2–41 Modern Fed. Jury Inst.-Crim. P 41.01, 41–8 (2009).

13. Ala. Code § 13A-6-2 (2010); 17–A Me. Rev. Stat. Ann. § 202 (2010); Minn. Stat. § 609.05, Subd. 2 (2009); Ohio Rev. Code Ann. § 2903.02 (LexisNexis 2010); see also United States v. Heinlein, 490 F.2d 725 (D.C. Cir. 1973); Witherspoon v. State, 2009 Ala. Crim. App. LEXIS 57, 4 (Ala. Crim. App. 2009): State v. Lopez, 845 P.2d 478, 481 (Ariz. Ct. App. 1992); State v. Spates, 405 A.2d 656, 600 (Conn. 1978); Hassan-El v. State, 911 A.2d 385, 391 (Del. 2006); Lee v. United States, 699 A.2d 373, 385 (D.C. 1997); Durden v. State, 297 S.E.2d 237, 241–42 (Ga. 1982); Hulme v. State, 544 S.E.2d 138, 141 (Ga. 2001); State v. Hokenson, 527 P.2d 487, 492 (Idaho 1974); People v. Jenkins, 545 N.E.2d 986, 994 (Ill. App. Ct. 1989); People v. Brown, 388 N.E.2d 1253, 1256 (Ill. App. Ct. 1979); Booker v. State, 386 N.E.2d 1198 (Ind. 1979); Sheckles v. State, 684 N.E.2d 201, 205 (Ind. Ct. App. 1997); State v. Campbell, 755 P.2d 7, 9 (Kan. 1988); State v. Branch, 573 P.2d 1041, 1043 (Kan. 1978); State v. Kalathakis, 563 So. 2d 228, 231 (La. 1990); Commonwealth v. Baez, 694 N.E.2d 1269, 1271 (Mass. 1998); Watkins v. State, 726 A.2d 795 (Md. Ct. Spec. App. 1999); State v. Day, No. A07–0455 (Minn. Ct. App. June 10, 2008) (foreseeability required for accomplices only); State v. Mahkuk, 736 N.W.2d 675, 682 (Minn. 2007) (same); State v. Blunt, 863 S.W.2d 370, 371 (Mo. Ct. App. 1993); State ex rel. Murphy v. McKinnon, 556 P.2d 906, 910 (Mont. 1976); State v. Weinberger, 671 P.2d 567, 569 (Mont. 1983); State v. Martin, 573 A.2d 1359, 1369 (N.J. 1990); State v. Bonner, 411 S.E.2d 598, 600 (N.C. 1992); People v. Matos, 634 N.E.2d 157 (N.Y. 1994); Kinchion v. State, 2003 OK CR 28, 81 P.3d 681 (Crim. App. 2003); Malaske v. State, 2004 OK CR 18, 89 P.3d 1116 (Crim. App. 2004); Commonwealth v. Tate, 401 A.2d 353 (Pa. 1979); In re Leon, 410 A.2d 121 (R.I. 1980); Gore v. Leeke, 199 S.E.2d 755, 758 (S.C. 1973); Graham v. State, 346 N.W.2d 433, 436 (S.D. 1984) (dictum); State v. Severs, 759 S.W.2d 935, 938 (Tenn. Crim. App. 1988); State v. Jackson, 976 P.2d 1229 (Wash. 1999); State v. Diebold, 277 P. 394, 396 (Wash. 1929); State v. Weisengoff, 101 S.E. 450 (W. Va. 1919); see also 1–6 Me. Jury Ins. Man. § 6–33 (2010); S. C. Requests to Charge Crim. § 2–3 (2007); 1–3 Tenn. Crim. Jury Inst. 3.01.

14. 18 U.S.C.S. § 1111 (LexisNexis 2010); Cal. Penal Code § 189 (Deering 2010); Del. Code Ann. tit. 11, § 635 (2010); D. C. Code § 22–2101 (LexisNexis 2010); Ga. Code.Ann. § 16–5–1 (2010); Idaho Code.Ann. § 18–4003 (2010); 720 Ill. Comp. Stat. Ann. 5/9–1 (LexisNexis 2010); Ind. Code § 35–42–1–1 (LexisNexis 2010); Iowa Code Ann. § 707.2 (2010); Kan. Stat. Ann. § 21–3401 (2010); La. Rev. Stat. Ann. § 14:30.1 (2010); Md. Code Ann., Crim. Law § 2–201 (LexisNexis 2010); Mass. Gen. Laws ch. 265, § 1 (2010); Minn. Stat. § 609.19 (2010); Miss. Code Ann. § 97–3–27 (2010); Neb. Rev. Stat. Ann. § 28–303 (LexisNexis 2010); Nev. Rev. Stat. Ann. § 200.030 (LexisNexis 2009); N.C. Gen. Stat. § 14–17 (2010); Okla. Stat. Ann. tit. 21 § 701.8 (2010); 18 Pa. Cons. Stat. § 2502 (2010); R.I. gen. Laws § 11–23–1 (2010); S.C. Code Ann. § 16–3–10 (2009); S.D. Codified Laws § 22–16–4 (2009); Tenn. Code Ann. § 39–13–202 (2010); Tex. Penal Code Ann. § 19.02 (Vernon 2003); Utah Code Ann. § 76–5–203 (2009); Va. Code Ann. § 18.2–32 (2010); W. Va. Code Ann. § 61–2–1 (LexisNexis 2010); Wis. Stat. Ann. § 940.03 (2005); Wyo. Stat. Ann. § 6–2–101 (2010); Commonwealth v. Garner; 795 N.E.2d 1202, 1209–10 (Mass. 2003); Lowry v. State, 657 S.E.2d 760, 763 (S.C. 2008); State v. Norris, 328 S.E.2d 339, 343 (S.C. 1985); Gore v. Leeke, 199 S.E.2d 755, 759 (S.C. 1973).

15. Wyo. Stat. Ann. § 6–2–101 (2010).

16. Del. Code Ann. tit. 11, § 271(2) (2010); Ga. Code Ann. § 16–2–20 (b)(3) and (b) (4) (2009); 720 Ill. Comp. Stat. Ann. 5/5–2(c) (LexisNexis 2010); Ind. Code § 35–41–2–4 (2010); Kan. Stat. Ann. § 21–3205 (1) (2009); Minn. Stat. § 609.05 (2009); 18 Pa. Cons. Sat. § 306(c)(1) (2010); S.D. Codified Laws § 22–3–3 (2009); Tenn. Code Ann. § 39–11–402 (2) (2010); Tex. Penal Code Ann. § 7.02(2) (Vernon 2003); Utah Code Ann. § 76–2–202 (2009); Wis. Stat. Ann. § 939.05(2)(b) (2010); Wyo. Stat. Ann. § 6–1–201(a) (2009). See also People v. Beeman, 35 Cal. 3d 547 (1984). See also 1–11 Modern Fed. Jury Inst. – Crim. P.11.01, 11–2 (2009) (Aiding and Abetting or intend to aid or encourage it); 1–3 Crim. Jury Inst. for the D.C. 3.200 (2009); Md. Crim. Pattern Jury Inst. 6:01 (2007); Ma. Sup. Ct. Crim. Prac. Jury Inst. § 2.11(8) (2004) (intend to aid conduct, while sharing mental element required for offense); Okla. Jury Inst. – Crim. § 2–5 (2009); 1–3 Va. Model Jury Inst. – Crim. Inst. No. 3.100 (2009); A few jurisdictions also require that accomplices have the culpability required for the offense: Ma. Sup. Ct. Crim. Prac. Jury Inst. No. 2.11 (8) (2004); 18 Pa. Cons. Stat. § 306 (d) (2010); Utah Code Ann. § 76–2–202 (2009).

17. Iowa Code § 703.2 (2010); Kan. Stat. Ann. § 21–3205(2) (2009); Minn. Stat. § 609.05 (2) (2009).

18. Mares v. State, 939 P.2d 724 (Wyo. 1997).

19. Wyo. Stat. Ann. § 6–1–201 (2009).

20. 18 U.S.C.S. § 1111 (LexisNexis 2010); D.C. Code § 22–2101 (LexisNexis 2010); Idaho Code Ann. § 18–4003 (2010); Ind. Code § 35–42–1–1 (LexisNexis 2010); Iowa Code Ann. § 707.2 (2010); Kan. Stat. Ann. § 21–3401 (2010); La. Rev. Stat. Ann. § 14:30.1 (2010); Neb. Rev. Stat. Ann. § 28–303 (LexisNexis 2010); 18 Pa. Cons. Stat. § 2502 (2010); S.D. Codified Laws § 22–16–4 (2009); Tenn. Code Ann. § 39–13–202 (2010); Utah Code Ann.

§ 76–5–203 (2009); W. Va. Code Ann. § 61–2–1 (LexisNexis 2010); Wis. Stat. Ann. § 940.03 (2005); Wyo. Stat. Ann. § 6–2–101 (2010).

21. Pa. Suggested Stan. Crim. Jury. Inst. 15.2502 (B) (2008).

22. Wilson-Bey v. United States, 903 A.2d 818 (D.C. 2006)(quoting Professor Wayne LaFave).

23. State v. Gleason, 88 P.3d 218 (Kan. 2004); State v. Oimen, 516 N.W.2d 399 (Wis. 1994).

24. 18 U.S.C.S. § 1111 (LexisNexis 2010); Idaho Code Ann. § 18–4003 (2010); Ind. Code § 35–42–1–1 (LexisNexis 2010); Kan. Stat. Ann. § 21–3401 (2010); Neb. Rev. Stat. Ann. § 28–303 (LexisNexis 2010); 18 Pa. Cons. Stat. § 2502 (2010); S.D. Codified Laws § 22–16–4 (2009); Tenn. Code Ann. § 39–13–202 (2010); Utah Code Ann. § 76–5–203 (2009); W. Va. Code Ann. § 61–2–1 (LexisNexis 2010); Wyo. Stat. Ann. § 6–2–101 (2010).

25. Drug offenses: D.C. Code § 22–2101 (LexisNexis 2010); Ind. Code § 35–42–1–1 (LexisNexis 2010); Kan. Stat. Ann. § 21–3401 (2010); La. Rev. Stat. Ann. § 14:30.1 (2010); Utah Code Ann. § 76–5–203 (2009); W. Va. Code Ann. § 61–2–1 (LexisNexis 2010). Theft offenses: Kan. Stat. Ann. § 21–3401 (2010); Tenn. Code Ann. § 39–13–202 (2010); Wis. Stat. Ann. § 940.03 (2005).

26. See Kan. Stat. Ann. § 21–3205 (2) (2010).

27. See State v. Branch, 573 P.2d 1041, 1042–43 (Kan. 1978).

28. See State v. Chism, 759 P.2d 105, 110 (Kan. 1988); State v. Gleason, 88 P.3d 218, 229 (Kan. 2004).

29. State v. Howard, 30 S.W.3d 271 (Tenn. 2000); State v. Richmond, 90 S.W.3d 648 (Tenn. 2002).

30. State v. Mickens, 123 S.W.3d 355 (Tenn. Crim. App. 2003); State v. Simerly, Lexis 230 (Tenn. Crim. App. Mar. 11, 2004); State v. Winters, 137 S.W. 3d 641, 659 (Tenn. Crim. App. 2003).

31. Mickens, 123 S.W.3d, 370, citing 2 LaFave & Scott, 1986, § 7.5(b)

32. State v. Hoang, 755 P.2d 7, 11 (Kan. 1988).

33. Commonwealth v. Waters, 418 A.2d 312, 318 (Pa. 1980).

34. Iowa Code § 703.2 (2009); United States v. Heinlein, 490 F.2d 725, 735 (D.C. Cir. 1973); Wilson-Bey v. United States, 903 A.2d 818, 838 (D.C. 2006); Sheckles v. State, 684 N.E.2d 201, 205 (Ind. Ct. App. 1997); Vance v. State, 620 N.E.2d 687, 690 (Ind. 1993); State v. Hokenson, 527 P.2d 487, 492 (Idaho 1974); State v. Smith, 98–2078 (La. 10/29/99), 748 So. 2d 1139, 1143 (1999); Graham v. State, 346 N.W.2d 433, 435–36 (S.D. 1984).

35. See Cal. Penal Code § 189 (Deering 2010); Del. Code Ann. tit. 11, § 635 (2010); Ga. Code Ann. § 16–5–1 (2010); 720 Ill. Comp. Stat. Ann. 5/9–1 (LexisNexis 2010); Md. Code Ann., Crim. Law § 2–201 (LexisNexis 2010); Mass. Gen. Laws. Ch. 265, § 1 (2010); Minn. Stat. § 609.19 (2010); Miss. Code Ann. § 97–3–27 (2010); Nev. Rev. Stat. Ann. § 200.030 (LexisNexis 2009); N.C. Gen. Stat. § 14–17 (2010); Okla. Stat. Ann. tit. 21 § 701.8 (2010); R.I. gen. Laws § 11–23–1 (2010); S.C. Code Ann. § 16–3–10 (2009); Tex. Penal Code Ann.

§ 19.02 (Vernon 2003); Va. Code Ann. § 18.2–32 (2010); Commonwealth v. Garner; 795 N.E.2d 1202, 1209–10 (Mass. 2003); Gore v. Leeke, 199 S.E.2d 755 (S.C. 1973).

36. Ma. Superior Ct. Crim. Prac. Jury Inst. § 2.1.1 n.4 (C), § 2.3.4 (2004).

37. See Minn. Stat. § 609.05 (2) (2009); State v. Mahkuk, 736 N.W.2d 675, 682 (Minn. 2007).

38. People v. Cavitt, 91 P.3d 222, 227 (Cal. 2004).

39. 1–500 Judicial Council of Cal. Crim. Jury Inst. 540C.

40. People v. Beeman, 674 P.2d 1318, 1323 (Cal. 1984).

41. See Del. Code Ann. tit. 11, § 635 (2010); Ga. Code Ann. § 16–5–1 (2010); 720 Ill. Comp. Stat. Ann. 5/9–1 (LexisNexis 2010); Md. Code Ann., Crim. Law § 2–201 (Lexis-Nexis 2010); Miss. Code Ann. § 97–3–27 (2010); N.C. Gen. Stat. § 14–17 (2010); Okla. Stat. Ann. tit. 21 § 701.8 (2010); R.I. gen. Laws § 11–23–1 (2010); S.C. Code Ann. § 16–3–10 (2009); Tex. Penal Code Ann. § 19.02 (2009); Va. Code Ann. § 18.2–32 (2010); Gore v. Leeke, 199 S.E.2d 755 (S.C. 1973).

42. Four of the remaining jurisdictions (Del. Code Ann. tit. 11, § 635 (2010); Ga. Code Ann. § 16–5–1 (2010); S.C. Code Ann. § 16–3–10 (2009); Tex. Penal Code Ann. § 19.02 (2009))have no enumerated felonies at all. Oklahoma (Okla. Stat. Ann. tit. 21 § 701.8 (2010)) predicates collective liability on its enumerated felonies. Virginia (Va. Code Ann. § 18.2–32 (2010) has enumerated felonies, but all of them are dangerous by our criteria.

43. See Del. Code Ann. tit. 11, § 271 (2010); Ga. Code Ann. § 16–2–20(b)(3) (2010); 720 Ill. Comp. Stat. Ann. 5/5–2 (c) (LexisNexis 2010); Tex. Penal Code Ann. § 7.02 (a)(2) (Vernon 2003). See also State v. Francis, 459 S.E.2d 269, 272 (N.C. 1995); Okla. Jury Inst. – Crim. § 2.5 (2009); State v. Medeiros, 599 A.2d 723,726 (R.I. 1991). See also Md. Crim. Pat. Jury Inst. 6:01 (2007); 2 Ga. Jury Inst. – Crim. § 1.42.10; 1–3 Va. Model Jury Inst. – Crim. Inst. No. 3.100 (intent to aid).

44. Hassan-El v. State, 911 A.2d 385, 395 (Del. 2006); Claudio v. State, 585 A.2d 1278, 1282 (Del. 1991).

45. People v. Bongiorno, 192 N.E. 856, 858 (1934); People v. Burke, 407 N.E.2d 728, 730 (Ill. App. Ct. 1980); People v. Brown, 388 N.E.2d 1253, 1257 (Ill. App. Ct. 1979).

46. Gore v. Leeke, 199 S.E.2d 755, 757 (S.C. 1973); S.C. Request to Charge, § 2–3 (2007).

47. 1–3 Va. Model Jury Inst. – Crim. Inst. No. 3.160 ("concert of action").

48. Haskell v. State, 243 S.E.2d 477 n.4 (Va. 1978).

49. See State v. Bonner, 411 S.E.2d 598 (N.C. 1992).

50. See State v. Medeiros, 599 A.2d 723, 726 (R.I. 1991).

51. Tex. Penal Code Ann. § 7.02 (b) (2010).

52. Moffett v. State, 2008–KA–00175–COA, ¶ 39 (Miss. Ct. App. 2009).

53. See Oxendine v. State, 350 P.2d 606 (Okla. 1960).

54. Okla. Jury Inst. – Crim. § 4–93 (2009).

55. Williams v. State, 578 S.E.2d 858, 860 (Ga. 2003).

56. Md. Crim. Pattern Jury Inst. 4.17.7 (2007) ("Homicide—First Degree Felony Murder, Comment").

57. Mumford v. State, 313 A.2d 563, 566 (Md. Ct. Spec. App. 1974).

58. Watkins v. State, 726 A.2d 795 (Md. Ct. Spec. App. 1999)

59. Ohio Rev. Code Ann. § 2903.02 (2010); 17–A Me. Rev. Stat. Ann. § 202 (2010); Mo. Rev. Stat. § 565.021 (2009) ("killed as a result of").

60. Okla. Stat. tit. 21, § 701.7 (2010).

61. Ohio Rev. Code Ann. § 2901.01 (2010).

62. Ohio Rev. Code Ann. § 2923.03 (2010).

63. See State v. Kimble, 2008 Ohio 1539, 2008 Ohio App. LEXIS 1357, ¶ 30 (Ohio Ct. App. 2008).

64. 17–A Me. Rev. Stat. Ann. § 202 (2010); Mo. Rev. Stat. § 565.021 (2010); Okla. Jury Inst. – Crim. § 4–65 (2009).

65. 17–A Me. Rev. Stat. Ann. § 202 (2010).

66. 17–A Me. Rev. Stat. Ann. § 57(3)(A) (2010).

67. 1–6 Me. Jury Inst. Man. § 6–33 (2010) (emphasis added).

68. 17–A Me. Rev. Stat. Ann. § 202 (2010).

69. Mo. Rev. Stat. § 562.036 (2009).

70. Mo. Rev. Stat. § 562.041 (2009).

71. See State v. Blunt, 863 S.W.2d 370, 371 (Mo. Ct. App. 1993).

72. Okla. Stat. tit. 21, § 701.7 (2010).

73. Okla. Jury Inst. – Crim. § 4–60 (2009).

74. Okla. Jury Inst. – Crim. §§ 4–64, 4–65 (2009).

75. See Ala. Code § 13A-6–2 (2010); Conn. Gen. Stat § 53a-54c (2010); Mont. Code Ann. § 45–5–102 (2010); N.Y. Penal Law § 125.25 (Consol. 2010); N.D. Cent. Code § 12.1–16–01 (2010); Or. Rev. Stat. § 163.115 (2009); Wash. Rev. Code Ann. § 9A.32.030 (Lexis-Nexis 2010); an eighth jurisdiction with a similar statute, Arkansas, punishes extreme indifference murder rather than felony murder.

76. Conn. Gen. Stat § 53a–54c (2010); Mont. Code Ann. § 45–5–102 (2010); N.Y. Penal Law § 125.25 (Consol. 2010); N.D. Cent. Code § 12.1–16–01 (2010); Or. Rev. Stat. § 163.115 (2009); Wash. Rev. Code Ann. § 9A.32.030 (LexisNexis 2010);

77. Ala. Code § 13A-2–23 (2010); Conn. Gen. Stat § 53a-8 (2010); Mont. Code Ann. § 45–2–302 (2010); N.Y. Penal Law § 20.00 (Consol. 2010); N.D. Cent. Code § 12.1–03–01 (2010); Or. Rev. Stat. § 161.155 (2010); Wash. Rev. Code Ann. § 9A.08.020 (LexisNexis 2010).

78. Ala. Code § 13A-6–2 (2010); Conn. Gen. Stat § 53a-54c (2010); N.Y. Penal Law § 125.25 (Consol. 2010); N.D. Cent. Code § 12.1–16–01 (2010); Or. Rev. Stat. § 163.115 (2009); Wash. Rev. Code Ann. § 9A.32.030 (2010); State v. Weinberger, 671 P.2d 567, 568 (Mont. 1983); State ex rel. Murphy v. McKinnon, 556 P.2d 906, 910 (Mont. 1976); State v. Russell, 2008 MT 417, 347 Mont. 301, 198 P.3d 271.

79. Conn. Gen. Stat § 53a–16b (2010); N.Y. Penal Law § 125.25(3)(b),(c),(d) (Con-

sol. 2010); N.D. Cent. Code § 12.1–16–01(c) (2)(3)(4) (2010); Or. Rev. Stat. § 163.115(3) (b),(c),(d) (2009); Wash. Rev. Code Ann. § 9A.32.030 (c)(ii),(iii),(iv) (2010).

80. Conn. Gen. Stat § 53a–12 (2010); N.Y. Penal Law § 25.00 (2010); N.D. Cent. Code § 12.1–01–03 (3) (2010); Or. Rev. Stat. § 161.055 (2) (2009); Wash. Rev. Code Ann. § 9A.32.030 (1)(c) (2010).

81. Ala. Code § 13A–6–2 (2010).

82. State v. Valeriano, 468 A.2d 936, 938 (Conn. 1983).

83. State v. Jackson, 976 P.2d 1229, 1238 (Wash. 1999).

84. See State v. Weinberger, 206 Mont. 110, 671 P.2d 567 (1983).

85. State v. Cox, 879 P.2d 662, 668 (1994); see also State ex rel. Murphy v. McKinnon, 556 P.2d 906 (Mont. 1976).

86. People v. Giro, 90 N.E. 432 (N.Y. 1910); People v. Giusto, 99 N.E. 190 (N.Y. 1912).

87. People v. Hernandez, 624 N.E.2d 661 (N.Y. 1983).

88. Alaska Stat. § 11.41.110 (2010); Ariz. Rev. Stat. § 13–1105 (2010); Colo. Rev. Stat. § 18–3–102 (2010); Fla. Stat. Ann. § 782.04 (LexisNexis 2010); N.J. Stat. Ann. § 2C:11–3 (West 2010).

89. But not Alaska. Alaska Stat. § 11.41.110(a)(3) (2010).

90. Ariz. Rev. Stat. § 13–301 (2010); Alaska Stat. § 11.16.110 (2) (2009); Colo. Rev. Stat. § 18–1–603 (2010); N.J. Stat. Ann. § 2C:2–6 (c)(1) (West 2010); Ariz. Jury Inst. – Crim. 3d 3.01 (2009); Fl. Stan. Jury Inst. Crim. Cases § 3.5(a) (2009).

91. N.J. Stan. Crim. Jury Inst. 2C:11–3a(3) (2009).

92. State v. Lopez, 845 P.2d 478, 481 (Ariz. Ct. App. 1992).

93. State v. Rutledge, 4 P.3d 444, 446 (Ariz. Ct. App. 2000).

94. State v. Lopez, 845 P.2d 478, 481–82 (Ariz. Ct. App. 1992).

95. Auman v. People, 109 P.3d 647, 657 (Colo. 2005).

Chapter 11

1. Binder, 2007, 103–04.

2. Moore, 1997, 71; Fletcher, 1978, 461.

3. Michael & Wechsler, 1937, 715–16.

4. Finkelstein, 2005, 218–40.

5. Id., 224–25, 231, 238–39 (criticizing cases of Murphy v. State, 665 S.W.2d 116 (Tex. Crim. App. 1983), and People v. Billa, 102 Cal. App. 4th 822 (2002), which reject application of the merger doctrine to arson).

6. Finkelstein, 2005, 218–19.

7. Hawkins, 1716, 83.

8. States with ungraded felony murder statutes: NY (1829–60 and after 1873), MS (1839–57), MO (before 1879), IL, GA, NJ. States with third-degree felony murder provisions: MN, WI, FL. States with common law felony murder rules: KY, LA, SC.

9. People v. Rector, 19 Wend. 569, 592 (Sup. Ct. Jud. of N.Y. 1838).

10. Foster v. People, 50 N.Y. 598, 603 (1872).

11. Buel v. People, 78 N.Y. 492, 497 (1879).

12. People v. Deacons, 109 N.Zy. 374 (1888); People v. Miles, 143 N.Y. 383 (1894)

13. People v. Hüter, 77 N.E. 6, 9 (N.Y. 1906).

14. See People v. Spohr, 100 N.E. 444, 446 (1912; People v. Moran, 158 N.E. 35 (1927); People v. Wagner, 156 N.E. 644, 646 (1927); People v. Lazar, 2 N.E.2d 32 (1936); People v. Luscomb, 292 N.Y. 390, 55 N.E.2d 469 (1944).

15. State v. Jennings, 18 Mo. 435 (1853); State v. Nueslein, 25 Mo. 111, 126 (1857).

16. State v. Shock, 68 Mo. 552, 563–64 (1878).

17. Id., 561–62.

18. Id., 562.

19. See Mo. Rev. Stat. § 1232 (1879).

20. Mask v. State, 36 Miss. 77 (1858).

21. State v. Alexander, 8 S.E. 440, 441 (S.C. 1889).

22. See Boyle v. State, 15 N.W. 827, 832 (Wis. 1883); Hammond v. State, 35 Wis. 315 (1874); Collins v. State, 12 So. 906, 909 (Fla. 1893).

23. 1893 N.C. Pub. Laws ch. 85; State v. Covington, 23 S.E. 337, 353 (N.C. 1895).

24. State v. Capps, 46 S.E. 730 (N.C. 1904).

25. See State v. Roselli, 198 P. 195 (Kan. 1921).

26. State v. Fisher, 243 P. 291, 293 (Kan. 1926).

27. See State v. Severns, 148 P.2d 488, 491 (Kan. 1944).

28. See Tarter v. State, 359 P.2d 596, 602 (Okla. Crim. App. 1961).

29. State v. Moffitt, 431 P.2d 879, 894 (Kan. 1967).

30. State v. Clark, 460 P.2d 586, 590 (Kan. 1969).

31. State v. Essman, 403 P.2d 540, 545 (Ariz. 1965).

32. State v. Miller, 520 P.2d 1113 (Ariz. 1974); State v. Miniefield, 522 P.2d 25 (Ariz. 1974).

33. Or. Rev. Stat. § 163.020 (repealed 1971).

34. State v. Reyes, 308 P.2d 182, 192 (Or. 1957).

35. State v. Branch, 415 P.2d 766, 768 (Or. 1966); see also State v. Shirley, 488 P.2d 1401 (Or. Ct. App. 1971).

36. State v. Morris, 405 P.2d 369 (Or. 1965); State v. Tremblay, 479 P.2d 507, 510 (Or. Ct. App. 1971).

37. People v. Carmen, 228 P.2d 281, 286 (Cal. 1951).

38. People v. Robillard, 358 P.2d 295, 300 (Cal. 1960).

39. People v. Hamilton, 362 P.2d 473, 485 (1961); People v. Talbot, 414 P.2d 633, 641 (1966).

40. People v. Ireland, 450 P.2d 580, 590 (1969).

41. People v. Wilson, 462 P.2d 22, 28 (Cal. 1969).

42. People v. Sears, 465 P.2d 847, 852–53 (Cal. 1970).

43. People v. Wesley, 10 Cal. App. 3d 902, 907 (1970).

44. People v. Burton, 491 P.2d 793, 801–02 (Cal.1971).

45. People v. Smith, 35 Cal. 3d 798, 891 (Cal. 1984); People v. Benway, 164 Cal. App. 3d 505, 512 (Cal. Ct. App. 1985).

46. See People v. Taylor, 11 Cal. App. 3d 57, 64 (Ct. App. 1970).

47. See People v. Mattison, 481 P.2d 193, 198–99 (1971). Cf. People v. Calzada, 13 Cal. App. 3d 603 (Ct. App. 1970) (rejecting an independent purpose test in favor of an independent act test).

48. See Robles v. State, 188 So. 2d 789, 792 (Fla. 1966).

49. See State v. Harris, 421 P.2d 662, 665 (Wash. 1966).

50. Id., 664.

51. See State v. Trott, 289 A.2d 414, 418 (Me. 1972).

52. 1978 Alaska Sess. Laws ch.164, 6; 1978 Ariz. Sess. Laws 729; 1974 Conn. Acts 496; 1974 Colo. Sess. Laws 251–53; 1976 Ind. Acts 730; 1976 Iowa Acts 555–56; 1972 Kan. Sess. Laws 482; 1975 ME Laws 1294–95; 1977 Neb. Laws 96; 1978 N.J. Laws 540–41; 1965 N.Y. Laws 2387–88; 1973 N.D. Laws 254–55; 1971; Or. Laws 1903; 1974 Pa. Laws 216–17; 1979 S.D. Sess. Laws 200; 1973 Utah Laws 607; 1982 Wyo. Sess. Laws 523.

53. 1977 Ala. Laws 836–37; 1970 Del. Laws c. 186 § 1; 1971 Fla. Laws 838; 1968 Ga. Laws 1276; 1961 Ill. Laws 2003; 1963 Minn. Laws 1200; 1983 Mo. Laws 926–27; 1963 Mont. Laws 1355; 1973 Tex. Gen. Laws 913; 1975 Va. Acts 21–22; 1975 Wash. Sess. Laws 833–34. New Mexico also adopted a categorical felony murder rule (1963 N.M. Laws 834–35), but, as noted, its application was eventually conditioned on depraved indifference.

54. See Malone v. State, 232 S.E.2d 907, 908 (Ga. 1977); TX, MO.

55. Massie v. State, 553 P.2d 186, 191 (Okla. Crim. 1976); State v. Lucas, 759 P.2d 90, 98–99 (Kan. 1988); State v. Prouse, 767 P.2d 1308, 1313 (Kan. 1989); People v. Smith, 678 P.2d 886, 891 (Cal. 1984).

56. People v. Hansen, 885 P.2d 1022, 1028, 1030 (Cal. 1995).

57. People v. Robertson, 95 P.3d 872, 880–81 (Cal. 2004); People v. Randle, 111 P.3d 987, 999 (Cal. 2005).

58. People v. Chun, 203 P.3d 425, 443 (Cal. 2009).

59. People v. Gutierrez, 28 Cal. 4th 1083 (2002).

60. People v. Farley, 46 Cal. 4th 1053 (2009).

61. Id., 1117–20.

62. Kan. Stat. Ann. § 21–3436 (2009).

63. Commonwealth v. Quigley, 462 N.E.2d 92, 95 (1984). quoting LaFave & Scott, 1972, 559.

64. Barnett v. Alabama, 783 So. 2d 927, 7 (Ala. Crim. App. 2000).

65. State v. Williams, 199 S.E.2d 409 (N.C. 1973); State v. Swift, 226 S.E.2d 652, 668–69 (N.C. 1976); State v. Mash, 287 S.E.2d 824, 826 (N.C. 1982); State v. Wall, 286 S.E.2d 68, 71 (N.C. 1982); State v. King, 340 S.E.2d 71, 73 (N.C. 1986).

66. State v. Jones, 538 S.E.2d 917 (N.C. 2000).

67. Id., 926 n.3.

68. Faraga v. State, 514 So. 2d 295 (Miss. 1987); Smith v. State, 499 So. 2d 750 (Miss. 1986).

69. Faraga v. State, 514 So. 2d 295 (Miss. 1987), 303.

70. See People v. Viser, 343 N.E.2d 903, 909 (1975).

71. People v. Morgan, 758 N.E.2d 813, 838 (Ill. 2001).

72. E.g., People v. Boyd, 825 N.E.2d 364, 369–70 (Ill. App. Ct. 2005).

73. See State v. Beeman, 315 N.W.2d 770, 775 (Iowa 1982).

74. Id., 776–77.

75. State v. Heemstra, 721 N.W.2d 549, 558 (Iowa 2006).

76. See State v. Hanes, 729 S.W.2d 612, 617 (Mo. Ct. App. 1987).

77. State v. Rogers, 976 S.W.2d 529 (Mo. Ct. App. 1998).

78. State v. Williams, 24 S.W.3d 101, 117 (Mo. Ct. App. 2000).

79. Garret v. State, 573 S.W.2d 543, 545 (Tex. Crim. App. 1978).

80. See Wray v. State, 642 S.W.2d 27, 29–30 (1982) (overturned on other grounds).

81. Murphy v. State, 665 S.W.2d 116, 119–20 (Tex. Crim. App. 1983).

82. See Aguirre v .State, 732 S.W.2d 320, 324–25 (Tex. Crim. App. 1987).

83. Ex parte Easter, 615 S.W.2d 721 (Tex. Crim. App. 1981); Bergahn, 696 S.W.2d 948 (Tex. App. 1985).

84. Rodriguez v. Texas, 953 S.W.2d 342, 350 (1997); accord Johnson v. Texas, 4 S.W. 3d 254 (Tex. Crim. App. 1999).

85. Lawson v. Texas, 64 S.W.3d 396, 397 (Tex. Crim. App. 2001).

86. Chao v. State, 604 A.2d 1351, 1361 (Del. 1992).

87. Williams v. State, 818 A.2d 906, 908 (Del. 2002).

88. 74 Del. Laws. 246 (2004); Del. Code Ann. tit 11, §§ 635, 636 (2010).

89. In re Shawn Andress, 56 P.3d 981, 985 (Wash. 2002).

90. Wash. Rev. Code § 9A.32.050 (2010); 2003 Wash. Sess. Laws 3.

91. Andress, 56 P.3d, 988.

92. 1968 Ga. Laws 1276.

93. Malone v. State, 232 S.E.2d 907, 908 (Ga. 1977); see also Edge v. State, 414 S.E.2d 463, 465 (Ga. 1992).

94. Baker v. State, 225 S.E.2d 269, 271 (1976).

95. Id., 271–72.

96. Lewis v. State, 396 S.E.2d 212, 213 n.2 (Ga. 1990).

97. Miller v. Martin, 2007 U.S. Dist. LEXIS 13112, 48.

98. See Holt v. State, 278 S.E.2d 390 (Ga. 1981)(child abuse).

99. Fisher v. State, 786 A.2d 706 (Md. 2001).

100. Roary v. State, 867 A.2d 1095, 1100–1101 (Md. 2005).

101. 1963 Minn. Laws 1200.

102. State v. Morris, 187 N.W.2d 276 (Minn. 1971); State v. Smith, 203 N.W.2d 348

(Minn. 1972); State v. Carson, 219 N.W.2d 88 (Minn. 1974); Kochevar v. State, 281 N.W.2d 680, 686 (Minn. 1979); State v. Loebach, 310 N.W.2d 58, 65 (Minn. 1981); State v. Abbott, 356 N.W.2d 677, 680 (Minn. 1984); State v. Jackson, 346 N.W.2d 634, 636 (Minn. 1984); State v. French, 402 N.W.2d 805, 808 (Minn. Ct. App. 1987).

103. See State v. Burkhart, 2004 MT 372, 325 Mont. 27, 103 P.3d 1037.

104. Cotton v. Commonwealth. 546 S.E.2d 241 (Va. Ct. App. 2001).

105. Id., 244.

106. State v. O'Blasney, 297 N.W.2d 797 (S.D. 1980).

107. State v. Reams, 636 P.2d 913, 918 (Or. 1981); State v. Tremblay, 479 P.2d 507 (Or. Ct. App. 1971); People v. Miller, 297 N.E.2d 85, 87–88 (N.Y. 1973); State v. Foy, 582 P.2d 281, 289 (Kan. 1978) citing Miller, 520 P.2d 1113; State v. McGuire, 638 P.2d 1339, 1342 (Ariz. 1981); State v. Hankins, 686 P.2d 740, 744 (Ariz. 1984); People v. Farley, 46 Cal. 4th 1053 (2009).

108. State v. Reams, 636 P.2d 913, 918 (Or. 1981); State v. Tremblay, 479 P.2d 507 (Or. Ct. App. 1971); People v. Miller, 297 N.E.2d 85, 87–88 (N.Y. 1973); State v. Foy, 582 P.2d 281, 289 (Kan. 1978), citing Miller, 520 P.2d, 1113; People v. Farley, 46 Cal. 4th 1053 (2009).

109. Smith v. State, 499 So. 2d 750, 754 (Miss. 1986); Blango v. United States, 373 A.2d 885, 888 (D.C. 1977).

110. Parker v. State, 731 S.W.2d 756, 759 (Ark. 1987).

111. State v. Rueckert, 561 P.2d 850, 857 (Kan. 1977).

112. State v. Champagne, 198 N.W.2d 218, 227 (N.D. 1972).

113. State v. Miniefield, 522 P.2d 25, 28 (Ariz. 1974); Murphy v. State, 665 S.W.2d 116, 119–120 (Tex. Crim. App. 1983).

114. AK, AZ, CO, CT, DC, ID, IN, IA, KS, LA, ME, NE, NJ, NY, ND, OH, OR, PA, SD, TN, UT, WV, WI, WY, US.

115. The Kansas code specifically excludes assaults that merge with the act causing death. Kan. Stat. Ann. § 21–3436 (2009). The Iowa code includes willful injury as a predicate felony, Iowa Code § 702.11 (2009), but the Iowa courts have excluded willful injuries of the deceased. State v. Heemstra, 721 N.W.2d 549, 558 (Iowa 2006).

116. See Malani, 2002; Wis. Stat. Ann. § 940.03 (2010).

117. Ohio Rev. Code Ann. § 2903.02 (2010); Ohio Rev. Code Ann. § 2901.01(9) (2010), Ohio Rev. Code Ann. § 2903.11 (2010).

118. Ohio's new (1998) felony murder statute conditions murder on causing death in the course of any first- or second-degree felony of violence other than involuntary manslaughter. In a 2006 case a trial judge dismissed a murder charge predicated on a felonious assault, reasoning that involuntary manslaughter also included causing death in the course of the felony of assault. The decision relied on a misreading of the statute as requiring that the killing (rather than the predicate felony) not constitute manslaughter. An appeals court issued an advisory opinion pointing out the interpretive error. Neither decision addressed the merger issue, which remains open. (State v. Brodie, 847 N.E.2d 1268 (Ohio Ct. App. 2006).

119. La. Rev. Stat. Ann. § 14:30 (2009).

120. La. Rev. Stat. Ann. § 14:37.1 (2009).

121. 18 U.S.C.S. § 1111 (2010); D.C. Code § 22–2101 (2010); Idaho Code Ann. § 18–4003 (2010); Kan. Stat. Ann. § 21–3436 (2009); La. Rev. Stat. Ann. § 14:30 (2009); Ohio Rev. Code Ann. § 2903.02 (2009); Or. Rev. Stat. § 163.115 (2009); Tenn. Code Ann. § 39–13–202 (2010); Utah Code Ann. § 76–5–203 (2009); Wyo. Stat. Ann. § 6–2–101 (2010).

122. Kan. Stat. Ann. § 21–3436 (2009); Kan. Stat. Ann. § 21–3609 (2009).

123. 18 U.S.C.S. § 1111(a) (2010).

124. Or. Rev. Stat. § 163.115(J) (2009)

125. Tenn. Code Ann. § 39–15–401 (2010).

126. D.C. Code § 22–2101 (2010); D.C. Code § 22–1101 (2010) (1st deg. Cruelty to children).

127. Wyo. Stat. Ann. § 6–2–503 (2010).

128. Ohio Rev. Code Ann. § 2919.22 (2009).

129. Ohio Rev. Code Ann. § 2901.21(B) (2009).

130. Utah Code Ann. § 76–5–109.1 (2009).

131. Idaho Code Ann. § 18–4003(d) (2010).

132. Idaho Code Ann. § 18–907(e) (2010).

133. La. Rev. Stat. Ann. § 14:93(A)(1) (2009).

134. Md. Code Ann., Crim. Law § 2–201 (2010); Cal. Penal Code § 189 (2010).

135. Cal. Penal Code § 189 (2010).

136. 720 Ill. Comp. Stat. Ann. 5/9–1 (LexisNexis 2010); 720 Ill. Comp. Stat. Ann. 5/2–8 (2010); People v. Morgan, 758 N.E.2d 813, 838 (Ill. 2001).

137. Minn. Stat. § 609.185 (2010). Another enumerated felony, an aggravated battery in violation of a protective order, seems defensible as a form of depraved indifference murder; Minn. Stat. § 609.185 (6) (2010).

138. Okla. Stat. Ann. tit. 21 § 701.7(b) (2010). Another Oklahoma predicate felony— shooting with intent to kill—supplies enough culpability for murder in Oklahoma, which permits no mitigation of intentional killings. Okla. Stat. Ann. tit. 21 § 711 (2010).

139. See Barnett v. Alabama, 783 So. 2d 927, 7 (Ala. Crim. App. 2000); People v. Chun, 203 P.3d 425, 443 (Cal. 2009); People v. Morgan, 758 N.E.2d 813, 838 (Ill. 2001); State v. Jones, 538 S.E.2d 917, 925 (N.C. 2000); Tarter v. State, 359 P.2d 596, 602 (Okla. Crim. App. 1961); Massie v. State, 553 P.2d 186 (Okla. Crim. 1976).

140. State v. Wall, 286 S.E.2d 68, 71 (N.C. 1982); State v. King, 340 S.E.2d 71, 73 (1986).

141. Faraga v. State, 514 So. 2d 295, 312–13 (Miss. 1987).

142. See Roary v. State, 867 A.2d 1095 (Md. 2005); State v. Morris, 187 N.W.2d 276 (Minn. 1971); State v. French, 402 N.W.2d 805 (Minn. 1987). See State v. Burkhart, 2004 MT 372, 325 Mont. 27, 103 P.3d 1037; Wash. Rev. Code Ann. § 9A.32.050(b) (2010).

143. Cotton v. Commonwealth, 546 S.E.2d 241, 244 (Va. Ct. App. 2001).

144. Cordova v. State, 6 P.3d 481 (Nev. 2000) (defendant shot through a door on be-

ing asked to identify himself). The offense was defined by Nev. Rev. Stat. Ann. § 202.285 (2009).

145. Cordova, 6 P.3d, 484, citing People v. Hansen, 885 P.2d 1022 (Cal. 1994) overruled by People v. Chun, 203 P.3d 425, 443 (Cal. 2009). The offense was defined by Cal. Penal Code § 246 (2009).

146. Florida's 1966 Robles decision, holding that merger is unnecessary in a state enumerating all predicate felonies, no longer applies to its current code, which predicates third-degree murder on unenumerated felonies. Fla. Stat. Ann. § 782.04(4) (2010).

147. Faraga v. State, 514 So. 2d 295 (Miss. 1987); Miss. Code Ann. § 97–5–39(2)(a) (2009).

148. See Cotton v. Commonwelath, 546 S.E.2d 241 (Va. Ct. App. 2001); Va. Code Ann. § 18.2–371.1 (2010).

149. See Fisher v. State, 786 A.2d 706 (Ma. 2001); Md. Code Ann., Crim. Law § 3–601(a)(2) (2010).

150. See State v. Anderson, 513 S.E.2d 296 (N.C. 1999); N.C. Gen. Stat. § 14–318.4 (2009); N.C. Gen. Stat. § 14–17 (2010).

151. Fla. Stat. Ann. § 782.04 (2010); Fla. Stat. Ann. § 784.045 (2010) (definition of aggravated battery); Fla. Stat. Ann. § 827.03 (1) (2) (2010) (provisions defining child abuse and aggravated child abuse).

152. Fla. Stat. Ann. § 782.04 (2010) (murder); Fla. Stat. Ann. § 782.04 (2010) (elder abuse); Nev. Rev. Stat. Ann. § 200.030 (2009) (murder); Nev. Rev. Stat. Ann. § 200.5092 (2009) (elder abuse).

153. See Ga. Code Ann. § 16–5–1 (2010); Malone v. State, 232 S.E.2d 907, 908 (Ga. 1977); Mo. Rev. Stat. § 565.021 (2009); State v. Williams, 24 S.W.3d 101, 112; Tex. Penal Code Ann. § 19.02 (2009).

154. Commonwealth v. Quigley, 462 N.E.2d 92, 95 (Mass. 1984).

155. Holt v. State, 278 S.E.2d 390 (Ga. 1981); Ex parte Easter, 615 S.W.2d 719 (Tex. Crim. App.) (1981); Bergahn v. State, 696 S.W.2d 943, 948 (Tex. App. 1985).

156. Ga. Code Ann. § 16–5–70 (2010).

157. Tex. Penal Code Ann. § 22.04 (2009).

Chapter 12

1. Commonwealth v. Flanagan, 7 Watts & Serg. 415 (Pa. 1844); People v. Scott, 6 Mich. 287, 293 (1859); Moynihan v. State, 70 Ind. 126, 130 (1880).

2. State v. Cooper, 13 N.J.L. 361, 370 (1833); People v. Foren, 25 Cal. 361, 366 (1864).

3. 118 Mass. 36, 44 (1875).

4. AL, DE, ME, NJ, PA, TX.

5. CA, ID, IA, MS, NV, RI, SC, VA, US.

6. CA, MA, MN, NV.

7. AL, DE, GA, IL, MD, MO, MT, NC, OK, RI, SC, TX, VA.

8. AK, AZ, CO, CT, DC, ID, IN, IA, KS, LA, ME, NE, NJ, NY, ND, OH, OR, PA, SD, TN, UT, WV, WN, WY, US.

9. AL, CA, FL, IL, MD, MN, MS, MT, NV, NC, OK, RI, VA, WA.

10. AZ, CA, CO, CT, FL, ID, IN, IA, IL, KS, ME, MS, MT, NE, NV, NJ, NY, ND, PA, RI, SD, TN, UT, WV, WY, US.

11. AK, AZ, DC, FL, IN, KS, LA, OH, OK, RI, UT, WV.

12. KS, TN, WI.

13. AL, AZ, CA, CT, DC, DE, GA, ID, IL, IN, KS, LA, MA, MD, ME, MO, MT, NE, NV, NJ, NY, NC, OH, OK, PA, RI, TN, TX, UT, VA, WA, WV.

14. AZ, CA, CT, DC, ID, IL, IN, KS, LA, ME, MT, NE, NV, NJ, NY, OH, OK, PA, RI, TN, UT, WV. Jurisdictions with potentially non-dangerous felonies and without foreseeability requirements are AK, CO, FL, IA, MS, ND, SD, WI, WY, US.

15. CO, FL, IA, MS, OR, SC, SD, WY, US.

16. MA, MN, OR.

17. ME, MO, OH, OK.

18. AZ, AL, CA, CT, DC, DE, GA, ID, IL, IN, IA, LA, ME, MS, MN, MO, MT, NJ, NY, NC, OK, RI, SC, SD, TX, VA, WA.

19. CO, CT, ME, NY, NJ, ND, OR, WA.

20. GA, PA, UT, WV, NE, NV.

21. AK, AZ, CO, FL, NJ.

22. AL, AZ, CO, CT, DC, FL, ID, IL, IN, KS, MA, MD, ME, MO MT, NV, NJ, NY, NC, ND, OH, OK, OR, PA, TN, TX, VA, WA, WV, US.

23. CA, DE, IA, MS, MN, NE, WY.

24. AL, CA, KS, IA, IL, MA, NC, OK, and possibly MS.

25. GA, MD, MN, MT, TX, WA, WI.

26. Thus Ohio courts should determine that the statutory exclusion of manslaughter as a predicate felony also bars aggravated assault. The Louisiana legislature should revise its drive-by-shooting felony to require more recklessness; the Louisiana and Idaho legislatures should define more aggravated forms of child abuse and predicate felony murder only on these; the Oklahoma legislature should require clearer endangerment of human life for its shooting-into-a-building predicate felony.

BIBLIOGRAPHY
OF SECONDARY SOURCES

Abbott, Jack Henry, *In the Belly of the Beast: Letters from Prison* (Random House 1981).

Ackerman, Bruce A., *Social Justice in the Liberal State* (Yale University Press 1980).

Adlerstein, Jo Anne C., Felony-Murder in the New Criminal Codes, 4 *Am. J. Crim. L.* 249 (1975–1976).

Alexander, Larry, Reconsidering the Relationship Among Voluntary Acts, Strict Liability, and Negligence in Criminal Law, 7 *Soc. Phil. & Pol'y* 84, Spring 1990.

Alexander, Larry, Crime and Culpability, 5 *J. Contemp. Legal Issues* 1 (1994).

Alexander, Larry, Insufficient Concern: A Unified Conception of Criminal Culpability, 88 *Cal. L. Rev.* 931 (2000).

Alexander, Larry, & Kessler, Kimberly D., Mens Rea and Inchoate Crimes, 87 *J. Crim. L. & Criminology* 1138 (1997).

Almond, Gabriel, & Verba, Sidney, *The Civic Culture* (Princeton University Press 1963).

Andenaes, Johannes, General Prevention—Illusion or Reality?, 43 *J. Crim. L. Criminology & Police Sci.* 176 (1952).

Andenaes, Johannes, The General Preventive Effects of Punishment, 114 *U. Pa. L. Rev.* 949 (1966).

Anderson, Elizabeth, *Value in Ethics and Economics* (Harvard University Press 1993).

Anooshian, John S., Note, Should Courts Use Principles of Justification and Excuse to Impose Felony-Murder Liability?, 19 *Rutgers L.J.* 451 (1988).

Aquinas, Thomas, *Summa Theologiae*, II-II (Blackfriars 1975).

Arent, Albert E., & MacDonald, John W., The Felony Murder Doctrine and Its Application Under the New York Statutes, 20 *Cornell L.Q.* 288 (1934).

Arrow, Kenneth J., *Social Choice and Individual Values* (2d ed., Wiley 1963).

Arrow, Kenneth J., Extended Sympathy and the Possibility of Social Choice, 67 *Am. Econ. Rev.* 219 (1977).

Ashworth, A.J., Transferred Malice and Punishment for Unforeseen Consequences, in *Reshaping the Criminal Law* 77 (P.R. Glazebrook ed., Stevens & Sons 1978).

Ashworth, Andrew, Criminal Attempts and the Role of Resulting Harm Under the Code, and in the Common Law, 19 *Rutgers L.J.* 725 (1988).

Askin, Kelly Dawn, *War Crimes Against Women: Prosecution in International War Crimes Tribunals* (M. Nijhoff Publishers 1997).

Augustine, Epistle 47 (to Publicola), reprinted in 33 *Patrologiae Cursus Completus, Series Latina* 184 (J.P. Migne ed., *Lutetiæ Parisiorum* 1861).

Austin, John, *Lectures on Jurisprudence* (Robert Campbell ed., London, John Murray 5th ed. 1885).

Bacon, Francis, The Elements of the Common Laws of England (1596), reprinted in 4 *The Works of Francis Bacon* 1 (C. & J. Rivington 1826).

Baier, Donald, Note, Arizona Felony Murder: Let the Punishment Fit the Crime, 36 *Ariz. L. Rev.* 701 (1994).

Bailey, Greg, Note, Death by Automobile as First Degree Murder Utilizing the Felony Murder Rule, 101 *W. Va. L. Rev.* 235 (1998).

Balkin, J.M., The Crystalline Structure of Legal Thought, 39 *Rutgers L. Rev.* 1 (1986).

Banner, Stuart, *The Death Penalty: An American History* (Harvard University Press 2002).

Barkow, Rachel E., The Political Market for Criminal Justice, 104 *Mich. L. Rev.* 1713 (2006).

Baumeister, Michel F., & Capone, Dorothea M., Admissibility Standards as Politics—The Imperial Gate Closers Arrive!!!, 33 *Seton Hall L. Rev.* 1025 (2003).

Beccaria, Cesare, *On Crimes and Punishments* (David Young ed. & trans., Hackett Publ'g Co. 1986) (1764).

Beckman, Gail McKnight, Three Penal Codes Compared, 10 *Am. J. Leg. Hist.* 148 (1966).

Bentham, Jeremy, *An Introduction to the Principles of Morals and Legislation* (J.H. Burns & H.L.A. Hart eds., Univ. of London 1970) (1789).

Binder, Guyora, Representing Nazism: Advocacy and Identity at the Trial of Klaus Barbie, 98 *Yale L.J.* 1321 (1989).

Binder, Guyora, Felony Murder and Mens Rea Default Rules: A Study in Statutory Interpretation, 4 *Buff. Crim. L. Rev.* 399 (2000).

Binder, Guyora, Meaning and Motive in the Law of Homicide, 3 *Buff. Crim. L. Rev.* 755 (2000).

Binder, Guyora, The Poetics of the Pragmatic: What Literary Criticisms of Law Offers Posner, 53 *Stan. L. Rev.* 1509 (2001).

Binder, Guyora, Punishment Theory: Moral or Political?, 5 *Buff. Crim. L. Rev.* 321 (2002).

Binder, Guyora, The Rhetoric of Motive and Intent, 6 *Buffalo Crim. L. Rev.* 1 (2002).

Binder, Guyora, The Origins of American Felony Murder Rules, 57 *Stanford L. Rev.* 90 (2004).

Binder, Guyora, The Meaning of Killing, in *Modern Histories of Crime and Punishment* 88 (Markus D. Dubber and Lindsay Farmer eds., 2007).

Binder, Guyora, The Culpability of Felony Murder, 83 *Notre Dame L. Rev.* 965 (2008).

Binder, Guyora, Victims and the Significance of Causing Harm, 28 *Pace L. Rev.* 713 (2008).

Binder, Guyora, & Smith, Nicholas J., Framed: Utilitarianism and Punishment of the Innocent, 32 *Rutgers L.J.* 115 (2000).

Binder, Guyora, & Weisberg, Robert, Cultural Criticism of Law, 49 *Stan. L. Rev.* 1149 (1997).

Binder, Guyora, & Weisberg, Robert, *Literary Criticisms of Law* (Princeton University Press 2001).

Bishop, Joel Prentiss, *Commentaries on the Criminal Law* (Little, Brown 1856).

Bishop, Joel Prentiss, *Commentaries on the Criminal Law* (2d ed., Little, Brown 1858).

Blackstone, William, *Commentaries on the Laws of England* (W.E. Dean 1853) (1765–69).

Blackstone, William, *Blackstone's Commentaries* 1 (photo. reprint Rothman reprints 1969) (St. George Tucker ed., William Young Birch & Abraham Small 1803) (1969).

Blackstone, William, *Commentaries on the Laws and Customs of England* (photo. reprint University of Chicago Press 2002) (1765–69).

Blinka, Daniel, Trial by Jury on the Eve of the Revolution: The Virginia Experience, 71 *U.M. K.C. L. Rev.* 529 (2003).

Block, Michael K., & Lind, Robert C., An Economic Analysis of Crimes Punishable by Imprisonment, 4 *J. Legal Stud.* 479 (1975).

Block, Richard, *Violent Crime: Environment, Interaction and Death* (Lexington Books 1977).

Blumenthal, Jeremy A., Law and the Emotions: The Problems of Affective Forecasting, 80 *Ind. L.J.* 155 (2005).

Boyce, Ronald N., Dripps, Donald A., & Perkins, Rollin M., *Criminal Law and Procedure: Cases and Materials* (11th ed., Thomson Reuters/Foundation Press 2010).

Brackenridge, Hugh Henry, *Law Miscellanies* (photo. reprint Arno Press 1972) (1814).

Bracton, Henry de, *On the Laws and Customs of England* (Samuel E. Thorne ed., Harvard Univ. Press 1968) (1235).

Bradford, William, *An Enquiry How Far the Punishment of Death Is Necessary in Pennsylvania* (T. Dobson 1793).

Brandt, Richard B., *A Theory of the Good and the Right* (Oxford: Clarendon Press 1979).

Brandt, Richard B., *Morality, Utilitarianism, and Rights* (Cambridge University Press 1992).

Brink, David O., Utilitarian Morality and the Personal Point of View, 83 *J. Phil.* 417 (1986).

Brown, Elizabeth Gaspar, *British Statutes in American Law, 1776–1836* (University of Michigan Law School 1964).

Brownmiller, Susan, *Against Our Will* (Fawcett Columbine 1993) (1975).

Chapin, Bradley, *Criminal Justice in Colonial America, 1606–1660* (University of Georgia Press 1983).

Chipman, Nathaniel, *A Dissertation on the Act Adopting the Common and Statute Laws of England, in Reports and Dissertations, in Two Parts* (Anthony Haswell 1793).

Clark, William L., & Marshall, William L., *A Treatise on the Law of Crimes* (6th ed., Callaghan 1958) (1900).

Cloud, Morgan, & Johnson, Phillip E., *Criminal Law: Cases, Materials, and Text* (7th ed., West Group 2002).

Coase, R. H., The Problem of Social Cost, 3 *J.L. & Econ.* 1 (1960).

Coffee, John Collins, Jr., Corporate Crime and Punishment: A Non-Chicago View of the Economics of Criminal Sanctions, 17 *Am. Crim. L. Rev.* 419 (1980).

Coke, Edward, *The Third Part of the Institutes of the Laws of England* (Hein Co. 1986) (1644).

Cole, Dana K., Expanding Felony-Murder in Ohio: Felony-Murder or Murder-Felony?, 63 *Ohio St. L.J.* 15 (2002).

Cole, Kevin, Killings During Crime: Toward a Discriminating Theory of Strict Liability, 28 *Am. Crim. L. Rev.* 73 (1990).

Crompton, Richard, *L'office et Aucthorite de Justices de Peace* (Richard Tottell 1587) (1583).

Crum, Charles, Causal Relations and the Felony-Murder Rule, 1952 *Wash. U. L.Q.* 190.

Crump, David, & Crump, Susan Waite, In Defense of the Felony Murder Doctrine, 8 *Harv. J.L. & Pub. Pol'y* 359 (1985).

Dallison, William, *Law Cases,* 6 Ed. 6 et 1, 2, 3, 4, & 5 Ph. & Mariae, fols. 40–41 (William Lambarde transcriber, n.d.) (unpublished material, on file with the British Library, Harleian Manuscript No. 5141).

Dalton, Michael, *The Countrey Justice* (corrected and enlarged ed., Societie of Stationers 1619) (1618).

Dalton, Michael, *The Countrey Justice* (6th ed., The Assignes of John More 1635) (1618).

Dan-Cohen, Meir, *Harmful Thoughts: Essays on Law, Self, and Morality* (Princeton University Press 2002).

Darley, John M., On the Unlikely Prospect of Reducing Crime Rates by Increasing the Severity of Prison Sentences, 13 *J. L. & Pol'y* 189 (2005).

Davis, Michael, How to Make the Punishment Fit the Crime, 93 *Ethics* 726 (1983).

Davis, Michael, Why Attempts Deserve Less Punishment than Complete Crimes, 5 *Law & Phil.* 1 (1986).

Davis, Michael, Criminal Desert and Unfair Advantage: What's the Connection?, 12 *Law & Phil.* 133 (1993).

Diamond, John L., The Myth of Morality and Fault in Criminal Law Doctrine, 34 *Am. Crim. L. Rev.* 111 (1996).

Dickey, Walter, Schultz, David, & Fullin, James L., Jr., The Importance of Clarity in the Law of Homicide: The Wisconsin Revision, 1989 *Wis. L. Rev.* 1323.

Dilloff, Anthony M., Transferred Intent: An Inquiry into the Nature of Criminal Culpability, 1 *Buff. Crim. L. Rev.* 501 (1998).

Donohue, John J., & Wolfers, Justin, Uses and Abuses of Empirical Evidence in the Death Penalty Debate, 58 *Stan. L. Rev.* 791 (2005).

Doob, Anthony, & Webster, Cheryl Marie, Sentence Severity and Crime: Accepting the Null Hypothesis, 30 *Crime and Justice* 143 (2003).

Dressler, Joshua, *Understanding Criminal Law* (3d ed., Lexis/Nexis 2001).

Dressler, Joshua, *Understanding Criminal Law* (4th ed., Lexis/Nexis 2006).

Dressler, Joshua, *Cases & Materials on Criminal Law* (4th ed., Thomson/West 2007).

Dripps, Donald, Fundamental Retribution Error, 56 *Vand. L. Rev.* 1383 (2003).

Duff, R.A., *Intention, Agency, and Criminal Liability: Philosophy of Action and the Criminal Law* (Blackwell 1990).

Duff, R.A., *Criminal Attempts* (Clarendon Press 1996).

Duff, R.A., Subjectivism, Objectivism, and Criminal Attempts, in *Harm and Culpability* (A.P. Semester & A.T.H. Smith eds., Oxford University Press 1996).

Dworkin, Ronald, No Right Answer?, 53 *N.Y.U. L. Rev.* 1 (1978).

Dworkin, Ronald, *Taking Rights Seriously* (Harvard University Press 1978).

Dworkin, Ronald, *A Matter of Principle* (Harvard University Press 1985).

Dworkin, Ronald, *Law's Empire* (Harvard University Press 1986).

East, Edward Hyde, *A Treatise of the Pleas of the Crown* (A. Strahan 1806) (1803).

Ehrlich, Isaac, Participation in Illegitimate Activities: A Theoretical and Empirical Investigation, 81 *J. Pol. Econ.* 521 (1973).

Eigenberg, Helen M., Rape in Male Prisons: Examining the Relationship Between Correctional Officers' Attitudes Toward Male Rape and Their Willingness to Respond to Acts of Rape, in *Prison Violence in America* (Michael Braswell et al. eds., 2d ed. Anderson Publishing 1994).

Elster, John, Rationality and Addition, in *Drugs and the Limits of Liberalism* (Pablo De Greiff ed., Cornell University Press 1999).

Eskridge, William N., *Dynamic Statutory Interpretation* (Harvard University Press 1994).

Feinberg, Joel, Problematic Responsibility in Law and Morals, 71 *Phil. Rev.* 340 (1962).

Feinberg, Joel, The Expressive Function of Punishment, 49 *Monist* 397 (1965).

Feinberg, Joel, *Doing and Deserving: Essays in the Theory of Responsibility* (Princeton University Press 1974) (1970).

Feinberg, Joel, *Harm to Others* (Oxford University Press 1984).

Ferzan, Kimberly Kessler, Opaque Recklessness, 91 *J. Crim. L. & Criminology* 597 (2001).

Ferzan, Kimberly Kessler, Don't Abandon the Model Penal Code Yet! Thinking Through Simons's Rethinking, 6 *Buff. Crim. L. Rev.* 185 (2002).

Finkel, Norman J., *Commonsense Justice* (Harvard University Press 1995).

Finkelstein, Claire O., Duress: A Philosophical Account of the Defense in Law, 37 *Ariz. L. Rev.* 251 (1995).

Finkelstein, Claire O., Excuses and Dispositions in Criminal Law, 6 *Buff. Crim. L. Rev.* 317 (2002).

Finkelstein, Claire O., Merger and Felony Murder, in *Defining Crimes: Essays on the Spe-*

cial Part of the Criminal Law (R.A. Duff and Stuart P. Green eds., Oxford University Press 2005).

Fitzherbert, Anthony, *The Boke of Justyces of Peas* (2d ed., 1510) (1506), *available online at: http://gateway.proquest.com/openurl?ctx_ver=Z39.88–2003&res_id=xri:eebo&rft_id =xri:eebo:image:8491* (Univ. of Mich. 1999).

Fitzherbert, Anthony, *The Newe Booke of Justyces of Peas* (T. Petit 1541).

Fletcher, George, The Metamorphosis of Larceny, 89 *Harv. L. Rev.* 469 (1976).

Fletcher, George P., *Rethinking Criminal Law* (Little, Brown 1978).

Fletcher, George, Reflections on Felony-Murder, 12 *Sw. U. L. Rev.* 413 (1981).

Foster, Michael, *A Report of Some Proceedings on the Commission for the Trial of the Rebels in the Year 1746, in the County of Surry; and of Other Crown Cases: To Which Are Added Discourses upon a Few Branches of the Crown Law* (2d ed. 1776).

Frankowski, Stanislaw, Mens Rea and Punishment in England: In Search of Interdependence of the Two Basic Components of Criminal Liability (A Historical Perspective), 63 *U. Det. L. Rev.* 393 (1986).

Gabel, Leona C., Benefit of Clergy in England in the Later Middle Ages, 14 *Smith C. Stud. Hist.* 1 (1928).

Gallie, W.B., Essentially Contested Concepts, 56 *Proc. Aristotelian Soc'y* 167 (1956).

Galligan, D.J., The Return to Retribution in Penal Theory, in *Crime, Proof, and Punishment: Essays in Memory of Sir Rupert Cross* (Colin Tapper ed., Butterworths 1981).

Galston, William, Defending Liberalism, 76 *Am. Pol. Sci. Rev.* 621 (1982).

Galston, William, *Liberal Purposes* (Cambridge University Press 1991).

Gardbaum, Stephen A., Why the Liberal State Can Promote Moral Ideals After All, 104 *Harv. L. Rev.* 1350 (1991).

Gardbaum, Stephen, Liberalism, Autonomy, and Moral Conflict, 48 *Stan. L. Rev.* 385 (1996).

Gardner, John, The Gist of Excuses, 1 *Buff. Crim. L. Rev.* 575 (1998).

Gardner, Martin, The Mens Rea Enigma: Observations on the Role of Motive in the Criminal Law, Past and Present, 1993 *Utah L. Rev.* 635.

Garvey, Stephen P., What's Wrong with Involuntary Manslaughter?, 85 *Tex. L. Rev.* 333 (2006).

Gauthier, David, *Morals by Agreement* (Clarendon Press 1986).

Gegan, Bernard E., Criminal Homicide in the Revised New York Penal Law, 12 *N.Y.L.F.* 565 (1966).

Geimer, William S., The Law of Homicide in North Carolina: Brand New Cart Before Tired Old Horse, 19 *Wake Forest L. Rev.* 331 (1983).

Gerber, Rudolph J., The Felony Murder Rule: Conundrum Without Principle, 31 *Ariz. St. L.J.* 763 (1999).

Glazebrook, P.R., Criminal Law Reform: England, in 1 *Encyclopedia of Crime and Justice* 400 (Joshua Dressler ed., 2d ed., 2002).

Goebel, Julius, Jr., *History of the Supreme Court of the United States* (Macmillan Company 1971).

Goodenow, John, *A Review of the Question Whether the Common Law of England, Respecting Crimes and Punishments, is in Force in the State of Ohio* (Butler & Lambdin's Letter Press Print. Office 1817).

Goodenow, John, *Historical Sketches of the Principles and Maxims of American Jurisprudence, in Contrast with the Doctrines of the English Common Law on the Subject of Crimes and Punishments* (photo. reprint W.S. Hein 1972) (1819).

Goodin, Robert E., *Utilitarianism as a Public Philosophy* (Cambridge University Press 1995).

Gordon, Robert W., Legal Thought and Legal Practice in the Age of American Enterprise, 1870–1920, in *Professions and Professional Ideologies in America* (Gerald Geison ed., 1983).

Green, Thomas A., The Jury and the English Law of Homicide, 1200–1600, 74 *Mich. L. Rev.* 413 (1976).

Green, Thomas A., *Verdict According to Conscience: Perspectives on the English Criminal Trial Jury, 1200–1800* (University of Chicago Press 1985).

Greenawalt, Kent, Punishment, in 4 *Encyclopedia of Crime and Justice* (Sanford H. Kadish ed., Free Press 1983).

Gross, Hyman, *A Theory of Criminal Justice* (Oxford University Press 1979).

Hale, Matthew, *Pleas of the Crown* (the Assigns of Richard Atkyns and Edward Atkyns 1678).

Hale, Matthew, *The History of the Pleas of the Crown* (Sollom Emlyn ed., E. and R. Nutt 1736).

Hall, Ford, The Common Law: An Account of Its Reception in the United States, 4 *Vand. L. Rev.* 791 (1951).

Hall, Jerome, *Theft, Law, and Society* (Little, Brown 1935).

Hall, Jerome, Negligent Behavior Should Be Excluded from Penal Liability, 63 *Colum. L. Rev.* 632 (1963).

Hampton, Jean, The Moral Education Theory of Punishment, 13 *Phil. & Pub. Aff.* 208 (1984).

Hampton, Jean, The Retributive Idea, in Jeffrie G. Murphy & Jean Hampton, *Forgiveness and Mercy* (Cambridge University Press 1988).

Hampton, Jean, Mens Rea, *Soc. Phil. & Pol'y*, Spring 1990.

Hampton, Jean, Correcting Harms Versus Righting Wrongs: The Goal of Retribution, 39 *UCLA L. Rev.* 1659 (1992).

Hampton, Jean, *The Intrinsic Worth of Persons: Contractarianism in Moral and Political Philosophy* (Daniel Farnham ed., Cambridge University Press 2007).

Hancock, Catherine, The Perils of Calibrating the Death Penalty Through Special Definitions of Murder, 53 *Tul. L. Rev.* 828 (1979).

Haque, Adil, Lawrence v. Texas and the Limits of Criminal Law, 42 *Harvard Civil Rights-Civil Liberties L. Rev.* 1 (2007).

Harcourt, Bernard E., The Collapse of the Harm Principle, 90 *J. Crim. L. & Criminology* 109 (1999).

Harel, Alon, & Segal, Uzi, Criminal Law and Behavioral Law and Economics: Observations on the Neglected Role of Uncertainty in Deterring Crime, 1 *Am. L. & Econ. Rev.* 276 (1999).

Harris, Angela, & Lee, Cynthia, *Criminal Law* (Thomson/West 2005).

Harsanyi, John, *Rational Behavior and Bargaining Equilibrium in Games and Social Situations* (Cambridge University Press 1977).

Hart, Henry M., Jr., The Aims of the Criminal Law, 23 *Law & Contemp. Probs.* 401 (1958).

Hart, Henry M., & Sacks, Albert, *The Legal Process: Basic Problems in the Making and Application of Law* (Foundation Press 1957).

Hart, H.L.A., Prolegomenon to the Principles of Punishment, 60 *Proc. of Aristotelian Soc'y* 1 (1960).

Hart, H.L.A., Intention and Punishment, 4 *Oxford Rev.* 5 (Feb. 1967).

Hart, H.L.A., *Punishment and Responsibility: Essays in the Philosophy of Law* (Clarendon Press 1968).

Hart, H.L.A., & Honoré, Tony, *Causation in the Law* (2d ed., Clarendon Press 1985).

Haskins, George Lee, *Law and Authority in Early Massachusetts* (Macmillan 1960).

Hausman, Daniel M., & McPherson, Michael S., *Economic Analysis and Moral Philosophy* (Cambridge University Press 1996).

Hawkins, William, *A Treatise of the Pleas of the Crown* (E. Nutt 1716).

Hawkins, William, *A Treatise of the Pleas of the Crown* (photo. reprint Arno Press 1972) (2d ed. 1724).

Hay, Douglas, Property, Authority, and the Criminal Law, in Douglas Hay, Peter Linebaugh, John G. Rule, & E.P. Thompson, *Albion's Fatal Tree: Crime and Society in Eighteenth-Century England* (Pantheon Books 1975).

Helvetius, Claude, *De L'Esprit* (photo. reprint 1970, B. Franklin) (1759).

Herzog, Don, *Happy Slaves: A Critique of Consent Theory* (University of Chicago Press 1989).

Hindelang, Michael J., Dunn, Chris, Aumick, Allison, & Sutton, Paul, *U.S. Dep't of Justice, Sourcebook of Criminal Justice Statistics—1974* (1975).

Hippard, James J., The Unconstitutionality of Criminal Liability Without Fault: An Argument for a Constitutional Doctrine of Mens Rea, 10 *Hous. L. Rev.* 1039 (1973).

Hobbes, Thomas, A Dialogue Between a Philosopher and a Student of the Common Laws of England (1681), reprinted in 6 *The English Works of Thomas Hobbes of Malmesbury* 87 (William Molesworth ed., 1840).

Hoecker, Thomas R., Comment, Felony Murder in Illinois, 1974 *U. Ill. L.F.* 685.

Hoffheimer, Michael H., Murder and Manslaughter in Mississippi: Unintentional Killings, 71 *Miss. L.J.* 35 (2001).

Hohfeld, Wesley, Some Fundamental Legal Conceptions as Applied in Judicial Reasoning, 23 *Yale L.J.* 16 (1913).

Holcomb, Richard Brooks, Note, Predicate Offenses for First Degree Felony Murder in Virginia, 57 *Wash. & Lee L. Rev.* 561 (2000).

Holmes, Oliver Wendell, *The Common Law* (Mark DeWolfe Howe ed., Harvard Univ. Press 1963) (1881).

Holmes, Oliver Wendell, *The Common Law* (Neill H. Alford, Jr. et al. eds., Gryphon Eds., Ltd. 1982) (1881).

Horder, Jeremy, Gross Negligence and Criminal Culpability, 47 *U. Toronto L.J.* 495 (1997).

Horwitz, Morton J., *The Transformation of American Law, 1780–1860* (Harvard University Press 1977).

Houck, Kara M., Note, People v. Dekens: The Expansion of the Felony-Murder Doctrine in Illinois, 30 *Loy. U. Chi. L.J.* 357 (1999).

Huigens, Kyron, Virtue and Inculpation, 108 *Harv. L. Rev.* 1423 (1995).

Huigens, Kyron, Virtue and Criminal Negligence, 2 *Buff. Crim. L. Rev.* 431 (1998).

Hume, David, *An Enquiry Concerning Human Understanding* (Tom L. Beauchamp ed., Clarendon Press 2000) (1748).

Hurd, Heidi M., Why Liberals Should Hate "Hate Crime Legislation," 20 *Law and Philosophy* 215 (2001).

Hurd, Heidi M., & Moore, Michael S., Punishing Hatred and Prejudice, 56 *Stan. L. Rev.* 1081 (2004).

Hurley, S.L., *Natural Reasons* (Oxford University Press 1989).

Hurnard, Naomi D., *The King's Pardon for Homicide Before A.D. 1307* (Clarendon Press 1969).

Hutson, H. Range, Anglin, Deirdre, & Pratts, Michael J., Jr., Adolescents and Children Injured or Killed in Drive-By Shootings in Los Angeles, 330 *New England J. Med.* 324 (1994).

Jefferson, Thomas, A Bill for Proportioning Crimes and Punishments (1779), in *Public Papers* (Merrill D. Peterson ed., Library of America 1984).

Johnson, Eric A., Criminal Liability for Loss of a Chance, 91 *Iowa L. Rev.* 59 (2005).

Kadish, Sanford H., The Model Penal Code's Historical Antecedents, 19 *Rutgers L.J.* 521 (1988).

Kadish, Sanford H., Foreword: The Criminal Law and the Luck of the Draw, 84 *J. Crim. L. & Criminology* 679 (1994).

Kadish, Sanford H., & Schulhofer, Stephen J., *Criminal Law and Its Processes: Cases and Materials* (5th ed., Little, Brown 1989).

Kadish, Sanford H., Schulhofer, Stephen J., & Steiker, Carol, *Criminal Law and Its Pro-*

cesses: Cases and Materials (8th ed., Wolters Kluwer Law & Business/Aspen Publishers 2007).

Kahan, Dan M., Ignorance of Law *Is* an Excuse—But Only for the Virtuous, 96 *Mich. L. Rev.* 127 (1997).

Kahan, Dan M., The Secret Ambition of Deterrence, 113 *Harv. L. Rev.* 414 (1999).

Kahan, Dan M., & Nussbaum, Martha C., Two Conceptions of Emotion in Criminal Law, 96 *Colum. L. Rev.* 269 (1996).

Kaplan, John, Weisberg, Robert, & Binder, Guyora, *Criminal Law* (4th ed., Aspen Publishers 2000).

Kaplan, John, Weisberg, Robert, & Binder, Guyora, *Criminal Law* (6th ed., Aspen Publishers 2008).

Kant, Immanuel, *Metaphysical Elements of Justice 80* (John Ladd trans., Hackett Publ'g Co. 2d ed. 1999) (1797).

Kant, Immanuel, *Groundwork for the Metaphysics of Morals* (Alan W. Wood ed. & trans., Yale Univ. Press 2002) (1785).

Katz, Jack, *Seductions of Crime* (Basic Books 1988).

Kaye, J.M., The Early History of Murder and Manslaughter—Part I, 83 *Law Q. Rev.* 365 (1967).

Kaye, J.M., The Early History of Murder and Manslaughter—Part II, 83 *Law Q. Rev.* 569 (1967).

Keedy, Edwin R., History of the Pennsylvania Statute Creating Degrees of Murder, 97 *U. Pa. L. Rev.* 759 (1949).

Kelman, Mark, Interpretive Construction in the Substantive Criminal Law, 33 *Stan. L. Rev.* 591 (1981).

Kelman, Mark, Strict Liability: An Unorthodox View, 4 *Encyclopedia of Crime and Justice* 1512 (Sanford H. Kadish ed., Free Press 1983).

Kelman, Mark, The Necessary Myth of Objective Causation Judgments in Liberal Political Theory, 63 *Chi.-Kent L. Rev.* 579 (1987).

Kelman, Mark, Hedonic Psychology and the Ambiguities of "Welfare," 33 *Phil. & Pub. Aff.* 391 (2005).

Kennedy, Duncan, A Semiotics of Legal Argument, 42 *Syracuse L. Rev.* 75 (1991).

Kessler, Kimberly D., The Role of Luck in the Criminal Law, 142 *U. Pa. L. Rev.* 2183 (1994).

Kutz, Christopher, *Complicity: Ethics and Law for a Collective Age* (Cambridge University Press 2000).

LaFave, Wayne R., *Criminal Law* (3rd ed., Thomson/West 2000).

LaFave, Wayne R., *Criminal Law* (4th ed., Thomson/West 2003).

LaFave, Wayne R., *Criminal Law* (5th ed., Thomson/West 2010).

LaFave, Wayne R., & Scott, Austin W., Jr., *Handbook on Criminal Law* (West Pub. Co. 1972).

LaFave, Wayne R., & Scott, Austin W., Jr., *Substantive Criminal Law* (West Pub. Co. 1986).

Lambarde, William, *Eirenarcha* (2d ed., 1588) (1581).

Langbein, John H., *The Origins of Adversary Criminal Trial* (Oxford University Press 2003).

Lanham, David, Felony Murder—Ancient and Modern, 7 *Crim. L.J.* 90 (1983).

Lawson, Robert G., Criminal law Revision in Kentucky: Part I—Homicide and Assault, 58 *Ky. L.J.* 242 (1970).

Lee, Cynthia, *Murder and the Reasonable Man* (New York University Press 2003).

Lee, Youngjae, Desert and the Eighth Amendment, 11 *U. Pa. J. Const. L.* 101 (2009).

Levy, Leonard W., *Freedom of Speech and Press in Early American History* (Harper & Row 1963).

Lieber, Francis, *Legal and Political Hermeneutics* (3d ed., F.H. Thomas and Co. 1880) (1839).

Lijtmaer, Martin, The Felony Murder Rule in Illinois, 98 *J. Crim. L. & Criminology* 621 (2008).

Liptak, Adam, Serving Life for Providing Car to Killers, *N.Y. Times*, Dec. 4, 2007, A1.

Livingston, Edward, *A System of Penal Law for the State of Louisiana* (J. Kay 1833).

Locke, John, *Two Treatises of Government* (Peter Laslett ed., Cambridge Univ. Press 1988) (1698).

Lockwood, Daniel, Issues in Prison Sexual Violence, in *Prison Violence in America* (Michael Braswell et al. eds., 2d ed. Anderson Publishing 1994).

Loewenstein, George, & Schkade, David, Wouldn't It Be Nice? Predicting Future Feelings, in *Well-Being: The Foundations of Hedonic Psychology* (Daniel Kahneman et al. eds., 1999).

Loewy, Arnold H., *Criminal Law in a Nutshell* (4th ed., West Pub. Co. 2003).

Macaulay, Thomas Babington, Notes on the Indian Penal Code (1837), reprinted in 7 *The Miscellaneous Works of Lord MaCaulay* 221 (Lady Trevelyan ed., Phila., Univ. Library Ass'n 1890).

Macedo, Stephen, *Liberal Virtues: Citizenship, Virtue, and Community in Liberal Constitutionalism* (Clarendon Press 1990).

Mackie, J.L., Causes and Conditions, 2 *Am. Phil. Q.* 245 (1965)

MacKinnon, Catharine A., *Feminism Unmodified: Discourses on Life and Law* (Harvard University Press 1987).

Madison, James, Report to the General Assembly of Virginia (1800), reprinted in *The Kentucky-Virginia Resolutions and Mr. Madison's Report of 1799* (Va. Comm'n on Constitutional Gov't ed., 1960).

Malani, Anup, Does the Felony-Murder Rule Deter Crime: Evidence from FBI Crime Data, unpublished working paper, 2002.

Mannheimer, Michael J., Not the Crime but the Cover-Up: A Deterrence-Based Rationale for the Premeditation-Deliberation Formula, 86 *Ind. L.J.* 879 (2011).

Marcus, Paul, Book Review, 73 *J. Crim. L. & Criminology* 811 (1982).

Marowe, Thomas, De Pace Terre et Ecclesie & Conseruacione Eiusdem (1503), reprinted in 7 *Oxford Studies in Social and Legal History* 286 (Paul Vinogradoff ed., Clarendon Press 1924).

McAdams, Richard H., Relative Preferences, 102 *Yale L.J.* 1 (1992).

Michael, Jerome, and Wechsler, Herbert, Rationale of the Law of Homicide: I, A 37 *Colum. L. Rev.* 701 (1937).

Michaels, Alan C., Acceptance: The Missing Mental State, 71 *S. Cal. L. Rev.* 953 (1998).

Michaels, Alan C., Constitutional Innocence, 112 *Harv. L. Rev.* 828 (1999).

Michie, Thomas Johnson, *A Treatise on the Law of Homicide* (The Michie Co. 1914).

Mill, John Stuart, *On Liberty* (Alburey Costell ed., Harlan Davidson Inc. 1947) (1859).

Miller, William Ian, Choosing the Avenger: Some Aspects of the Bloodfeud in Medieval Iceland and England, 1 *Law & Hist. Rev.* 159 (1983).

Miller, William Ian, *Bloodtaking and Peacemaking* (University of Chicago Press 1990).

Miller, William Ian, *Humiliation and Other Essays on Honor, Social Discomfort, and Violence* (Cornell University Press 1993).

Moore, Michael, *Placing Blame: A General Theory of the Criminal Law* (Clarendon Press 1997).

Moreland, Roy, Kentucky Homicide Law with Recommendations, 51 *Ky. L.J.* 59 (1962).

Moreland, Roy, A Reexamination of the Law of Homicide in 1971: The Model Penal Code, 59 *Ky. L.J.* 788 (1971).

Morris, Clarence, Duty, Negligence, and Causation, 101 *U. Pa. L. Rev.* 189 (1952).

Morris, Herbert, Persons and Punishment, 52 *Monist* 475 (1968), reprinted in Herbert Morris, *On Guilt and Innocence* 31 (University of California Press 1976).

Morse, Stephen J., Reason, Results, and Criminal Responsibility, 2004 *U. Ill. L. Rev.* 363.

Mueller, Gerhard, *Crime, Law, and the Scholars* (Heinemann Educational 1966).

Murphy, Jeffrie G., *Kant: The Philosophy of Right* (Mercer Univ. Press 1994) (1970).

Murphy, Jeffrie G., *Retribution, Justice, and Therapy* (Wilfrid Sellars & Keith Lehrer eds., Springer 1979).

Murphy, Liam B., *Moral Demands in Nonideal Theory* (Oxford University Press 2000).

Nagel, Thomas, *Mortal Questions* (Cambridge University Press 1979).

Nagel, Thomas, *The View from Nowhere* (Oxford University Press 1986).

Nat'l Comm'n on Reform of Fed. Crim. Laws, Final Report of the National Commission on Reform of Federal Criminal Laws (1971).

Neal, Patrick, Liberalism & Neutrality, 17 *Polity* 664 (1985).

Nelson, William, *Americanization of the Common Law: The Impact of Legal Change on Massachusetts Society, 1760–1830* (2d ed., University of Georgia Press 1994).

Note, Felony Murder as a First Degree Offense: An Anachronism Retained, 66 *Yale L.J.* 427 (1957).

Note, Felony Murder: A Tort Law Reconceptualization, 99 *Harv. L. Rev.* 1918 (1986).

Nourse, Victoria, Passion's Progress: Modern Law Reform and the Provocation Defense, 106 *Yale L.J.* 1331 (1997).

Nourse, Victoria, The New Normativity: The Abuse Excuse and the Resurgence of Judgment in the Criminal Law, 50 *Stan. L. Rev.* 1435 (1998).

Nourse, Victoria, Heart and Minds: Understanding the New Culpability, 6 *Buff. Crim. L. Rev.* 361 (2002).

Nozick, Robert, *Anarchy, State, and Utopia* (Basic Books 1974).

Packer, Herbert L., *The Limits of the Criminal Sanction* (Stanford University Press 1968).

Packer, Herbert L., Criminal Code Revision, 23 *U. Toronto L.J.* 1 (1973).

Palmer, Robert C., The Federal Common Law of Crime, 4 *Law & Hist. Rev.* 267 (1986).

Pillsbury, Samuel, *Judging Evil: Rethinking the Law of Murder and Manslaughter* (New York University Press 1998).

Pirsig, Maynard E., Proposed Revision of the Minnesota Criminal Code, 47 *Minn. L. Rev.* 417 (1963).

Polinsky, Mitchell, & Shavell, Steven, The Optimal Tradeoff Between the Probability and Magnitude of Fines, 69 *Am. Econ. Rev.* 880 (1979).

Polinsky, Mitchell, & Shavell, Steven, On the Disutility and Discounting of Imprisonment and the Theory of Deterrence, 28 *J. Legal Stud.* 1 (1999).

Pollock, Frederick, & Maitland, Frederick W., *The History of English Law before the time of Edward I* (photo. reprint Cambridge University Press 1968) (2d ed. 1898).

Pound, Roscoe, The Place of Judge Story in the Making of American Law, 48 *Am. L. Rev.* 676 (1914).

Presser, Stephen B., *The Original Misunderstanding* (Carolina Academic Press 1991).

Preyer, Kathryn, Crime, the Criminal Law, and Reform in Post-Revolutionary Virginia, 1 *Law & Hist. Rev.* 53 (1983).

Preyer, Kathryn, Jurisdiction to Punish: Federal Authority, Federalism, and the Common Law of Crimes in the Early Republic, 4 *Law & Hist. Rev.* 223 (1986).

Radin, Max, A Short Way with Statutes, 56 *Harv. L. Rev.* 388 (1942).

Radzinowicz, Leon, 1 *A History of English Criminal Law and Its Administration from 1750* (Stevens 1948).

Radzinowicz, Leon, 3 *A History of English Criminal Law and Its Administration from 1750* (Stevens 1957).

Radzinowicz, Leon, 4 *A History of English Criminal Law and Its Administration from 1750* (Stevens 1968).

Railton, Peter, Alienation, Consequentialism, and the Demands of Morality, 13 *Phil. & Pub. Aff.* 134 (1984).

Rantoul, Robert, Jr., Oration at Scituate, Massachusetts, 4 July, 1836, reprinted in *Readings in American Legal History* 472 (Mark DeWolfe Howe ed., Harvard Univ. Press 1949).

Rawls, John, Two Concepts of Rules, 44 *Phil. Rev.* 3 (1955), in *Philosophical Perspectives on Punishment* 82 (Gertrude Ezorsky ed., SUNY Press 1972).

Rawls, John, *A Theory of Justice* (rev. ed., Harvard University Press 1999).

Rawls, John, *Political Liberalism* (Columbia University Press 2005).

Raz, Joseph, *The Morality of Freedom* (Clarendon Press 1986).

Reinsch, Paul Samuel, The English Common Law in the Early American Colonies, in 1 *Select Essays in Anglo-American Legal History* (Ernst Freund et al. eds., Little, Brown 1907).

Robinson, Paul H., *Criminal Law* (Aspen Law & Business 1997).

Robinson, Paul H., & Darley, John M., *Justice, Liability, and Blame: Community Views and the Criminal Law* (Westview Press 1995).

Robinson, Paul H., & Darley, John M., The Utility of Desert, 91 *Nw. U. L. Rev.* 453 (1997).

Robinson, Paul H., & Grall, Jane A., Element Analysis in Defining Criminal Liability: The Model Penal Code and Beyond, 35 *Stan. L. Rev.* 681 (1983).

Rosen, Allen D., *Kant's Theory of Justice* (Cornell University Press 1996).

Ross, Alf, *On Guilt, Responsibility, and Punishment* (University of California Press 1975).

Ross, W.D., *The Right and the Good* (Philip Stratton-Lake ed., Clarendon 2002).

Roth, Nelson, & Sundby, Scott, The Felony-Murder Rule: A Doctrine at Constitutional Crossroads, 70 *Cornell L. Rev.* 446 (1985).

Rothman, Kenneth J., Causes, 104 *Am. J. Epidemiology* 587 (1976).

Russell, William Oldnall, *A Treatise on Crimes and Misdemeanors* (J. Butterworth 1819).

Russell, William Oldnall, & Prentice, Samuel, *A Treatise on Crimes and Misdemeanors* (5th ed., T. & J. W. Johnson & Co. 1877).

Sachs, Leslie G., Casenote, Due Process Concerns and the Requirement of a Strict Causal Relationship in Felony Murder Cases: Conner v. Director of Division of Adult Corrections, 23 *Creighton L. Rev.* 629 (1990).

Sayre, Francis Bowes, Mens Rea, 45 *Harv. L. Rev.* 974 (1932).

Scarre, Geoffrey, *Utilitarianism* (Routledge 1996).

Schick, Frederic, *Understanding Action* (Cambridge Univ. Press, 1991).

Schick, Frederic, *Making Choices* (Cambridge Univ. Press, 1997).

Schulhofer, Stephen J., Harm and Punishment: A Critique of the Results of Conduct in the Criminal Law, 122 *U. Pa. L. Rev.* 1497 (1974).

Searle, John, *The Construction of Social Reality* (Simon and Schuster 1995).

Seibold, Jeanne H., The Felony-Murder Rule: In Search of a Viable Doctrine, 23 *Cath. Law.* 133 (1978).

Seidman, Louis Michael, Soldiers, Martyrs, and Criminals: Utilitarian Theory and the Problem of Crime Control, 94 *Yale L.J.* 315 (1984).

Simon, Jonathan, *Governing Through Crime: How the War on Crime Transformed Democracy and Created a Culture of Fear* (Oxford University Press 2007).

Simon, Michelle, Whose Crime Is It Anyway?: Liability for the Lethal Acts of Nonparticipants in the Felony, 71 *U. Det. Mercy L. Rev.* 223 (1994).

Simons, Kenneth W., Rethinking Mental States, 72 *B.U. L. Rev.* 463 (1992).

Simons, Kenneth W., When Is Strict Criminal Liability Just?, 87 *J. Crim. L. & Criminology* 1075 (1997).

Sinclair, Andrew, *Era of Excess* (Harper & Row 1964) (1962).

Singer, Joseph William, The Legal Rights Debate in Analytical Jurisprudence from Bentham to Hohfeld, 1982 *Wis. L. Rev.* 975.

Starke, Richard, *The Virginia Justice* (Purdie and Dixon 1774).

Stephen, James Fitzjames, *A History of the Criminal Law of England* (Macmillan and Co. 1883).

Stephen, James Fitzjames, *Digest of the Criminal Law* (Macmillan 1926).

Stephen, Serjeant, *New Commentaries on the Laws of England* (Edward Jenks ed., 16th ed., Butterworth & Co. 1914).

Stuntz, William J., The Pathological Politics of Criminal Law, 100 *Mich. L. Rev.* 505 (2001).

Sunstein, Cass R. & Vermeule, Adrian, Is Capital Punishment Morally Required? Acts, Omissions, and Life-Life Tradeoffs, 58 *Stan. L. Rev.* 703 (2005).

Sutherland, John Gridley, *Statutes and Statutory Construction* (3d ed., Frank Horack ed., Callaghan & Co. 1943).

Swift, Zephaniah, *A System of the Laws of the State of Connecticut* (John Byrne 1795).

Tadros, Victor, *Criminal Responsibility* (Oxford University Press 2005).

Thode, E. Wayne, The Indefensible Use of the Hypothetical Case to Determine Cause in Fact, 46 *Tex. L. Rev.* 423 (1968).

Thorpe, Francis Newton, *The Federal and State Constitutions, Colonial Charters, and Other Organic Laws of the States, Territories, and Colonies Now or Heretofore Forming the United States of America* (Govt. Print. Off. 1909).

Tobias, J.J., *Crime and Police in England 1700–1900* (Gill and Macmillan 1979).

Tomkovicz, James J., The Endurance of the Felony-Murder Rule: A Study of the Forces that Shape Our Criminal Law, 51 *Wash. & Lee L. Rev.* 1429 (1994).

Torcia, Charles E., *Wharton's Criminal Law* (15th ed., Lawyers Cooperative 1994).

Toulmin, Harry, & Blair, James, *A Review of the Criminal Law of the Commonwealth of Kentucky* (photo. Reprint W. W. Gaunt 1983) (1804).

Vidmar, Neil, & Hans, Valerie P., *American Juries,* (Prometheus Books 2007).

Warren, Charles, *The Supreme Court in United States History* (rev. ed., Little, Brown 1947).

Webb, George, *The Office and Authority of a Justice of the Peace* (photo. reprint W. W. Gaunt 1969) (1736).

Wechsler, Herbert, The Challenge of a Model Penal Code, 65 *Harv. L. Rev.* 1097 (1952).

Wechsler, Herbert, Codification of Criminal Law in the United States: The Model Penal Code, 68 *Colum. L. Rev.* 1425 (1968).

Wechsler, Herbert, & Michael, Jerome, A Rationale of the Law of Homicide, 37 *Colum. L. Rev.* 701 (1937).

Weinreb, Lloyd, *Criminal Law; Cases, Comments, Questions* (7th ed., Foundation Press 2003).

Wharton, Francis, *A Treatise on the Law of Homicide in the United States* (Kay & Brother 1855).

Wharton, Francis, *A Treatise on the Law of Homicide in the United States* (Phila., Kay & Bro. 2d ed. 1875).

Williams, Bernard, *Moral Luck: Philosophical Papers, 1973–1980* (Cambridge University Press 1982).

Wilson, James Q., & Abrahamse, Allan, Does Crime Pay?, 9 *Just. Q.* 359 (1992).

Wolfgang, Marvin, *Patterns in Criminal Homicide* (University of Pennsylvania 1958).

Wolfgang, Marvin E., *Victim-Precipitated Criminal Homicide, in Crime and Justice at the Millennium 293* (Robert A. Silverman et al. eds., 2002).

Wright, Richard W., Causation in Tort Law, 73 *Calif. L. Rev.* 1735 (1985).

Wyatt-Brown, Bertram, *Southern Honor* (Oxford University Press 1982).

Zaibert, Leo, *Five Ways Patricia Can Kill Her Husband: A Theory of Intentionality and Blame* (Open Court 2005).

Zimmerman, Michael J., Luck and Moral Responsibility, 97 *Ethics* 374 (1987).

Zimring, Franklin E., *Crime Is Not the Problem: Lethal Violence in America* (Oxford University Press 1997).

Zimring, Franklin E., and Zuehl, James, Victim Injury and Death in Urban Robbery: A Chicago Study, 15 *J. Legal Stud.* 1 (1986).

INDEX

Critical Perspectives on Crime and Law
Edited by Markus D. Dubber

Mona Lynch, *Sunbelt Justice: Arizona and the Transformation of American Punishment*
2009

Vera Bergelson, *Victims' Rights and Victims' Wrongs: Comparative Liability in Criminal Law*
2009

Wayne A. Logan, *Knowledge as Power: Criminal Registration and Community Notification Laws in America*
2009

Markus D. Dubber and Mariana Valverde, editors, *Police and the Liberal State*
2008

David Alan Sklansky, *Democracy and the Police*
2007

Markus D. Dubber and Lindsay Farmer, editors, *Modern Histories of Crime and Punishment*
2007

Markus D. Dubber and Mariana Valverde, editors, *The New Police Science: The Police Power in Domestic and International Governance*
2006